D0023501

Free Jazz and Free Improvisation
An Encyclopedia
Volume II: K–Z

TODD S. JENKINS

GREENWOOD PRESS
Westport, Connecticut • London

Library of Congress Cataloging-in-Publication Data

Jenkins, Todd S., 1968–
     Free jazz and free improvisation : an encyclopedia / Todd S. Jenkins.
       p. cm.
     Includes bibliographical references (p.) and index.
     ISBN 0–313–29881–5 (set : alk. paper) — ISBN 0–313–33313–0 (v. 1 : alk. paper) —
     ISBN 0–313–33314–9 (v. 2 : alk. paper)
       1. Free jazz — Dictionaries.   2. Improvisation (Music)   I. Title
     ML102.J3J46   2004
     781.65′136′03—dc22   2004047531

British Library Cataloguing in Publication Data is available.

Library of Congress Catalog Card Number: 2004047531
ISBN: 0–313–29881–5 (set code)
        0–313–33313–0 (v. 1)
        0–313–33314–9 (v. 2)

First published in 2004

Greenwood Press, 88 Post Road West, Westport, CT 06881
An imprint of Greenwood Publishing Group, Inc.
www.greenwood.com

Printed in the United States of America

The paper used in this book complies with the
Permanent Paper Standard issued by the National
Information Standards Organization (Z39.48–1984).

10 9 8 7 6 5 4 3 2 1

Contents

K

Kaiser, Henry (b. Oakland, CA, 11 September 1952): guitarist. A member of the Bay Area's prominent Kaiser family, young Henry got into music almost as an act of defiance and has become one of the most respected performers in his field. He was influenced by Derek Bailey, with whom he recorded the duo *Wireforks* (1995, Shanachie); the avant-rock of Captain Beefheart, in whose Magic Band Kaiser played briefly in the 1980s; the Grateful Dead; and musics of Africa, Asia and the Mississippi Delta.

In 1977, Kaiser's debut album, *Ice Death*, was released by Parachute, the same label that brought John Zorn into public attention. Series of recordings followed on Metalanguage (*With Friends Like These*, 1979) and SST (*Those Who Know History Are Doomed to Repeat It*, 1989). *Lemon Fish Tweezer* (1992, Cuneiform) is a look back at Kaiser's early career. He established professional relationships with the members of Rova (*Daredevils*, 1979, Metalanguage), working with them repeatedly as a player and composer, and with ex-Magic Band drummer John French (*Crazy Backwards Alphabet*, 1992, SST) and guitarist/bassist Fred Frith. Kaiser, French, and Frith partnered with British folk-rock guitarist Richard Thompson for a pair of cult-classic albums, and the four have done a number of projects together outside that collective.

Besides acoustic and electric guitars, Kaiser has explored banjo, shamisen, and other ethnic instruments. With slide guitarist David Lindley, he studied the music of Madagascar and issued compelling compilations on Shanachie. In 1998, Kaiser and Wadada Leo Smith teamed for a tribute to Miles Davis, *Yo, Miles!* (Shanachie). He has performed with Diamanda Galas and Sergei Kuryokhin, among others, and in 2001, he spent several weeks in Antarctica performing for scientists stationed there.

Kaplan, Ori (b. Tel Aviv, Israel, 1 October 1969): saxophonist. Kaplan studied music at Mannes College in New York City and graduated in 1996. His first ensemble in America was Trio Plus with tubaist/bassist Tom Abbs and drummer Geoff Mann

(*Realms*, 1999, CIMP). Trombonist Steve Swell later rounded the group into a strong quartet (*Delirium*, 2000, CIMP). The recent Shaat'nez Band includes Mann, bassist Adam Roberts, pianist Andrew Bemkey, drummer Tamir Muskat, and tuba player Marcus Rojas (*Le Magus*, 2002, Knitting Factory Works). Kaplan has been a member of Jump Arts, ethno-punkers Gogol Bordello, and William Parker's Little Huey Creative Music Orchestra, and has collaborated with Alan Silva, Roy Campbell, Karen Borca, and the Pink Noise Saxophone Quartet. He leads his own Percussion Ensemble, which performed with Susie Ibarra on *Gongol* (2001, Knitting Factory Works).

Karayorgis, Pandelis: pianist. Born in Greece, Karayorgis performs somewhere toward the middle of the expanse between melodic Paul Bley and percussive Cecil Taylor. In the 1980s, he studied with Bley, Ran Blake, and Dave Holland at the New England Conservatory, and he chose to remain in Boston afterward. Most of his own records have been cut for Leo, beginning with his debut, *In Time* (1993). He is a regular collaborator with Mat Maneri and reedmen Eric Pakula and Guillermo Gregorio (*Approximately*, 1995, HatOlogy), and was a member of the Mandala Octet. One of his best is *Lift & Poise* (1996, Leo) with Mat and Joe Maneri and bassist John Lockwood.

Kelley, Greg (b. Boston, MA, September 1973): trumpeter and electronic experimenter. Kelley studied trumpet at the Peabody Conservatory in Baltimore, then returned to Boston's improvised music scene in 1996. Two years later he and saxophonist Bhob Rainey formed the duo nmperign, with which they have toured much of the world. Kelley has performed and recorded with electronics wizard Jason Lescalleet, Anthony Braxton, Eddie Prévost, John Butcher, Pauline Oliveros, Paul Lovens, Lê Quan Ninh, Soul-Junk, and other experimenters. A hallmark of Kelley's solo and group performances is the electronic manipulation of his trumpet sounds for exotic textural effects. *Forlorn Green* (2001, Erstwhile), a duo with Lescalleet, demonstrates his wide technical palette.

Kessler, Kent: bassist. A regular partner of reedman Ken Vandermark, Kessler came up in free music through Hal Russell's NRG Ensemble beginning in the late 1970s. He is an expert technician with a booming sound that can slice through the chaotic environments in which Kessler finds himself. NRG was his principal gig until the mid-1990s. When Vandermark replaced the late Russell in 1992, Kessler began collaborating with the reedman on side projects: the DKV Trio with drummer Hamid Drake; Steam; the Steelwool Trio; the Albert Ayler tribute band, Witches and Devils; and most prominently, the Vandermark 5. Kessler has also worked with Peter Brötzmann's Chicago bands, Misha Mengelberg, Joe McPhee, Mats Gustafsson, Georg Graewe, trombonist Jeb Bishop's trio, and hometown hero Fred Anderson, among others.

King Übü Örchestrü: European ensemble. One of the more impressive big bands to come in the wake of the Globe Unity Orchestra, Wolfgang Fuchs's King Übü

Örchestrü has recorded only twice (1992's *Binaurality* and 2001's live *Trigger Zone*, both on FMP) but has built a positive reputation for their large-ensemble improvisations. The band's lineup has included Luc Houtkamp, saxophonist Peter Van Bergen, Günter Christmann, Radu Malfatti, Paul Lytton, tubaist Melvyn Poore, Philipp Wachsmann, and bassist Torsten Müller.

Kirk, Rahsaan Roland (Roland T. Kirk; b. Columbus, OH, 7 August 1936; d. Bloomington, IN, 5 December 1977): reedman, composer, and bandleader. Kirk was one of the most colorful figures in jazz's history, a blind eccentric who played two or three horns at once, wore his full arsenal of instruments around his neck, and whose understanding of the spectrum of jazz history was on a par with Charles Mingus and Muhal Richard Abrams. An incredible technician who did not even let a severe stroke keep him from performing for long, Kirk displayed a wild sense of humor but was dead serious about the importance of music to society and particularly the black culture.

Kirk was blinded in an accident when he was two, a tragedy he revisited musically in *The Inflated Tear* (1967, Atlantic) but did not let hinder him permanently. As a child, he learned to play the trumpet and bugle, moving to clarinet and C-melody saxophone in his teens. By age fifteen, Kirk was a professional tenor saxophonist, playing with local R&B bands. Early on, he mastered the discipline of "circular breathing," permitting him to play for extended stretches without having to draw in a breath. Not long thereafter, in a music store basement, he discovered two rare horns left over from the Spanish Civil War: the manzello, a slightly curved form of soprano saxophone, and stritch, a straight alto sax with an extra-large bell. In a gesture typical of his astounding genius, Kirk was able to modify the horns so he could play them simultaneously along with his tenor sax or clarinet. He claimed that he was inspired to do so by a dream, the same justification for his assumption of the mysterious moniker Rahsaan. Those oddball horns remained part of his armory, and Kirk exhibited his early prowess with them on his debut recording, *Triple Threat* (1956, King; issued on CD as *Early Works*, Rhino). One of Kirk's later crowd-pleasing stunts was his simultaneous performance of "Going Home" and "Sentimental Journey" on two different horns, demonstrating his ability to think in two directions at once.

After gigging around Louisville, Kirk packed up for Chicago in 1960. He struck a one-shot deal with blues powerhouse Chess Records, which resulted in his second disc, *Introducing Roland Kirk*. Chess's better distribution got Kirk more attention than his King debut, and word began to spread about the blind phenomenon. A German tour the following year culminated in an invitation to join Charles Mingus's band, which further assisted Kirk's rise to fame. As intolerant as Mingus tended to be, he found plenty of joy in Kirk's outlandish playing, use of sirens and whistles, and quirky stage presence. Kirk performed on two classic Mingus albums, *Oh Yeah!* and *Tonight at Noon* (both 1961, Atlantic). The latter disc included Mingus's ambitious, free-minded title track on which Kirk was able to flaunt his own unfettered spirit. Though his service with Mingus only lasted about three months, the two men made lasting impressions on each other.

From 1961 onward, Kirk usually worked as a leader of his own units and continued to develop his special skills. "You Did It, You Did It," a slow blues from *We Free Kings* (1961, Mercury), was a landmark of jazz flute technique, with Kirk spitting out notes and vocalizing with pure, raw passion. *Rip, Rig and Panic* (1965, Limelight) was one of his freest, most energetic settings. Gradually Kirk began to add hybrid instruments of his own devising: black mystery pipes and black puzzle flute, made from lengths of plastic tubing; the slidesophone and trumpophone, brass horns with sax mouthpieces; not to mention kalimba, wolf whistles, English horn, piccolo, clarinets, nose flute, harmonica, and others. Kirk's explorations on these instruments and his experiments with tone color, timbre, and song form were inspirational to the free musicians who followed him.

In the 1970s, Kirk became a social activist, founding the Jazz and People's Movement to publicize black music and arts through television appearances and disruptive but peaceful tactics. In 1975, Kirk was paralyzed by a stroke and lost the use of one side of his body. Nevertheless, he developed a method to play all his horns one-handed and continued to play until felled by a final stroke in 1977. Never a "free jazz" musician in the strictest sense, Kirk was inarguably influential to the movement due to his fearless pursuit of new sounds and opportunities.

Klucevsek, Guy (b. 26 February 1948): accordionist. One of the few free performers to specialize in his instrument (only Tony Cedras, Andrea Parkins, and the more classically minded Pauline Oliveros rank higher in the field), Klucevsek has added a nostalgic yet avant-garde timbre to free sessions since the mid-1980s. He has worked with John Zorn, Laurie Anderson, Don Byron, and Anthony Braxton, accompanied the Kronos Quartet, took part in Dave Douglas's project Charms of the Night Sky (self-titled, 1998, Winter & Winter; *A Thousand Evenings*, 2000, RCA) with Mark Feldman and bassist Greg Cohen, and led the Accordion Tribe, a full ensemble of squeeze-boxers. Klucevsek has composed and played for dance troupes, performed on the audiobook edition of Annie Proulx's *Accordion Crimes*, and released several albums (*Flying Vegetables of the Apocalypse*, 1991, Experimental, and *Stolen Memories*, 1996, Tzadik, are both excellent).

Knitting Factory: music venue on Leonard Street in New York City's TriBeCa District, which has fostered many developments in jazz and improvised music. Founded by Michael Dorf and Louis Spitzer in 1987, the "Knit" has become one of the city's prime musical landmarks for its policy of scruffy openness. Originally housed in a fairly run-down building at 47 E. Houston Street, the Knit moved to 74 Leonard Street in the late 1990s. Besides the avant universe, which at the time centered on John Zorn, the Knit has presented cutting-edge jazz, rock, techno, and uncategorizable artists since its doors opened. Knitmedia also administers and distributes four record labels: Knitting Factory Works, specializing in new recordings by avant-garde artists; Knit Classics, which has reissued discs from Rashied Ali's Survival label catalog, along with albums by Dizzy Gillespie and other jazzers; the psychedelic-pop imprint Shimmy Disc; and JAM: Jewish Alternative Music, dealing in albums by contemporary Jewish performers.

In 1988, the Knit founded the annual "What Is Jazz?" Festival, which has since become the mainstreamed Bell Atlantic Jazz Festival. Besides the Main Performance

Space, the New York Knit houses several smaller stages: the Old Office, Tap Bar, and Alterknit Theater. In the late 1990s, the Knitting Factory experienced some rough times, exacerbated by Zorn's boycotting of the venue after a dispute with Michael Dorf. Those strains delayed but did not prevent the opening of the Los Angeles Knitting Factory in 1999, which was a grave disappointment to West Coast avant-jazz fans because it very rarely books anyone other than local rock bands and DJs. Since Dorf broke with the company in 2003, the New York Knitting Factory has also ceased most of its jazz-oriented bookings.

Koglmann, Franz (b. Mödling, Austria, 1947): trumpeter, composer, and bandleader. Koglmann studied trumpet and flügelhorn in school and, like many of his contemporaries, embraced free music as a young adult. In 1973, he founded Pipe Records, a label that issued a handful of albums by Bill Dixon, Steve Lacy, and some Europeans. Lacy, Koglmann, and Dixon all performed on *Opium/For Franz* (1976), which was reissued in 2001 by Koglmann's latest label, between the lines. In the 1970s, the trumpeter performed with Georg Graewe's GrubenKlangOrchester, the Improvising Music Orchestra, and the Reform Art Unit. From his Chamber Jazz Ensembles, Koglmann spun off the Pipetet, which recorded *Schlaf Schlemmer, Schlaf Magritte* (HatArt) in 1984. The contract with Werner Uehlinger's label was quite fruitful, resulting in some of Koglmann's best records: *The Use of Memory* (1990), *L'Heure Bleue* (1991), *Cantos I-IV* (1993), *O Moon My Pin-Up* (1997), and a project with altoist Lee Konitz, *We Thought about Duke* (1995). *L'Heure Bleue*, an especially entertaining disc, features Koglmann's Monoblue Quartet (with reedman Tony Coe, guitarist Burkhard Stangl, and bassist Klaus Koch) and four duets with Misha Mengelberg. Since 1972, he has received a number of awards for artistic excellence from the city of Vienna and the Austrian government. The between the lines label debuted in 1999 with Koglmann's *Make Believe*, featuring Coe and Brad Shepik.

Komeda, Krzysztof (Krzysztof Trzcinski; b. Poznan, Poland, 1931; d. 1969): pianist and composer. A doctor by official profession, Komeda was more renowned as a composer of scores for Ingmar Bergman and Roman Polanski than as a jazz musician, but he was equally gifted at both tasks. "Komeda" was a pseudonym used to throw off the Communist authorities, who did not approve of jazz. He gave a renowned performance at the 1956 Sopot Festival and became interested in free jazz a few years later. Among his earliest associates were Tomasz Stánko and Swedish tenorman Bernt Rosengren. *Astigmatic* (1965, Polonia) was Komeda's greatest recorded achievement, although he cut many excellent tracks that have been obscured over time. Altoist Zbigniew Namyslowski and violinist Michal Urbaniak were among Komeda's attentive sidemen. The pianist was injured in an auto accident in Los Angeles after completing the haunting score for Roman Polanski's *Rosemary's Baby*. He recovered from a coma and returned home but died of complications a few months later. Since the mid-1990s, Komeda's recordings have been reissued by the Power Brothers and Polonia labels; the latter's large series, *The Complete Recordings of Krzysztof Komeda*, is essential to understanding the tragic genius's work.

Kondo, Toshinori (b. Mabari City, Shikoku, Japan, 15 December 1948): trumpeter. Kondo's style updates the various elements of Miles Davis's playing, particularly his electric experiments, but it's not likely that Miles would have approved. Kondo is an extreme improviser, regularly doing battle with Peter Brötzmann in his tentet and Die Like A Dog Quartet (see entries), but he tempers his commitment to freedom with Eastern insight into peacefulness.

Kondo was largely influenced by Davis, Dizzy Gillespie, and Charlie Parker when he embraced jazz in the 1960s. He played in a hard-bop outfit, the Funky Beaters, and got into free jazz when artists like Milford Graves, Steve Lacy, and Derek Bailey visited Japan and played with local musicians. Kaoru Abe, Masayuki Takayanagi, and Motoharu Yoshizawa utilized the trumpeter in their free jazz experiments in the 1970s. In 1982, Kondo recorded *The Last Supper* for Po Torch, then came to New York and immersed himself in free improvisation there for some time. Eventually, however, he made Amsterdam his home, although he does not regularly participate in the Dutch jazz circles. He first recorded with Brötzmann in 1981 (*Alarm*, FMP); in 1992 he joined the saxophonist's tentet, then Die Like A Dog the following year. Kondo's more off-the-wall collaborations have included Borbetomagus, Henry Kaiser, and DJ Krush.

Konk Pack: trio of keyboardist Thomas Lehn, saxophonist Tim Hodgkinson, and drummer Roger Turner. Founded in the 1990s, their recordings include *Big Deep* (1999) and *Warp Out* (2001, both Grob).

Konnex: German label, established in 1984 by Manfred Schiek. Recorded artists include Dennis Gonzalez, Charlie Mariano, Rolf and Joachim Kühn, Peter Brötzmann, Sonny Fortune, Anthony Braxton, Cecil Taylor, John Stevens, Albert Mangelsdorff, Arthur Blythe, Tomasz Stánko, and Thomas Borgmann.

Kono, Masahiko (b. Kawasaki, Japan, 7 December 1951): trombonist. Kono began his studies on flute but switched to trumpet in 1971 while studying with Toshinori Kondo. Five years later, he took up the trombone, which remains his principal horn. Influenced by free greats like Roswell Rudd, Paul Rutherford, and George Lewis, Kono became one of Japan's leading free trombonists. He toured Japan with the quartet Tree, then worked in Kondo's tense Evolution Ensemble Unit. Kono spent three months in New York in 1980, making the rounds with William Parker, Milford Graves, and other up-and-coming free jazzmen. Upon returning home, Kono put his new experiences to the test with Kondo, pianist Katsuo Itabashi, and drummer Shoji Hano. He also backed visiting American and European freemen for a few years before returning to New York in 1983. He chose to remain there and eventually gained American citizenship. Since the 1980s, he has performed with Lewis, Parker's Little Huey Creative Music Orchestra, John Zorn, Fred Frith, Jemeel Moondoc's Jus' Grew Orchestra, Ken McIntyre, Ellen Christi, Cecil Taylor's large ensembles, Zusaan Kali Fasteau, and William Hooker. Kono occasionally returns to Japan for special events and spent two months in Mexico studying local musical styles.

Kowald, Peter (b. Meiningen, Germany, 21 April 1944; d. Brooklyn, NY, 20 September 2002): bassist. Kowald was one of Europe's principal free musicians, a beloved man and consummate performer who approached his music with an estimable passion. He began playing bass at age sixteen and spent time working with Peter Brötzmann in early free settings. In 1966, the two men were hired by Carla Bley and Michael Mantler for a European tour, which not only better educated them in American jazz forms but also spread their names around America's music circles. Later Kowald performed with Irène Schweizer and Pierre Favre, then became a founding member and occasional director of the Globe Unity Orchestra. In 1973, he began playing with Alexander von Schlippenbach, Evan Parker, and Paul Lovens in an extension of their trio explorations (*Hunting the Snake*, rec. 1975, issued 2000, Atavistic).

The bassist left Globe Unity in 1978 to join the London Jazz Composers Orchestra, with which he remained until 1985. He also helped to found the FMP (Free Music Production) label. Kowald performed and recorded with dozens of European and American freemen over the years, cut several impressive discs of his own (the solo *Was Da Ist*, 1994, FMP, is a must-hear *tour de force*), and collaborated with dance troupes, poets, and visual artists. *Touch the Earth—Break the Shells* (1997, FMP) is a superior document of his live ensemble dynamics, and *Duos: Europa America Japan* (1986, FMP) collects various pairings. Kowald was a principal catalyst of the Sound Unity Festival in 1984, a precursor to the Vision Festival, and was thereby a central character in *Rising Tones Cross*, Ebba Jahn's documentary about Sound Unity. He died of a heart attack at William Parker's home in September 2002.

Krauss, Briggan (b. St. Paul, MN, 6 August 1969): alto saxophonist. Krauss's family relocated to Oregon when he was a youth, and he initially learned the saxophone from his musician father (in fact, he continues to play his dad's horn today, along with occasional baritone sax and clarinet). Krauss attended Cornish College of the Arts in Seattle and began his professional career in that city. Babkas, his trio with Brad Schoeppach (later Shepik) and drummer Aaron Alexander, was Krauss's first highly visible gig. They were signed to the Songlines label in 1993. He began working with Wayne Horvitz's band Pigpen a year or so later.

In 1995, Krauss moved to New York and joined the Downtown movement centered around the Knitting Factory. His brusque tone and technical abilities made Krauss an asset in whichever settings he found himself. In the Big Apple, he performed with the Pink Noise Sax Quartet, Myth-Science (a Sun Ra cover band), Satoko Fujii's big band, E-Z Pour Spout, and Jerry Granelli's Badlands. Krauss joined slide trumpeter Steven Bernstein's Sex Mob in 1995; the group has since reaped a large fanbase for their daring but fun-filled excursions. The Resonance Impeders, a trio with bassist Chris Dahlgren and drummer Jay Rosen, debuted on CIMP in 1997. He has recorded with Andrea Parkins and drummer Kenny Wollesen, vocalist Jay Clayton, and DJ Logic. Krauss has also led bassless trios, first with Chris Speed and Michael Sarin (*Good Kitty*, 1997), then with Wollesen and Horvitz (*300*, 1998).

Kühn, Joachim (b. Leipzig, Germany, 15 March 1944): pianist, composer, brother of clarinetist Rolf Kühn. He began his piano studies as a child and kept up his studies through college. In 1961, Kühn practically gave up classical music in order to front jazz combos. In 1964, he played with his brother Rolf while leading his own trio. He stepped into jazz-rock fusion in the 1970s, gigging with violinist Jean-Luc Ponty, guitarist Jan Akkerman, and drummer Billy Cobham. Kühn's profile was significantly lower in the 1980s, though he recorded several strong albums for the CMP label. He came back powerfully in the next decade, interpreting "The Threepenny Opera" with bassist Jean-François Jenny-Clark and drummer Daniel Humair (1998) and recording in duo with Ornette Coleman (*Colors: Live from Leipzig*, 1997, both on Verve). Though not strictly a free player, Kühn has contributed well to certain free sessions.

Kuryokhin, Sergei (b. Murmansk, Russia, 16 June 1954; d. 9 July 1996): pianist and composer, a prominent figure in Russian free improvisation. He was mostly self-taught but did study piano and choral conducting in college. After working with reedman Anatoly Vapirov in the late 1970s, Kuryokhin encountered Vladimir Chekasin and began to investigate free jazz under his tutelage. He also developed a following as keyboardist for the rock band Aquarium, where he met guitarist Boris Grebenshikov. Kuryokhin's "Pop Mechanics" concepts were related to Lester Bowie's transmogrifications of American pop music into odd beasts of his own design, farfetched yet respectful.

Two solo albums recorded a decade apart principally represent Kuryokhin. *The Ways of Freedom* (1981, Leo) shows him utilizing classical principles as much as jazz and making good use of the piano's pedals so that he nearly duets with himself. "Theory and Practice" and "Rules of the Game" both operate on specific structural principles; "No Exit" and "Archipelago" find him suspended between Taylor and Mengelberg. The deep resonances wrought by his pedal technique build a plushy wall around certain passages, giving them a synthetically processed feel. *Some Combination of Fingers and Passion* (1991, Leo) is better. Kuryokhin relies on the same methodology, but in the decade since the prior session, he matured into a more tasteful, organized player. "Blue Rondo A La Russ—A Tribute to Dave Brubeck" depicts the cool-school giant in a funhouse mirror with an odd take on his unusual time signatures and blocky approach. On "Passion and Feelings," further pedal tides result in a polychromatic tapestry of sound greater than its parts.

By the time Kuryokhin died in July 1996, he had developed a passionate cult following but had not broken out into the market as far as he deserved. His death came a couple of months before a scheduled tour with Keshavan Maslak (aka Kenny Millions) and Otomo Yoshihide. Those friends recorded a loving tribute, *Without Kuryokhin* (1998, LongArms). Some of his long-unavailable music on Leo is available in the anthology *Golden Years of Soviet New Jazz, Vol. 1* (2001, Leo), along with rare recordings by other artists.

L

Lacy, Steve (Steven Norman Lackritz; b. New York, NY, 23 July 1934): soprano saxophonist, composer, and bandleader. He changed his last name to Lacy in the early 1950s when job opportunities began to appear. Lacy is a special case in jazz for numerous reasons, one being that he has almost always concentrated specifically on the soprano sax. He was the first jazz musician to do so since Sidney Bechet swung on the straight horn in the 1920s and 1930s. Lacy's adeptness on soprano inspired John Coltrane to try it out; ironically, Trane sold thousands of copies of *My Favorite Things* and immediately eclipsed Lacy's smaller public profile. If Lacy were revenge minded, he would have attained it by now; the number of records he has appeared on, and mostly led, surpasses three digits.

Like Roswell Rudd, whom he continually encountered around the city, Lacy began his career in Dixieland bands playing soprano sax and clarinet with Henry "Red" Allen, Rex Stewart, and other jazz forefathers. His first recording was a 1954 date led by Dick Sutton, which has long been forgotten. After his Dixie days, he dropped the clarinet in favor of the straight sax, and in 1955 he landed a job with Cecil Taylor's courageous unit. His tenure with the iconoclastic pianist only lasted a couple of years, then he fell back into slightly more mainstream projects: *Gil Evans + Ten*, led by the brilliant cool-school arranger, and his own bebop-laden debut *Soprano Sax* (both recorded in 1957, Prestige).

For a while, Monk was a much greater influence on Lacy than Taylor had been, and the chance to work in Monk's quartet in 1960 was a dream realized. In 1961, Lacy and Rudd formed a quartet with Henry Grimes and Denis Charles, which performed Monk's tunes exclusively. *School Days* (1975, Emanem; reissued 2000, HatHut) was recorded in March 1963 at a live show by the group. The renditions are pretty straightforward, ironic since all four men went on to become giants of free jazz. The hornmen, at least, never denied their lasting love for Monk's works.

Lacy found himself growing tired of the New York scene with so many young cats coming up the ranks of free jazz and trying to outdo each other for the few available jobs. He began to check out the rest of the world to see if better opportunities could be found. In October 1966, he found himself in Buenos Aires, Argentina, with a few of Europe's best: Italian trumpeter Enrico Rava and South African expatriates Johnny Dyani and Louis Moholo, who had taken up residence in England. That fortuitous circumstance led to *The Forest and the Zoo* (1966, ESP), which contains two twenty-minute improvisations by the quartet. A lack of dynamic range keeps this session from reaching the energetic heights of Taylor or Ayler by a long shot, but Moholo and Rava try their best. It is a valuable historical session with plenty of excellent interplay.

In 1970, Lacy decisively moved to Paris, where he remained until a teaching position at the New England Conservatory called him back to America in 2002. Along the way, Lacy became almost obsessed with the notion of music emulating the characteristics of objects or motions. His composition and album titles began reflecting these inspirations: "Stabs," "Trickles," "Ducks," "Clinkers," "Blinks," "Chirps," "The Door," "The Rent." On most of his several "Duck" tunes, Lacy quacks and squawks most birdlike; "Stabs" is riddled with sharp jabs of sound. With this philosophy, Lacy will certainly never lack for inspiration.

Lacy's solo efforts tend to be of a piece, each showing his pinpoint precision of intonation and delivery no matter what the underlying motif. One of the best to grace the market recently is *Hooky* (2000, Emanem), recorded in Montréal in March 1976. The acoustics of St.-Jean l'Évangéliste Church enabled Lacy to essentially duet with himself, in the manner of Europeans like Evan Parker. These tracks rank among his better solo conceptualizations, and the "Tao" suite is as spiritually uplifting as his music has ever been.

Lacy's group recordings are something else again though they, too, tend to be of consistent quality. Most of his ensemble efforts have been with his Parisian sextet, which will be addressed in a moment, but a few others stand out. *N.Y. Capers and Quirks* (1979, HatHut) is a rewarding trio set with Lacy, Boykins, and Charles evaluating five of the leader's multifaceted compositions. *One Fell Swoop* (1986, Silkheart) features Lacy with bassist Jean-Jacques Avenel, drummer Oliver Johnson, and Charles Tyler on alto and baritone. An ungainly take on Monk's "Friday the 13th," which has almost no chordal movement to speak of, showcases the hornmen's best traits: twisted harmonic logic, flexibility of tone. Tyler's baritone positively pounds on his tune "The Adventures Of," and Lacy's title track has great sectional movement.

Lacy recorded two albums with Franz Koglmann for the Pipe label in the 1970s. Both of those discs have been reissued on CD as *Opium/For Franz* (2001) on between the lines. Lacy's duels with the harmonically inventive trumpeter are uniformly captivating, particularly the two "Bowery" tracks and "For Franz," which adds Bill Dixon to the mix. "Bowery 1" begins with the deep, bluesy tones of Alan Silva's bowed bass, followed by a wistful melody from Lacy with supplementary muted statements by Koglmann. Gerd Geier's electronic chirpings and Aldo Romano's drums are more subtle.

In 1977, Lacy gathered the basic core of his sextet, a popularly acclaimed unit that remained active into the new century. Fellow saxophonist Steve Potts, pianist Bobby

Few, bassist Avenel, drummer Johnson (or, after 1990, John Betsch), and string player/ vocalist Iréne Aebi (Lacy's wife) have been the center of Lacy's attention since the 1980s. The excitement of two soprano saxes uniting or clashing in waves, teamed with the breezy strings and curious vocals of Aebi, makes a sound like no other in jazz. In time, Lacy's compositions began to move away from freedom to allow for ensemble coherence, a perfectly logical move, but there is abundant free activity to be heard.

The master tapes of *Prospectus* (1982, HatHut) were badly deteriorated when the time came for a CD issue, so much of the original two LPs' content had to be dumped. The title piece has since been recorded by the sextet on other sessions, but the original (with Aebi reciting from a French travel pamphlet, of all things) will be sorely missed on disc. The remaining tunes are available on *Clichés* (1999, HatHut), which features Johnson on drums and a guest spot by trombonist George Lewis. The Mingus stamp is audible on some arrangements, a nod to a key inspiration that Lacy shared with Gil Evans.

On *Two, Five, Six, Blinks* (1983, HatArt), the sextet reinterprets most of the same tunes as on *Clichés*. "The Whammies" is over nine minutes longer, giving Potts and Lacy a chance to dig into those bop mutations more firmly. Aebi's cello and violin work falls right into accord with the fluid Avenel. The bass player locks horns with Johnson on the rapid-fire "Blinks," which is based upon an old Dixieland motif by Kid Ory. Few is missing on some of the tracks; his presence on "Prospectus" and others fills out the sound nicely.

Aebi's voice can be abrasive, but she is charming on "Gay Paree Bop," which opens *The Gleam* (1986, Silkheart). Her buoyancy is echoed in the light tones of Lacy's soprano and Potts's alto, ending on a fun note. This enjoyable date tends to be over-looked, as does *The Door* (1988, Novus), with its title track inspired by the sound of knocking. Former Duke Ellington drummer Sam Woodyard sits in on the maestro's "Virgin Jungle," locking in with Aebi's lilting violin. Lacy enjoys returning to the same compositions time and again, Monk's and his own, not just to run carbon copies but to see what twists and turns can be inserted on the next go-round. These rehashes are not always successful, but the multiple renderings of "Blinks" and "Clichés" do benefit from additional goings-over.

Live at Sweet Basil (1991, Novus) was taped at the now-defunct New York club that hosted the Gil Evans Orchestra for many years. Despite a little sound trouble, the session is quite good. Aebi's voice is slightly out of tune early in "Prospectus" but straightens out in later returns. Though the five tracks are long, the interest level is high, the tension between Lacy and Potts on dueling sopranos is fascinating, and Avenel's dark resonance fills the room. A satisfying date, which can't quite be said for *Clangs* (1992, HatArt), a double sextet that takes forever to gel.

The year 1997 caught Lacy in the mood for duets. *Associates* (New Tone) is loaded to the brim with them; he has a different partner on each track, which gives a fresh scent to the disc. Japanese percussionist Masahiko Togashi opens on "Haze," with Lacy's soprano getting all prickly and fuzzy. Derek Bailey's edgy guitar brings out impatience and angst in the saxophonist's tone, the polar opposite of the soft "Pannonica" with Roswell Rudd. Few, Potts, and Aebi get their shots in, but their filial familiarity with Lacy's methods results in near complacency. George Lewis ("The Whammies") and Mal Waldron ("Epistrophy") provide the peaks on an uneven but

attractive program. Waldron is one of Lacy's oldest, dearest associates, and
Communiqué (1997, Soul Note) is perhaps their finest duo conference.

In 1999, Lacy recorded what might be his best work yet. *The Rent* (Cavity Search)
is a modest trio session with Avenel and Betsch, an unadorned unit that strips some
Lacy classics down to their glorious bare bones. Monk's hiccuppy "Shuffle Boil" sounds
fine and even more humorous without the piano filling out the harmonies, which lets
Avenel really show his stuff. Plenty of comfortable old favorites compose the set list.

One can hope that Lacy will return to the sextet format some time in the future,
given the financial success and lifelong camaraderies that came out of it, but these
recent duo and trio projects prove that he has much more in the oven to offer. His
return to America in 2002, to teach at the New England Conservatory, was a blessed
event to Lacy's hordes of American fans but might hinder hopes for regular sextet
reunions. At the time of this writing, Lacy was preparing interpretations of Beat poetry
for a quintet featuring George Lewis.

LaFaro, Scott (Rocco; b. Newark, NJ, 3 April 1936; d. Geneva, NY, 6 July 1961):
bassist. Few bass players have been on a par with LaFaro; only Mingus, Charlie Haden,
and Dave Holland leap immediately to mind. Though his career spanned only a few
short years before he was killed in a car accident, LaFaro made an indelible mark on
jazz and the state of the bass through his manual dexterity, melodic conceptions, and
unfailing intuition.

LaFaro did not even play bass regularly until his college years; he originally focused
on clarinet and tenor sax. In 1955, he joined Buddy Morrow's band for a year, then
left to work with Chet Baker. Until 1959, LaFaro was on the road and in the studio
with many mainstream jazz greats: Benny Goodman, Barney Kessel, Cal Tjader, and
others. In 1959, he met pianist Bill Evans and joined his trio with drummer Paul
Motian, becoming Evans's ideal partner. Their level of interaction bordered on the
miraculous, and their triumphant dates at the Village Vanguard (*Sunday at the Village
Vanguard*, 1961, Riverside) sealed the trio's reputation for all time. LaFaro also took
time to explore free jazz with Ornette Coleman in the early 1960s, appearing on the
important *Art of the Improvisers* (1959) and landmark *Free Jazz: A Collective Improvisation* (1960, both Atlantic), the latter of which paired him with Charlie Haden. The
bright young bassist also worked briefly with Stan Getz until his death, a tragic event
that sent Evans into a deep depression and cut short LaFaro's promising career.

Lake, Oliver (b. Marianna, AR, 14 September 1942): alto saxophonist, composer,
and bandleader. Soulful, forceful, and versed in Caribbean styles, classical music, and
other forms, Lake is a unique voice on alto sax. He began his music studies on drums
and did not learn to play sax until after high school. He graduated from Lincoln
University in 1968, then worked as a schoolteacher in St. Louis while gigging around
town. Lake was a founding member of the Black Artists Group (BAG), a performance
collective modeled after Chicago's AACM. He made his debut record in 1971 for the
Freedom label (*Ntu: The Point from Which Freedom Begins*). Charles Bobo Shaw, Julius
Hemphill, Joseph Bowie, and other BAG members worked with Lake in America and,
from 1972 until 1974, in Paris.

Upon his return to the United States, Lake moved to New York and soon recorded with Anthony Braxton. In 1976, he, Hemphill, Hamiet Bluiett, and David Murray formed the World Saxophone Quartet, which has been one of Lake's main gigs since. (See the entry for World Saxophone Quartet.) However, he continued to work as a leader; *Clevont Fitzhubert (Was a Friend of Mine)* (1981, Black Saint) is one of Lake's most enduring sessions. In that same year, he founded the reggae-influenced Jump Up, which began recording for Gramavision. In the 1990s, Lake recorded with Borah Bergman, Andrew Cyrille, Pheeroan Ak Laff, and pianist Donal Fox. His own records became progressively more ambitious; *Movement, Turns & Switches* (1996) featured strings, and *Matador of 1st and 1st* (1997, both on Passin' Thru) was a solo venture of alto, percussion, and poetry.

Lancaster, Byard (William; b. Philadelphia, PA, 6 August 1942): saxophonist and flautist. Based in his hometown for many years, Lancaster is a tremendous improviser whose technique reveals a steeping in soul and blues (he worked for a while with Memphis Slim in France) as well as the avant-garde. Lancaster worked with pianist Dave Burrell and bassist Sirone in the Untraditional Jazz Improvisational Team as far back as 1965, the same year that he began working with Sunny Murray. Later employers included Bill Dixon, Sun Ra, and McCoy Tyner. He was an essential part of several aggregations organized in the mid-1970s within the New York loft community, including Murray's Untouchable Factor and pianist Sonelius Smith's Flight to Sanity. Lancaster was one of the most commanding sax players on the *Wildflowers* album series that documented the loft scene.

Most of Lancaster's own recordings are now difficult to come by. He has often been relegated to obscurity within the genre, despite some excellent performances and records. In 2001, he teamed up with fellow Philly saxman Odean Pope on the outstanding *Philadelphia Spirit in New York* (CIMP). His enjoyment of playing in the streets and subways has gotten Lancaster arrested more than once; the last incident, in October 2002, brought the plight of street buskers to national attention.

Lasha, Prince (William B. Lawsha; b. Fort Worth, TX, 10 September 1929): altoist, flautist, and composer. Respectably talented and deeply inspired by Ornette Coleman, Lasha's career has largely been defined by only a few recordings. He had performed with Coleman in the early 1950s and moved to California several years before the free pioneer. He met altoman Sonny Simmons and struck up an excellent collaboration wherein the two often alternated between flutes and altos. *The Cry* (1962, Contemporary, reissued by Original Jazz Classics) gives an interesting look at how Lasha interpolated Coleman's free concepts into his own band. Simmons is a good foil, bluesier and more tense than his partner. Gary Peacock and Mark Proctor, alternating on bass, team well with drummer Gene Stone in driving the horns to explore beyond the chord progressions.

The following year Lasha and Simmons both worked with Eric Dolphy, contributing to the sessions that were released as *Conversations* (1963, FM) and *Iron Man* (1963, Douglas). Lasha also performed with the sextet of Elvin Jones and Jimmy Garrison in that year. A now obscure 1965 recording, *Inside Story* (issued 1981, Enja), was an enlightening document of how strong Lasha's flute talents were in the company of Herbie Hancock, bassist Cecil McBee, and drummer Jimmy Lovelace. In 1967, Lasha and Simmons reunited for *The Firebirds* (Contemporary), an impressive set that revealed a definite maturation of their free-bop conceptions. With Bobby Hutcherson, Charles Moffett, and bassist Buster Williams on hand, the reedmen wrought an exciting set of originals that has long been underappreciated. The session unfortunately seemed to mark the end of Lasha's heyday; he released very few new albums afterward, none after 1983, and has not been heard from since.

Last Exit: free jazz-rock quartet consisting of Sonny Sharrock, Peter Brötzmann, Ronald Shannon Jackson, and bass guitarist Bill Laswell. Each member brought their own special touches to form the unmistakable chaos of Last Exit: Laswell's vibrant, dub-inflected bass tones, Jackson's overwhelming polyrhythms, Sharrock's volcanic metal guitar lines, and Brötzmann's torrential horn parts blended together to form a passionate unit like no other.

The group made a huge impact starting with their eponymous debut album in 1986 (discussed in the front matter of this book), but their recordings were inconsistent. *The Noise of Trouble* (1987, Enemy) features marginal interplay with Japanese reedman Akira Sakata, as well as a poorly conceived guest spot by pianist Herbie Hancock. *Köln* (ITM, 1986) and *Cassette Recordings '87* (Enemy/Celluloid, 1987) are dissatisfying; Laswell is often reduced to near inaudibility on the latter, and Brötzmann uncharacteristically seems to go at it by rote despite his rawness. The sole studio album, *Iron Path* (Venture, 1988), is severely understated compared with the live discs. Still, Last Exit reached incredible peaks, and their promise hardly seemed spent by the time of Sharrock's death in May 1994.

Laster, Andy (b. 1961): saxophonist, composer, and bandleader. Laster studied jazz at Seattle's Cornish Institute but came home to New York in 1985. He had not built much of a profile downtown before releasing his debut disc, *Hippo Stomp* (1989, Sound Aspects), to good acclaim. He became as respected for his compositional skills as for his adept blowing. A couple of years later, Laster assembled the group Hydra, which made its first, self-titled album for Sound Aspects in 1994. The following year, the band was signed to Songlines, along with his ponderously named Interpretations of Lessness. Laster worked in various other ensembles: the Pink Noise Sax Quartet with Briggan Krauss, Erik Friedlander's Topaz, Orange Then Blue, and New and Used. He has also performed with Mark Helias; Hank Roberts; Fred Ho; Satoko Fujii; Phil Haynes; the Julius Hemphill Sextet (replacing the leader on alto); Bobby Previte's Weather Clear, Track Fast; the early-jazz repertory Ballin' the Jack; and country crooner Lyle Lovett. His most recent disc is *Window Silver Bright* (2002, New World).

Laswell, Bill (b. Salem, IL, 12 February 1955): electric bassist and one of the most in-demand producers in modern music. Laswell began on guitar in his youth but moved to the bass so he could play with funk bands around Detroit. He came to New York in 1978 and soon met Gong leader Daevid Allen. The backup band Laswell had cobbled for Allen became known as Material and started doing their own dates in 1979 (*Material*, Temporary Music). Their next album, *One Wish* (1980, Celluloid), marked the debut of Whitney Houston on record, while *Memory Serves* (1982, Enemy) saw a movement away from R&B into free-funk territory. Laswell issued his debut as a leader, *Baselines* (1982), on his Celluloid label.

Laswell's credits began to pile up quickly: John Zorn, Fred Frith, ex–Talking Heads singer David Byrne, Laurie Anderson, the Golden Palominos, Peter Gabriel, Mick Jagger. In 1983, he won a Grammy for producing Herbie Hancock's electric hit "Rockit." Laswell joined Curlew for a while but moved on to Last Exit where he gained some of his most intense experience in improvisation (see entry for Last Exit). Along the way, he produced albums for African artists, Cream drummer Ginger Baker, the Last Poets, soul diva Nona Hendryx, and Pharoah Sanders. Laswell issued more recordings under his own name and dabbled in hip-hop sounds with Praxis. In 1990, he formed the Axiom label, featuring techno and ambient music as well as free jazz by artists like Henry Threadgill. Laswell has stepped up his output as a leader and producer, exploring everything from dub to free jazz to ambience.

Lê Quan, Ninh (b. Paris, France, 1961): percussionist and electronic musician. In the 1980s, he studied at Versailles Conservatory and received awards for his work there. He has worked with various contemporary music ensembles, written for the theater, and commissioned compositions from George Lewis, Jean-Pierre Drouet, Vinko Globokar, and other modern writers. From 1987, he worked frequently with Peter Kowald, including stints with the bassist's Ort Ensemble and Global Village. Carlos Zingaro, Daunik Lazro, and Butch Morris have also been regular partners of the percussionist; he has appeared on a number of Morris's "conductions" projects for the New World label. His resumé further includes concerts and records with Ned Rothenberg, Paul Lovens, Phil Minton, Elliott Sharp, Zeena Parkins, Mario Schiano, Günter Müller, Myra Melford, and Tristan Honsinger. He has developed a computer music system for multimedia improvisational projects.

Léandre, Jöelle (b. Aix-en-Provence, France, 12 September 1951): bassist and vocalist. Léandre studied piano and bass as a young girl, and she was accepted to the Conservatoire National Superieur de Musique de Paris with honors. In 1976, she went to the Center for Creative and Performing Arts in Buffalo to study contemporary music with Morton Feldman. John Cage's music was particularly inspirational to Léandre at the time. Soon thereafter, she explored the improvisation scene in downtown New York and was inspired to delve further into that type of music. She became enthralled with Derek Bailey, Irène Schweizer, Anthony Braxton, and George Lewis. She has taken part in Bailey's Company projects and worked with Schweizer in the European Women's (formerly Feminist) Improvising Group, along with doing sessions with Evan Parker, Lol Coxhill, Peter Kowald, Fred Frith, William Parker, Jon Rose, and Barre Phillips. She presently performs in Canvas Trio with Rüdiger Carl and Carlos Zingaro. *Paris Quartet* (1987, Intakt) and her duo with Zingaro, *Écritures* (1990, In Situ), are excellent.

Lee, Jeanne (b. New York, NY, 29 January 1939; d. Tijuana, Mexico, 25 October 2000): vocalist. One of the most truly impressive free singers, Lee possessed an astonishing flexibility and deep soulfulness that enabled her to blend in with most any ensemble. It is said that much of her best work was never recorded; a shame, since she has not been served very well by the music industry.

Lee originally studied dance at Bard College in upstate New York, where she met pianist Ran Blake. They collaborated as a duo, and Lee's voice immediately impressed those who heard the pair. After a European tour, she moved to California in 1964 and met future Frank Zappa saxophonist Ian Underwood. She married David Hazelton, her first husband, not long thereafter and met her second husband, Gunter Hampel, while touring Europe again in 1967. With Hampel, she recorded nearly two dozen albums, including the influential *Eighth of July 1969* (Birth).

Lee's resumé eventually included projects with Cecil Taylor, Archie Shepp, Sunny Murray, Marion Brown, Anthony Braxton, Andrew Cyrille, Carla Bley, Marilyn Crispell, Jane Bunnett, Peter Kowald, Enrico Rava, and Bob Moses. In the 1980s, she began composing works for jazz and dance ensembles, and taught at conservatories in Europe throughout the 1990s. In 2000, Lee contracted colon cancer, which quickly claimed her life.

Lee, Peggy: cellist. Lee and her husband, drummer Dylan van der Schyff, are among the principal improvisers in Canada. Classically trained, Lee has devoted much of her young life to avant-garde music so far. She has performed with François Houle, the NOW Orchestra, Carlos Zingaro, Barry Guy, Scott Fields, John Butcher, Phil Durrant, and others. *These Are Our Shoes* (1999, Spool) was the debut recording of Lee's own ensemble.

Lehn, Thomas (b. Detmold, Germany, 1958): pianist and synthesizer player. He studied at the Detmold Hochschule für Musik in his youth, then continued his studies in Köln. There he participated in several jazz workshops under George Russell, Gunter Hampel, and Keith Tippett, exploring the music further outside of school. In 1982, he began his career as a solo performer of avant-garde and classical piano music and later moved into the world of analog synthesizers. On Moogs and other vintage keyboards, Lehn has performed and recorded with John Butcher, Günter Christmann (*Vario-34*, 1993, Blue Tower), Gerry Hemingway (*Tom and Gerry*, 1997, Erstwhile), MIMEO, Eugene Chadbourne (*C Inside*, 1999, Grob), John Russell, Keith Rowe, and a number of trios (Phil Durrant/Radu Malfatti, John Butcher/guitarist Andy Moor, Peter van Bergen/Gert-Jan Prins, Phil Minton/Axel Dörner, Konk Pack, and VCO-1). *Feldstärken* (1999, Random Acoustics) is a recommended solo effort. Lehn still regularly participates in a number of new music groups and multimedia events.

Leimgruber, Urs (b. Lucerne, Switzerland, 1952): saxophonist and composer. A resident of Paris since 1988, he has been active in European contemporary music since the early 1970s. He has been a member of the electric free band Om, Ensemble Bleu, and the acclaimed quartet Reflexionen. He has performed and recorded with the likes of Joe McPhee, Tim Berne, Steve Lacy, Marilyn Crispell, and Louis Sclavis.

Leimgruber has led his own groups and has done various mixed-media productions. His best records include *Reflexionen* (1983, Timeless), *L'enigmatique* (1991, HatArt), and *Quartet Noir* (1998, Victo, with Joëlle Léandre, Marilyn Crispell, and drummer Fritz Hauser).

Leo Records: label established by Leo Feigin in 1981 to expose Russian improvised music to the world. Many of the Russian sessions were recorded in secret and smuggled out of the country for release. Besides documenting the Ganelin Trio, Igor Bril, and other like-minded Soviet players, the label has issued recordings by American avant-gardists like Amina Claudine Myers, Anthony Braxton, Marilyn Crispell, Sun Ra, and Cecil Taylor. A sister imprint, Golden Years of New Jazz, handles reissues of American, European, and Russian free jazz, while Leo Lab delves into less jazzy outward territories.

Lewis, George (b. Chicago, IL, 14 July 1952): trombonist and composer. Lewis has been a pioneer in free jazz and electronic improvisation, utilizing computer technology in live and recorded performances. He studied with Muhal Richard Abrams under the AACM's auspices and became one of its youngest members in the early 1970s. Lewis graduated from Yale with a philosophy degree but has devoted his life to avant-garde music. His enormous resumé includes recordings with Abrams, Anthony Braxton, Evan Parker, Steve Lacy, Barry Altschul, Bill Laswell, Derek Bailey, John Zorn, and even Count Basie.

Lewis's debut as a leader was the aptly titled *Solo Trombone Album* (1976, Sackville), which demonstrated his stylistic debt to Albert Mangelsdorff. He has since modified his approach to include electronics; in one unique show, his trombone playing triggered a CD-ROM photo album of family members. His *Homage to Charles Parker* (1979, Black Saint) is one of the greatest documents of post-Ayler free jazz, an incredible conception that builds upon Bird's bebop legacy and carries it all the way into the future. Lewis has held residencies in electronic music at Amsterdam's STEIM and Paris's IRCAM, as well as the Banff Center for the Arts in Canada.

Lindberg, John (John Arthur Lindberg III; b. Royal Oak, MI, 16 March 1959): bassist, composer, and bandleader. Lindberg is an intuitive and flexible bassist who brings just a touch of classical austerity to his music at times. He studied in Ann Arbor, spent time in St. Louis with the Human Arts Ensemble, and began working with Anthony Braxton in 1978. The following year he became a founding member of the String Trio of New York, with violinist Billy Bang and guitarist James Emery. In 1980, he performed with ex–Cecil Taylor alumni Jimmy Lyons and Sunny Murray, and continued to work with the drummer off and on during the decade. Lindberg has led well over a dozen sessions; *Dimension 5* (1981, Black Saint) and *Tree Frog Tonality* (2000, between the lines) are two strong releases. Lindberg paid homage to a prime influence on 1997's *Luminosity: Homage to David Izenzon* (Music & Arts) and has backed up Susie Ibarra, Tim Berne, Ray Anderson, and Wadada Leo Smith.

Lindsay, Arto (b. Brazil, 28 May 1953): guitarist and vocalist. Even when Lindsay was playing pop music in his homeland, he infused it with the quirky twists that still characterize his style. He came to New York City in the mid-1970s and founded the No Wave rock group DNA in 1977. In the early 1980s, he led the noise-pop band Ambitious Lovers and was a founding member, if only briefly, of the Lounge Lizards (see entry) and the Golden Palominos. Lindsay was associated for several years with John Zorn (*Locus Solus*, 1983, Rift; reissued 1995, Tzadik), which increased his improvising credentials, and with Japenese electronic composer Ryuichi Sakamoto (*Collection: 1981–1987*, 1999, MIDI). Since the 1990s, Lindsay has toned down his experimentalism slightly, playing more acoustic guitar and producing sessions for Laurie Anderson, Carlinhos Brown, and Vinicius Cantuaria. The twenty-six short pieces on *Arto Lindsay* (1995, Knitting Factory Works) are representative of his cut-and-slash guitar style. *Subtle Body* (1996, Bar None) contains some of his best Brazilian-influenced musings.

Liof Munimula: Chicago-based improvising trio. The principals are Michael Zerang on drums and percussion, Don Meckley on shortwave radio and invented instruments (such as the hydrokalimba and typewriter mbira), and Daniel Scanlan on violin and trumpet. Their sole recording to date is 1988's *The Jonah Syndrome* (Garlic), but a boxed set of live performances is rumored to be in development. (The band's name is "aluminum foil" backward.)

Little, Booker (Jr.; b. Memphis, TN, 2 April 1938; d. New York, NY, 5 October 1961): trumpeter and free-jazz pioneer. At the time of his death from uremia, Little had begun to move toward free jazz in the same manner as his cohort Eric Dolphy, particularly his use of phrasing and intervals. Little studied at the Chicago Conservatory and kept busy with bop tenorman Johnny Griffin's band and the MJT+3. A tenure with Max Roach got him interested in harder edged, more politicized music. He recorded *Africa/Brass* with John Coltrane, then continued working with Dolphy in sessions led by the reedman (*At the Five Spot*, 1961, Prestige) and himself (*Out Front*, 1961, Candid). The latter album is the most forward-looking of Little's too-sparse output.

Logan, Giuseppi (b. Philadelphia, PA, 22 May 1935): saxophonist and bandleader. Logan was an early herald of free jazz in New York, having come to the Big Apple from Boston seeking to make an impact on the city's music scene. He was not a brilliant technician but certainly knew how to inspire those around him. Like Coltrane, Logan had worked with Earl Bostic's R&B band, and like Cecil Taylor, he attended New England Conservatory. His quartet performed in the "October Revolution in Jazz," and he recorded a series of unusual albums for ESP (*The Giuseppi Logan Quartet*, 1964; *More Giuseppi Logan* and *At Town Hall*, 1965), which featured him on alto, tenor, flute, bass clarinet, piano, and Pakistani oboe. The first is the strongest. Logan also worked as a sideman for Byard Lancaster, Patty Waters, and Roswell Rudd.

For all of his experience, Logan's technique was not considered strong enough for him to hold down stable gigs as a musician. He was also woefully unequipped to work through the wheelings and dealings of the New York jazz scene, which held him back further. Logan finally faded into oblivion, a casualty of the mindset that an interest in free improvising might be enough to sustain a career in America's most creative city. He is believed to have died in California sometime in the early 1990s, but even that is uncertain. Ironically, his ignorance of how to survive in the business did not keep Logan from influencing scores of more successful players with whom he came in contact.

Lonberg-Holm, Fred (b. 1962, Delaware): cellist. Lonberg-Holm studied classical cello and modern composition, the latter with Morton Feldman and Anthony Braxton. He resided in Sweden during part of his youth and later made his way to New York. There he performed with Braxton's Creative Music Orchestra, John Zorn, Anthony Coleman, the avant group God Is My Co-Pilot, and his own units, including Peep. In the 1990s, he moved to Chicago and fell into Ken Vandermark's circle of influence. Lonberg-Holm is a member of Peter Brötzmann's Chicago Tentet and performs regularly with Vandermark, Michael Zerang, Jim O'Rourke, Boxhead Ensemble, and Kevin Drumm. He has received several commissions for compositions and presently leads Pillow and Terminal 4. *A Valentine for Fred Katz* (2002, Atavistic) is a loving tribute to the cellist who helped bring the instrument into jazz prominence with Chico Hamilton's 1950s bands.

London Improvisers Orchestra: large improvising ensemble, born from a 1997 tour by American cornetist/composer Lawrence "Butch" Morris. Morris hired members of the London Music Collective for his "London Skyscraper" project, a "conduction" in which he directed the band with hand signals through group improvisations. Evan Parker, Steve Beresford, and a number of younger players enjoyed the project so much that they decided to pursue similar paths. The group began gathering once a month at the Red Rose Club for rehearsals and concerts. Simon H. Fell, Philipp Wachsmann, trumpeter Ian Smith, and vocalist Terry Day (fresh from a ten-year retirement) are among the chief constituents. The ranks also include composers who write specifically for the ensemble, among them Caroline Kraabel, Alex Ward, and David Leahy.

In 1999, Martin Davidson, the head of Emanem Records, began recording the LIO's adventures. Their first two-disc set was *Proceedings*, taped that same year with thirty-one musicians on hand. Several tracks are navigable group improvisations, some conducted in the Morris fashion. "Monster's Milk" is the centerpiece, an expertly conceived panorama of tonal divergences between strings and horns. Fell's "Ellington 100 (Strayhorn 85)" is an odd aberration of a Duke ballad. A good-sized booklet of performances notes offers insights into the LIO's mission.

The Hearing Continues (2001, Emanem) is a more cohesive statement. Louis Moholo, Veryan Weston, mallet player Orphy Robinson, and West Indies–born trumpeter Harry Beckett are included. David Leahy's "Prior to Freedom" is based upon the understanding that most of the performers played some other form of music before they got into free improv. The instruction is for everyone to play in the style they worked in "prior to freedom." Classical, Dixieland, rock, and other influences come belching out in a hilarious cacophony, which has some odd semblance of order. On "How Can You Delude Yourself?", silence may never occur without being immediately filled with sound, and no more than three performers can play at one time.

London Jazz Composers' Orchestra (LJCO): collective formed in 1970. Intrigued by the musical possibilities explored by the Jazz Composers' Orchestra Association in America, a group of British improvisers, including Evan Parker and Barry Guy, developed their own organization to facilitate free improvisation in a larger ensemble setting. The LJCO has been among the most successful groups when it comes to integrating free jazz into larger situations, although its early days were tumultuous.

Ode (1972, Incus), the LJCO's debut, balanced freedom with quality Guy compositions and Buxton Orr's attentive conducting. Guy's subsequent works became progressively more difficult for the performers to handle, as is often the case with avant-garde experiments. As the bassist gradually doled out control and writing duties to other members, a sense of unity and purpose returned to the orchestra, which was reflected in its improved performances. By the time of the reasonably solid *Stringer* (1983, FMP), the ratio of jazz to free improv had leveled off. *Harmos* (1989) and *Theoria* (1991, both Intakt), the latter featuring Irène Schweizer on her fiftieth birthday, represent the LJCO's pinnacles on disc. *Double Trouble II* (1995, Intakt), with both Schweizer and Marilyn Crispell on piano and Pierre Favre on drums, is another excellent endeavor.

Lounge Lizards: New York ensemble. Founded in 1981 by the Lurie brothers, saxophonist John and pianist Evan, the Lounge Lizards are a smart postmodern outfit who love to cross the borders between free jazz, swing, circus music, pop, *film noir*, and whatnot. The group was originally gathered for a gig at an arts community downtown, but the Luries liked the results and decided to keep the band together. John Lurie also held a lucrative side gig, scoring and acting in Jim Jarmusch films like *Stranger in Paradise* and *Down by Law*.

The original lineup included the wacko Brazilian guitarist Arto Lindsay, drummer Anton Fier, and bassist Steve Piccolo (*Lounge Lizards*, 1981, EG; *Live 79-81*, 1985, Roir). That configuration did not last long before Fier and Lindsay left to form the Golden Palominos. The group floundered for a bit, working with less interesting players and collaborating with the London Philharmonic and producer Teo Macero before hitting their stride with *Big Heart: Live in Tokyo* (1986, Polygram). The personnel then included the Lurie brothers, guitarist Marc Ribot, saxophonist Roy Nathanson, trombonist Curtis Fowlkes, bassist Eric Sanko, and drummer Dougie Bowne. In 1987, that same lineup recorded the excellent *No Pain for Cakes* (Polygram). Its follow-up, *Voice of Chunk* (Strange & Beautiful), was conceived as a mail-order-only album in its LP format but saw wider release on CD. Their most recent recording is *Queen of All Ears* (1998, Strange & Beautiful), with a radically different lineup including cello and percussion.

Lovens, Paul (b. Aachen, Germany, 6 June 1949): drummer and percussionist. A European adjunct to America's Milford Graves, Lovens tends to become an equal part of the process instead of sticking to the pulse. Self-taught, he began his pro career as a teenager. Since the early 1970s, he has worked with most of the premier players and groups in European free music; perhaps his most significant performances have been with the Globe Unity Orchestra, Alex von Schlippenbach's trio (*Elf Bagatellen*, 1990, FMP), and the Berlin Contemporary Jazz Orchestra. In 1976, Lovens founded the Po Torch label. He plays in combo settings often and has partnered with dancers, visual artists, theater troupes, and filmmakers. He has done duets with Schlippenbach (*Stranger Than Love*, 1984, Po Torch), Cecil Taylor (*Regalia*, 1988, FMP), Eugene Chadbourne, and other improvisers.

Lowe, Frank (b. Memphis, TN, 24 June 1943; d. 19 September 2003): tenor saxophonist. Lowe was a player of fearsome power, given to fits of raw musical emotion with a hard blues undertone. Woefully neglected in the jazz business, he nonetheless kept up the pace and created some of the most bracing free jazz of the past quarter-century. He began playing the saxophone at age twelve and attended the University of Kansas. After a brief spell on the West Coast, Lowe went to New York and worked with the principal figures of free jazz's first and second waves: Don Cherry, Archie Shepp, Alice Coltrane, and Rashied Ali. In 1973, Lowe and Ali recorded the crushing *Duo Exchange* (Survival), and the tenorman cut his name debut for the then-fading ESP label, *Black Beings*. The record features Joseph Jarman, a young William Parker, drummer Rashid Sinan, and a violinist billed as "The Wizard" (possibly Billy Bang with whom Lowe worked through much of the 1980s, or Leroy Jenkins). Lowe's next two albums, *Fresh* (1975, Freedom) and *The Flam* (1975, Black Saint) continued his streak of excellence. Later in life he saw low points (1978's *Doctor Too-Much*, Kharma) and more triumphs (discs for Soul Note and CIMP). Recent achievements included the two *Legend Street* collaborations with Joe McPhee (1996, CIMP), albums with the reed sextet SaxEmble and poet Jayne Cortez, and *The Philip Wilson Project* (1994, ITM), a tribute to the late drummer. Lowe died of cancer at age sixty.

Lussier, René: guitarist. Lussier is one of Montréal's finest improvisers, a fearless experimenter in the spirit of Fred Frith and Henry Kaiser. Frith has been an inspiration to Lussier since the days of Henry Cow and a frequent partner since the 1986 Festival International de Musique Actuelle de Victoriaville (FIMAV). The recording of their duo set *Nous Autres* inaugurated the Victo record label in 1987. The pair also collaborated in the Keep the Dog ensemble, with saxophonist Jean Derome. Lussier began playing guitar in high school and joined the group Conventum after graduation. The project marked the first of many collaborations with guitarist André Duchesne. After the ensemble's demise, Lussier got into heavier avant-garde work with the Grand Orchestre de Montréal, where he met Derome and began composing for films. The friends formed the group Ambiances Magnétiques and a record label by the same name, with Duchesne and clarinetist Robert Lepage (*Theorie Des Ensembles*, 1992). *Le Trésor de la Langue* (1989) is an outstanding example of *musique actuelle*, layering music and spoken words in creative, arresting ways. In the 1990s, Lussier was a member of Derome's Les Dangereux Zhoms but quit to concentrate on his own projects. He has won several national awards and is also a respected engineer and music editor.

Lyons, Jimmy (b. Jersey City, NJ, 1 December 1933; d. New York, NY, 19 May 1986): alto saxophonist, composer, and bandleader. Lyons was raised mostly by his grandparents, who ran a chicken restaurant at Harlem's famous Hotel Woodside. Lyons was surrounded by visiting musicians for most of his youth and studied drums with his uncle. In 1947, he got his first sax from Ellington reedman Buster Bailey, a friend of his mother.

Brief, informal lessons with pianists Elmo Hope, Al Walker, and Thelonious Monk and saxophonist Rudy Rutherford helped to shape Lyons's understanding of jazz and musical structure. Like most altoists in the late 1940s and 1950s, Lyons derived inspiration from Charlie Parker; in fact, his technique became so amazing and precise that he was occasionally held up as the possible successor to Parker's throne. That firm grounding in bebop added an important, accessible element to his later free work.

Lyons played at occasional dances and other social functions, but his first serious professional gig came with Cecil Taylor in 1961. The two men developed a tremendous friendship and artistic rapport that helped Lyons navigate the pianist's devilishly complex music. The sporadic gigs available to Taylor's group were frustrating for everyone involved, but the two friends worked together, off and on, for the rest of Lyons's life. His Parker-inspired alto sax tone eventually evolved into a more abstracted sound, now more reminiscent of Eric Dolphy but instantly recognizable as Lyons's own. (See Cecil Taylor's entry.)

Lyons occasionally worked as a music teacher to compensate for the general lack of work. He taught at the Narcotic Addiction Control Center for a year, then held posts at Antioch (with Taylor and Cyrille) and Bennington (with Bill Dixon), where he directed the Black Music Ensemble. In 1969, Lyons recorded his first session as a leader (*Other Afternoons*, BYG), but he did not gather his own regularly working unit until 1978. That unusual ensemble featured bassoonist Karen Borca, who contributed a most surprising, otherworldly sound to the leader's impressively structured music. *Wee Sneezawee* (1983, Black Saint) was one of Lyons's best efforts as a leader, with a great band including Borca, Raphé Malik, William Parker, and drummer Paul Murphy. A similar lineup, with Enrico Rava and Jay Oliver in place of Malik and Parker, made the even better *Give It Up* (Black Saint) in 1985. An earlier session, *Jump Up* (1980, HatArt), teamed the active altoist with Sunny Murray and John Lindberg. On all of these releases, Lyons was in secure command with a detached, not to say standoffish, air about his playing. His excellent recording streak was brought to an abrupt end by his death, which nearly devastated his close friend and partner, Cecil Taylor.

Lytton, Paul (b. London, England, 8 March 1947): drummer and percussionist. A close counterpart to Paul Lovens, with whom he has been teamed, compared, and confused, Lytton is the motor that drives Evan Parker's incredible trio with bassist Barry Guy (see Parker's entry). Lytton came up in European free music in the late 1960s and helped to found musicians' cooperatives in London and Aachen, Germany. His first record was *An Electric Storm* (1968, Island [Japan]), with the ensemble White Noise. His association with Parker began in the early 1970s and continues to this day. In 1975, Lytton moved to Belgium, where he and Lovens founded their Po Torch record label. Besides his projects with Parker (including the brilliant duo *Ra 1+2*, 1976, Ring), Lytton has played and recorded with the London Jazz Composers Orchestra, Barry Guy's New Orchestra (*Inscape–Tableaux*, 2000, Intakt), the King Übü Orchestrü, Hans Schneider, Wolfgang Fuchs, Ken Vandermark (*English Suites*, 1999, Wobbly Rail), the Territory Band, Philipp Wachsmann, Marilyn Crispell, and his own projects. Lytton is also a renowned builder of musical instruments.

M

M(atsubara), Sachiko: electronic musician. A highly unusual performer, even among the electroacoustic community, Sachiko M is a virtuoso with samplers and sine-wave generators. She often plays the sampler without samples, using its built-in test tones and ambient noise to generate sounds. She was a member of Otomo Yoshihide's group Ground Zero from 1994 to 1997 and has since become one of the busiest EAI improvisers in the world. She still works with Otomo today, administering the Amoebic label and playing in the duo Filament and the trio I.S.O. with percussionist and electronic musician Ichiraku Yoshimitsu (see the entry for I.S.O.) Her work with Toshimaru Nakamura and his no-input mixing board represents a pinnacle of improvisational "music" with almost no sounds generated at all. She has performed with Hoahio, singer Amy Yoshida, poire_z, Andrea Neumann, Rhodri Davies, and Günter Müller as well.

Malaby, Tony (b. Tucson, AZ, 1964): tenor saxophonist. He studied at University of Arizona and William Paterson College in New Jersey, absorbing mainstream jazz at the former, more avant-garde music at the latter. He was hired by organist Joey DeFrancesco in 1992, which led to gigs with Marty Ehrlich, bassist Michael Formanek, a couple of Charles Mingus tribute bands, and Satoko Fujii's Orchestra. Formanek and drummer Tom Rainey have been steady partners since, recording *Cosas* (1993, Nine Winds) with trombonist Joey Sellers. Malaby waxed the adventurous *Sabino* (Arabesque) in 2000. He has recorded more mainstream jazz with trumpeter Fred Forney, his former mentor at Arizona, and outward-looking fare with Pandelis Karayorgis and Mat Maneri (*Disambiguation*, 2002, Leo). Thus far, Malaby is one of the most promising voices on tenor sax in the new millennium.

Malfatti, Radu (b. Innsbruck, Austria, 16 December 1943): trombonist and composer. After studying with Eje Thelin at the Graz Music Academy, Malfatti began his career playing mainstream and free jazz around Central Europe in the early 1970s with Paul Rutherford, Arjen Gorter, Paul Lovens, and Peter Kowald. He moved to London in 1972 and worked with Chris McGregor's Brotherhood of Breath, saxophonist Elton Dean's Ninesense, and other ensembles. During the 1980s, as he moved around Europe and finally settled in Köln, Malfatti grew disillusioned with the state of improvised music in Europe and began to seek alternative forms of expression.

One of the most avant hornmen on the continent, Malfatti has pushed John Cage's concepts of silence to new extremes with extremely sparse performances in which he might not play a single note for several minutes at a time. He was briefly a member of the Wandelweiser Group, which specialized in such silence-based ideas, and the collective Polwechsel. In more recent years, he has been a member of the Dedication Orchestra, King Übü Örchestrü, Georg Graewe's GrubenKlangOrchester, Franz Koglmann's Pipetet, the ICP Tentett, and London Jazz Composers Orchestra. Malfatti has recorded with Joe McPhee, Steve Lacy, Burkhard Stangl, Harry Miller, Louis Moholo, and in trio with Phil Durrant and Thomas Lehn on two albums (*Beinhaltung*, 2000, Fringes; *Dach*, 2001, Erstwhile). He has recorded only sporadically as a leader since the 1970s (*Thrumblin'*, 1976, FMP) and has received commissions for new-music compositions. Some critics have dubbed his style "reductionism," reflecting his attempts to weed out all unnecessary communication.

Malik, Raphé: trumpeter. One of the better brass players to venture into Cecil Taylor's territory, Malik's confident style and limpid tone were a complement to Jimmy Lyons's bluesy boppishness within Taylor's coruscating worlds. Born near Boston, he studied at the University of Massachusetts and then spent time in Paris in the early 1970s, encountering the expatriate members of the AACM and BAG, Frank Wright, and other freemen. Malik was tapped for Taylor's Carnegie Hall presentation in 1974 and maintained the association through the 1980s. His tenure with Taylor is perhaps best documented on three releases in 1978 (*3 Phasis* and *Cecil Taylor Unit*, New World; *One Too Many Salty Swift and Not Goodbye*, HatArt) with Lyons, Sirone, Ramsey Ameen, and Ronald Shannon Jackson. Malik has worked as a sideman with Lyons (*Wee Sneezawee*, 1983, Black Saint), the Full Metal Revolutionary Jazz Ensemble, Glenn Spearman (*Free Worlds*, 1994, Black Saint), Joel Futterman, and Alan Silva's large Sound Visions Orchestra. He also played a role in Rova's revisitation of *John Coltrane's Ascension* (1995, Black Saint). Malik's first album as a leader was 1994's *Sirens Sweet & Slow*, on the obscure Outsounds label. He has since made strong discs for Eremite (*The Short Form*, 1997), FMP (*21st Century Texts*, 1999), Boxholder, and other small imprints.

Maneri, Joe (b. Brooklyn, NY, 1927): alto saxophonist, composer, and bandleader, father of Mat Maneri. His first horn was the clarinet, taught to him by a local cobbler. Maneri performed at Catskills resorts after graduating high school, then studied music with a personal concentration on the twentieth-century avant-garde composers. Schoenberg's serialism and the vast possibilities of microtonal music fascinated Maneri, and at the age of twenty, he began looking into a fusion of dodecaphony and jazz. In this, Maneri was an early pioneer of Third Stream music, although he has remained in the shadows of Gunther Schuller and George Russell. He continued his serialism studies under Joseph Schmidt and wrote a piano concerto for conductor Eric Leinsdorf while performing in jazz and ethnic ensembles. Maneri had the opportunity to record for Atlantic in 1962 but was frustrated when the album was never released. (It finally surfaced in 1998 as *Paniots Nine*, Avant.)

Maneri continued to play in relative obscurity until 1970, when he landed a teaching position at the New England Conservatory. This gave him not only the chance to share his ideas and experiments with a new generation, but also the financial wherewithal to continue his investigations of microtonal music. He did not record again until 1989, when he cut *Kavalinka* (1991) for the Northeastern label. That record was a trio session with percussionist Masashi Harada and Maneri's son, Mat, on violin. The trio format has remained one of Maneri's best outlets for expression. He released a good number of albums during the 1990s on ECM (*Three Men Walking*, 1995, with son Mat and Joe Morris), Leo Lab (*Get Ready to Receive Yourself*, 1993), and the Hat labels (*Dahabenzapple*, 1993, HatArt; *Coming Down the Mountain*, 1997, HatOlogy).

Maneri, Mat (b. Brooklyn, NY, 1969): violinist and violist, son of Joe Maneri. He began studying violin and viola at age five and later, at the New England Conservatory, studied jazz techniques with Dave Holland, Bob Moses, and Miroslav Vitous. At age fourteen, he began working professionally with the klezmer band Shirim and branched into jazz from there; he is also interested in Greek, African, and Indian musical styles. His specially made instruments include baritone violin, five-string viola, and six-string electric violin. Besides his father's albums and his own (starting with *Acceptance*, 1998, HatHut), Maneri has performed and recorded with Pandelis Karayorgis, Joe Morris, William Parker, Mark Dresser, Ellery Eskelin, Borah Bergman, and other free jazzmen. Matthew Shipp has become a more frequent partner, blending well with Maneri on *Blue Decco* (2000, Thirsty Ear).

Mangelsdorff, Albert (b. Frankfurt, Germany, 5 September 1928): trombonist. One of the continent's most popular improvisers, Mangelsdorff pioneered the use of multiphonics on the trombone. He had performed as a violinist and guitarist before deciding to take up the trombone, which he played in bop settings throughout the 1950s. Mangelsdorff moved into the avant-garde in the early 1960s and has since established himself as one of Europe's most adventurous trombonists. Besides his solo albums and group projects under his own name, he has performed as a member of both Globe Unity and the United Jazz and Rock Ensemble. On his classic disc *Now, Jazz Ramwong* (Pacific Jazz, 1965), Mangelsdorff combined jazz with Thai and Indian elements. In 1976, he recorded a concert with electric bassist Jaco Pastorius and drummer Alphonse Mouzon, issued as *Trilogue: Live* (MPS/Pausa). Mangelsdorff has performed and recorded with the cream of European and American improvisors, among them John Lewis, Rolf and Joachim Kühn, Ian Carr, Randy Brecker, Lee Konitz (*Art of the Duo*, 1983, Enja), Lester Bowie, Peter Brötzmann, Stan Getz, John Lindberg, Raphé Malik, and Don Cherry.

Marclay, Christian (b. San Rafael, CA, 1955): turntable artist. A vital fixture of the Downtown New York scene, Marclay was among the first to assimilate turntable artistry into free improvisation. Inspired by the arty activities of Fluxus and John Cage while studying at Massachusetts College of Art, he began to investigate the sonic possibilities of turntables beyond the developing hip-hop scene around 1979. Some of his works have been "serious" art pieces: an unengraved vinyl disc he entitled *Record Without Grooves* (1987, Ecart Editions), a gallery show where visitors walked on LPs spread all over the floor and could buy the damaged results later, and his Cage tribute, a sort of "Frankenrecord" assembled from the fragments of several shattered LPs. He has collaborated with John Zorn, Butch Morris (*Current Trends in Racism in Modern America*, 1985, Sound Aspects), Thurston Moore, Kronos Quartet, Otomo Yoshihide, and David Moss (*Dense Band*, 1985, Moers Music). *Records 1981–1989* (1997, Atavistic) is a collection of some of his best efforts.

Maroney, Denman: composer and "hyperpianist." That description, from Maroney himself, is a fitting indicator of his animated performance methods. His debut, *Hyperpiano* (1998, Mon$ey Music), represents his preparation of the piano and manner of playing inside the instrument. He has worked with bassist Mark Dresser for over a decade, beginning with *Force Green* (1994, Soul Note) and has contributed to sessions by Dave Douglas and Jon Rose. He has been a member of Tambastics and the Absolute Ensemble.

Masada: ensemble led by alto saxophonist John Zorn, at the forefront of the Radical Jewish Culture art movement. The most consistent format has been that of a quartet with Zorn, trumpeter Dave Douglas, bassist Greg Cohen, and drummer Joey Baron. The group performs original music inspired by Jewish klezmer, free jazz, and other elements. Their tunes invariably bear Hebrew titles, and their studio albums have been titled after the letters of the Hebrew alphabet. The name comes from an ancient hill fortress where a valiant group of Jews fought against a Roman legion and opted to commit mass suicide rather than be conquered. At times, Zorn has augmented the group with strings (*Bar Kokhba*, 1996, Tzadik) or electric guitars to perform specialized compositions. Over a dozen live and studio albums have been issued under the Masada heading, mostly on Zorn's label Tzadik. *Live in Sevilla 2000* captures one of their most scintillating performances.

Masaoka, Miya (b. Washington, DC): koto player. Her Japanese cousin got her interested in the koto when she was young, and Masaoka studied its technique and history while living in the San Francisco Bay Area. She performed with Henry Kaiser, Pharoah Sanders, and Wadada Leo Smith while honing her improvising chops. She graduated from San Francisco State University in 1990 and studied under Alvin Curran at Mills College afterward. Some of her multimedia performances at this time included strippers (*What Is the Difference Between Stripping & Playing the Violin?*, 1998, Victo) and buzzing live bees.

In the late 1990s, Masaoka attached an electronic interface to her koto, leading to participation in some of Steve Coleman's M-BASE projects and duets with George

Lewis. She debuted on disc in 1996 with *Compositions/ Improvisations* (Orchard), followed by *Trio: Masaoka, Robair, Dunn* (1996, Rastascan) with drummer Gino Robair and bassist Trevor Dunn. One of her most popular albums, *Monk's Japanese Folk Song* (1997, Dizim) featured the free-pedigreed rhythm team of Reggie Workman and Andrew Cyrille. In that year, she joined Fred Frith and Larry Ochs in Maybe Monday (*Digital Wildlife*, 2001, Winter & Winter). Masaoka has also recorded with Jon Rose, John Butcher, the Toshiko Akiyoshi Jazz Orchestra, and fusion violinist L. Subramaniam.

Maslak, Keshavan (a.k.a. Kenny Millions): reedman. An often flamboyant entertainer, Maslak has had a colorful career that has spanned polka bands, fusion, and the extreme avant-garde. Born to Ukrainian immigrant parents, Maslak learned about Eastern European musics from his grandfather and began playing polkas and mazurkas before high school. In his teen years, he got into jazz and R&B, subsequently studying both jazz and classical music at the University of Michigan and North Texas State University. Maslak toured for a while with a Motown revue and then settled in San Francisco, where he performed with Charles Moffett and learned about free jazz from the ex–Ornette Coleman Trio drummer. In New York, Maslak began performing theatrical avant-garde music with Laurie Anderson and Philip Glass, and free jazz with artists like Burton Greene. He relocated to Amsterdam from 1978 to 1982, during which time he underwent a personality switch as a performer. He formed a hybrid free-funk-soul band called Loved By Millions (self-titled album, 1981, ITM), and assumed the stage name "Kenny Millions." He also participated in "traditional" free groups like the ICP Orchestra (*Japan Japon*, 1982, ICP). Maslak eventually moved to Florida and opened a Japanese restaurant while continuing to perform freely. His resumé includes concerts and recordings with Chet Baker, Paul Bley (*Romance in the Big City*, 1993, Leo), Sunny Murray, and others. (Note: The record issued by Leo in 1981 under the title *Loved By Millions* should not be confused with the contemporaneous ITM record by the so-named band. The Leo album is a good trio date with Sunny Murray and John Lindberg.)

Matchless: label founded by AMM member Eddie Prévost to document the music of that ensemble, its individual constituents, and key European improvisers. The company also includes a publishing division, Copula.

Mateen, Sabir (b. Philadelphia, PA): reeds player. Mateen has had an impressive career on both American coasts, having debuted with Horace Tapscott's Pan-Afrikan People's Arkestra in 1980. Almost a decade later, Mateen went to New York and immediately began working with legendary free drummer Sunny Murray. The pair eventually cut an invigorating duo set, *We Are Not at the Opera* (1998, Eremite). In the early 1990s, Mateen met Tom Bruno while the drummer was performing in a subway station. They formed a good working partnership, recording the duo disc *Getting Away with Murder* (1995, Eremite) in Grand Central Station. Their collaboration evolved into the quartet Test, with hornman Daniel Carter and bassist Matthew Heyner, which also began in the subway underground and has grown into one of the most exciting and inventive bands in contemporary free jazz. Aside from Test and Murray, Mateen has worked with Steve Dalachinsky, Alan Silva, Raphé Malik, the One World Ensemble, Thurston Moore, Zusaan Kali Fasteau, and drummers Marc Edwards and William Hooker. He has recorded a couple of sessions under his own name, the first being 1997's *Divine Mad Love* (Eremite).

Mattos, Marcio (b. Rio de Janeiro, Brazil, 20 March 1946): bassist and cellist. Mattos studied guitar as a teenager and later taught himself the cello and bass. He studied electronic music, jazz, and improvisation at the Villa-Lobos Institute before moving to Great Britain in 1970. One of his earliest associations was with the Spontaneous Music Ensemble (*The Source – From and Towards*, 1970, Tangent; *Plus Equals*, 1975, Emanem). Mattos worked with Eddie Prévost's quartet for many years, as well as several of saxophonist Elton Dean's groups. He has been a member of Georg Graewe's GrubenKlangOrchester, Bardo State Orchestra (Mattos is a practicing Buddhist), Company, Tony Oxley's Celebration Orchestra, the Electric String Trio, Stefano Maltese's Open Music Ensemble, and the London Improvisers Orchestra. Other projects include albums with Keith Tippett, Marilyn Crispell, Dewey Redman, Maggie Nicols, the Chris Burn Ensemble, John Butcher, George Haslam, Philipp Wachsmann, Lol Coxhill, and two trios: Axon, with Phil Minton and Martin Blume, and one with Graewe and Michael Vatcher. With Steve Beresford, he has recorded scores for animated films (*Lihaa*, 1990, Tzadik). Mattos has also collaborated with dance companies and electroacoustic groups across Europe, and is a talented ceramicist.

Maya Recordings: Kilkenny, Ireland–based label established in 1992 by Barry Guy and violinist Maya Homburger to document free improvisations, extended compositions, and baroque works. The catalog includes albums by both of the founders, Barre Phillips, and Evan Parker.

Mazzon, Guido (b. Milan, Italy, 1946): trumpeter. Originally a clarinetist, Mazzon learned to play the trumpet to participate in a local brass band. His study of jazz began in 1964, and a few years later, he began investigating free music along with his compositional studies. He was a founder of Gruppo Contemporaneo, a Milan-based ensemble that worked along similar lines to Gruppo Romano Free Jazz and Willem Breuker's later Kollektief. In the 1970s, he led his own trio, quartet, and the Precarious Orchestra. Later Mazzon was a charter member of the Italian Instabile Orchestra, featured prominently on all of their recordings thus far. He has often collaborated with trumpeter Alberto Mandarini (*Trumpet Buzz Duo*, 1995, Splasc(h)), pianist Umberto Petrin, Mario Schiano, and Andrea Centazzo. He has recorded many sessions over the past three decades, but most of Mazzon's own albums are not available on CD. *Other Line* (1990, Splasc(h)) is a good introduction to his clear, vibrant approach.

McBee, Cecil (Tulsa, OK, 19 May 1935): bassist. McBee has been one of the most invigorating presences in jazz since the mid-1960s but has only started to receive his full due in the past decade or so. He studied the clarinet in his teens but moved to the bass at age seventeen. He taught music and led a military band for a time, then appeared with singer Dinah Washington. He spent one year working with Paul Winter in Detroit, then went to New York in 1962. There, McBee connected with several advanced jazzmen: Sam Rivers, Andrew Hill, Keith Jarrett, Wayne Shorter, Jackie McLean, Charles Tolliver, Pharoah Sanders, Alice Coltrane, Yusef Lateef. His work with Charles Lloyd in 1966 gained McBee more recognition and recording opportunities. In the 1970s, he performed with Abdullah Ibrahim, Arthur Blythe, and Chico Freeman on the free edge, and Art Pepper and Joanne Brackeen in more "inside" situations. He debuted as a leader with *Mutima* (1974, on Tolliver's label, Strata-East) and has led a half-dozen sessions since that time. His relationships with Freeman and Blythe led to membership in The Leaders, a "supergroup," which included Lester Bowie, Don Moye, and pianist Kirk Lightsey. In the 1980s, McBee worked mostly as a high-profile sideman and made records with Kenny Barron, Muhal Richard Abrams, Ray Anderson, tenorman George Adams, and others. His most recent album was the quintet date *Unspoken* (1997, Palmetto). McBee remains a first-call bassist in New York and Europe.

McCall, Steve (b. Chicago, IL, 20 September 1933; d. 24 May 1989): drummer and percussionist. McCall was inarguably one of the most gifted free drummers, an AACM founder who could keep up the barest hint of a pulse while roaring through high-intensity improvisations. Some of his earliest gigs were with Chicago bluesman Lucky Carmichael. In 1961, McCall joined Muhal Richard Abrams's Experimental Band and moved on to the AACM four years later. He kept active in hard bop combos while exploring the Association's concepts of free music. McCall relocated to Paris in 1967, like many of his contemporaries. One day he encountered Anthony Braxton coming out of a Parisian taxi and accepted his invitation to join the Creative Construction Company. (See Braxton's entry.) He also performed with Braxton on Gunter Hampel's landmark *8th of July, 1969* (1969, Birth).

McCall went back to Chicago in 1970. He gigged a bit with Dexter Gordon, then joined the trio Reflection, which became Air in 1975 once the members moved to New York. (See separate entry.) McCall built his reputation further on free dates with Abrams, David Murray, Arthur Blythe, Cecil Taylor, Roscoe Mitchell, Fred Anderson, and Chico Freeman. He died suddenly of a stroke at the age of fifty-five, robbing free jazz of one of its most vital, dynamic rhythmists.

McGregor, Chris (b. Umtata, South Africa, 24 December 1936; d. Ager, France, 26 May 1990): pianist, composer, and bandleader. The son of a Scottish missionary, McGregor was raised on a steady diet of hymns and traditional South African music, both of which left permanent marks on his character as a musician. He got into jazz at Cape Town College of Music, where he met some future members of The Blue Notes (see separate entry). McGregor spent a couple of years playing around the country and was constantly harassed for working with black musicians. In 1964, he and The Blue Notes attended the Antibes Jazz Festival and gained asylum in Europe. The band traveled through Switzerland and Denmark, then settled in London to instigate a new movement of African-inflected free jazz.

In 1970, McGregor debuted the Brotherhood of Breath, a free-spirited big band that added improvisers like Evan Parker and Paul Rutherford to The Blue Notes' personnel. While the band's live performances were almost universally praised, label troubles gave them difficulty on the mass market. Ogun, a label founded by bassist Harry Miller, documented some of the Brotherhood's better shows: *Live at Willisau* (1973) and *Live at Toulouse* (1977). McGregor moved to the south of France in the late 1970s and convened the Brotherhood only sporadically, preferring to concentrate on small groups and solo concerts (*In His Good Time*, 1978, Ogun). In 1981, McGregor attempted to revive the Brotherhood of Breath by contracting other European musicians, but the end result was nothing like the original deal. Discs like *Country Cooking* (1988, Venture) presented well-arranged, African-inspired compositions and arrangements, but they were marred by shaky ensemble work and weak soloing. McGregor only rarely appeared as a sideman on record, which included dates with Harry Beckett, Noah Howard, and Nick Drake.

McIntyre, (Kalaparusha) Maurice (b. Clarkville, AR, 24 March 1936): saxophonist. A founding member of the AACM, McIntyre's roots lie in R&B and flat-out blues. Brought up in Chicago, McIntyre began on drums and took up the saxophone before his teen years. He attended Chicago College of Music but did not like being restricted by all the theories laid in his lap. He was more interested in free exploration, and he found spiritual kinsmen in Roscoe Mitchell, Malachi Favors, and Muhal Richard Abrams. He joined Abrams's Experimental Band in 1961 and became an original AACM member in 1965. He participated in some of Delmark's early recordings of the AACM's efforts, and the label released his *Humility in the Light of Creator* in 1969. McIntyre's profound interest in the blues gave him an advantage that not many other AACMers could claim: it enabled him to work on the blues side of Delmark's roster, cutting records with J.B. Hutto, Little Milton, George Freeman, and other local bluesmen.

In the early 1970s, McIntyre moved to New York City and became involved in the loft-jazz movement. He played at Sam Rivers's Studio RivBea and taught at Creative Music Studio with Karl Berger and Ornette Coleman. McIntyre did some European concerts with Abrams, and in 1979, he landed a contract with Black Saint (*Peace and Blessings*). For most of the 1980s, McIntyre stayed away from the studio but continued to perform live around New York and Europe. *Dream Of . . .* (1998, CIMP), with bassist Michael Logan and Pheeroan Ak Laff, was his first disc in nearly two decades, and it showed that McIntyre had lost little or none of his prowess over the years. In that same year, he joined the "supergroup" Bright Moments (*Return of the Lost Tribe*, 1998, Delmark).

McIntyre, (Makanda) Ken (Kenneth Arthur; b. Boston, MA, 7 September 1931; d. Harlem, NY, 13 June 2001): reeds player. McIntyre (no relation to Maurice, above) was an undersung pioneer of free jazz, having first recorded with Eric Dolphy in 1960 (*Looking Ahead*, New Jazz) shortly before Ornette Coleman's *Free Jazz* session. McIntyre was a recent graduate of the Boston Conservatory when he came to New York in 1960 seeking like-minded souls with whom to experiment. *Stone Blues* (1960,

New Jazz), his first record, did not have nearly the impact of the session with Dolphy a few months later. McIntyre worked as an educator for many years, recording on his own (*Way Way Out*, 1963, United Artists) and with Bill Dixon (*Bill Dixon's 7-Tette*, 1962, Savoy), Cecil Taylor (*Unit Structures*, 1966, Blue Note), and other freemen.

McIntyre was a superb technician on the alto and tenor saxes, bass clarinet, flute, oboe, and even bassoon. Unfortunately, those skills did not get presented very often on disc. McIntyre recorded a handful of albums for the Steeplechase label in the 1970s, including the excellent *Hindsight* (1974), but he mostly stuck to teaching except for singular projects with trombonist Craig Harris, Carla Bley, Beaver Harris, and Nat Adderley. In the early 1990s, he adopted the name Makanda as a nod to his African heritage and studies. *A New Beginning* (2001, Passin' Thru) was his first recording as a leader in almost a decade; it was also his last, as a heart attack soon felled him at age sixty-nine.

McLean, Jackie (John Lenwood McLean Jr.; b. New York, NY, 17 May 1932): alto saxophonist, composer, and educator. Like many of his contemporaries, McLean came from a musical family; his father John played guitar with Tiny Bradshaw's band. Young Jackie literally grew up in the midst of bebop, living in the same neighborhood as Thelonious Monk and Bud Powell, who were close family friends. He began playing the alto sax at age fifteen, and it has remained his sole instrument. McLean kicked off his recording career at age nineteen, appearing on Miles Davis's *Dig* (1951, Prestige) alongside young tenorman Sonny Rollins. Four years later, he cut his debut as a leader, *The Jackie McLean Quartet* (1955, Ad Lib), which featured his enduring "Little Melonae." Fruitful stints with Art Blakey's Jazz Messengers and tenorman Gene Ammons furthered his reputation as a young lion to watch.

McLean's impressive technique floored bebop fans and musicians, yet he continued to evolve until he was entirely happy with his personal sound. He has been known to disavow the quality of his recordings up until 1959, when he made *Jackie's Bag* for Blue Note. By that time, McLean had already become aware of Ornette Coleman's innovations and was inspired to look deeper into freedom. Eric Dolphy was another principal inspiration. *New Soil* (1959, Blue Note), recorded after *Jackie's Bag* but released before, bore some of the earliest evidence of the altoist's freeing-up. It was not until 1962 that McLean took the full leap into free exploration, issuing the quartet session *Let Freedom Ring* (Blue Note) with Coleman's drummer, Billy Higgins, on hand to guide the way. The record served as a palpable bridge between hard bop and free jazz, demonstrating that established beboppers could embrace freedom as earnestly as its pioneers.

McLean continued to dabble in free jazz on a string of Blue Note albums: the outstanding *One Step Beyond* and *Destination Out!* (both 1963) with like-minded trombonist Grachan Moncur III and vibist Bobby Hutcherson; *It's Time*, *Action* (both 1964), and *Right Now!* (1965) with trumpeter Charles Tolliver. Coleman himself guested on *New and Old Gospel* (1967), playing trumpet instead of alto, resulting in some utterly brilliant interplay despite the lack of melodicism in Coleman's blowing. *'Bout Soul* (1967) had as its centerpiece a poetry recitation by Barbara Simmons and was perhaps McLean's freest effort of all. With that session, the altoist seemed to have burned himself out on free playing. He closed out his Blue Note contract with the fairly straightforward *Demon's Dance* (1967) and has rarely looked back toward freedom since that time. In 1968, he entered his enduring career in education and has continued to make excellent hard-bop albums, sometimes in the company of his son René (*Dynasty*, 1988, Triloka). McLean presently heads the jazz department at Hartt School of Music in Connecticut.

McPhee, Joe (b. Miami, FL, 3 November 1939): trumpeter, saxophonist, composer, and bandleader. McPhee is one of the few jazzmen to concentrate on performing on both trumpet and reeds, along with Hal Russell, Daniel Carter, and Ornette Coleman (though it is easy to argue for Coleman's exclusion from those ranks). In fact, McPhee played the trumpet since childhood but did not take up the sax until the age of twenty-six. He has spent most of his life in Poughkeepsie, New York, but has worked so often with European musicians and labels that many people assume McPhee is an expatriate. His style is a rich blend of American jazz and European avant, and his recordings reveal a passionate love for jazz traditions tempered with a relentless need to press onward.

McPhee is an admirer of philosopher Dr. Edward de Bono, author of *Future Positive* and other books about the nature of thinking. De Bono's concepts, dubbed Po, center upon thinking about matters in a positive or potential light instead of perceiving them literally. The "Po" designation stems from keywords such as *po*sitive, hypoth*esis, *po*ssible, and *po*etic, which relate to his optimistic philosophy. In 1981, McPhee developed the concept he calls "Po Music" based upon the artistic application of de Bono's theories. The fundamental principle of Po Music is to keep a final objective in mind without worrying about the paths taken to get there. This concept throws McPhee's musical possibilities wide open, permitting travel in a number of conceivable directions in order to attain the final goal. He expresses himself eloquently and provocatively in conversations, liner notes, poetry, and his bracing music.

McPhee's family background was rich in jazz. His father was a trumpet player who appreciated jazz greatly but did not play it himself. Alfonso Cooper, the leader of the traditional jazz band Savoy Sultans, and trombonist Grachan Moncur III were relatives. McPhee also had many friends who were interested in jazz, so he was immersed in the music from a listening standpoint from an early age. He himself did not begin to play improvised music until the age of twenty-two, since his school and army bands discouraged improvisation. A group of army musicians with whom McPhee associated began to covertly explore jazz stylings, and soon he was hooked on Miles, Mingus, and the hard boppers. Shortly thereafter came an interest in the explorations of Albert Ayler, Ornette Coleman, Cecil Taylor, and his principal influence, John Coltrane. Witnessing Ayler and Coleman in action at Coltrane's funeral was one of the most profound experiences of his life.

Following his discharge, McPhee settled in New York City and taught Black Studies at Vassar College. In the mid-1960s, he made the acquaintance of trumpeter/valve trombonist Clifford Thornton. The two men became fast friends and collaborators, and it was at this time that McPhee began to learn the saxophone. He made his recording debut on Thornton's *Freedom and Unity* (1967, Third World). In 1969, McPhee recorded his own first album, the long-forgotten but recently reissued

Underground Railroad, for the CJR label, which was founded expressly for the purpose of recording McPhee's music. That was followed in 1970 by the classic *Nation Time* (CJR), which blended free jazz energy with funk and soul elements in an exotic mix. All three of the above albums have been reissued on CD by Atavistic.

McPhee actually holds the distinction of inaugurating *two* different record labels, as two years later Swiss producer Werner Uehlinger founded the legendary HatHut imprint for that purpose. *Black Magic Man* (1971), taped at the same concert as *Nation Time*, was the very first release on the label, assigned catalog letter A. Between 1975 and 1982, McPhee recorded eleven albums for HatHut. He developed lasting associations with several top European improvisers, among them André Jaume and Raymond Boni, who have been at the core of most of McPhee's units for over twenty years.

In 1971, bassist Tyrone Crabb quit the music business to pursue political interests, leading McPhee to try out a bassless band. This was a frightening prospect, particularly for a form where having *two* bassists in the group had become as commonplace as one. His trio with pianist Mike Kull and percussionist Harold E. Smith was sparing, light-toned even when Kull concentrated on left-hand playing, and completely unique. *Trinity* (1971, CJR, reissued by Atavistic) finds the trio looking further into the legacies of McPhee's inspirations—Coltrane, Ayler, Mississippi blues—on three long tracks. *Survival Unit II: At WBAI's Free Music Store* (1996, HatArt) is a strong live disc from October 1971, which adds Thornton and saxophonist Byron Morris to the group.

Tenor/Fallen Angels (1977, Hatology) is McPhee's first solo saxophone performance, now an established rite of passage that can make or break one's career. He had nothing to worry about, being a tonal innovator on the level of Anthony Braxton and Evan Parker. Some of his tireless, rip-roaring solos were still rough around the edges, but McPhee's fearlessness in spinning sounds off the top of his head and heart makes up for the few shaky spots. He sounds, simply, like no one else on the horn when he lets it all hang out. Double discs were necessary for *Graphics* (1977, HatHut), on which he played trumpet, pocket trumpet, soprano saxophone, and percussion in addition to the tenor. McPhee is equally courageous on this session, playing two trumpets at once on parts of "Legendary Heroes" and paying simultaneous homage to Sidney Bechet and Steve Lacy on three soprano sax features. A much later solo recording, *As Serious as Your Life* (1996, Hatology), confirms the hornman's profound maturation. A number of friends and inspirations are acknowledged in that set: Miles Davis, avant-garde composer Conlon Nancarrow, Sun Ra, Gershwin, and Coltrane are handled with utmost respect.

Starting with 1979's *Old Eyes and Mysteries* (HatHut), McPhee began to gain a bit more notoriety. The personnel, not uniform across all tracks, includes multi-instrumentalist Milo Fine, guitarists Boni and Steve Gnitka, Jaume and Urs Leimgruber on the reeds, cellist Jean-Charles Capon, bassist Pierre-Yves Sorin, and drummer Fritz Hauser. "Eroc Tinu" ("unit core" spelled backwards), an appreciation of Cecil Taylor, is rich with the dedicatee's percussiveness. The impetuous Boni dissects and reassembles John Lewis's classic "Django." The four sections of "Women's Mysteries" are beautiful but unstructured, so that McPhee and associates can explore those mysteries in infinite detail.

Topology (1981) also changes personnel with almost every track, not that the vacillation hurts the product. The first sounds heard are the vigorously bowed cello and bass on "Age," toppled by Boni's abrasive guitar and the leader's wailing tenor. Charles Mingus's "Pithecanthropus Erectus," a genuine forefather of free jazz, begins straight with bassman François Mechali and Irène Schweizer laying down the groove beneath McPhee and Radu Malfatti. On "Blues for New Chicago" McPhee uses half-valve effects on trumpet, painting a skim impression of the blues over a mysteriously sparse landscape. The graphically notated "Topology" begins with Boni's prog-rock guitar sounds zooming and echoing about the room, sculpting the aural equivalent of 3-D shapes. The guitarist detunes and taps out military drum rolls on the strings to announce the arrival of McPhee's straight-toned trumpet and Jaume's overblown tenor. The piece evolves through many forms to end up at home base again.

Oleo and a Future Retrospective (1987, HatHut) combines two sessions onto one outstanding CD. Sonny Rollins's bebop standard "Oleo" is reconfigured twice, with Boni hacking slices out of the otherwise straight theme. "Pablo," dedicated to painter Picasso, cellist Casals, *and* poet Neruda, is a gorgeous selection that places François Mechali's Latin-flavored bass in the seat of honor. "A Future Retrospective" is a four-part solo feature for McPhee, with the titles set in a specific sequence to echo a statement by Eric Dolphy: "When You Hear Music"/"After It's Over"/"It's Gone in the Air"/"You Can Never Capture It Again."

Linear B (1990, HatHut) is inspired by the decoded language of the ancient Minoan people. The language has a special meaning for McPhee: one horse-head symbol represents the syllable "po," which ties in with DeBono's philosophies. The standards this time are Wayne Shorter's timeless "Footprints," as close to the Miles Davis fashion as McPhee could comfortably maneuver, and "Here's That Rainy Day" kicked up a notch. Boni's guitar weirdness is tempered by fellow six-stringer Christy Doran, a straighter musician who balances out these tottering performances. "Imagine a World Without Art" is deliberately disturbing, calculated to make us think about the title's implications; the two-minute "Little Pieces" are duets with various band members.

Back in 1960, drummer Max Roach composed his infamous black liberation suite, "We Insist—Freedom Now!" In 1994, McPhee recorded his reply to that period sentiment, *Sweet Freedom—Now What?* (1995, HatHut), a trio with two fast friends, Canadian pianist Paul Plimley and bassist Lisle Ellis. McPhee's record is not only a loving homage to Roach's importance, it addresses the difficult questions that faced American blacks after the civil rights movement wound down. McPhee plays tenor and soprano saxes and alto clarinet. Plimley and Ellis, as familiar with each other as dog-eared books, were able to turn their attention comfortably to the leader's directions while staying attuned to one another. It is so typical of McPhee's irony that some of Roach's best works—"Driva Man," "Garvey's Ghost"—are venerated by a trio completely lacking a drummer, but the gambit works.

On October 19, 1995, the day that Don Cherry died, McPhee was scheduled to play a concert in Seattle. As legend has it, McPhee called for "Spirit Traveler," his dedication to Cherry, to be the set's opener before he even found out that the great trumpeter had passed away. That fact, coupled with McPhee's wonderfully brittle playing on pocket trumpet, gives *Common Threads* (1996, Deep Listening) a spiritual aura.

Violinist Eyvind Kang is forcefully melodic, cellist Loren Dempster more of a background supporter, yet they link up with repeated success.

McPhee has renewed his partnership with violinist David Prentice at times, churning out three enterprising albums in 1996 alone. *Legend Street One* and *Two* (both on CIMP) feature a quartet with Frank Lowe and Charles Moffett. Dolphy's "Something Sweet, Something Tender" begins the second disc on a rather downbeat tone. "What We Do" draws from Ornette Coleman's melodic-harmonic experiments; McPhee and Prentice parallel each other while Lowe playfully kicks at their heels. A duo with Prentice, *Inside Out* (1996, CIMP), pushes the walls further out to give the players infinite elbowroom. In fact, several tracks were recorded in the woods outside of the studio! Birdsongs and other natural noises enhance the session's sheer beauty, beginning with the austere "Haiku" suite.

Elan Impulse (1991, In Situ) is an adventure in jazz nostalgia with French reedman Daunik Lazro; he and McPhee skate past the spirits of Duke, Cage, and Coltrane, wave at Steve Lacy in warm greetings, and even get into old-fashioned swing. A *Meeting in Chicago* (1997, Okkadisk) pits McPhee against two of the Windy City's finest, Ken Vandermark and Kent Kessler. On *Brass City* (1996, Okkadisk), McPhee meets Jeb Bishop, a Vandermark 5 member. Only two tracks, part five of "The Brass City" and "The Rozwell Incident" (honoring Roswell Rudd), bear any clearly appreciable structure. All of the others are in-depth exposés of the sonic potential buried within the brass instruments. *Grand Marquis* (2000, Boxholder) is an uneven but rewarding duo with drummer Johnny McLellan, experimenting with satisfying mainstream jazz like McPhee hasn't done in years.

McPhee maintains a full schedule of live performances, playing in the major festivals and clubs worldwide. McPhee's most recent project is Trio X with bassist Dominic Duval and drummer Jay Rosen, the effective "house rhythm section" of the CIMP label. They have recorded three critically acclaimed albums and have quickly risen to prominence in the free scene. *Rapture* (1998, Cadence Jazz) adds vocalist and violinist Rosi Hertlein, the centerpiece of which is a long, fervent delivery of the black national anthem, "Lift Every Voice and Sing." The bassist's huge ears enable him to lock onto the entertaining drums, flittering violin, or bombastic tenor at will, making Duval the real anchor. *On Tour: Toronto/Rochester* (2001, Cadence Jazz) is a bone-crunching live set by Trio X and includes ironic takes on "My Funny Valentine," "Trail of Tears," and "Monkin' Around," among others.

McPhee's Bluette is an unusual quartet: two hornmen, McPhee and Joe Giardullo, and two bassists, Duval and Michael Bisio. The group is given to slow, ardently thoughtful musings; these men have some profound notions about music. Bluette is documented on two albums recorded on the same day, *In the Spirit* (1999) and *No Greater Love* (2000, both CIMP). The first is a collection of spirituals, standards, and two originals, "Birmingham Sunday" (linked with Ellington's "Come Sunday") and "Astral Spirits." Bisio and Duval are distinctive bassists, but the horns blend into a rich meld when they wish to. Giardullo is a former student of George Russell's Lydian Concept, and on *Specific Gravity* (2001, Boxholder), he and McPhee look deeply into his own expansive theories as a duo. This is a nice pairing: Giardullo is too talented to remain as obscure as he has been, and Joe McPhee is richly deserving of the recognition that came to him fairly late.

Melford, Myra (b. Glencoe, IL, 5 January 1957): pianist, composer, and bandleader. Although, like almost every other free-leaning pianist of her generation, Melford often is compared to Cecil Taylor, her principal influence was the similarly percussive but more soulful Don Pullen. Melford grew up outside of Chicago and was immersed in the blues from childhood. She studied boogie-woogie and swing piano styles as a youth, and jazz piano under Art Lande at Evergreen College in Washington. After studying gamelan and African music at Seattle's Cornish Institute, she went to New York and met Pullen and Henry Threadgill, both of whom she admired, as well as Butch Morris, Leroy Jenkins, and other major freemen. Melford made an intensive study of Threadgill's unique compositional style and Pullen's piano technique, which she then put to the test in a duo with flautist Marion Brandis.

In the late 1980s, Melford formed her first trio, with bassist Lindsay Horner and drummer Reggie Nicholson. The trio made immediate waves upon the release of *Jump* (1990, Enemy), a blissfully exciting disc that featured her well-constructed compositions like "Frank Lloyd Wright Goes West to Rest" (Melford had once lived in a home designed by Wright). It was followed by *Now and Now* (1991, Enemy) and *Alive in the House of Saints* (1993, HatOlogy, 2 CDs). The last disc, recorded in Germany, presents some of the trio's best renditions of Melford staples like "Live Jump" and "Frank Lloyd Wright. . . ." Later in the 1990s, Melford hired Dave Douglas as the hornman for her group The Same River, Twice, named for an Alice Walker story. The band's self-titled album (1996, Gramavision), featuring Chris Speed, Erik Friedlander, and Michael Sarin, further displayed her awesome prowess as a pianist and composer. Melford has worked under the leadership of Douglas, Jenkins, Morris, Threadgill, Joseph Jarman, Chris Jonas, trumpeter Frank London, and Scott Fields. She is a member of Equal Interest with Jarman and Jenkins. In 2000, Melford studied North Indian music and harmonium in Calcutta on a Fulbright Scholarship. Her most recent ensemble is Crush, with electric bassist Stomu Takeishi and drummer Kenny Wollesen (*Dance beyond the Color*, 2000, Arabesque).

Mengelberg, Misha (or Misja; b. Kiev, Ukraine, 4 June 1935): pianist, composer, and bandleader. Since his father, famed conductor Karel Mengelberg, relocated the family to Amsterdam in the 1940s to avoid political persecution, the pianist has been a Dutch citizen for most of his life. He studied the piano in his youth and fell under the spell of Thelonious Monk and Charlie Parker while still in his teens. Monk remained one of the pianist's greatest influences, along with cult favorite Herbie Nichols. Mengelberg originally studied architecture in college but gave it up in favor of the Royal Conservatory. His formal studies and an encounter with John Cage broadened the scope of his musical understanding but did little to change his love for jazz or his slowness on the keyboard. To this day, Mengelberg's piano playing is marked by an unhurried fastidiousness largely absent in Cecil Taylor's followers. His experimental compositions did not sit well with his instructors much of the time, a frustrating situation that did not prevent him from looking further outward.

In his mid-twenties, not long after winning the Loosdrecht Jazz Competition, Mengelberg met Han Bennink and saxophonist Piet Noordijk, young musicians following the same exploratory paths as the pianist. With Noordijk and Bennink, he formed a group that became fairly popular backing visiting jazzmen from other nations.

Eric Dolphy's *Last Date* (1964, Fontana) brought Mengelberg, Bennink, and bassist Jacques Schols to America's attention.

Two years later, the pianist's quartet was invited to perform at the Newport Jazz Festival, where the crowd received them with reasonable acclaim. *The Misja* [sic] *Mengelberg Quartet as Heard at the Newport Jazz Festival 1966* (Dutch Artone) became the pianist's first album under his own leadership. Upon his return home, Mengelberg judged a music competition where he was impressed by young Willem Breuker. The reedman began to collaborate with Bennink regularly, and within a couple of years, the three had developed the concept of the Instant Composers Pool (ICP). (See the Instant Composers Pool entry.)

Breuker and Mengelberg worked together for several years at encouraging the Dutch government to give more subsidies to jazz and improvising musicians. The eventual result of their toil was the BIMHuis, an Amsterdam venue, and STEIM (Studio for Electro-Instrumental Music), which held educational programs to increase the profile of the electronic avant-garde. Mengelberg was president of both BIM and STEIM until the end of the 1970s.

Besides the ICP projects, Mengelberg has released recordings under his own name every few years since the early 1980s, occasionally revising material he had performed with the Pool. *Three Points and a Mountain . . . Plus* (1979, FMP) is a tremendous meeting with Peter Brötzmann and Han Bennink. The reedman is uncharacteristically restrained on this Berlin session, opting for more controlled dynamics and melodicism instead of his trademark fury. Mengelberg has the clearly dominant hand, shaping some tracks into nostalgic forms with boogie-woogie and bebop flourishes. Bennink is his usual volcanic self on drums, and he even contributes some angular reedwork as a contrast to Brötzmann's epic tone.

In 1984, the same year that the ICP recorded its set of Herbie Nichols compositions, Mengelberg convened a quintet with Bennink, Steve Lacy, Arjen Gorter, and George Lewis for a foray into the underappreciated pianist's songbook. *Change of Season: The Music of Herbie Nichols* (1984, Soul Note) is an interesting companion piece to the ICP album and Mengelberg's earlier Monk/Nichols set with Roswell Rudd, *Regeneration* (1981, Soul Note). The quintet on *Change* cuts a middle path between the ICP and Nichols's own trio discs. Lacy and Lewis seem at home negotiating these difficult compositions; perhaps, as Americans, they were a bit more familiar with Nichols's work to begin with. *Dutch Masters* (1987, Soul Note) again features Lacy, Lewis, and Bennink, with cellist Ernst Reijseger replacing Gorter. A delightful take on Monk's quirky "Off Minor" is one highlight, as are Mengelberg's staples "Reef" and "Kneebus."

The pianist's solo works have been few and far between but usually magical. *Impromptus* (1988, FMP) is a classically oriented collection of improvisations on which Mengelberg tends to accompany himself with strange vocalizations, in the manner of Keith Jarrett. Most are four minutes or less in length, but the finale stretches lushly over fifteen minutes. His subtle, unhurried keyboard style is most evident in situations like this. *Solo* (2000, Buzz) provides a better indication of his dissident humor, as he starts down certain paths and then digs deliberate potholes to make his followers stumble. Brötzmann, Wagner, and Bill Evans all get name-checked in the titles and contents of certain tracks, and, of course, Monk's spirit is omnipresent.

Since the 1980s, Mengelberg has worked more frequently with American jazzmen. His trio with bassist Brad Jones and drummer Joey Baron is a particular favorite. Baron possesses a good deal of Han Bennink's wit and high spirits. Those traits proved valuable in his past work with John Zorn, who produced the trio's *Who's Bridge* (1994) for his Avant label. Mengelberg's flexibility as both a pianist and composer are prominent here. A more recent gem is *No Idea* (1998, DIW), also produced by Zorn. With the exception of the leader's boppish title tune, the album is filled with anarchistic jazz reduxes of Nichols, Ellington, Kurt Weill, and Cole Porter.

A less traditional trio is presented on *Instant Discoveries, No. 5* (1997, X-OR), with Mats Gustafsson and Gert-Jan Prins. The standard assaulted this time around is Jerome Kern's "I've Told Every Little Star," mutated into an ugly fairy tale by Gustafsson's energy blasts. Prins's twinkling electronics and gargantuan percussion complement the forceful sax, while Mengelberg is as spare in his thoughts as a monk at meditation.

In 1998, Mengelberg and some European cohorts traveled to Chicago to spend a few days working with the Windy City's improvising cadre, including several members of Brötzmann's Chicago Tentet. *Two Days in Chicago* (1999, HatArt) presents both live and studio recordings of the passions that resulted. Besides the brilliant improvised tracks, which range from solo piano to several quartets, the troupe tackles Monk's "Eronel," "Round Midnight," and "Off Minor."

Brad Jones, Han Bennink, and Dave Douglas make up Mengelberg's entourage on the wide-ranging *Four in One* (2001, Songlines). The disc begins with "Hypochristmutreefuzz," the pianist's wacky, hiccuping theme that caught listener's ears when Eric Dolphy blasted through it on bass clarinet. Douglas manages to convey some of the blissful Dolphy character in his ecstatic solo. "Reef" and "Kneebus" are present once more; the pianist invariably performs the tunes in that same order, a wise choice since transition from one to the other is easy and letter-perfect. And, of course, Monk abounds. Bennink is exceptionally relaxed here, holding back on all the shouts and frantic pounding, no doubt to the relief of the resourceful but stable Jones.

Meniscus: Minneapolis-based record label, founded in 1999 by Jon Morgan. The catalog features Gino Robair, Paul Lovens, Frank Gratkowski, Georg Graewe, and other improvisers.

Metheny, Pat (b. Lee's Summit, MO, 12 August 1954): guitarist, composer, and bandleader. Metheny first got into jazz after hearing Ornette Coleman's *New York Is Now!* in 1966, then checking out his brother's Charlie Parker and Miles Davis records. Wes Montgomery, Jim Hall, and Gary Burton's work with guitarist Larry Coryell inspired Metheny to take up the guitar himself. Fortuitously, he got the chance to sit in with Burton at the state fair, which led to joining the vibraphonist's group and teaching at Berklee College of Music.

Metheny's first album under his own name, *Bright Size Life* (1976, ECM), included a medley of Ornette Coleman's "Round Trip" and "Broadway Blues." However, instead of aping Coleman's free-jazz style, the guitarist opted for a light, slightly echoed tone that rested easy on the listeners' ears. Soon afterward, he assembled the famous Pat Metheny Group, with keyboardist Lyle Mays, bassist Mark Egan, and drummer

Danny Gottlieb. The PMG were quickly the darlings of the press and public, and Metheny's atmospheric musical style came to be a defining sound of the ECM label. Since that time, the PMG has often reconvened with some personnel switches, and more recently Metheny has worked in a trio with bassist Larry Grenadier and drummer Jorge Rossy. For the purposes of this book, Metheny's most interesting work from the free-jazz standpoint has been with Coleman (*Song X*, 1985, Geffen) and the altoist's sidemen, Charlie Haden and Billy Higgins (*Rejoicing*, 1983, ECM). Metheny also recorded an album of free, noisy explorations on solo guitar (*Zero Tolerance for Silence*, 1992, Geffen), which was critically lambasted.

Microscopic Septet: avant-jazz ensemble. Formed in 1981 by soprano saxophonist Philip Johnston, the group was renowned for their fluid conception and sense of group dynamics. Its personnel included altoist John Zorn (replaced by Don Davis), tenorman Paul Shapiro, baritone saxophonist Dave Sewelson, pianist Joel Forrester, bassist/tubaist Dave Hofstra, and drummer Richard Dworkin. Johnston never added any brass players because he so enjoyed the reeds-and-rhythm situation. Because the Septet was misunderstood by the press and not well promoted, despite their inarguably strong level of creativity and musicianship, they folded in 1992 after just four albums, none of which seem to be currently available on CD. Since the breakup, most of its members have remained active. Johnston presently works with the Unknown and Transparent Quartet, and scores films; both Sewelson and Hofstra have been members of William Parker's Little Huey Creative Music Orchestra; and Forrester and Hofstra work in People Like Us.

Middletown Creative Orchestra: ensemble. Founded at Wesleyan University by a number of Anthony Braxton's students, the Middletown Creative Orchestra is one of the more adventurous big bands on the East Coast today. The group's personnel have included altoists Seth Misterka and Jackson Moore, bassist Jonathan Zorn (no relation to the reedman/composer), bass clarinetist James Fei, oboist Rafael Cohen, and accordionist Pete Cafarella. *10.6.97* (1997, Newsonic) documents the ensemble's somewhat academic explorations of Braxton's difficult compositional methods.

Miller, Harry (b. Cape Town, South Africa, 25 April 1941; d. Holland, 1983): bassist. Miller expatriated several years before The Blue Notes, becoming one of the first South Africans to move into the British jazz community. He played with Manfred Mann and R&B bands for a while, then got a cruise-ship job that took him to New York regularly. In the early 1960s, he absorbed as much of the British and Big Apple jazz scenes as he could, appreciating Thelonious Monk and Cecil Taylor on equal levels. After he left the ship gig, Miller worked with the bands of Mike Westbrook and John Surman. After The Blue Notes broke up, he was asked by Chris McGregor to play bass in his Brotherhood of Breath big band, which Miller accepted. He then participated in Keith Tippett's Centipede (*Septober Energy*, 1971, Neon) and the trio Ovary Lodge, and gigged with pianist Stan Tracey, reedman Alan Skidmore, Radu Malfatti, and prog band King Crimson. Miller and Louis Moholo formed fiery trios with Mike Osborne and Peter Brötzmann. He also backed singer Julie Driscoll (later

Tippetts), flautist Bob Downes, and guitarist Mike Cooper. In 1974, Miller and his wife, Hazel, established the Ogun record label to document what was going on at the leading edge of European jazz, especially in the South African expat community. The boxed set *Collection* (1999) presents Miller's work as a leader on the label. In the early 1980s, he formed the short-lived Isipingo (*Family Affair*, 1980, Ogun). Miller moved to Berlin, then to the Netherlands, where he recorded with Dutch jazz powerhouses like Han Bennink (*Down South*, 1983, Varajazz) before his death in a car accident.

MIMEO: improvising ensemble. The name is short for Music in Movement Electronic Orchestra, a reflection of the group's birth at the 1997 Music in Movement Festival. Electronic musicians Hans Falb and Gerlinde Koschik and reedman Peter van Bergen developed the traveling festival in that year, and MIMEO was born from the experiments and collaborations that resulted. *Queue* (1998, Grob, reissued by Perdition Plastics) documented the three shows on the tour. After the festival's demise, some of the participants decided to keep MIMEO alive as a working project. The final roster of members included Keith Rowe, Phil Durrant, Thomas Lehn, Gert-Jan Prins, Cor Fuhler, Fennesz, Peter Rehberg, Jérôme Noetinger, Kaffe Matthews, Marcus Schmickler, Rafael Toral, and Markus Wettstein. Since then, two more albums have been released: *Electric Chair and Table* (2000, Grob) and *The Hands of Caravaggio* (2002, Erstwhile), the latter in conjunction with pianist John Tilbury of AMM.

Minafra, Pino (b. Ruvo, Italy, 1951): trumpeter and founder of the Italian Instabile Orchestra. Minafra was raised in Apulia, the "heel" of the Italian boot, where he sang in the church choir and studied trumpet as a youth. After some jobs in brass bands and classical groups, Minafra began playing jazz around 1980 and received acclaim for his first group, Praxis. In the mid-1980s, he began promoting concerts around the south of Italy and recording with his quintet and sextet (*Colori*, 1986, Splasc(h); *Sudori*, 1995, Victo). The Italian Instabile Orchestra was born in 1990, with the flamboyant trumpeter in the forefront on flügelhorn, plastic-pipe didgeridoo, and omnipresent megaphone. Minafra has also recorded with tubaist Michel Godard (*Castel del Monte*, 2001, Enja), La Banda, Peter Kowald, and in a trio with Ernst Reijseger and Han Bennink (*Noci . . . Strani Frutti*, 1991, Leo).

Minasi, Dom (b. New York, NY, 6 March 1943): guitarist. Minasi is an interesting player, capable of negotiating the tightest corners of bebop, then veering off into open improvisation with the freedom of his main inspirations, John Coltrane and Cecil Taylor. In the mid-1970s, Minasi had a brief contract with Blue Note (*When Joanna Loved Me* and *I Have the Feeling I've Been Here Before*, both 1975) but faded away into near-oblivion for a number of years before returning to the scene via the CIMP label (*Finishing Touches*, 1999). Minasi has played in duos with pianist Michael Jefry Stevens, bassist Ed Schuller, and reedman Blaise Siwula, in an acclaimed trio with drummer Jackson Krall and bassist Ken Filiano, and DDT with cellist Tomas Ulrich and Dominic Duval (later replaced by Filiano). *Goin' Out Again* (2002, CDM) presents Minasi's sharp interpretations of standards like "Autumn Leaves" and "All

Blues," recast in his own image; *Takin' the Duke Out* (2001, CDM) frees up the Ellington repertoire.

Minton, Phil (b. Torquay, U.K., 2 November 1940): trumpeter and vocalist. Minton rides on the extreme edge of freedom as a vocalist, emitting sounds familiar, unusual, and unfathomable through his remarkable larynx with a Dada flair. He is also a gifted trumpeter, though that talent has tended to take a back seat to his vocal notoriety.

Minton began his career as a jazz trumpeter in his late teens. He was hired as both a hornman and singer for Mike Westbrook's ensemble in the mid-1960s, after which time he moved around the Canary Islands and Sweden for a few years. During the 1970s, he returned to Westbrook's band and became more renowned as a free improviser, vocally in particular. From 1975, he gave solo performances of his extreme vocal antics (*A Doughnut in Both Hands (1975–1982)*, Emanem) and worked in a voice trio with Maggie Nicols and Julie Tippetts. Minton has since performed and recorded with Lindsay Cooper, Peter Brötzmann, Company, John Butcher, pianist Veryan Weston, Roof, his own quartet, and Axon, a trio with Martin Blume and Marcio Mattos. Minton has also worked with theatrical groups, an apt setting for such an exotic, creative character. One of his most enticing projects was *Songs from a Prison Diary (Poems by Ho Chi Minh)* (1993, Leo).

Mitchell, Roscoe (Jr.; b. Chicago, IL, 3 August 1940): reeds player, percussionist, composer, and bandleader. A founding member of the AACM and the Art Ensemble of Chicago, Mitchell is one of the most creative, distinctive saxophonists in the business. He is largely responsible for the vogue of solo sax performances among free jazzmen, having progressed beyond the groundwork laid by his AACM compadre Anthony Braxton. An excellent technician on all the reeds, his tone on alto sax is especially distinctive, and he constantly seems to be thinking ahead to the next note or phrase. Mitchell has a notable interest in contemporary classical music, which has led to some entertaining collaborations, particularly with vocalist Tom Buckner and accordionist/composer Pauline Oliveros.

Mitchell took up the reeds in high school and later played with Albert Ayler in an Army band stationed in Germany. In 1961, back in Chicago, he enrolled in Wilson Junior College where he met a number of musicians who were interested in exploring the new free jazz coming out of New York. Like many of his classmates, Mitchell went to Muhal Richard Abrams to study his advanced jazz concepts. Soon the reedman was playing in the Experimental Band, and three years later he joined the ranks of the new AACM.

From within the Association's membership, Mitchell gathered his first sextet: tenorman Maurice McIntyre, trumpeter Lester Bowie, trombonist/cellist Lester Lashley, bassist Malachi Favors, and drummer Alvin Fielder. This group recorded *Sound* (1966), the first AACM project to be released by local label Delmark Records. As discussed under the AACM's separate entry, the album was a shock to jazz's system, full of silences and unexpected noises and barely resembling anything previously acknowledged as "jazz." Mitchell also began giving solo performances on saxophone around this time, inspired by Joseph Jarman's similar efforts. In the following year,

Mitchell debuted the first lineup of his Art Ensemble, with Bowie, Favors, and drummer Philip Wilson. Over the next couple of years, the group's personnel changed, first with Jarman replacing Wilson, then Don Moye coming in on drums, and finally the permanent lineup of the Art Ensemble of Chicago was in place. (See the Art Ensemble's entry.)

From 1969 to 1971, the AEC resided in Paris, successfully helping to establish a new wave of creativity on the continent. Upon returning to America, Mitchell spent some time in St. Louis before heading back to the Chicago area. In 1973, he recorded *1973 Solo Saxophone Concerts* (Sackville), the first of several hard documents of his solo excursions. The following year, Mitchell went to East Lansing, Michigan, where he had a hand in implementing an AACM-inspired arts organization, the Creative Arts Collective. Its members, including the reliable rhythm team of bassist Jaribu Shahid and drummer Tani Tabbal, have played a part in many of Mitchell's later projects, such as the *Sound and Space Ensembles* (1983, Black Saint, with unusual reeds specialist Gerald Oshita) and his current Note Factory. The latter group, a nonet, has recorded some of the leader's more coolly complex works on *This Dance Is for Steve McCall* (1992, Black Saint) and *Nine To Get Ready* (1999, ECM).

Some of Mitchell's recordings have stretched to the outmost reaches of the academic avant-garde, pursuing avenues of definite creativity but dubious marketability. On *L-R-G/The Maze/S II Examples* (1978, Chief), the first piece is a sort of stylistic collage for trio; the second, a bizarre setting for percussion octet; the third, a solo soprano work of extreme quietness and tonal ambiguity. His later trio with pianist Borah Bergman and vocalist Tom Buckner trod on intriguing new lands as well. On the other end of the continuum is his nicely accessible quintet with Shahid, Tabbal, trumpeter Hugh Ragin, and guitarist Spencer Barefield (*3 x 4 Eye*, 1981; *Live at the Knitting Factory*, 1987, both Black Saint). Mitchell has continued to evolve his solo reeds vocabulary, with an intriguing use of overdubbing on recordings like the double-disc *Sound Songs* (1997, Delmark), which suffers a little from the static academicism that seems to have settled into his work.

Moers Music: Moers, Germany-based jazz label, created in 1974 to document performances at the Moers Festival. Among the featured artists are Anthony Braxton (who inaugurated the imprint), John Surman, the World Saxophone Quartet, John Carter, Sunny Murray Trio, Leo Smith, Fred Anderson, Barry Altschul, Günter Christmann, the Music Revelation Ensemble, Alfred Harth, Rova, Roscoe Mitchell, Ray Anderson, the Vienna Art Orchestra, Fred Frith, Richard Teitelbaum, and Evan Parker with Paul Lytton.

Moffett, Charles (b. Fort Worth, TX, 6 September 1929; d. 14 February 1997): drummer and patriarch of a potent jazz family. Moffett began his career as a trumpeter; he played the trumpet while in high school with Ornette Coleman, then switched to drums in college. After nearly a decade as a high school teacher, Moffett moved to New York in 1961 and joined Coleman's new trio with bassist David Izenzon. During the altoist's downtime, the drummer performed with Sonny Rollins, Eric Dolphy, and Archie Shepp to good acclaim. After the Coleman trio's European tour, Moffett moved briefly to Oakland, where he ran a music school before returning to New York. Aside from occasional gigs with men like Frank Lowe, he concentrated mostly on teaching for the remainder of his life. *The Gift* (1969, Savoy) is the principal document of Moffett as a leader. His legacy is carried on by his gifted children: trumpeter Mondre, reedman Charles, Jr., vocalist Charisse, drummer Cody, and bassist Charnett.

Moholo, Louis (b. Cape Town, South Africa, 10 March 1940): drummer and percussionist. Self-taught, Moholo was one of the African expatriates who helped to revitalize European jazz in the mid-1960s. Chris McGregor hired him as the Blue Notes' drummer in 1962, and Moholo made the fateful trek to Europe two years later that resulted in the band's expatriation and overwhelming success. He was carried over to the Brotherhood of Breath. Moholo formed a bond with bassist Harry Miller, performing in his group Isipingo and other settings.

In 1978, Moholo recorded an excellent octet date, *Spirits Rejoice!* (Ogun), featuring Evan Parker and Kenny Wheeler. *Tern* (1982, FMP) was an artistic triumph that is due for reissue by Atavistic. Later in the 1980s, Moholo put together a brand new octet, Viva la Black (*Freedom Tour: Live in South Africa 1993*, Ogun), which included trumpeter Claude Deppa and percussionist Thebe Lipere. He and Lipere have worked in trio with Derek Bailey, and Moholo has also performed with Iréne Schweizer, Peter Brötzmann (*The Nearer the Bone, the Sweeter the Meat*, 1979, FMP), Cecil Taylor, Evan Parker (*Foxes Fox*, 1999, Emanem), and the Dedication Orchestra. His traditionally African approach to the drums, combined with his fearless interest in new directions, has made Moholo one of the premier improvisers in avant-garde jazz for nearly forty years.

Moncur, Grachan, III (b. New York, NY, 3 June 1937): trombonist and composer. Aside from Roswell Rudd, Moncur was perhaps the most impressive trombonist to venture into free jazz. His father, the bassist for the famous Savoy Sultans swing band, encouraged Moncur to pursue music early on. He took up the trombone at age eleven and was an impressive technician by the time he finished school. He is the cousin of Joe McPhee, upon whom he was a strong influence.

Moncur played with Ray Charles's band from 1959 to 1962, then served briefly in the Art Farmer–Benny Golson Jazztet before joining altoist Jackie McLean's group. That experience put Moncur at the forefront of the hard bop/free-jazz crossover that McLean spearheaded. His tunes and powerful tone were central to two of McLean's best Blue Note albums, *One Step Beyond* and *Destination Out!* (both 1963). In that same year, Moncur recorded his debut as a leader, *Evolution*, also for Blue Note. The equally exciting *Some Other Stuff* followed it in 1964. Both of those sessions showcase both his technical skills and his impressive gifts as a composer. A boxed set of his tracks with McLean is expected from Mosaic in 2003.

In 1966, Archie Shepp effectively featured the paired trombones of Moncur and Rudd in his group (*Mama Too Tight*, Impulse). Moncur performed with Marion Brown and bop tenormen Benny Golson and Joe Henderson in the mid-1960s as well. In 1968, Moncur, Dave Burrell, and Beaver Harris formed the 360 Degree Music Experience, and Moncur continued to partner with both men outside of that unit. The year 1969 saw the recording of three profound discs for the French label BYG: Burrell's overpowering noise experiment *Echo*, and Moncur's own *New Africa* and *Aco Dei de Madrugada*.

In the 1970s, Moncur became an educator and spent less time in the recording studio. He was a member of the Jazz Composers Orchestra Association and recorded *Echoes of Prayer* for the JCOA label in 1974. Since then he has rarely led his own units, concentrating on teaching and sideman work for singer Cassandra Wilson, Frank Lowe, Bobby Hutcherson, organist Big John Patton, and the Paris Reunion Band with Henderson, trumpeter Nat Adderley, and pianist Kenny Drew.

Moondoc, Jemeel (b. 1951): alto saxophonist, composer, and bandleader. Grossly underrated as an improviser, the impressively gifted Moondoc did not receive his fair due until the mid-1990s, when a gracious boom of interest led to a well-deserved resurgence in his career. He studied piano, clarinet, and flute as a child before taking the alto sax as his principal instrument. Around the turn of the 1970s, he studied at college under Cecil Taylor and quickly gained a new interest in free jazz. After moving to New York, Moondoc founded his own label, Muntu, and hired a quartet he called Ensemble Muntu: trumpeter Roy Campbell and two ex-Taylor sidemen, William Parker and drummer Rashid Bakr. (This same lineup, with Daniel Carter replacing Moondoc, presently forms Other Dimensions in Music.) *The Evening of the Blue Men* (1981, Muntu) is now scarce but worth hunting down. Moondoc made a guest appearance on Parker's own debut, *Through Acceptance of the Mystery Peace* (1979, Centering; reissued 1998, Eremite).

In the early 1980s, Moondoc landed a contract with Soul Note Records, which put out a trio session with Fred Hopkins and Ed Blackwell (*Judy's Bounce*, 1981) and a sextet set with Parker, Campbell, Ellen Christi, Khan Jamal, and Denis Charles (*Kostanze's Delight*, 1983). *Nostalgia in Times Square* (1985, Soul Note), now out of print, teamed the altoman, Parker, and Charles with pianist Rahn Burton and guitarist Bern Nix. Moondoc assembled the first incarnation of his big band, the Jus' Grew Orchestra, during the 1980s but soon folded it up due to financial concerns. Moondoc basically retired from music at that time, taking a job as an architectural assistant.

In 1996, Moondoc was lured back into the studio by Eremite Records, which has since released six albums featuring the saxophonist. The first, *Tri-P-Let* (1996), is a highly musical trio session with bassist John Voigt and drummer Laurence Cook. *Fire in the Valley*, issued the same year, captures the trio in fine form at the Massachusetts festival. *New World Pygmies, Vol. 1* (1998) presents Moondoc and Parker in duo; *Volume 2* (2002) adds drummer Hamid Drake to the mix. That trio is also featured on Ayler Records' *Live at Glenn Miller Café, Vol. 1* (2002). The Jus' Grew Orchestra received its due on *Spirit House* (2001), one of the best free big-band discs in recent memory, with a group including Nix, Campbell, Voigt, trombonist Steve Swell, and tenorman Zane Massey. The altoist's engaging melodic sensibility is voiced differently on *Revolt of the Negro Lawn Jockeys* (2001), with Voigt, Jamal, trumpeter Nathan Breedlove, and drummer Codaryl (Cody) Moffett. On the evidence of these releases, Moondoc's power as a writer and improviser has been undiminished, and perhaps even strengthened, by his unfair absence from the marketplace.

Moore, Michael (b. Eureka, CA, 1954): reedman. Moore moved to Amsterdam in the mid-1970s after studying at the New England Conservatory under Jaki Byard. He has become one of the Netherlands' most prized improvisers, one of the few non-natives to really be assimilated into the brotherhood of New Dutch Swing. Misha Mengelberg and Han Bennink have been among his best partners. The Clusone Trio (see separate entry), with Bennink and cello player Ernst Reijseger, was Moore's highest-profile gig of the 1990s. He has been a member of Mengelberg's ICP Orchestra and the combo Available Jelly, and has appeared on over fifty albums in the past quarter-century.

Moore has issued several recordings on his own Ramboy label, including *Home Game* (1988) with the all-American lineup of pianist Fred Hersch, drummer Gerry Hemingway, trumpeter Herb Robertson, and bassist Mark Helias; *Tunes for Horn Guys* (1995), with a Dutch quintet of four reeds and Wolter Wierbos's trombone; and *Jewels and Binoculars: The Music of Bob Dylan* (2000), a surprisingly pleasing session with bassist Lindsay Horner and drummer Michael Vatcher. Moore has also recorded for Franz Koglmann's label, between the lines (*Monitor*, 1999; *Air Street*, 2002).

Moore, Thurston (b. Coral Gables, FL, 25 July 1958): guitarist and vocalist. Best known as the frontman of the alternative rock-noise band Sonic Youth, Moore has been a mover and shaker in free music since the 1980s. Drawing inspiration from artists like Lou Reed and the MC5, Moore came into the avant-garde courtesy of composer Glenn Branca, who used his otherworldly guitar skills on his earthshaking electric guitar symphonies (*Symphony No. 1 [Tonal Plexus]*, 1983, Roir). He formed Sonic Youth in 1981 with guitarist Lee Ranaldo, bassist Kim Gordon (later his wife), and drummer Steve Shelley. Outside of the band, he has made his own recordings (*Psychic Hearts*, 1995, Geffen; *Piece for Jetsun Dolma*, 1996, Victo; *Lost to the City*, 1997, Intakt); collaborated with Borbetomagus, punk singer Lydia Lunch, Nels Cline (*Pillow Wand*, 1997, Little Brother), William Hooker, Christian Marclay, William S. Burroughs, and the rock bands Dim Stars, Ciccone Youth, and Even Worse; and engineered rock and improvisational recording sessions. A dependable spokesman for free jazz, Moore wrote the liner notes for the *Jazzactuel* collection (2001, Charly) and has encouraged his audiences to look into free music.

Mopomoso: concert series, held the third Sunday of every month at the Red Rose in Holloway, London, England. The name is short for "Modernism, Post-Modernism, So What?" Inaugurated around 1986, the series has included such performers as Chris Burn, John Russell, Lol Coxhill, Phil Minton, and John Edwards, all of whom can be heard on *Mopomoso Solos 2002* (Emanem, 2004).

Mori, Ikue (b. Tokyo, Japan, 1953): drummer and drum machine programmer. Mori came to New York in 1977, when the No Wave rock/jazz/improv scene was taking off. She joined Arto Lindsay in DNA as the band's drummer, then worked with Fred Frith, cellist Tom Cora, and John Zorn, who has released all of Mori's self-led sessions on his Tzadik and Avant labels. Mori gave up on the drum kit in mid-decade, focusing instead on the new developments in drum machines and sampler technology. In 1990, Mori began creating soundtracks for indie filmmaker Abigail Child (*B-Side*, 1998, Tzadik), and soon kicked off her career as a leader (*Death Praxis*, 1992, Tzadik). Her finest moment thus far is the impressive *Hex Kitchen* (1995, Tzadik). Partners in concert and on record include Zorn, vocalist Mike Patton (both on *Hemophiliac*, 2002, Tzadik/Ipecac), Sonic Youth, trombonist Jim Staley, Susie Ibarra (*Songbird Suite*, 2002, Tzadik), Mark Dresser, Jim O'Rourke, and Mephista with Ibarra and pianist Sylvie Courvoisier. The arresting *One Hundred Aspects of the Moon* (2000, Tzadik) features violinist Eyvind Kang, cellist Erik Friedlander, and keyboardist Anthony Coleman.

Morris, Joe (b. New Haven, CT, 13 September 1955): guitarist, composer, and bandleader. Self-taught, Morris's guitar technique often seems to draw as much from the bebop tradition of Jim Hall and Wes Montgomery as from avant-gardists like Sonny Sharrock or Derek Bailey. He successfully bridges the often wide gap between jazz melodicism and free expression.

Morris's interest in contemporary music and composition was peaked in his teen years when he listened to Gerry Hemingway's local radio show, which featured everyone from Cecil Taylor to traditional African musicians, and attended a series of Yale workshops given by Duke Ellington, Karlheinz Stockhausen, and other innovators. In the mid-1970s, Morris spent time in Boston and Europe, trying to break into avant-garde music with little success. His partnership with multi-instrumentalist Lowell Davidson finally cemented Morris's reputation and provided the inspirational spark needed to direct his career. Around 1981, Morris established the Riti label to release his albums, and in the mid-1990s, he was signed to Soul Note where he debuted with *Symbolic Gesture* (1994).

His subsequent curricula vitae includes work with Ken Vandermark (*Like Rays*, 1996, with pianist Hans Poppel), Whit Dickey, Matthew Shipp, William Parker (all three together on *Elsewhere*, 1997, Homestead), Butch Morris, Joe and Mat Maneri, Billy Bang, Eugene Chadbourne, Roy Campbell, Paul Hession, Rob Brown, Raphé Malik, Joe McPhee, John Butcher, Peter Kowald, Ivo Perelman, and other freemen. Morris has lectured and taught at Harvard, Berklee, the New England Conservatory, and several European institutions, and leads his own trio, quartet, sextet, and Many Rings Ensemble. He often performs as a solo artist on guitars, mandolin, and banjo ukelele (*No Vertigo*, 2001, Leo). Morris has recorded for over a dozen labels including Okkadisk, Aum Fidelity, Knitting Factory Works, Incus, Leo, ECM, and No More.

Morris, Lawrence "Butch" (b. Long Beach, CA, 10 February 1947): cornetist, composer and conductor. The brother of bassist Wilber Morris, he was part of the small but fertile California free scene in the 1970s, working with Frank Lowe, Horace Tapscott, Bobby Bradford, and others. Morris lived in New York briefly in 1975, performing with Hamiet Bluiett and Charles Tyler and establishing a long-running relationship with David Murray. Morris lived in Paris for the next two years, where he worked with Steve Lacy, then returned to New York. He has been an essential part of several of Murray's recordings and ensembles, as well as leading his own dates.

Morris has developed a new style of direction known as "conduction," using hand signals to direct his band's performances. He is a talented and creative cornetist, but since the mid-1980s that gift has taken a back seat to his composition and conduction projects. Morris has recorded the results of over a dozen conduction experiments for New World (several albums in 1996 alone; see the boxed set *Testament: A Conduction Collection*) and other labels, with varying success. *Dust to Dust* (1991, New World), including Andrew Cyrille, Myra Melford, bassoonist Janet Grice, and violinist Jason Hwang, is a triumph. *Burning Cloud* (1993, FMP) is a fine, meditative trio with trombonist/flautist J.A. Deane and Lê Quan Ninh.

Morris, Wilber (b. Los Angeles, CA, 27 November 1937; d. Livingston, NJ, 8 August 2002): bassist, older brother of Butch Morris. He studied drums as a child but moved to playing bass during his service in the Air Force. Morris met Pharoah Sanders and Sonny Simmons while stationed in San Francisco, then became involved in Horace Tapscott's circle upon moving to Los Angeles. Times were slow and opportunities scarce on the West Coast, and in 1978, Wilber moved to New York City. He soon formed partnerships with David Murray and Billy Bang, which sustained him for several years. In 1981, he formed the trio Wilber Force, with Charles Tyler (replaced by Murray later on) and Denis Charles. Teaching jobs and regular work with Murray kept Morris active throughout the 1990s. He collaborated with Noah Howard, Thomas Borgmann, Ken McIntyre, Bob Ackerman, Frode Gjerstad, and Roy Campbell during that decade, along with a trio with Rashied Ali and Bobby Few, and his own One World Ensemble. Morris suffered two bouts with cancer; the second claimed his life at age sixty-four.

Moss, David (b. New York, NY, 21 January 1949): percussionist and vocalist. Moss came up within the free music community in Downtown New York, performing with Arto Lindsay in both the Ambitious Lovers and the Golden Palominos, and with Eugene Chadbourne and Tom Cora. Moss issued his first record, *Coessential* (Bent), in 1978 and began venturing to Europe in the early 1980s. In 1985, Moss formed his Dense Band (self-titled, 1985, Moers) with Lindsay, Cora, John Zorn, Fred Frith, Christian Marclay, and Wayne Horvitz. He was commissioned twice by New American Radio, and in 1991 was granted a Guggenheim Fellowship and other honors, which led him to an intended one-year residency in Berlin. Moss opted to stay in Germany, where he has received acclaim for his percussion and vocal skills. *Texture Time* (1993, Intakt) and the live *All at Once at Any Time* (1995, Victo) are some of his better albums. Moss has been awarded the the Preis der Deutschen Schallplatten Kritik twice, the Horspiel des Monats once. He has worked with the band Direct Sound, Uri Caine (*Goldberg Variations*, 2000, Winter & Winter), Jon Rose, and a number of dancers.

Motian, Paul (Stephen Paul Motian; b. Philadelphia, PA, 25 March 1931): drummer, percussionist, composer, and bandleader. Motian has frequently crossed the line between free jazz and post-bop during a colorful career that took off in the mid-1950s. A drummer since the age of twelve, Motian toured the northeast with a big band for several years before moving to New York. There he performed bebop, modal, and cool jazz with Thelonious Monk, Gil Evans, George Russell, Lennie Tristano, Coleman Hawkins, Roy Eldridge, Mose Allison, and like performers before being hired by pianist Bill Evans in 1959. The Evans Trio, completed by bassist Scott LaFaro, was an incredibly intuitive group characterized by attentive listening and reaction on the part of all three performers.

Motian began playing with Paul Bley in 1963 and quickly became interested in the pianist's free methods (*Turns*, 1964, Savoy). He left Evans's trio not long thereafter and wound up with Keith Jarrett in 1966 (*Life Between the Exit Signs*, 1967, Vortex). His relationship with the brilliant Jarrett lasted off and on for over a decade, during which time Motian loosened up his drum technique drastically, becoming more of a complementary player than a simple accompanist.

In 1972, Motian debuted as a leader with *Conception Vessel* (ECM), an exciting affair with Jarrett, Charlie Haden, Leroy Jenkins, flautist Becky Friend, and guitarist Sam Brown. Brown and Haden were carried over to the 1974 session, *Tribute* (ECM), with Carlos Ward and second guitarist Paul Metzke, on which the band interpreted compositions by Motian, Haden, and Ornette Coleman. Motian continued in the free vein through the 1970s, recording with Charles Brackeen on *Dance* (1977, with David Izenzon) and *Le Voyage* (1979, both ECM, with Jean-François Jenny-Clark on bass). Beginning in the early 1980s, the drummer's concepts became more grounded; his albums lost their free edginess and began to resemble much of ECM's other material, not necessarily a bad thing. A long period with Joe Lovano as a sideman helped to establish the tenorman's own career, and Jim Pepper and Dewey Redman also contributed their tenor skills to Motian's bands in the 1980s and 1990s.

In 1992, Motian kicked off his *Electric Bebop Band* (1992, JMT), which initially featured tenorman Joshua Redman, bassist Stomu Takeishi, and guitarists Kurt Rosenwinkel and Brad Schoeppach (Shepik). Their first album was shaky and inconclusive, but the band's future improved dramatically with some personnel changes: the ever-reliable Steve Swallow in for Takeishi, and Redman replaced by the pairing of Chris Potter and Chris Cheek (*Flight of the Blue Jay*, 1998, Winter & Winter). Motian has continued to record with Joe Lovano, sometimes in a trio with guitarist Bill Frisell, and pianist Geri Allen, but the Electric Bebop Band appears to now be his main priority as he continues to evolve as a singular drum innovator and composer of promise.

Moye, (Dougaufana Famoudou) Don (b. Rochester, NY, 23 May 1946): drummer and percussionist. Since 1969, Moye has been most famous as the mercurial drummer for the Art Ensemble of Chicago. Moye studied at Wayne State University and joined Detroit trumpeter Charles Moore's free ensemble at that time. After the group toured Europe in 1968, Moye chose to stay at Paris's American Center for Students and Artists for a while and gig with fellow Americans such as Sonny Sharrock and Steve Lacy. In 1970, he became the Art Ensemble's first regular drummer since Philip Wilson two years prior. His skills with his enormous array of drums and ethnic percussion instruments added stability and a new sense of rhythmic excitement to the band's experiments. (See the Art Ensemble's entry.)

Upon returning to America, Moye worked with the remnants of the Black Artists Group in St. Louis before joining his cohorts in Chicago. There he became involved with the AACM, fronted the Malinke Rhythm Tribe, and duetted at times with Steve McCall. In 1974, Moye performed in Montreux with pianist Randy Weston's African-influenced band; in the following year, he took the name "Famoudou" in acknowledgment of his roots (sometimes supplementing it further with "Dougaufana") and recorded his solo album *Sun Percussion* for the Art Ensemble's own AECO label. Later in the 1970s, Moye often performed in duo with Joseph Jarman (*Egwu-Anwu*, 1978, India Navigation; *Black Paladins*, 1979, Black Saint), and in settings with Don Pullen, vibist Jay Hoggard, and reedmen Chico Freeman and Hamiet Bluiett. Moye became a member of The Leaders in 1984.

Müller, Günter (b. München, Germany, 1954): drummer, electronic musician, and founder of the For 4 Ears label, based in Switzerland. Müller is one of the busiest improvisers in Europe, performing with poire_z, Jim O'Rourke (*Slow Motion*, 1992, For 4 Ears), Carlos Zingaro, Richard Teitelbaum, the trio Nachtluft (*Telefonia*, intercontinental recording via satellite link-up in 1989, For 4 Ears), and others. His drum kit features electronic enhancements that permit him to alter the sound of his drums in live performance. He debuted on record with *Planet Oeuf* (1985, XOPF) and has since appeared on nearly fifty recordings. Müller's prior collaborators include Paul Lovens, Keith Rowe, Joëlle Léandre, guitarist Taku Sugimoto, Alfred Harth (*Plan Eden*, 1987, Creative Works), Otomo Yoshihide, Sachiko M (both on *Filament 2*, 1998), Butch Morris (*Tit For Tat/Conduction #70*, 1996, both For 4 Ears), Lê Quan Ninh, and Christian Marclay.

Muñoz, Tisziji (b. Brooklyn, New York, 15 July 1946): guitarist. A spiritually attuned performer of great technical skill and concentration, Muñoz has gradually emerged as one of the avant-garde's most interesting voices on guitar. He draws much inspiration from John Coltrane but has adapted the master's ideas to his own deeply personal style. He has collaborated with both free and mainstream jazzmen like Pharoah Sanders, Rashied Ali, Nick Brignola, Dave Liebman, Bob Moses, and even David Letterman's music director, Paul Shaffer. After working in Sanders's bands for about six years, Muñoz debuted as a leader with *Rendezvous with Now* (1978, India Navigation). He presently runs his own label, Anami Music, on which he releases CDs and cassettes.

Murphy, Paul (b. Worcester, MA, 1949): drummer and percussionist. Murphy was a child prodigy of sorts, having studied with Gene Krupa and Louis Bellson before his teen years. He performed around Washington, D.C., during high school and college, often with Billy Taylor, then moved to California at age twenty-one. He split his time between Los Angeles and the San Francisco area, experimenting with new jazz forms with tenorman Art Baron and pianist Mary Ann Driscoll. In 1974, he met Jimmy Lyons, who brought Murphy to New York and relied upon his drum services regularly for over a decade. Murphy sometimes led his own quintet with Driscoll, trumpeter

Dewey Johnson, and two of Lyons's other sidemen, bassist Jay Oliver and bassoonist Karen Borca. Following Lyons's death, Murphy spent some time as a house drummer on the Las Vegas Strip. In 1987, he returned to the Bay Area, where he worked with Glenn Spearman and William Parker in the impressive Trio Hurricane (*Live at Fire in the Valley*, 1997, Eremite). Since 1990, Murphy has resided in Washington once more, recording various discs for the Mapleshade label under the leadership of Joel Futterman, Eddie Gale, pianist Larry Willis, and singer Kendra Shank.

Murray, David (b. Berkeley, CA, 19 February 1955): reedman, composer, and bandleader. Murray's influences, to whom he has paid frequent tribute throughout his career, include boppers and preboppers Coleman Hawkins, Ben Webster, and Lester Young, and free jazzmen like Ayler, Shepp, and Dolphy. He crosses back and forth between these schools of jazz thought, infusing his straighter playing with adventurous harmony and his freer playing with a firm sense of the music's roots. Murray's bass clarinet playing has evolved well beyond the point where Dolphy left the cumbersome beast, becoming even more melodic and flowing over time.

Born to a guitarist father and pianist mother, Murray performed in church and grade school before joining his first band, Notations of Soul, at the age of thirteen. During his time at Pomona College, where he studied under Bobby Bradford, Murray switched to the tenor sax and soon made it his main horn. With his friend Stanley Crouch, Murray moved to New York in 1975 and opened the Studio Infinity loft-space. He and Crouch performed in a trio with bassist Mark Dresser for a time, exploring the ground previously tread by the late Ayler. Murray's debut album, *Flowers for Albert* (1976, India Navigation) was a dedication to the free tenorman. The rhythm section on the date was bassist Fred Hopkins and drummer Philip Wilson, two former Chicagoans who helped Crouch spread Murray's name around the scene. In that same year, Murray became a founding member of the World Saxophone Quartet, with ex-St. Louis freemen Julius Hemphill, Oliver Lake, and Hamiet Bluiett. (See the WSQ's separate entry.)

Theatrical magnate Joseph Papp commissioned Murray to assemble his first big band, which fared well in the fickle jazz market. From its ranks, Murray gathered his famed octet, the setting for many of his best recordings. In 1978, Murray was contracted to Black Saint Records and soon became one of their best-selling artists, beginning with that year's *Interboogieology*. His career expanded further, particularly as a recording artist. He is now one of the most extensively recorded musicians in modern memory, with a discography that nearly rivals those of Anthony Braxton and Steve Lacy in length. More important than the quantity is the fairly dependable quality of his albums; for the sheer volume of tape he has consumed in the studio, Murray's output has been reasonably consistent. Among his most successful releases for the Black Saint have been *Ming* (1980), *Home* (1981), and *The Hill* (1986). The first album features one of his best octet lineups: Murray on tenor and bass clarinet, Henry Threadgill, Olu Dara, Butch Morris, George Lewis, Anthony Davis, Wilber Morris, and Steve McCall. Besides Black Saint, Murray has recorded for a number of other labels: the Italian imprints Cecma and Horo, Japan's DIW (which has since led to a contract with Columbia), Enja, Red Baron, Sound Hills, Sound Aspects, Bleu Regard, and others.

In the late 1980s, Murray, like many of his fellow freemen, began concentrating more on standards and less on original materials, though favorites like "Ming," "The Hill," and "Hope Scope" have been revisited many times throughout his career. His skills as a composer and arranger have developed dramatically over the past decade or so, breathing a new vitality into his recordings. He has also spread his interests into the music of other cultures, working with the Gwo-Ka musicians of Guadeloupe on excellent albums like *Yonn-Dé* (2002, Justin Time). In favoring other forms, Murray has often set aside his free jazz skills, but he returns to those avant-garde extremes with reasonable frequency. Since the 1980s, he has often performed alongside Dave Burrell to good effect (*In Concert*, 1991; *Windward Passages*, 1993, both Black Saint), duetted with pianists Donal Fox and John Hicks, and collaborated with bluesman Doyle Bramhall, vocalists Teresa Brewer and Leon Thomas, The Skatalites, and Music Revelation Ensemble.

Murray, Sunny (James Marcellus Arthur; b. Idabel, OK, 21 September 1937): drummer, composer, and bandleader. His most enduring legacy is his recordings with Cecil Taylor, but Murray has taken part in many outstanding projects as a leader and sideman since the 1960s. When he moved to New York City in 1956, he rode both sides of the embryonic free-jazz fence: mainstream, almost stolid gigs with stride pianist Willie "The Lion" Smith and traditional trumpeter Henry "Red" Allen alternated with more daring jobs for Ted Curson and Jackie McLean. Murray decided early that the burgeoning free sound was the way to go, even while the movement still had no name. He began to develop his personal style of drumming melodically instead of functioning as a rhythmic floorboard, though he never forgot how to keep up a groove. By the time he was hired by Taylor in 1959, the drummer's conceptions had already begun to change the face of jazz drumming for good. Murray's value to Taylor, Albert Ayler, and Archie Shepp is inestimable. His approach to percussion was a trademark of quality free jazz, throwing open the doors to musical democracy for drummers and bassists who followed him. His considerable talents as a writer of spacious compositions have been less appreciated, but his own recordings flaunt that side rather well.

Murray's first project as a leader was *Sunny's Time Now* (1965, Jihad, reissued by DIW), which included important contributions by Ayler and Don Cherry. The long anthem "Justice" is priceless in hindsight, and Leroi Jones (pre–Amiri Baraka) recites one of his typically inciteful poems on "Black Art." More famous is the follow-up on ESP, *Sunny Murray Quintet* (1966), with bassist Alan Silva, saxophonists Byard Lancaster and Jack Graham, and trumpeter Jacques Coursil. Silva was a flawless partner, striking the same balance of rhythm and melodicism with a ceaseless flow of fresh ideas. Graham is a capable altoist, but Lancaster and Coursil are brighter stars.

The drummer cut no less than three albums for the BYG label in 1969, beginning with *Sunshine*. Lester Bowie, Malachi Favors, and Roscoe Mitchell of the Art Ensemble of Chicago were in town, as were altoist Arthur Jones, pianist Dave Burrell, and the criminally underrecorded tenorman Kenneth Terroade. On the urgent "Red Cross," the band immediately hits a peak of intensity that most musicians take several minutes to achieve. The horns blast out long, high alarums followed by an insistent, blaring low-register line within the crash and scream of free play. *Homage to Africa* (1969, BYG), recorded the same day as *Sunshine*, adds Grachan Moncur III and trumpeter Clifford Thornton to the unit for the hair-raising "R.I.P." The drummer's third BYG set, (Never Give a Sucker) An Even Break (1969), pares things down to a manageable foursome of Murray, Favors, Lancaster, and Terroade. The saxophonists rock the house, and Murray's poetry reading is interesting.

In the 1970s, Murray moved to Philadelphia but remained active in New York circles as well, performing in both cities with his Untouchable Factor project. Recording opportunities were rather scarce, a symptom of the times, but the Untouchable Factor can be heard on "Something's Cookin'" on the Wildflowers collection (1977, Douglas/Casablanca, reissued 1999, Knit Classics). The lineup includes Murray, Lancaster, Philly vibist Khan Jamal, bassist Fred Hopkins, and guest tenorist David Murray. The tune has a beautiful, leisurely melody delivered by the saxmen as Hopkins plucks delectable commentaries. The drummer dishes out restrained tumbles and fills that fit right in line with the theme, but once the horns are finished, the rhythm begins to mutate into something almost devilish.

In the 1980s, Murray often performed in a quintet with Grachan Moncur III and promising younger faces: altoist Steve Coleman, William Parker, and pianist Curtis Clark. Eventually, however, the quixotic drummer moved to France to pursue other options. He found plenty of concert work as a sideman for others, renewing his partnership with Alan Silva along the way. It was not until 1996 that he released another album of his own: 13 Steps on Glass (Enja), a somewhat unstable session with saxophonist Odean Pope and bassist Wayne Dockery. The more consistent Illuminators (1996, Audible Hiss) teams Murray with Ayleresque saxophonist Charles Gayle, whose overwhelming volatility is a suitable match for the drummer. Gayle's notions of melody within freedom line up well with those of Murray and Ayler, resulting in a seriously musical collaboration with a lot of fire inside. Gayle's bebop-oriented piano playing is a revelation in itself, giving Murray something new to dance with.

Sabir Mateen, who relocated from the West Coast to New York in the 1990s, is a saxophonist of incredible promise. Appropriate, then, that the ever-encouraging Murray opted to record with him in a duo setting. The title of We Are Not at the Opera (1998, Eremite) is one of those "no kidding" sarcasms that comes up at times about this kind of music. This is a much freer session than the date with Gayle; Mateen discards melodies as quickly as they come up in favor of exhilarating spontaneous interaction. A keen attention to dynamics and use of silence keeps this album from becoming a plastic-wrapped migraine. The turn of the millennium saw Murray still residing in France and working as steadily as possible.

Music and Arts: nonprofit label cataloguing important American and European jazz and free musicians, including Duke Ellington, Anthony Braxton, Peter Brötzmann, Marilyn Crispell, and Barry Guy.

Music Improvisation Company: see **Bailey, Derek**.

Music Now Festival: New York City festival, founded in 2000 and held at select venues around Brooklyn's South Side. A smaller gathering than the Vision Festival, Music Now has presented a rewarding cross section of artists from across the city, including drummer Marc Edwards's trio, Ras Moshe's Sanctified, reedman Seth Misterka, Test, and several other groups featuring Test members Daniel Carter (Transcendentalists, Freedomland, Saturn Return) and Matthew Heyner (IZITITIZ, reedman Louis Belogenis's trio).

Music Revelation Ensemble: see **Ulmer, James Blood**.

Musica Elettronica Viva (MEV): electronic improvising group founded in Rome, Italy, in 1966. MEV was more of a loose collective, like Company or ICP, than a set band of performers; at one point, there were separate branches in Rome, Paris, and New York. The original body of members included Richard Teitelbaum, Alvin Curran, Frederic Rzewski, Jon Phetteplace, Allen Bryant, and Giuseppe Chiari. Their first efforts were in the spirit of Fluxus, occult art pieces featuring run-down organs, miked olive oil cans, Teitelbaum's Moog synth, and Rzewski's glass plate. In 1967, the group recorded *Spacecraft* (1970, Mainstream), their first major collaborative recording, with altoist Ivan Vandor. The live *The Sound Pool* (1969, BYG) mostly featured noise and disassociated voices; *Unified Patchwork* (1977, Horo), a more accessible work, included Teitelbaum; Rzewski; Curran; and guests Steve Lacy on soprano sax; Garrett List on trombone, voice, and electronics; and vibraphonist Karl Berger. MEV gradually dissolved into nothingness as its members took on other projects, but their recordings remain inspirational documents of radical electronic experimentation.

N

Nakamura, Toshimaru: guitarist and electronic musician. Nakamura is a kindred spirit to Sachiko M, with whom he has worked (*Do*, 1999, Erstwhile). His principal tool is his "no-input" mixing board, used to create feedback and tiny electronic sounds that are amplified tremendously. He named his 2000 album on Zero Gravity after this, his favored instrument. He founded his ensemble A Paragon of Beauty in 1992 and began sporadic trips to Berlin in 1994 to interact with Europe's finest improvisers. He has collaborated with Taku Sugimoto, Tetuzi Akiyama (both appear on the live *The Improvisation Meeting at Bar Aoyama*, 1999, Reset), dancer Kim Ito, drummer Jason Kahn, and other interdisciplinary performers.

Namtchylak, Sainkho (b. Tuva, Soviet Union): vocalist. Namtchylak is an unusual case, a "throat singer" from the Asian people of Tuva, trained to produce about seven octaves of multiphonics through the larynx. The end effect can be bizarre, chilling, or strangely beautiful, depending on the setting. Namtchylak has brought the Tuvan style to new ears through collaborations with improvisers in America and Europe, musicians who are used to accommodating the most exotic sounds.

Although women have traditionally been forbidden to study Tuvan vocal technique, Namtchylak learned it from her grandmother. After being rejected at the local college, she went to Moscow to study and was intrigued by the idea of improvisation. She returned home to join Sayani, the state folk ensemble, but not long thereafter went back to Moscow, where she formed the experimental group Tri-O. She appeared on the 1993 collection *Out of Tuva* (Crammed Discs), which introduced Tuva's vocal music to most of the Western world. However, two years prior, Namtchylak had debuted on FMP with *Lost Rivers*. She was soon residing in Vienna and performing regularly. She was assaulted and left in a coma for a couple of months in 1997 and made a slow but complete recovery.

On *Mars Song* (1996, Victo), a live recording from the Toronto Music Gallery, Namtchylak duets with the deeply sympathetic Evan Parker. Both are highly physical performers versed in coloration via multiphonics. Logically, they find much common ground to explore as a duo. The record is not for the faint of heart; the primal gutterations and visceral saxophone skitters are inevitably frightening. The better choice for beginners is *Stepmother City* (2000, Ponderosa), a Tuvan/techno/hip-hop melange. Also good are her albums with the Moscow Composers Orchestra (*Italian Love Affair*, 1995, Leo), New Age harpist Andreas Vollenweider (guest spot on *Book of Roses*, 1992, Columbia), and saxophonist Vladimir Rezitsky (*Hot Sounds from the Arctic*, 1995, Leo). Sometimes she is billed simply as Sainkho.

Nato: French record label distributed by Harmonia Mundi. Its catalog and that of its sister label Chabada, including free improvisation and film music, documents artists like Lol Coxhill, Steve Beresford, and Tony Coe (in their trio, the Melody Four, and like arrangements), Evan Parker, and other improvisers.

Naughton, Bobby (Robert; b. Boston, MA, 25 June 1944): vibraphonist, pianist, and composer. Naughton is not as prominent a player as his talents warrant. He has been a member of Leo Smith's New Dalta Akhri and collaborated with Anthony Braxton, Roscoe Mitchell, Charlie Haden, George Lewis, Hugh Ragin, Kenny Wheeler, and others. He issued a couple of albums as a leader on the Otic label (*Understanding*, 1973; *Nauxtagram*, 1980) but has never received the break needed for higher visibility.

Nessa: record label founded by Chuck Nessa after his departure from Delmark. Nessa, one of the first people to turn Bob Koester on to the AACM's jazz innovations, was a producer of some of Delmark's earliest recordings from the movement. Nessa decided to found his own label in 1967, at the suggestion of Roscoe Mitchell. The label debuted with Lester Bowie's set *Numbers 1 and 2*, a precursor to the Art Ensemble of Chicago. Nessa Records continued to record artists like the Art Ensemble and Charles Tyler throughout the 1980s before fading for financial reasons. Chuck Nessa revived the imprint in the 1990s, issuing a five-disc limited-edition boxed set of early Art Ensemble recordings (*The Art Ensemble 1967/68*, 1993) including some interesting alternate takes.

Neumann, Andrea: pianist and "pianoharpist," meaning she has performed on the interior frame of a piano without the supporting structure. An innovator along the lines of Denman Maroney, Neumann has taken the art of inside-the-piano performance to new heights (*Innenklavier*, 2002, A Bruit Secret). She has recorded with Sven-Åke Johansson and Axel Dörner (*Barcelona Series*, 2001, HatOlogy), Not Missing Drums Project (*Offline Adventures*, 1999, Leo Lab), Otomo Yoshihide (*Ensemble Cathode*, 2002, IMJ), and the Berlin-based group Phosphor (2001, Potlatch). *In Case of Fire Take the Stairs* (2002, IMJ) pits Neumann against Sachiko M's dense sine-wave manipulations, while Kaffe Matthews digitally processes their efforts into new forms.

New Dalta Akhri: ensemble conception devised by trumpeter Leo Smith. He has tagged the moniker onto several of his projects with configurations ranging from duo to quintet, depending upon Smith's purposes and musical vision at the time. Past line-ups have included drummer Pheeroan Ak Laff, pianist Anthony Davis, and saxophon-ists Henry Threadgill and Oliver Lake. Unlike many titular group leaders, Smith does not pressure himself to hold down the lead in all things. Rather, he prefers to let the individual players interpret his compositions as they see fit, providing the musical framework with little elbowing along. New Dalta Akhri's *Go In Numbers* (1982, Black Saint) features a quartet that includes Smith on trumpet, flügelhorn and atenteben flute; Dwight Andrews on tenor, soprano, and flute; Bobby Naughton on vibes; and Wes Brown on bass and odurogyaba flute. This particular ensemble admirably utilizes the level of introspective freedom in Smith's compositions.

New Music Distribution Service (NMDS): distribution company founded by Carla Bley and Michael Mantler as a function of the Jazz Composers Orchestra Association. NMDS was created to assist independent labels, particularly those that handled avant-garde artists, in distributing their wares around North America. Unfortunately, the organization was plagued with financial difficulties, with a large number of art-ists never being paid for their wares. When NMDS finally ceased operation around 1990, many indie labels once again found American distribution of their products to be nearly unattainable.

New Orchestra Workshop: see **NOW Orchestra**.

New Phonic Art (NPA): French improvising ensemble. Founded in the late 1960s, NPA was one of the better experimental groups to come out of Europe in that era. Unfortunately, they were woefully underdocumented despite the promising level of creativity they exhibited. The quartet included reedman Michel Portal, trombonist Vinko Globokar, pianist Carlos Roque Alsina, and percussionist Jean-Pierre Drouet. The members often referred to ethnic musical forms in their usage of alphorn, bandoneon, and the double-reed zurle in addition to electric organ. The principal document of their investigations is *New Phonic Art* (1971, Wergo), which has spo-radically been reissued.

New Winds: all-horn trio, originally consisting of clarinetist J.D. Parran, saxophon-ist Ned Rothenberg, and flautist Robert Dick. Dedicated to exploring the tonal and rhythmic possibilities of horns without rhythm, the trio debuted in 1986 with *The Cliff* (Sound Aspects). Parran remained with New Winds for a number of concerts and two more albums (*Traction*, 1991, Sound Aspects; *Digging It Harder from Afar*, 1995, Victo; the latter live record spans five years in the trio's life). Parran left in 1998 and was replaced by trumpeter Herb Robertson, whose presence radically altered the group's sound and dynamic. The later lineup is documented on *Potion* (1998, Victo).

New York Art Quartet: ensemble founded in 1964. The lineup included John Tchicai (fresh from the New York Contemporary Five), Roswell Rudd, Milford Graves, and bassist Lewis Worrell. Their self-titled album (1964, ESP) featured a strong guest spot by poet Amiri Baraka on "Black Dada Nihilismus"; *Mohawk* (1965, Fontana) was the undersung follow-up. As influential as the NYAQ was to younger musicians, it only lasted a short time before its members moved on to other projects. The founders reunited, with Reggie Workman in for the late Worrell, in 1999 for the well-received album *35th Anniversary* (DIW).

New York Contemporary Five: mid-1960s free ensemble. Their original lineup, with Archie Shepp, Don Cherry, John Tchicai, bassist Don Moore, and drummer J. C. Moses, recorded their debut album for Storyville in 1963. One year later, Moore and Moses were replaced by Sun Ra bassman Ronnie Boykins and rising drum artist Sunny Murray for *Archie Shepp and the New York Contemporary Five* (1964, Savoy), on which the band shared space with Bill Dixon's septet. Trumpeter Ted Curson was a guest on the later date, which was the NYC5's last recording before its dissolution.

Newton, James (b. Los Angeles, CA, 1 May 1953): flautist. Newton is one of the few jazz artists to specialize in the flute. Though he has explored absolute freedom in his music, Newton rarely brings forth a sound from his horn that is not traditionally beautiful in some way.

Newton began his musical career as an electric bassist, interpreting the music of Motown and Jimi Hendrix in local bands. In high school, he learned the saxophone, then took up the flute after hearing what Rahsaan Roland Kirk and Eric Dolphy had done with it in jazz settings. He studied classical music at Cal State Los Angeles and later investigated free jazz with Arthur Blythe, David Murray, and drummer Stanley Crouch in the ensemble Black Music Infinity. Horace Tapscott was a key influence, drawing Newton into his small circle of associates. Newton's debut as a leader was *Solomon's Sons* (1977) on the Circle label.

In 1978, the Infinity members moved to the more fertile grounds of New York City. Newton began working with pianist Anthony Davis regularly, sometimes in an exceptionally beautiful trio with cellist Abdul Wadud (*I've Known Rivers*, 1982, Gramavision) and the octet Episteme. Blythe, Murray, and John Carter were frequent partners, and Newton briefly held a spot in Cecil Taylor's big band. Recordings for the European labels BVHaast and Moers preceded a sinecure contract with India Navigation (*Paseo Del Mar*, 1978), which further spread Newton's influence. *Axum* (1981, ECM) was a particular triumph for the flautist, a brilliant solo excursion inspired by the ancient East African kingdom. That session, one of Newton's most popular recordings, brought him further notoriety in the late 1990s when he sued the rap group Beastie Boys for using a sample of "Choir" in one of their records. He has continued to issue outstanding albums (*The African Flower*, 1985, Blue Note, proffers his adaptations of Ellington's music) while instructing at CalArts, the University of California at Irvine, and his alma mater, Cal State L.A. Newton has been commissioned to compose classical works and continues to work as a sideman, notably with Andrew Cyrille (*X Man*, 1993, Black Saint).

Newton, Lauren (b. Coos Bay, OR): vocalist and composer. Best known for a long-time association with the Vienna Art Orchestra, Newton is one of the most esteemed vocalists in the new music. She graduated from the University of Oregon in 1974 and then attended the Stuttgart School of Music. Newton decided to remain in Europe and worked with the Vienna Art Orchestra from 1980 (*Concerto Piccolo*, HatArt) to 1989. She functioned as a horn as much as a traditional vocalist in the setting, pouring forth swooping scats or streams of nonsense syllables with the greatest of ease. The first recording issued under her own name was the critically acclaimed *Timbre* (1983, HatArt; reissued as *Filigree*, 1998, HatOlogy). Away from the VAO and her own recordings, Newton has worked with Jon Rose, Jöelle Léandre, Not Missing Drums Project, Anthony Braxton (*Composition No. 192*, 1996, Leo), poet Ernst Jandl, Christy Doran, and contemporary classical art ensembles. *The Lightness of Hearing* and *Out of Sound* (both 2002) are her most recent recordings for Leo.

Nicols, Maggie (b. Edinburgh, Scotland, 24 February 1948): vocalist. Trained in voice and dance, Nicols worked in both fields from her teen years. In the mid-1960s, she became interested in jazz and landed a job with pianist Dennis Rose, eventually coming around to free improvisation. Nicols was invited to join the Spontaneous Music Ensemble early in its life, and she was part of their lineup at the first Total Music Meeting in Berlin in 1968. Other gigs of the period included the ensemble Voice with singers Brian Ely, Phil Minton, and Julie Tippetts, and duos with percussionist Ken Hyder (*In the Stone*, 1998, Impetus) and pianist Pete Nu. Minton and Tippetts found a place for Nicols in Keith Tippett's mega-big-band Centipede, which recorded *September Energy* in 1971 (Neon). Nicols and Tippetts worked as a duo later in the decade, around the time that Nicols's interests in feminism grew stronger. She helped to form the Feminist Improvising Group, Ova, and the women's arts workshop Contradictions. With Irène Schweizer and Joëlle Léandre she works in the trio Les Diaboliques; her resumé also includes work with Trevor Watts's Moiré Music, Lol Coxhill, Gunter Sömmer, Phil Minton, Jon Rose, Iskra 1903, Cat's Cradle, Tony Oxley's Dedication Orchestra, the London Jazz Composers Orchestra, and her daughter, Aura Marina. *Transitions* (2002, Emanem), with saxophonist Caroline Kraabel, proved that Nicols had lost little creativity over three decades.

Nine Winds: label founded in 1977 by Vinny Golia (see entry). The award-winning label, noted for its high-quality products, specializes in new jazz, improvised, and modern classical recordings from the American West Coast. The catalog of over 100 releases includes records by Golia; bass artist Bertram Turetzky; pianists Paul Plimley, Wayne Peet, and Tad Weed; percussionists Alex Cline and Dick Berk; reedmen Steve Adams and Kim Richmond; guitarists Larry Koonse and Nels Cline; and the ensembles Big World, Continuum, Quartetto Stig, New Orchestra Workshop, and Mark Harvey's Aardvark Jazz Orchestra. Golia and his staff also provide production, promotion, and consultation services to West Coast musicians.

Ninh, Lê Quan: see **Lê Quan, Ninh.**

nmperign: duo of trumpeter Greg Kelley and soprano saxophonist Bhob Rainey. The name derives from a Latin phrase, "igNotuM PER IGNotius" (the unknown through the more unknown). As Rainey describes it, "The concept has never been rigorously defined but has always involved attention, investigation, humor, and a complex ethical palette that has something to do with the way we want to live our lives." Besides touring the United States, Europe, and Japan under the nmperign banner, the men have collaborated with Axel Dörner, Masashi Harada, and others. Recordings include their debut on Twisted Village (1998), two collaborations with electronics manipulator Jason Lescalleet (*in which the silent partner-director is no longer able to make his point with the industrial dreamer*, 1999, and *Love Me Two Times*, 2002 [2 CDs], both Intransitive) and a disc with shakuhachi artist Philip Gelb, Lescalleet, and Tatsuya Nakatani (*This Is nmperign's Second CD*, 1999, Twisted Village).

No More: record label based in Woodmere, New York. Founded by Alan Schneider, its catalog includes albums by William Parker, Matthew Shipp, Frank Lowe, Mat Maneri, Anthony Braxton, Rob Brown, and others.

Nommonsemble: quartet of drummer/leader Whit Dickey, pianist Matthew Shipp, altoist Rob Brown, and violinist Mat Maneri. The name derives from the Kiswahili word *nommo*, which roughly refers to some verbal, visual, or musical communication that plants a seed of thought and growth in the listener. The quartet debuted with *Life Cycle* (2001, Aum Fidelity).

Norton, Kevin (b. Brooklyn, NY, 21 January 1956): drummer and percussionist. Raised in Staten Island, Norton grew up around a profusion of musical styles (his father worked for Columbia Records). He studied jazz with Mike Sgroi, Milt Hinton, and Barry Altschul at Hunter College and afterward devoted special effort to mallet studies. His resumé includes work in klezmer, rock, blues, and gospel bands as well as mainstream and free-jazz settings. Norton has held fruitful partnerships with Anthony Braxton and guitarist James Emery, playing a particularly vital role in Braxton's "Ghost Trance" projects since 1995.

Not Missing Drums Project: improvising ensemble co-led by saxophonist/keyboardist Joachim Gies and cellist/keyboardist Thomas Böhm-Christl. As one might gather from the name, their aesthetic involves the absence of drum support in performance. It has been a difficult sell at times, with some shaky ground covered on early albums, but *The Gay Avantgarde* (2000, Leo) is a high mark. On that disc, mezzosoprano Ute Döring delivers a loose, Nietzsche-worded song cycle backed by the group, featuring trombonist Jörg Huke. Lauren Newton and Andrea Neumann have collaborated with the Project in the past.

NOW Orchestra: ensemble centered on Canada's New Orchestra Workshop. Formed in 1987 by saxophonist Coat Cooke, the group draws from Vancouver, Seattle, and adjacent regions. Its members include drummer Dylan van der Schyff, cellist Peggy Lee, pianist Paul Plimley, reedman Graham Ord, and trumpeter Bill Clark. The NOW Orchestra has collaborated with such luminaries as Butch Morris, Marilyn Crispell, Vinny Golia, and George Lewis; the last two are featured on *WOWOW* (1991, Spool) with vocalist Kate Hammett-Vaughn and reedman Paul Cram.

NRG Ensemble: group founded by Hal Russell in the late 1970s. Russell, a former bebop drummer of solid repute, learned to play the saxophone late in his career and formed NRG Ensemble to explore his notions of free jazz. The early members included saxophonist Mars Williams, bassist Kent Kessler, multi-instrumentalist Brian Sandstrom, and percussionist Steve Hunt, with Williams usually playing saxophones and trumpet. The group debuted in 1981 with a self-titled release on Nessa, somewhat lacking in focus but showing definite promise. By the recording of *The Finnish/ Swiss Tour* (1990, ECM), their indubitably quirky style of freedom had won fans worldwide. Following the leader's death in 1992, Russell's spot was filled by reedman Ken Vandermark. *The Hal Russell Story* (1993, ECM) ended up as a sensitive posthumous reflection upon the bandleader's unique career. The excellent *This Is My House* (Delmark), issued two years later, confirmed Vandermark's suitability as a replacement. (See also Russell's entry.)

O

Ochs, Lawrence (b. New York, NY, 3 May 1949): saxophonist, composer, and bandleader. (See also Rova.) Ochs studied both the trumpet and saxophones in his younger days but soon settled upon the reeds. He founded the Rova Saxophone Quartet in 1978, the same year that he established the enterprising Metalanguage record label. The group debuted in that year with *Cinema Rovaté*, the first presentation of Ochs's bright ideas for rhythmless settings. Ochs has also run the Twelve Stars recording studio in the San Francisco area, composed for theater and film, and landed a number of commissions for original compositions. In the 1980s, he worked in reedman Glenn Spearman's Double Trio, one of the Bay Area's premier free groups. Presently Ochs participates in Rova and two prominent trios: the new-music ensemble Room, and What We Live with bassist Lisle Ellis and drummer Donald Robinson (see What We Live's entry). Ochs took part in *Yo Miles!* (1998, Shanachie) with Henry Kaiser and Wadada Leo Smith (both of whom he has worked with in other settings), Fred Frith's *Digital Wildlife* (2001, Winter & Winter), and projects with the Scott Fields Ensemble. *The Secret Magritte* (1995, Black Saint) was Ochs's first disc under his own name.

Ogun: British label founded in 1974 by South African expatriates Harry and Hazel Miller. Ogun's catalog includes records by the Brotherhood of Breath, Mike Osborne, John Surman, Keith Tippett, Elton Dean, Lol Coxhill, Evan Parker, John Stevens, and Trevor Watts. In the 1990s, Ogun joined forces with the Cadillac label and is now engaged in both a reissue program and the release of new material.

Okkadisk (or Okka): Chicago-based label founded by Bruno Johnson in 1994. Johnson's principal vision is simply to record the musicians he admires playing the music they love, a goal he put into action after seeing Fred Anderson perform. The label's roster also includes Ken Vandermark (in various situations, including the DKV Trio), Marilyn Crispell, Aaly Trio, and Peter Brötzmann's Chicago Octet and Tentet.

Old and New Dreams: quartet of Ornette Coleman alumni. Inspired by the visions instilled in them by Coleman, bassist Charlie Haden, tenorman Dewey Redman, trumpeter Don Cherry, and drummer Ed Blackwell reunited in 1980 to perform and record Coleman's compositions and their own original music. On their eponymous debut disc (1976, Black Saint) O&ND interpreted Coleman's "Handwoven," Redman's enticing "Dewey's Tune" and the title track, Haden's "Chairman Mao," and two excellent works from Cherry. The combination of Cherry's world-music inclinations, Blackwell's flawless rhythms, Haden's folkiness, and Redman's biting zeal resulted in an auspicious debut. The band recorded a second self-titled album, this time on ECM, in 1979, which featured Coleman's classics "Lonely Woman" and "Open or Close." *Playing* (1980, ECM), captured live in Austria, includes "Happy House," "New Dream," and "Broken Shadows" along with Cherry's "Mopti," Redman's "Rushour," and Haden's "Playing."

In the 1980s, Blackwell began suffering kidney trouble, requiring daily dialysis. An Atlanta festival in 1987, held as a benefit for the ailing drummer, marked the swansong of Old and New Dreams. Blackwell's "Togo" was the centerpiece of the middling live set (alternately titled *One for Blackwell*, or *A Tribute to Blackwell*, 1987, Black Saint) that also included "Dewey's Tune" and three pieces by Coleman. While the spirit is nice, neither Blackwell nor Cherry seemed up to the task.

Oliveros, Pauline (b. Houston, TX, 20 May 1932): accordionist, electronic musician, and composer. Oliveros is one of the principal architects of Deep Listening, an artistic philosophy that blends electronics and improvisation with meditation and intent listening exercises in order to train one's ears and mind. The aesthetic developed out of her experiments with environmental and natural sounds, dubbed "Sonic Meditations."

Oliveros learned music from her mother and grandmother, and later attended San Francisco State College. She played French horn in a new-music ensemble with minimalist composer/pianist Terry Riley while expanding her accordion skills. In the 1960s, Oliveros helped establish the Tape Music Center at Mills College in Oakland, then taught for many years at the University of California, San Diego. *Deep Listening* (1989, New Albion) was the first official document of her complex, often exceedingly quiet investigations into sensory expansion, though she began working on the concept in 1971. Oliveros continues to espouse her theories through the Deep Listening Band (*Ready Made Boomerang*, 1991, New Albion), in which she also sings and plays percussion, and a charitable foundation. Recently she has collaborated with other fringe artists like shakuhachi player Philip Gelb and drummer Susie Ibarra.

O'Rourke, Jim (b. Chicago, IL, 1969): guitarist, composer, and producer. O'Rourke has worked in situations from the academic avant-garde to flat-out rock, often preparing his guitar with paper clips, rubber bands, and other such alterations. He began studying the guitar at age six and became interested in electronic music and the avant-garde while attending DePaul University. In the early 1990s, he released several experimental albums on tiny labels with weak distribution but struck gold by meeting Derek Bailey. The invitation to participate in a Company Week festival spread O'Rourke's reputation around American and European improv circles. Since the early 1990s, he has performed with the avant-rock group Gastr del Sol, Illusion of Safety, Henry Kaiser, Eddie Prevost, Keith Rowe, Japanese guitarist KK Null, Stereolab, and Mayo Thompson's Red Krayola, and written commissioned works for Rova and Kronos Quartet. *Terminal Pharmacy* (1995, Tzadik) is a strong solo album that demonstrates his eclectic approach, while *I'm Happy, and I'm Singing, and a 1, 2, 3, 4* (2001, Mego) captures his live electroacoustic hijinks.

Organ of Corti: California-based label under the aegis of the Cortical Foundation. An anxiously awaited project is the proposed reunion of Derek Bailey, Tony Oxley, and Gavin Bryars as the seminal free group Joseph Holbrooke.

Osborne, Mike: alto saxophonist. Once one of Europe's most promising altoists, Osborne has almost been forgotten now, having left the music business in 1982 due to ill health. He made impressive contributions to Chris McGregor's Brotherhood of Breath in the 1970s, appeared on John Surman's self-titled debut in 1968 (Deram), and played with Surman and Alan Skidmore in the innovative saxophone trio S.O.S. With bassist Earl Freeman and drummer Louis Moholo, the three saxmen cut Osborne's *Shapes* (1972, reissued 1995, Future Music). He supported Harry Beckett (*Warm Smiles*, 1972, RCA), guitarist Mike Cooper, and The Trio (*Conflagration*, 1971, Dawn). Osborne's foremost album was *All Night Long* (1975, Ogun), which is difficult to come by. The recent issue (under John Stevens's name) of *Live at the Plough* (rec. 1979, issued 2001, Ayler), a trio date with bassist Paul Rogers, presents an opportunity to evaluate Osborne as a performer and composer, albeit twenty-odd years after his departure.

Ostertag, Bob (b. Albuquerque, NM, 19 April 1957): electronic musician and composer. Like many teens, he picked up the electric guitar in high school. While at Oberlin, he began his studies in electronic music, building a modular synthesizer. He was hired by Anthony Braxton in 1978 for the touring Creative Music Orchestra, and following the band's sojourn through Europe, Ostertag settled in New York City. The Downtown scene was just beginning to catch fire at the time, and he fell into the main circle with Eugene Chadbourne and John Zorn. Chadbourne issued Ostertag's debut album, *Early Fall* (1979), on his Parachute label, and the guitarist appeared on some of Zorn's earliest game-piece projects like *Pool* (1980, Parachute).

Ostertag experimented with various electric sound production methods while pursuing his interest in social and political activism. In 1980, while making some field recordings of Sandinista rebels in Nicaragua, he became convicted to follow activism as his principal line of work. By 1982, Ostertag had abandoned his music career to work as an adviser on Central American political matters. He continued in that vein until 1988, when Fred Frith lured him back into music with his band Keep The Dog. Ostertag began to catch up on musical technology that had bypassed him over the years, particularly the use of samplers. After tentative investigations with Zorn and Frith on *Attention Span* (1990, Rift), he formed the quartet Say No More (1993, Rec Rec) with Phil Minton, Mark Dresser, and Gerry Hemingway. Ostertag was an odd fourth wheel in that group, grabbing samples of the other musicians and stringing them together into new compositions. Ostertag has more recently started using laptop computers in performance. He has continued to collaborate with Frith while participating in gay-rights activism and multimedia events.

Oswald, John (b. Toronto, Canada, 30 May 1953): alto saxophonist, electronic musician, and composer. Oswald is perhaps principally known for his notorious 1996 CD *Plunderphonics*, which collected a vast number of music and sound samples into new compositions. Mere possession of the disc was illegal in most of the United States and Canada, so allegedly flagrant were the copyright violations. Despite the headaches, he has continued to experiment with the creative potential of samples. *Grayfolded: Transitive Axis* (1995, Swell/Artifact) strings together samples of various versions of the Grateful Dead's free-rock anthem "Dark Star"; *Nine Examples of Plunderphonic Techniques* (1992, Musicworks) is a how-to of the art form.

   A member of the CCMC, Oswald is a talented altoist who has performed or composed for such projects as Henry Kaiser's *Ice Death* (1977, Parachute), poet Paul Haines's *Darn It!* (1994, American Clavé), Derek Bailey's *Play Backs* (1998, Bingo), the Kronos Quartet's *Short Stories* (1993, Nonesuch), and the free ensemble Pitch, which habitually performs in darkness. *Bloor* (2001, CIMP) unites him with David Prentice on violin and Dominic Duval on bass. Oswald has written for dance companies and is a research director for the Mystery Laboratory experimental studio in Toronto.

Other Dimensions In Music: quartet of trumpeter Roy Campbell, reedman Daniel Carter, bassist William Parker, and drummer Rashid Bakr. Campbell and the rhythmists had originally performed together in Jemeel Moondoc's quartet, Ensemble Muntu, in the early 1970s. That they should reunite nearly two decades later, with another highly promising reedman in their ranks, was a well-timed masterstroke. ODIM has since become one of New York's most popular and promising free outfits, clearly inspired by Cecil Taylor but reaching out to all aspects of modern black music. Their self-titled debut (1989, Silkheart) declared their stance with its wealth of bop-centered improvisation and a dedication to Sly Stone. The next album, *Now!* (1998, Aum Fidelity), displays a more consistent level of free interplay, and the sorrowful "Tears for the Boy Wonder (for Winton Marsalis)" features an emotional conversation between Campbell's wah-muted trumpet and Parker's moaning bowed bass. The half-hour "For the Glass Tear/After Evening's Orange" is a titanic spotlight for Carter and the trumpeter. Their third release, *Time Is of the Essence—The Essence Is*

Beyond Time (2000, Aum Fidelity) is an exciting live set with guest Matthew Shipp on piano. Its seven simply numbered tracks present some of their most outlandish improvisations yet, with Campbell's effulgent tone almost evoking Lester Bowie at times.

Otomo, Yoshihide (b. Yokohama, Japan, 1 August 1959): guitarist, composer, and electronic musician. Otomo's interest in electronics started in childhood, when he built radio receivers and oscillators from kits. As a youth, he experimented with tape composition, played in rock bands, then got into free jazz upon hearing saxophonist Kaoru Abe. His first recording was 1977's *Moon Ray Three* (on the scarce Blind label). In the early 1980s, Otomo studied Chinese ethnic musics in Hainan, then performed around local clubs as a free improviser. His duo with saxophonist Junji Hirose brought him wider attention, and Otomo was soon participating in a number of ensembles: ORT, No Problem, Player Piano, his own noise-rock band Ground Zero (*Ground-0, No. 0*, 1991, Lost Space), and the Double Unit Orchestra. Otomo experiments with turntables in the spirit of Christian Marclay and has worked with Altered States, drummers Chris Cutler and Samm Bennett, Jon Rose, screamer/vocalist Yamatsuka Eye, Voice Crack, and Günter Müller. A good starting point to explore Otomo's music is *Live!* (1995, Blast First).

Oxley, Tony (b. Sheffield, England, 15 June 1938): drummer, percussionist, and bandleader. Oxley, Derek Bailey, and bassist Gavin Bryars were members of the early free ensemble Joseph Holbrooke from 1963 to 1966. Removed by miles from the bur- geoning London free scene, the band members developed their own unique approaches to the music. In 1966, Oxley and Bailey moved to London, where Oxley became the house drummer at Ronnie Scott's club. His first recorded appearance was *Experiments with Pops* (1967, Major Minor), with pianist Gordon Beck's quartet. Oxley later formed the important Incus label with Bailey and Evan Parker, although he and Parker even- tually ceased their involvement in the venture. Since then he has become Britain's premier free-improvising drummer.

The *Baptised Traveller* (1969, CBS) is by the quintet of Oxley, Bailey, Parker, Kenny Wheeler, and bassist Jeff Clyne. All of the tracks are composed to some degree, and the nexus is a fine reading of "Stone Garden" by alto saxophonist Charlie Mariano. Wheeler is melodic yet freewheeling, even this early in his career, while Bailey and Parker have already moved away from the period's loose conventions of free jazz. The guitarist remains in the habit of forming fairly melodic idea-strings, which he would soon abandon altogether. This session remains Oxley's best as a leader, a classic of European free music.

Oxley is as adept at bebop and straight jazz accompaniment as he is free improv, gifts that have brought innumerable opportunities for work. He is a member of Cecil Taylor's acclaimed Feel Trio with William Parker and has played with the London Jazz Composers Orchestra (*Ode*, 1972, Incus) and his Celebration Orchestra (*Ixesha*, 1994, Ogun). Oxley has continued to collaborate with performers like Bill Dixon

(*Vade Mecum* and *Vade Mecum II*, both 1993, Soul Note), Paul Bley (*Chaos*, 1994, Soul Note, with bassist Furio Di Castri), Derek Bailey, John Surman, and Tomasz Stánko (*Matka Joanna*, 1994, ECM). Part of his drumkit is amplified and includes springs, wires, kitchen devices, motors, and electronic effects. Oxley is also a respected painter.

P

Pachora: quintet led by saxophonist Matt Darriau. Pachora's music uniquely blends Eastern European influences (Gypsy, klezmer, Balkan) with modern jazz forms. Among the other members are reedman Chris Speed, guitarist Brad Shepik, bassist Skuli Sverrisson, and drummer Jim Black. *Ast* (1999, Knitting Factory Works) is Pachora's best recording to date.

Painkiller: extreme free improvising trio, formed in 1991 by altoist John Zorn, electric bassist Bill Laswell, and drummer Mick Harris, formerly of the grindcore rock band Napalm Death. Zorn assembled the group after studying the grindcore scene, wishing to assimilate that kind of intensity into jazz. The band's two official albums so far are *Guts of a Virgin* (1991, Mosh) and *Buried Secrets* (1992, Relativity). For live shows, former Faith No More/Mr. Bungle vocalist Mike Patton sometimes joins the trio.

Parachute: maverick record label from New York City, founded by Eugene Chadbourne but defunct since 1988. In the 1970s, Parachute unveiled many avant-rock and jazz artists, including John Zorn, Henry Kaiser, and Bob Ostertag, as well as humorists Shel Silverstein and Lowen & Navarro.

Parker, Evan (Shaw; b. Bristol, England, 5 April 1944): tenor and soprano saxophonist, one of the most instantly identifiable performers in modern music. His "Snake" technique, using false fingerings, circular breathing, and tone coloration, is as distinctive as his fingerprints, and he has graced a vast number of improvised music sessions.

John Coltrane was one of Parker's most significant influences when he became a professional musician in his early twenties. Originally, Parker practiced the modality, flowing lines, and emotionalism that characterized his idol's work. As Coltrane moved further into freedom, around the time that the Spontaneous Music Ensemble was formed, Parker followed suit in his own spontaneity but developed a more personal style. By the time he founded the Music Improvisation Company with Derek Bailey in 1968, Parker's sound was nearly a force unto itself.

In 1970, Bailey, Parker, and drummer Tony Oxley founded the Incus record label to document the current goings-on in British improvisation. Each man's career took off from that point, Parker landing chairs in the Globe Unity Orchestra and Chris McGregor's Brotherhood of Breath. That same year, Alex von Schlippenbach, the leader of Globe Unity, hired Parker and drummer Paul Lovens for a popular free-jazz trio (see Schlippenbach's entry). In the mid-1970s came Parker's equally arousing trio with bassist Barry Guy and drummer Paul Lytton.

Parker had made a number of solo recordings, starting with *Saxophone Solos* (1975, Chronoscope). While solo-horn discs are now an accepted norm in improvised music, few artists had attempted such a risky project since Anthony Braxton's *For Alto* set the standard. Parker was rather fearless by this time, however, and his performances on this album's fourteen "Aerobatics" are rational extensions of Braxton's innovations. Four earlier live pieces are the most energetic, but Parker's technique had improved significantly by the time the ten studio cuts were laid down. Some include fragments from Samuel Beckett's play "Krapp's Last Tape," theater just as demanding as the music it inspired Parker to create. Parker's solo records since have been consistently fascinating, showing the evolution of his style over the course of a quarter-century. On *Monoceros* (Latin for "one horn"; 1978, Incus), he continued to push the limits of one soprano sax with impressive improvisations ranging from four minutes to well over twenty in length. The Snake was beginning to take its definitive shape by now; Parker had learned how to pair multiphonics and circular breathing without his skull collapsing (*The Snake Decides*, 1986, Emanem, is also good).

On *Conic Sections* (1989, Ah Um), Parker nearly duets with himself, thanks to the cavernous acoustics of Holywell Cathedral where the album was waxed. On *Process and Reality* (1991, FMP), Parker uses multitracking technology instead of the space to carry on conversations with himself on sixteen shorter improvisations. "Fast Falls (for Mongezi Feza)," the longest, most passionate track, is dedicated to the Brotherhood of Breath's late trumpeter. On some pieces, Parker engages in thematic improv in the style of Cecil Taylor, working out fast and furious motivic variations. On the multitracked records, Parker vacillates between parallels of his prerecorded lines and deliberate altercations with them. At times, it seems a soundtrack to madness, with passages of lucid beauty interspersed.

His most recent solo release, *Lines Burnt in Light* (2001, PSI), inaugurates Parker's third independent label after Incus and Maya, the imprint named after his wife, baroque violinist Maya Homburger. It was recorded at St. Michael and All Angels Church, the acoustics of which cause Parker's hummingbird flutters and chicken squawks to resound like steeple bells. The music is delivered with a sweaty earnestness, in breathless tirades of breakneck note-streams that threaten to sunder the church's walls. Whereas on *Conic Sections* Parker allowed himself time to think about his responses to the echoes, here he treats his sound-ghosts with something approaching disregard.

In September 1984, Parker and Barry Guy teamed with AMM founders Eddie Prévost and Keith Rowe for *Supersession* (1984, Matchless), a half-hour ritual of electronically enhanced creativity. Parker and Guy provide the jazziest contributions, though Guy alters the sound of his acoustic bass through spontaneous electronic processing. Prévost supply steers the ship with mere hints of meter; Rowe assaults the very air they breathe with titanic screams of electric guitar. Through it all, The Snake darts around silences and between crashes.

Atlanta (1986, Impetus) captures the Parker/Guy/Lytton Trio live in that southern city. Guy's impressive chordal technique is essential, offering up instant idea threads. The bassist and drummer lock intuitively onto each other's patterns, forcing Parker to either join them or fight to the death. Usually the saxophonist wedges himself into a cozy niche (cozy being relative, of course) to flow in blessed accordance with his mates. By the time "The Snake as Road Sign" is going well, Lytton and Guy opt to move out of the way and let the man work his solo magic.

Not all the trio's experiments have been wholly successful. A case in point is *Breaths and Heartbeats* (1995, Rastascan), a rather painful affair. The album's focus is on the nature and patterns of bodily pulses, the rhythms of circulation, inspiration, and expiration. Parker's contributions are little more than quiet, staccato note repetitions of chafing length and little or no motion. Guy and Lytton seem uninspired, turning in equally static performances.

On April 10, 1994, Parker gave his *50th Birthday Concert* (1994, Leo) in the company of special friends. This disc offers the ideal comparison of his two principal trios. The first two tracks place him with Schlippenbach and Lovens, the pianist's liquid methodology feeding plenty of inspirational ideas to the reedman and drummer. Schlippenbach is almost as invigorating as Cecil Taylor, and the resulting cooperative music nearly raises the roof. On the three tracks by Parker/Guy/Lytton, differences become clear right away. Lytton and Lovens are drastically contrary drummers. Lovens is more melodic and linear; Lytton is more interested in the constant flux of sound and texture, less mindful of pulse. Guy's double- and triple-stops, pizzicato or arco, approach the density of a piano in his most inspired moments.

The same personnel are found on *2 x 3 = 5* (2001, Leo), except this time around, all five perform together on a single long track. Lovens and Lytton shine, instantly finding ways to unite their disparate approaches to the drums in service to the whole. Guy and Schlippenbach delve into conversation as deeply as Bill Evans and Scott LaFaro had forty years prior, following, prodding, dancing about each other like pixies. Parker is in firm command, bringing the fronts together in unity through democracy.

Pianist Marilyn Crispell guests with the trio on one track of *After Appleby* (2000, Leo). The inspirations of Braxton and Taylor are audibly stamped upon her playing, giving it a different character than Schlippenbach's more bop-grounded approach. The Tayloresque centerpiece, "Capnomantic Vortex," presents a formidable challenge, but Parker, Guy, and Lytton follow Crispell's beautiful lead around every twist and turn of the track's circular logic.

On occasion, Parker has recorded duos with his trio partners, coming up with compelling studies in texture and form. In duo with Lytton (*Ra 1 + 2*, 1978, Moers), he finds new realizations of rough and smooth in music: drums become more melodic, saxophone more percussive. A similar paradigm shift occurs when Parker and Guy team up on *Obliquities* (1994, Maya). Guy expertly forces the bass to operate as both a primary source of rhythm and a colead instrument. Parker takes a rare opportunity to relax on some cuts, basking in the drumless calm. On the opposite end is *Foxes Fox* (1999, Emanem) with Louis Moholo, Steve Beresford, and bassist John Edwards. Parker only plays on five tracks, and everyone is in a more mainstream attitude than usual. Moholo's African-derived drum patterns and Beresford's hot cascades of notes make this session especially enjoyable.

One of Parker's most sonically intriguing ventures has been the Electro-Acoustic Ensemble, documented on the adventurous *Drawn Inward* (1999, ECM). The core is Parker/Guy/Lytton, supplemented by Phil Wachsmann on violin and viola, and three "electronic sound-manipulators": Lawrence Casserly, Marco Vecchi, and Walter Prati. Their function is to create mechanical soundscapes through original synthesis and by processing the players' sounds. Wachsmann himself runs electronics when he is not dashing out striations of glimmering strings. Parker's playing is not quite as overboard as usual, perhaps because this atmosphere is so dense that further piling on would asphyxiate the listener. A new world of possibilities awaits the saxophonist in this bold setting, and it is expected that further electronic dabblings will provide even better fruit than this exceptional release.

Parker, William (b. The Bronx, NY, 1952): bassist, composer, and bandleader. Parker is one of the essential figures in contemporary free jazz, a catalyst for innumerable sessions since he started working with Cecil Taylor in the early 1970s. Highly respected as a bass player, leader, composer, and organizer, Parker has been a principal architect of improvised music over the past two decades. To create diverse textures, he uses a number of techniques on the bass: traditional walking; plucking the open strings with an effect like a West African kora; bowing squealing harmonics and sinuous, amelodic lines; or treating it as a percussion instrument as Taylor does with the piano.

Taylor was one of Parker's earliest associates following his studies with bass giants Wilbur Ware, Jimmy Garrison, and Richard Davis. The pianist first hired Parker for a Carnegie Hall performance around 1973, inspiring the bassist to look further into the avant-garde. Parker subsequently joined Jemeel Moondoc's band and continued to make a profound impact on contemporary free jazz.

Parker's first recording as a leader was *Through Acceptance of the Mystery Peace* (1979), originally issued on his own Centering label and reissued by Eremite in 1998. It includes tracks recorded as far back as 1974 ("Rattles and Bells and the Light of the Sun," with Moondoc, Charles Brackeen, Billy Bang, and three other players). Each of the five tracks is by a different ensemble; Parker composed but does not play on the title track, and he recites a poem over the violins of Bang and Ramsey Ameen on "Face Still Hands Folded." The record demonstrates Parker's early interest in es-caping the usual notions of jazz ensembles in favor of textural variation.

In the 1980s, Parker worked regularly with Taylor (see the pianist's entry) while building his own concepts of group improvisation. *In Florescence* (1989, A&M) is one of his best achievements within Taylor's unit, featuring a solo rendition of his com-position "Anast In Crisis Mouth Full of Fresh Cut Flowers." Parker presented a radi-cally different ensemble version of the tune on *In Order to Survive* (1995, Black Saint), an outstanding disc with pianist Cooper-Moore, Rob Brown, trumpeter Lewis Barnes, Grachan Moncur III, Denis Charles, and percussionist Jackson Krall. Parker later assembled a regular working group, also called In Order to Survive, along with his first big band (*Flowers Grow in My Room*, 1995, Centering).

In 1984, Parker and his wife, dancer Patricia Nicholson, coordinated the Sound Unity Festival, a racially mixed celebration of new music that held concerts at various venues around New York City. The festival and its featured performers are the subjects of Ebba Jahn's film *Rising Tones Cross*. Ten years later, the Parkers established the Improvisers Collective along with Krall, pianist Mark Hennen, and other artists. The Collective's objective was to present art of a spontaneous nature in a positive light in order to increase the visibility of such artists within the community. It was the Collective's inspiration that led to the annual Vision Festival (see separate entry), as well as Parker's Little Huey Creative Music Ensemble. It has become one of the premier large groups in improvised music, interpreting Parker's panoramic compositions with a respectable measure of freedom.

On *Mayor of Punkville* (2000, Aum Fidelity, 2 CDs), the spirit of Mingus permeates the arrangements; it is not a direct tribute by any stretch, yet his influence is undeniable. The Little Huey personnel includes Rob Brown, Ori Kaplan, and Charles Waters on alto saxes (with doubling); Chris Jonas on soprano sax; Darryl Foster on tenor and soprano; Dave Sewelson on bari sax; Roy Campbell, Richard Rodriguez, and Lewis Barnes on trumpets; Steve Swell, Masahiko Kono, and Alex Lodico on trombones; Dave Hofstra on tuba and bass; Cooper-Moore on piano; Andrew Barker on drums; and Parker on bass, piano, and conducting. Aleta Hayes sings on the blues-drenched "James Baldwin to the Rescue." "Oglala Eclipse" is a Mingusian tribute to various jazzmen of both black and Native American heritage. The nearly half-hour "I Can't Believe I Am Here" carries on the Mingus vibe with a long string of excellent soloists. On "Interlude #7 (Huey's Blues)," Parker's bass is so forceful he practically duets with Lewis Barnes, and Kono begins to assert himself just before an ill-timed fade. Sewelson and Parker's piano introduce the beautiful, Eastern-flavored suite "3 Steps to Nøh Mountain." Parker returns to bass for thunderous walking on the dark-souled title track, which mutates into a New Orleans rave-up halfway through. Jonas and Lodico particularly shine in solos and ensemble sections. The closing "Anthem" returns slightly to the Oriental feel, with a good dose of blues; bright-toned Rodriguez is in firm command. Recorded live at Tonic in New York City, the production suffers a bit from room ambience and coughs, but the performances are commendable.

Besides Little Huey, Parker has remained extremely active as a member of quartets led by David S. Ware and Matthew Shipp, as well as his own side projects. *Song Cycle* (2001, Boxholder) is a collaboration with singers Ellen Christi and Lisa Sokolov; *Zen Mountains/Zen Streets: A Duet for Poet & Improvised Bass* (1999, Boxholder) teams Parker with David Budbill; *Bob's Pink Cadillac* (Eremite, 2002) is a trio date with Perry Robinson on clarinet and drummer Walter Perkins; *Harras* (1996, Avant), another trio with Derek Bailey and John Zorn. With all these activities coming and going, Parker's discography has quickly swelled to become one of the largest in contemporary improvised music. Since the mid-1990s, he has recorded for Homestead (*Compassion Seizes Bed-Stuy*, 1996), Aum Fidelity (*Sunrise in the Tone World*, 1997), No More (*Lifting the Sanctions*, 1997), FMP (the exceptional *Posium Pendasem*, 1998), Thirsty Ear (*Painter's Spring*, 2000; *Raining on the Moon*, with vocalist Leena Conquest, 2002), and other imprints, along with participation in Other Dimensions in Music, Sonny Simmons's Cosmosamatics, Peter Brötzmann's Die Like A Dog Quartet and Chicago Tentet, and sideman work for Roy Campbell and Fred Anderson. If free music has a man for all seasons, it would have to be William Parker.

Parkins, Andrea (b. Detroit, MI): pianist, accordionist, and composer. Parkins is an incredible improviser who has carved out for the accordion a place of prominence in modern music. She uses samplers and analog synthesizers to alter the sound of her own instruments and those of her bandmates. Parkins is a key figure in two trios: Ellery Eskelin's group with drummer Jim Black (see Eskelin's entry) and her own trio with saxman Briggan Krauss and drummer Kenny Wollesen. Parkins has worked with John Zorn, Joe Gallant's Illuminati big band, and guitarist Joe Morris, among others. She is the sister of harpist Zeena Parkins.

Parkins, Zeena (b. Detroit, MI): harpist, accordionist, and composer. The sister of Andrea Parkins, Zeena is modern improvisation's principal voice on the harp. After studying piano, harp, and dance in her youth, Parkins attended Bard College in New York and attained her degree in Fine Arts. Upon moving to New York City, she immediately became immersed in the Downtown experimental scene. Opportunities for advancement came through John Zorn, Elliott Sharp, Butch Morris, and Fred Frith, who hired her for the radically avant Skeleton Crew with cellist Tom Cora. *Something Out There* (1987, No Mans Land) was her first record as a leader; later releases include *Isabelle* (1985, Tzadik), with her family-rich Gangster Band, and *No Way Back* (1998, Atavistic). Parkins has lectured on dance and music at colleges, and has written for films and performance groups via grants from Meet the Composer and the Rockefeller Foundation. Her more unusual collaborators have included Björk, Thurston Moore, and Hole.

Parran, J. D.: reeds player. He has been a faithful sideman to many leaders since the Black Artists Group, but Parran remains unjustly obscure in the business. He performs on the full range of clarinets, saxophones, and flutes, including bamboo saxes; the alto clarinet has been a specialty for years.

In the early 1970s, Parran was a BAG member and fixture of the Human Arts Ensemble (*Under the Sun*, 1973, Committee for Universal Justice/Freedom; *Funky Donkey, Vols. 1* and 2, rec. 1973, issued 2001, Atavistic Unheard Music). He joined the Butterfield Blues Band in 1974 and Leroy Jenkins's Mixed Quintet (1979, Black Saint) later in the decade. Subsequent employers have included Don Byron (*Plays the Music of Mickey Katz*, 1993, Nonesuch; *You Are #6*, 2001, Blue Note), Anthony Braxton (several sessions including *Ninetet [Yoshi's] 1997, Volume 1*, Leo), Lou Reed, Yoko Ono, Hamiet Bluiett's Clarinet Family (*Live in Berlin*, 1984, Black Saint), Peter Brötzmann, John Lennon, Edward Vesala, Stevie Wonder, John Lindberg, Brooklyn Poetry Choir, Julius Hemphill (*Big Band*, 1988, Elektra), Anthony Davis (*Hemispheres*, 1983, Gramavision), and Alan Silva (*Sound Visions Orchestra*, 2001, Eremite). Parran has participated in Company events and was a member of New Winds. He appeared in the film *Cotton Club* as a musician.

In 2001, Parran recorded his first session as a leader, *J. D. Parran and Spirit Stage* (Y'all Recordings), with poet Shirley LeFlore, vocalist Joan Bouise, guitarist Kelvyn Bell, trumpeter Stephen Haynes, accordion player Tony Cedras, vibist Bill Ware, bassist Brad Jones, and drummer Warren Smith. Parran is a director of the Harlem School of the Arts Institute of Jazz and African American Music Studies. He performs in Composicians, a trio with reedman Mixashawn Lee Rozie and trombonist Bill Lowe, and James "Jabbo" Ware's Me We and Them Orchestra (*Heritage Is*, 1995, Soul Note). Parran's compositions have been commissioned by Meet The Composer, the New York State Council on the Arts, the Jerome Foundation, and the National Endowment for the Arts.

Pavone, Mario (b. Connecticut, 1939): bassist. Pavone is best known for his productive tenures with altoist Thomas Chapin and Anthony Braxton in the 1990s. He only began playing the bass at the age of twenty-four, studying with classical and new-music icon Bertram Turetzky. Pavone studied both music and engineering in college, and in 1964, he was hired for his first professional tour by Paul Bley (*Canada*, 1968, Radio Canada). Attending John Coltrane's funeral inspired Pavone to forego his engineering ambitions and concentrate solely on music.

Pavone was a regular fixture on the New York loft jazz scene, working especially well with Bill Dixon in the 1970s. Later in the decade, he began working with Leo Smith, Ray Anderson, Pheeroan Ak Laff, and other artists in the Connecticut area. From there, Pavone and friends established the Creative Musicians' Improviser's Forum as a workshop and outlet for new musicians in New England. He continued his association with Bill Dixon into the 1980s, recording a number of albums for Soul Note (*Thoughts*, 1985; *Sons of Sisyphus*, 1988). Pavone ran his own label, Alarca, which only issued a few records over several years.

In 1989, Pavone became part of Thomas Chapin's new trio with drummer Steve Johns (later replaced by Michael Sarin). The significantly older bassist stood on equal grounds with his bandmates on a string of excellent albums such as *Third Force* (1990, Enemy) and *Night Bird Song* (1999, Knitting Factory Works). Pavone landed his own contract with New World in 1991, debuting on the label with *Toulon Days*; he has also recorded as a leader for Playscape (*Sharpeville*, 2000), Poetry, and Knitting Factory Works. With Braxton, he has worked in a number of settings, including *Seven Standards 1995* (Knitting Factory Works) with the reedman on piano.

Peacock, Annette (Coleman; b. Brooklyn, NY, 1941): vocalist, keyboardist, and composer. Peacock successfully bridged the divide between free jazz and rock long before such crossovers were in vogue. Both in performance and on record, she is starkly unadorned as both a singer and player, almost deadpan in her delivery.

Peacock was part of Timothy Leary's LSD cadre in the early 1960s and associated with Salvador Dali and Baba Ram Dass, all of which no doubt impacted her art. She toured Europe as Albert Ayler's pianist but never did record with him. At that time, Gary Peacock was Ayler's bassist; the two married, but their union only lasted a few years. Toward the end of the decade, she began working with pianist Paul Bley, composing interesting works for him as his ex-wife, Carla, had done. In 1970, Robert

Moog gave Peacock one of his prototype analog synthesizers. Fascinated by its possibilities, she and Bley (who later became her second husband) began exploring it avidly. In 1971, they recorded *The Bley/Peacock Synthesizer Show* (Polydor), which greatly helped to increase Moog's sales.

Through the 1970s and early 1980s, Peacock continued releasing albums of her stripped-down music: *I'm the One* (1972, RCA), *Improvise* (1973, America), *X-Dreams* (1978, See for Miles), *Sky Skating* (1982, Ironic). In 1978, she collaborated with Yes drummer Bill Bruford on *Feels Good to Me* (Polydor). All along, she was more influential to other musicians than to the buying public, and by the end of the 1980s, she had disappeared from the public eye.

In 1997, Marilyn Crispell recorded a collection of Peacock's compositions, *Nothing Ever Was, Anyway* (ECM); the honoree emerged from retirement to perform on "Dreams." David Bowie and Myra Melford both asked Peacock to collaborate, and in 2000, she produced an album by rock band Morcheeba. That same year saw her first record in over a decade, *An Acrobat's Heart* (ECM), supported by the Cikada String Quartet. Peacock has still been scarce on the scene since that project, but hopes are high for future appearances.

Peacock, Gary (b. Burley, ID, 12 May 1935): bassist. Peacock originally performed as a pianist but took up the bass in 1956 after his discharge from the army. Stationed in Germany, he chose to remain there to perform with locals and fellow Americans. Two years later, Peacock moved to Los Angeles and fell into the West Coast jazz scene with artists like Shorty Rogers, Don Ellis, Laurindo Almeida, and Paul Bley. In 1962, he and Bley moved to New York, where Peacock also performed cool, hot, and Third Stream jazz with Bill Evans, George Russell, Jimmy Giuffre, Roland Kirk, and Miles Davis.

In 1964, Peacock met Albert Ayler when both were members of the Jazz Composers Guild. They toured around Europe with drummer Sunny Murray and recorded the first free-jazz release on ESP-Disk Records, *Spiritual Unity*, in that year. Peacock remained busy with both the Ayler and Bley bands, also gigging on the side with Steve Lacy and Roswell Rudd; in several of those situations he frequently traded chairs with Henry Grimes. After leaving Ayler, Peacock returned to Miles Davis's side but departed before the trumpeter got into his primal fusion phase.

In 1969, Peacock took a sabbatical of sorts, residing in Japan for three years and focusing on nonmusical interests such as spirituality and science. He returned to college to study biology for four years, graduating in 1976, then returned to Paul Bley's trio with Barry Altschul for a brief time. Some of the trio's most impassioned playing can be found on *Japan Suite* (1978, Improvising Artists). In the late 1970s, Peacock began performing in a trio with Keith Jarrett and Jack DeJohnette, a richly rewarding position that has continued to bear fruit to the present day. He has also recorded some excellent sides with other pianists, among them Marc Copland, Warren Bernhardt, Richie Beirach, and Marilyn Crispell. Peacock has recorded about a dozen sessions as a leader, beginning with *Eastward* (1970, SME); his ECM albums such as *Tales of Another* (1977) are especially rich and inventive. He has taken part in Masabumi Kikuchi's Tethered Moon project in recent years.

People Band: British improv group, originally called the Continuous Music Ensemble. Members of several groups, including pianist Russell Hardy's trio with drummer Terry Day and bassist Terry Holman, founded it in 1965 at the Starting Gate pub in London. Those three men united with saxophonists George Khan and Lyn Dobson, pianist Mel Davis, trumpeter Mike Figgis, bassist Frank Flowers, and percussionists Tony Edwards and Eddie Edem to form a group dedicated to free improvisation, chance, and collage in the vein of Ornette Coleman, Charles Ives, and John Cage. Tapes from 1968 were produced by Charlie Watts and issued on Transatlantic in 1970 (*The People Band*); a more complete collection was compiled in 2003 on Emanem. Each member of the band played more than one instrument, in the Art Ensemble of Chicago spirit, and there were few, if any, formal structures used in their music. The group was associated with the People Show, an oddball collective of visual and performing artists, and toured Europe between 1968 and 1969. Anarchic to a fault, they were barred from performing at the Anarchists' Ball in 1969 due to the chaos their performance caused. By the mid-1970s, the People Band had begun to dissolve, its members pursuing other projects. Perhaps the most famous member today is Figgis, and that for his film direction (*Leaving Las Vegas, Internal Affairs*) rather than for his musical skill. Day, who began playing his drums with thin dowels and knitting needles, applied the People Band aesthetic to Alterations when that quartet was formed in 1978.

Perelman, Ivo (b. Sao Paulo, Brazil, 12 January 1961): tenor saxophonist. Perelman trained on a number of instruments in his youth: classical guitar, clarinet, cello, trombone, and piano. He took up the saxophone later in life and soon made the tenor sax his primary instrument. In 1989, Perelman veritably exploded onto the scene with the excellent *Ivo*, recorded for bassist Buell Neidlinger's K2B2 label. His debut featured a number of top fusion players including electric bassist John Patitucci, ex-Weather Report drummer Peter Erskine, and two fellow Brazilians: vocalist Flora Purim and percussionist Airto Moreira. This was surprisingly successful, considering that Perelman quickly moved into free jazz. His association with Cadence/CIMP, often with bassist Dominic Duval and drummer Jay Rosen, has been particularly rewarding; among his best records are *Bendito of Santa Cruz* (1996, Cadence Jazz), *Slaves of Job* and *Revelation* (both 1996, CIMP). Leo has been a similarly supportive label; Perelman has issued a half-dozen or so discs for them since 1996's *Strings*. He has collaborated with Joe Morris, Marilyn Crispell, Borah Bergman, and Matthew Shipp, to name but a few who have benefited from Perelman's tireless saxophonics.

Petrowsky, Ernst-Ludwig (b. Güstrow, Germany, 10 December 1933): reeds player. Petrowsky does not have quite the high profile of some of his cohorts like Peter Brötzmann. Nonetheless, he is one of the most reliable performers in European free music. A member of Zentralquartett with Conrad Bauer, Petrowsky has played and recorded with Globe Unity, George Gruntz's Concert Jazz Band, the European Jazz Ensemble, Kenny Wheeler, baritone saxist and tubaist Howard Johnson, Alex von Schlippenbach, Mario Schiano, Günter Christmann, and other improvisers. His recordings include 1973's *Just for Fun* (his debut on FMP) and the solo *tour de force* *Selb-Dritt* (1980, FMP).

Phalanx: quartet of saxophonist George Adams, guitarist James Blood Ulmer, bassist Sirone, and drummer Rashied Ali. The group added Ulmer's electric edge to the other members' more acoustically grounded freedom to produce a unique sound. Phalanx debuted on disc in 1985 with *Got Something Good for You* (Moers Music) and performed sporadically until Adams's death in 1992. Their other recordings, both fearless, are *Original Phalanx* (1987) and *In Touch* (1988, both DIW).

Phillips, Barre (b. San Francisco, CA, 27 October 1934): bassist. Phillips studied music from his youth but did not become a professional musician until he was twenty-five. In 1960, disillusioned with the lack of adventure in West Coast jazz, he moved to New York to seek out opportunities in the swelling avant-jazz scene there. He worked in various ensembles, including Don Ellis's experimental band and Eric Dolphy's quartet but first made a big impact at the 1965 Newport Jazz Festival, where he appeared with Archie Shepp. Following some further training at the hands of free jazz's second wave, Phillips moved to Europe in 1967 and finally settled in France. Since then he has worked regularly with the cream of the Continent, from Peter Brötzmann and Trevor Watts to the London Jazz Composers Orchestra. Since 1971, Phillips has recorded over a dozen albums under his own name; the solo masterpiece *Journal Violone II* (1979, ECM) remains a high point of his career. He has also worked with Vinny Golia, Masashi Harada, the Maneris, Evan Parker, and Paul Bley (the last two in a trio: *Sankt Gerold*, 2001, ECM).

Pilz, Michel (b. Bad Neustadt an der Saale, Germany, 28 October 1945): reedman. Pilz is a sharp, energetic sax, flute, and bass clarinet player whose associations with Manfred Schoof and Alex von Schlippenbach brought him attention in the mid-1960s. He was a member of both the Globe Unity Orchestra and the "kraut-rock" band Guru Guru, and has issued a handful of sessions as a leader or coleader (*Carpathes*, 1978, FMP, with Paul Lovens and Peter Kowald; *Jamabiko*, 1985, Musical Productions). Pilz works well with bass clarinetist Peter Schmid on the latter's *Schmilz* (2002, Creative Works).

Plimley, Paul (b. Vancouver, Canada, 1953): pianist and composer. Trained in classical music, Plimley has become one of the American West Coast's most prominent improvisers. Intensely personal as a performer, he draws from deep within himself to put the best effort into each performance. Of particular note is his long-standing partnership with bassist Lisle Ellis. The two burst onto Canada's improvisation scene in 1989 with an acclaimed concert at the Victoriaville festival. That year saw the release of *Both Sides of the Same Mirror*, Plimley's auspicious debut on the Nine Winds label. Plimley addressed Ornette Coleman's compositions on *Kaleidoscope* (1992, HatArt) and took part in the "Yo Miles!" project with Henry Kaiser and Wadada Leo

Smith. Since the early 1990s, Plimley has recorded with Kaiser, George Lewis, the NOW Orchestra, Joe McPhee, François Houle, Glenn Spearman, John Oswald, Miya Masaoka, Gregg Bendian, Barry Guy, and most of Canada's improvising musicians. Plimley's own recordings have been issued on Nine Winds, HatArt, Music & Arts (*Density of the Lovestruck Demons*, 1996), Victo (*Noir*, 1995), Maya (*Sensology*, 1995), and Songlines.

Po Torch: label administered by German drummer Paul Lovens. The catalog mostly consists of albums featuring Lovens with Paul Lytton, Alex von Schlippenbach, Paul Rutherford, and many other European improvisers. A true anomaly in the new century, Po Torch issues only albums on vinyl. Little has been released since the early 1990s.

poire_z: electronic improvising quartet, the meeting of Voice Crack (Andy Guhl and Norbert Möslang), electronic musician Erik M, and drummer Günter Müller. The quartet's first album was titled *poire_z* but credited to the four members. With the release of the live disc *Presque_Chic* (Sonoris) in 2001, poire_z was adopted as the ensemble's name. The music is noisy and amelodic, even at quiet levels, with Müller using electronic enhancement on his drums to level out the sound. On + (2002, Erstwhile) the quartet is joined by Otomo Yoshihide, Christian Marclay, and Sachiko M on different tracks for textural variation.

Polwechsel: improvising ensemble. Established in 1993 by Austrian bassist Werner Dafeldecker and cellist Michael Moser, the group explores every extreme of sound production from highest volume to tiniest clicks. Their music is generally structured in the modern avant-garde sense, with graphic templates set up to guide the players. Their debut album (*Polwechsel*, 1995, Random Acoustics) featured Dafeldecker, Moser, trombonist Radu Malfatti, and guitarist Burkhard Stangl, each performer playing as nonmelodically as possible in the interest of sheer sound and texture. Malfatti left the group in 1997 and was replaced by British saxophonist John Butcher, whose virtuosity and keen ear for cooperative improv changed the whole scope of Polwechsel. Their subsequent, consecutively numbered albums (1999, HatArt; 2001, Durian) showed that the ensemble's focus was continuing to mature. *Wrapped Islands* (2002, Erstwhile), a collaboration with guitarist Christian Fennesz, is their best to date.

Portal, Michel (b. Bayonne, France, 27 November 1935): reeds player. A founding member of New Phonic Art, Portal is one of France's best free improvisers. Some of his earliest work was done in support of singer Serge Gainsbourg, an odd but inspiring departure point for Portal's take on modern improvisation. He has performed with Jean-Luc Ponty, Eddy Louiss, Henri Texier, and most frequently with accordionist Richard Galliano and vocalist Barbara. Portal's albums are quite excellent almost on the whole, with *Arrivederci le Chouartse* (1980, HatArt) and *Dockings* (2000, Label

Bleu) at the highest peaks of achievement. He draws heavily from the example of Eric Dolphy, using rough-edged tones and intervallic jumps to good effect.

Positive Knowledge: husband-wife duo of saxophonist Oluyemi Thomas (b. Detroit, MI, 16 August 1952) and poet/vocalist Ijeoma Chinue Thomas (b. Washington, DC, 17 August 1950), based in the San Francisco Bay Area. The couple's performances and lyrics are inspired by the Baha'i faith. Mr. Thomas began playing the clarinet as a child, took up the saxophone later in life, and majored in both engineering and music at Washtenaw College. Mrs. Thomas studied dance and piano in her youth, and began writing poetry in her teen years. She studied art and art history at Hampton University in Virginia. Her writings have appeared in various literary journals and in the collection *Out of the Fire*. Collectively, their collaborators have included Cecil Taylor, Alan Silva, Roscoe Mitchell, William Parker, Kidd Jordan, Wadada Leo Smith, Peter Kowald, Charles Gayle, Anthony Braxton, Wilber Morris, and koto artist Miya Masaoka. The Thomases have worked together under the group name Positive Knowledge since the mid-1970s. Their best recording to date has been *Positive Knowledge Live in New York* (2003, Edgetone). Earlier releases included *Another Day's Journey* (1995), and *Invocation No. 9* (1996, both on Music & Arts).

Post Prandials: improvisational ensemble with Daniel Carter, guitarist Keith Nicolay, keyboardists Bob Aaron and John Burgos, and violinist/electronic musician John Hajeski (a.k.a. Busyditch). Their albums include *Switched-On Irresponsibility* (1996) and *Jamaica* (1997, both Artichoke/Tristero), the latter with Sabir Mateen.

Potlatch: Parisian record label founded by Jacques Oger in 1998. It has already distinguished itself with a goodly number of quality releases by the likes of Evan Parker, Derek Bailey, John Butcher, and Carlos Zingaro.

Previte, Bobby (b. Niagara Falls, NY, 16 July 1957): drummer and bandleader. Usually associated with John Zorn and the New York Downtown crowd, Previte is an impressive performer whose tastes as a leader tend more toward the commercial. He studied at SUNY-Buffalo, began his career there, and moved to New York City at the age of twenty-two. Zorn, Tom Waits, Jane Ira Bloom, and Marty Ehrlich were among the artists who benefited from Previte's amazing rhythmic skills. During this time, he established an enduring working relationship with keyboardist Wayne Horvitz.

He has led several bands, including Weather Clear, Track Fast (self-titled, 1990, Enja) with clarinetist Don Byron and pianist Anthony Davis, and Empty Suits (self-titled, 1990, Gramavision) with trombonist Robin Eubanks and electric bassist Jerome Harris. *Just Add Water* (2001, Palmetto) featured his ensemble Bump, with trombonists Joseph Bowie and Ray Anderson, tenorman Marty Ehrlich, bassist Steve Swallow, and Horvitz. More recently, he has worked with keyboardist Jamie Saft and DJ Olive as The Beta Popes, and acted in Robert Altman's *Short Cuts*.

Prévost, Eddie (Edwin; b. Hitchin, England, 22 June 1942): drummer and label head. Like many of his generation, Prévost came up in the trad and skiffle coteries in England. Hearing American jazz drummers like Max Roach and Ed Blackwell completely changed his outlook and led him into improvisational music. In 1965, he was a founding member of AMM (see entry), which has remained a constant light in his career. Along the way, he performed with American and British improvisers like Marilyn Crispell, Jim O'Rourke, Evan Parker, and Paul Rutherford as well as his own groups (*Now Hear This Then*, 1977, Spotlite; *Live, Vols. 1* and *2*, 1979, Matchless). Prévost has explored ambient and techno music with Experimental Audio Research, lectured at music workshops worldwide, and runs the Matchless label.

Prima Materia: ensemble led by drummer Rashied Ali and tenor saxophonist Louis Belogenis. Since 1994, Prima Materia has specialized in radically reworking some of the most inspirational music from the early days of free jazz: *Peace on Earth: The Music of John Coltrane* (1994), Coltrane's *Meditations* (1995), and *Albert Ayler's Bells* (1996, all on Knitting Factory Works). The other members of Prima Materia have included bassists William Parker and Joe Gallant, altoist Allan Chase, and pianist Greg Murphy. Ali's drumming is as impressive and driving as when he was backing Coltrane in the late 1960s, giving authentic power to the band's masterful revisitations.   •

Prins, Gert-Jan (b. Ijmuiden, Netherlands): percussionist and electronic musician. Prins is a specialist in noise and texture, evident on any of his recordings. He developed a technology he calls "etherloops," which applies radio principles to other electronic implements. Prins began improvising in 1984 with the ensemble Gorgonzola Legs and joined the avant-rock band Analecta in 1991 (*What You Hear Is Where You Are*, 1992, X-OR). He founded the X-OR label with Luc Houtkamp, his frequent partner in duos (*The Duo Recordings*, 1998) and in trios with Misha Mengelberg (*Instant Discoveries No. 3*, 1996) and Fred Van Hove (*Live in Canada '97*, 1997, all on The Field Recordings). Prins has performed with MIMEO, Cor Fuhler, United Noise Toys, and in other trio combinations with Mengelberg/Mats Gustafsson, Peter van Bergen/Thomas Lehn, and van Bergen/Fennesz (*Dawn*, 2000, Grob). Prins works frequently at the STEIM studio in Amsterdam.

PSF Records: Japanese improvisation label. Besides offering recordings by Japanese freemen like Kaoru Abe (*Jazz Bed*, 2000), Motoharu Yoshizawa, Masayuki Takayanagi, and Keiji Haino, the catalog also features live recordings of Western improvisers including Derek Bailey (*Fish*, 2001, with drummer Shoji Hano), Peter Brötzmann, Barre Phillips, AMM (*From a Strange Place*, 1995), and Borbetomagus.

Pukwana, Dudu (b. Port Elizabeth, South Africa, 18 July 1938; d. London, England, 28 June 1990): altoist and bandleader. Pukwana was one of the Blue Notes members who expatriated to Europe in 1964. Originally trained on piano, Pukwana took up the alto sax in 1956 and soon began impressing crowds with his performances with tenorman

Nick Moyake's Jazz Giants. When Chris McGregor heard Pukwana and Moyake play at the 1962 Johannesburg Jazz Festival, where Pukwana won first prize, the pianist immediately invited the altoist to join The Blue Notes. (See The Blue Notes entry.)

After settling in London in the mid-1960s, Pukwana and his associates moved into McGregor's big band, the Brotherhood of Breath, which became one of Britain's most popular groups. The altoman worked in various settings including the Incredible String Band and Toots & the Maytals, and established his own groups (Spear and Assagai) in the early 1970s (*Assagai*, 1971, Vertigo). He debuted as a leader with *In the Townships* (1973, Earthworks) and continued to perform in expatriate-based groups: Harry Miller's Isipingo, Louis Moholo's Spirits Rejoice, Johnny Dyani's ensembles, and African Explosion with trombonist Jonas Gwangwa and famed trumpeter Hugh Masekela. His own disc *Diamond Express* (1975, Freedom) crossed over into electric music while staying true to the African vibe he was comfortable with. In 1978, he established the group Zila and the Jika label to continue documenting the music of the African expats (*Zila Sounds*, 1981, Jika). Though he mostly put free music behind him, Pukwana did occasionally record improvised sessions: *Yi Yo Le* (1978, ICP) with Misha Mengelberg and Han Bennink, and *They Shoot to Kill* (1987, Affinity) with John Stevens, the latter dedicated to Dyani's memory. Pukwana died of liver failure in 1990 after his star had unfairly begun to fade.

Pullen, Don (b. Roanoke, VA, 25 December 1941; d. Orange, NJ, 22 April 1995): pianist, organist, composer, and bandleader. Pullen learned the piano early in life and was encouraged by his musical family. As a young adult, he relocated to Chicago, where he studied under Muhal Richard Abrams and took part in the early Experimental Band. His time in the Midwest was fairly short, as by 1964 he was gigging in New York with Giuseppi Logan. He connected famously with drummer Milford Graves, with whom Pullen began performing duo concerts in 1965. The pair made two recordings (*Nommo* and *Live at Yale*) the following year for their own SRP (Self-Reliance Project) label. The pianist then partnered with drummer Beaver Harris in the 360 Degree Music Experience and developed a lifelong friendship with Hamiet Bluiett that resulted in several excellent albums under the baritonist's leadership.

Pullen often stepped away from free music in order to flex his soul and blues muscles. Demonstrating his creative chops on electric organ, he backed artists like Big Maybelle, Ruth Brown, and Nina Simone in the late 1960s and early 1970s. From 1973 to 1975, Pullen performed with Charles Mingus's band, in which he met tenorman George Adams; a yearlong stint with Art Blakey's Jazz Messengers intersected his days with Mingus. Pullen recorded *Solo Piano Album* (1975) for Sackville and performed on a couple of Adams's records (*Don't Lose Control*, 1979, Soul Note). The friends eventually formed a blistering quartet with ex-Mingus drummer Dannie Richmond and bassist Cameron Brown. The unit became one of the most popular and impressive groups of the 1980s, drawing from the inspirations of Mingus, Monk, and other free and mainstream jazz (*Live at the Village Vanguard*, 1994, Soul Note).

In the 1990s, Pullen gathered his African-Brazilian Experience, a band that surprisingly delved into Native American musical styles as much as its titular inspirations (*Sacred Common Ground*, 1994, Blue Note). Pullen was active as a sideman in his last years, recording and performing with Hamiet Bluiett, Canadian soprano saxophonist Jane Bunnett, Kip Hanrahan, Mingus Dynasty, David Murray, and John Scofield. From the free jazz standpoint, his most interesting albums as a leader were recorded for Black Saint: *Warriors*, *Milano Strut* (both 1978), *Evidence of Things Unseen* (1983), *The Sixth Sense* (1985).

Q

Quintet Moderne: European improvising ensemble. The original personnel included drummer Paul Lovens, reeds player Harri Sjöström (later an impressive sideman with Cecil Taylor's quartet), violinist and electronic musician Philipp Wachsmann, trombonist Jari Hongisto, and bassist/cellist Teppo Hauta-aho. Hongisto was replaced by Paul Rutherford a couple of years on. *Ikkunan Takana (Behind the Window)* (1987, Bead) is their only full-length album to date, impressively textured and rife with creative impulses.

R

Ragin, Hugh (b. Houston, TX, 9 August 1951): trumpeter. Ragin took up the trumpet while in the eighth grade. Cat Anderson, Ellington's high-note trumpet man, was a particular inspiration. After touring Britain with the Houston all-city high school orchestra, Ragin studied music education at the University of Houston and Colorado State. In the interim, he studied privately with Donald Byrd and (briefly) Dizzy Gillespie. In December 1978, Ragin attended the Creative Music Workshop founded by Karl Berger in Woodstock, New York, where he studied with the resident Art Ensemble of Chicago. That experience and the prior inspiration of Anthony Braxton and Sun Ra led Ragin to pursue free jazz more seriously.

Roscoe Mitchell was especially impressed with the young trumpeter, and in 1979, he hired Ragin to play beside Leo Smith in his Creative Orchestra. The group went to the Moers Festival, where Ragin met Braxton again along with David Murray. A duo tour with Braxton and the recording of *Composition 98* (1991, HatArt) followed, then a big change of pace with service in Maynard Ferguson's big band. Murray began working with Ragin in 1984, and their association continued for years. Ragin has since performed with Roy Hargrove's big band, Mitchell's Note Factory nonet, pianist Marc Sabatella (*Gallery*, 1998, CIMP), and others. He has taught music at Colorado State and Oberlin College, and has released several albums including the fine *An Afternoon in Harlem* (1999, Justin Time) with Murray, pianist Craig Taborn, and Andrew Cyrille.

Rainey, Bhob (b. Philadelphia, PA, 19 April 1972): soprano saxophonist. Rainey studied with Gary Campbell and Gary Keller in the University of Miami's jazz program, then returned to Philly for a few years. In the city's clubs, he played both straight and free jazz with drummer Mickey Roker, pianist Uri Caine, and other hometown stalwarts. Bored with what he felt was a stagnating scene, Rainey went to New England Conservatory in 1996, where he obtained his master's degree in composition while studying under Joe Maneri, Ran Blake, and Paul Bley. In Boston, he performed with Mat Maneri, Nate McBride, and Pandelis Karayorgis before meeting trumpeter Greg Kelley. The two formed the duo nmperign in 1998 and have toured extensively, performing a quiet but dense form of improvised music with electronic enhancements. Rainey has recorded with pianist Dan DeChellis (*ink.*, 1998, Sachimay), Masashi Harada, Jack Wright, and Jason Lescalleet, among others.

Rainey, Tom: drummer. A ubiquitous percussionist on the contemporary New York scene, Rainey has contributed his powerful yet thoughtful drumming to a large number of sessions since the late 1980s. Among his best employers have been soprano saxophonist Jane Ira Bloom (*Modern Drama*, 1987, Columbia), violinist Mark Feldman, pianist Fred Hersch, Andy Laster, Herb Robertson, bandleader Klaus König, and pop/rock vocalist Michael McDonald. Rainey has had a particularly fertile association with altoist Tim Berne, who has utilized the drummer in projects like Big Satan, Bloodcount, and Paraphrase. Rainey is also a member of the improv groups Open Loose and New & Used.

Random Acoustics: label established in 1993 by German pianist Georg Graewe. Notable for using environmentally friendly cardboard packaging instead of plastic jewel boxes, the label's catalog includes albums by Graewe, Gerry Hemingway, Thomas Lehn, tubaist Melvyn Poore, and others. Its solo releases, among them fine works by Marcio Mattos and French hornist Martin Mayes, are particularly distinctive.

Rastascan: label founded in 1987 by percussionist Gino Robair. The catalog includes Robair's group Splatter Trio, his duets with Anthony Braxton, and sessions by Evan Parker, Peter Brötzmann, and other free players.

Rava, Enrico (b. Trieste, Italy, 20 August 1943): trumpeter, composer, and bandleader. Like his associate Steve Lacy, Rava began his jazz career as a Dixieland musician in the late 1950s. Once he heard Miles Davis, however, Rava switched from trombone to trumpet and decided to pursue more modern jazz forms. Gigs with cool trumpeter Chet Baker and hot Argentine tenorman Leandro "Gato" Barbieri pulled Rava in different directions, and it was his encounter with Lacy that finally pushed him toward the avant-garde. Lacy hired Rava and two South African expatriates, drummer Louis Moholo and bassist Johnny Dyani, to record *The Forest and the Zoo* (1966) for ESP. Rava's exemplary performance broke him out to American audiences in grand fashion, and in 1967 Rava moved to New York. The bright young trumpeter worked fairly steadily among the Big Apple's free community, nailing down crucial gigs with Cecil Taylor, Rashied Ali, Roswell Rudd, and Carla Bley's Jazz Composers Orchestra (*Escalator Over the Hill*, 1971, JCOA). Rava recorded *European Echoes* (1969, FMP) with Manfred Schoof during a brief visit to Europe, then returned to America for another seven years.

Rava's debut under his own name was *Il Giro del Giorno in 80 Mondi* (1972, Black Saint). The music is sort of an early free fusion with the guitar dipping into Miles

Davis's period funk, while Rava paid homage to Cecil Taylor on "C.T.'s Dance" and to Bley with a warm cover of her "Olhos de Gatos." The following year Rava paired with guitarist John Abercrombie, whose forsaken beauty complemented the trumpeter's unpredictability and vibrant tone. *Quotation Marks* (1973, Japo) teams that pair with Jack DeJohnette, keyboardist David Horowitz, Jeanne Lee, and others. Horowitz's keyboards date the session, but it is worth finding as a document of the Rava/Abercrombie hookup. *The Pilgrim and the Stars* (1975, ECM) features the Scandinavian rhythm team of bassist Palle Danielsson and drummer Jon Christensen. Rava's mates are veterans of the icy-cool ECM recording process, and this album is ripe with the label's typical chilly mystery.

Secrets (1986, Soul Note) is an excellent excursion with English pianist John Taylor, American drummer Bruce Ditmas, and two Italians: guitarist Augusto Mancinelli and bassist Furio Di Castri. Rava may have sounded at home in the ECM ether, and Taylor's piano style is highly reminiscent of ECM regular Keith Jarrett, but Giovanni Bonandrini's production draws out a different kind of glory. This was one of Rava's most cohesive units; the next albums, *Animals* (1987, Inak) and *Enrico Rava Quintet* (1989, Nabel), have new personnel and lack consistency.

Besides his occasional ventures into freedom, Rava has recorded several mainstream jazz albums. His vivid musical imagination has led him to interpret operas in jazz form (*Rava, L'Opera Va*, 1993, and *Carmen*, 1997, both on Label Bleu). He has paid adoring tribute to American trumpet icons: Bix Beiderbecke and Louis Armstrong on *For Bix and Pops* (2000, Philology), Chet Baker on *Shades of Chet* (1999, Via Veneto). *Rava String Band* (1984, Soul Note), a Colemanesque attempt at writing for a more orchestral setting, included Mancinelli, Tony Oxley, and Brazilian percussionist Nana Vasconcelos, as well as a string quartet.

Red Toucan: Quebecois record label, founded in 1993 by Michel Passaretti. The label, which has issued over two dozen discs thus far, specializes in rising experimental musicians and often issues the artists' first recordings. Their stable includes double-reed artist Kyle Bruckmann, John Butcher, Frank Gratkowski, Glenn Spearman's G-Force, Ian Smith, François Houle, and Jöelle Léandre. A sister label, Cactus, deals in less avant-garde music by artists such as pianist Michael Jefry Stevens and saxophonist Dave Liebman.

Redman, Dewey (Walter; b. Fort Worth, TX, 17 May 1931): tenor saxophonist and composer. In the new century, Redman is better known as the father of a young tenor lion, Joshua Redman, than for his cob-rough role in Ornette Coleman's 1970s ensembles. We might blame not only the mass market's age bias but also the stigma associated with Redman *pere*'s uncompromising performances in his nascent years. Shouting like some Delta bluesman through his horn, as capable of blasting piercing harmonics as of projecting truly beautiful tones, Redman had a sound that was perhaps more acceptable to audiences than the jagged brutality of Archie Shepp but distinctly different from John Coltrane's own human-cry emulations. Falling in the middle of the stream, Redman has tended to be unfairly overlooked by the partisans of jazz elegance and assertiveness alike.

Redman, barely one year younger than Coleman, began playing with his future employer in the high school band sax section. After graduation, Redman originally pursued a career in education, becoming a teacher in 1956 while Coleman was recording his first album for Contemporary Records in Los Angeles. Redman went as far as obtaining his master's degree from North Texas State University before moving to San Francisco in 1959 to seek a steadier job market. Redman fell into the city's germinating jazz scene and formed a friendship with Pharoah Sanders. The two worked together off and on for two years until Sanders moved to New York City.

Redman stayed in the Bay Area for a time, building his chops with friends like Sonny Simmons and Donald Rafael Garrett. His swing-grounded tone landed Redman more jobs than if he had pursued the aggressive approach of his contemporaries in New York. In 1966, Redman made his debut album, *Look for the Black Star* (Freedom), recording five original tunes in the company of Garrett, pianist Jym Young, and drummer Eddie Moore. Despite the label's decent distribution, the record did not exactly break Redman out to stunning acclaim. The free movement's acceptance of new voices was one of its definitive hallmarks, however, so when the saxman relocated to New York the following year he was readily accepted into the community. At age thirty-five, however, he was hardly looked upon as a spirited youngster.

Redman joined the Coleman band in 1967 and made an immediate impact as a model foil for the altoist. Both men pulled an almost human tone from their horns, and their ideas flowed seamlessly into one another once the tenorman had settled into his new niche. Redman generally deferred the authority to Coleman in their concerts and recording sessions but could burst boldly into the forefront when needed. (See Coleman's entry.)

Redman has always shown an affinity for clicking with outstanding bassists, as he had with Charlie Haden in the Coleman unit. Art Ensemble bassman Malachi Favors held the chair on Redman's second album, *Tarik* (1969, BYG), which bristles with exotic noises and tension. The leader blows the musette, a simple double reed, on the title track over Ed Blackwell's relentless drum groove and Favors's ostinato. "Lop-O-Lop," rooted in the blues, presents a more infectious side of Redman's tenor style.

In 1971, Redman began a turbulent relationship with Keith Jarrett in the pianist's American Quartet. Jarrett, Charlie Haden, and Paul Motian began working as a unit on Atlantic Records, recording the rock-tinged *Somewhere Before* (1968). After Redman was hired, the group jumped ship to Columbia (*Expectations*, 1971), then to Impulse, where they taped the less stable *Fort Yawuh* (1973) and *Treasure Island* (1974). At that time, Redman seemed fairly attuned to the pianist's expressive style, whereas Haden and Motian began to lose their cohesiveness with the leader.

Jarrett was a demanding individual, personally and in performance, so bickering was perhaps inevitable. A sense of discomfort spread through the quartet, first audible on *Bop-Be* and *Byablue* (both 1975, Impulse). Most of the tracks from those discs are available on *Silence* (Impulse), and while there are sections of beauty to be found, there is also a feeling that all is not well. The slow collapse continued on *The Survivor's Suite* (1975, ECM), which is fairly good despite the tensions, and the dismal *Eyes of the Heart* (1976, ECM). After that denouement, Redman wisely decided to forego Jarrett and get back to his own muse.

Redman's association with Impulse via Jarrett had led to the release of *The Ear of the Behearer* in 1973. As good as the Favors/Blackwell trio was, this larger unit permitted Redman to explore his concepts more ardently. The CD reissue includes four tracks from *Coincide* (1974, Impulse); it cuts out the noodling zither feature "Phadan-Sers" from the latter date, a wise choice, but also overlooks the interesting clarinet piece "Somnifacient." Eddie Moore, Redman's old bandmate from San Francisco, is back on drums and joined by Leroy Jenkins, Sirone, trumpeter Ted Daniel, cellist Jane Robertson, and percussionist Danny Robertson. Sirone's catchy descending lines on "Qow" are similar to Favors's ostinato on "Tarik," driving the band insistently on Redman's most memorable blues composition. "Boody" is a blues festival in itself, on which the leader wails passionately. Redman plays alto as much as tenor here, sounding quite unlike Coleman and very much his own self. Essential.

In 1978, the saxophonist looked up Eddie Moore again and restarted his own band for *Musics* (Galaxy), an underappreciated pearl in his discography. Pianist Fred Simmons and bassist Mark Helias are comfortable cohorts on Redman's originals and a surprisingly satisfying rendition of "Alone Again (Naturally)." In contrast is the weaker *The Struggle Continues* (1982, ECM) with Blackwell, Helias, and pianist Charles Eubanks. The operative term here is "struggle": excepting the reliable Blackwell, the players never seem to be on the same page. Redman's live duos with Blackwell (*In Willisau*, 1980, Black Saint) are much better, with the soul brothers in impeccable communication.

Since the 1980s, Redman's offerings have been few and far between. *Living on the Edge* (1989, Black Saint), with Moore, pianist Geri Allen, and bassist Cameron Brown, finds the saxophonist sounding more at ease than ever, nobly taking leads from the scintillating Allen much of the time. Two live albums from 1996, *Mostly Live* (Tiptoe) and *In London* (Palmetto), show that Redman's raw power has been further tempered by experience and maturity. And while *Momentum Space* (1999, Polygram), with Elvin Jones and Cecil Taylor, is marred by a grating disunity, their full-trio performances are as exciting as most anything Redman has done since the Coleman quartet.

Reichel, Hans (b. Hagen, Germany, 10 May 1949): guitar, daxophonist, composer and luthier. At age seven Reichel taught himself the violin. He performed in school orchestras, and as a teen was influenced by American and British rock music. He worked in several different musical settings but gave up the field while he studied graphic arts. In 1970, he submitted a tape of guitar music to the Frankfurt German Jazz Festival and was selected to appear as an up-and-coming performer. In 1973, Reichel released his first record, *Wichslinghauser Blues*, on FMP. A notable solo artist, he has also played with Europeans and Americans such as Sven-Äke Johansson, Paul Lovens, Tom Cora, and Fred Frith, including duos with the latter two. Reichel has invented some unusual instruments in his search for new sounds, among them being the bowed-wood daxophone and the odd "pick-behind-the-bridge" guitar, with playable string lengths extending beyond the bridge. He is a respected typographer, having designed several typeface series including Barmeno, Dax, Sari, and

Schmalhans. One of his most triumphant releases to date is *Lower Lurum* (1995, Rastascan), which features both the daxophone and his exotic mutant guitars.

Reijseger, Ernst (b. Bussum, Netherlands, 13 November 1954): cellist. Reijseger began playing the cello at eight and became interested in improvised music as a teenager after hearing the creative sounds of the Instant Composers Pool artists. Among his earliest collaborators were Derek Bailey and Michael Moore. In the 1980s, Reijseger joined the ICP Orchestra, worked with the Amsterdam and Arcado String Trios, and partnered with Dutch freemen Guus Janssen and Theo Loevendie. He received the Boy Edgar Prize, Holland's premier jazz award, in 1985 and was honored by the North Sea Jazz Festival in 1986 with their Bird Award. Since the late 1980s, Reijseger has worked with Gerry Hemingway in the drummer's quintet and a trio with Georg Graewe. He was a member of the Clusone Trio for that group's full existence (see separate entry), along with the improv group The Persons. Reijseger debuted as a leader with *Mistakes* (1979, Broken) and has regularly issued albums every few years. *Noci . . . Strani Frutti* (1991, Leo), *Et on ne Parle pas du Temps* (1995, FMP), and *I Love You So Much It Hurts* (2002, Winter & Winter) are among the best. He has also worked as a sideman with Karl Berger (*No Man Is An Island*, 1996, Knitting Factory Works) and pianist Uri Caine (adapting Bach to jazz on *The Goldberg Variations*, 2000, Winter & Winter).

Revolutionary Ensemble: free-jazz trio, active from 1971 to 1977. Formed by violinist Leroy Jenkins following the breakup of the Creative Construction Company, the Revolutionary Ensemble was a boldly adventurous group with uncommon instrumentation. Jenkins, bassist Sirone (formerly known as Norris Jones), and drummer Frank Clayton performed as a trio in New York. Jerome Cooper, a former Anthony Braxton sideman himself, replaced Clayton later that year. The men rehearsed vigorously to develop a rapport and empathy that is still rare by comparison, and this led to a sense of deliberate organization within their improvisations. All of the members sang and played various percussion devices, Sirone doubled on trombone now and then, and Cooper occasionally added piano, flute, and bugle flourishes to their performances. Like most AACM-inspired groups, the trio emphasized silence and space as much as dense ensemble interaction.

Most of the albums recorded between 1971 and the Revolutionary Ensemble's breakup in 1977 are difficult to come by, since they tended to be on independent labels with lousy distribution. *Vietnam* (1972, aka *Revolutionary Ensemble*) recorded for ESP, is an enduring classic. The sheer energy of the performances was likely inspired by the senseless war going on at the time, with passages of calm evoking the occasional cease-fire. Their second essential album is *The People's Republic* (1975, A&M), with more mainstream-appealing tracks and phenomenal bass work by Sirone. These discs show off the Ensemble's principal characteristic, the ability to craft music of unquestionable beauty even at high intensity and volume. For a unit with no regular horns, excepting the occasional trombone and bugle coloration, the Revolutionaries were an enticingly melodic improvisational group. A long-awaited reunion performance by the trio was scheduled for the Vision Festival in May 2004.

Ribot, Marc (b. Newark, NJ, 1954): New York Downtown–scene guitarist. Ribot studied with classical guitarist Frantz Casseus while honing his guitar style in garage bands. In 1978, he moved to New York to become a freelance backing player for jazz and soul acts. He was a founding member of the seminal group the Lounge Lizards, working with the band from 1984 to 1989. As he developed his unique blend of blues-based stylings and noise-rock, Ribot became involved in the ignited Downtown movement. He has occasionally led sessions (*Rootless Cosmopolitans*, 1990, Island), and recently fronted the Latin group Los Cubanos Postizos, but Ribot has mostly been a supporter for artists as diverse as John Zorn, Elliott Sharp, Elvis Costello, Tom Waits, and Anthony Coleman.

Riley, Howard (b. Huddersfield, Yorkshire, U.K. 1943): pianist and composer. One of Britain's most active free improvisers, Riley began his piano studies at age six and eventually studied at universities in Wales, York, and Indiana. In 1967, he debuted on disc in a trio with Barry Guy and drummer Jon Hiseman, from which his career in improv took off. His friendship and collaboration with Guy has lasted to the present day through a number of trio dates on up to the London Jazz Composers Orchestra (*Ode*, 1972, Incus). Tony Oxley and saxophonist Elton Dean have also been reliable partners. Riley has performed in duos with Keith Tippett and Jaki Byard (*Live at the Royal Festival Hall*, 1984, Leo), recorded many solo albums (including the thrice-overdubbed *Trisect*, 1980, Impetus), and gigged with Paul Rutherford, George Haslam, the Spontaneous Music Orchestra, tenorman Art Themen, Trevor Watts, and John Stevens. Riley has taught for over thirty years at the Guildhall School of Music and Goldsmith College, served a residency at the Buffalo Center for the Creative and Performing Arts, and has had compositions commissioned by the New Jazz Orchestra and other ensembles.

Rising Tones Cross: documentary by German filmmaker Ebba Jahn, about the 1984 Sound Unity Festival and its featured artists. Peter Kowald, Charles Gayle, and festival founder William Parker are the central figures in the film, which intersperses New York scenery and interview clips with performances by Kowald, Gayle, Parker's jazz/dance ensemble, John Zorn with Wayne Horvitz, Billy Bang's Forbidden Planet, the Charles Tyler Quintet, Don Cherry with the Sound Unity Festival Orchestra, the Jemeel Moondoc Sextet, Irène Schweizer with Rüdiger Carl, and Peter Brötzmann's ensemble. The interview segments reveal much about the lives and aspirations of these musicians, and the racial and social barriers they encountered. As a white German in New York for an extended period, Kowald's personal observations are especially poignant. The film was produced by FilmPals in New York and is distributed by Cadence/North Country.

Rivers, Sam (Samuel Carthorne Rivers; b. El Reno, OK, 25 September 1923): tenor saxophonist, flautist, composer, and bandleader. Besides being a prime catalyst for free jazz's evolution, particularly during the loft era, Rivers has been a valued sideman on many straight-ahead jazz sessions as well. His approach to the tenor sax is almost academic in its precision: firm, inflexible, and commanding.

Rivers was raised in a musical family; his father was a touring gospel musician, his mother an instructor at Shorter College in Little Rock, Arkansas. He studied the violin and piano from age five, dabbled in trombone a bit, and finally selected the tenor as his instrument of choice after appreciating greats like Lester Young and Don Byas. In 1947, Rivers began his studies at the Boston Conservatory of Music, followed by an inspirational period at Boston University, where he played with Herb Pomeroy, Quincy Jones, Jaki Byard, baritonist Serge Chaloff, and a number of other rising jazzmen.

In 1952, Rivers quit college and spent a few years working in Florida. He returned to Boston and Pomeroy's band in 1958, put together a bop quartet co-led by pianist Hal Galper, and built a friendship with pianist/writer Tadd Dameron, which resulted in Rivers's first recording date. A junior-high drum prodigy, Tony Williams, caught his ear and the two began working together in an avant-garde mode inspired by the new sounds of Cecil Taylor and Ornette Coleman. Rivers's musical mind was skewed more toward the academicism of Taylor than Coleman's bluesiness, but his synthesis of their concepts was pretty successful. In the early 1960s, Rivers began gigging with Taylor as well as Paul Bley, Bill Dixon, Archie Shepp, and other members of the Jazz Composers Guild.

In July 1964, Rivers was hired by Miles Davis for a tour, the sole recorded evidence being the uninspired *Miles in Tokyo* (1964, Columbia). That year would prove especially fortuitous for Rivers, as he performed on Tony Williams's debut, *Lifetime* (Blue Note), and landed his own contract with the label. *Fuschia Swing Song* (1964, Blue Note) was, in hindsight, an auspicious and brave debut, which featured Williams, Jaki Byard, and bassist Ron Carter navigating through the saxophonist's own elaborate material. Rivers recorded four more albums for Blue Note, his contract culminating with *Dimensions and Extensions* (1967). Even more cerebral than his first outing, the session is nevertheless grounded enough in hard bop to be accessible to less daring listeners. Trumpeter Donald Byrd is a bit of a mismatch, but the remaining musicians (reedman James Spaulding, trombonist Julian Priester, bassist Cecil McBee, and drummer Steve Ellington) get right with the program.

Rivers kept active within the Blue Note stable for most of the 1960s, recording with Bobby Hutcherson, Andrew Hill, Larry Young, and others. In 1969, he joined Taylor again for a successful tour of Europe. The bassless quartet, with Jimmy Lyons and Andrew Cyrille, is captured on *The Great Paris Concert* (1969, Black Lion). Rivers returned to New York and opened a music and dance studio space with his wife, Beatrice, which they later relocated to Soho and named Studio RivBea. Their loft was a primary venue for free jazz experimentation and performance in the 1970s, and the locale of the legendary *Wildflowers* series of recordings (1977, Douglas). Among Rivers's working ensembles at the time were his free trio, RivBea Orchestra, and Winds of Change woodwind ensemble. A contract with Impulse helped to document all the exciting directions in which Rivers's music was moving at the time.

Crystals (1977, Impulse) remains one of the most daunting albums in Rivers's discography. An orchestral session, there are over sixty musicians (yet no pianist!) present on the session, including Rivers, Clifford Thornton, Bill Barron, Grachan Moncur III, Andrew Cyrille, Ronnie Boykins, Hamiet Bluiett, Reggie Workman, and Ahmed Abdullah. Some of the compositions date back to 1959 but still sound far advanced today with their deft blending of collective improvisation and composed sections. Much of the music is frightening to inexperienced listeners but can be utterly cathartic once its energy and passion have washed away all resistance. It is a testimony to the tremendous scope of Rivers's vision and his fearlessness in pursuing it.

Rivers appeared on Dave Holland's classic *Conference of the Birds* (ECM) in 1972 and began working in a duo with Holland in 1976, the bass and cello brightly complementing his rigorous tenor, soprano, and flute work. Two self-titled volumes of their explorations were released that year by Improvising Artists, Paul Bley's label. Later in the decade, Rivers cut some good but poorly marketing discs for small labels, along with the appreciable *Contrasts* (1979) for ECM. He kept fairly active with live gigs but did little recording, taking what happened to come along to make ends meet (in 1977 he recorded separate dates with Barry Altschul and British rock howler Joe Cocker, a true indicator of his flexibility).

After an especially sparse period in the 1980s, during which time he moved to Florida and reconstituted the RivBea Orchestra, Rivers came back strong with a series of albums for FMP (*Portrait*, 1997). He worked in a duo with pianist Tony Hymas (*Winter Garden*, 1999, Nato) and made a huge impact on contemporary jazz with a pair of BMG/RCA Victor records by the RivBea All-Star Orchestra: *Inspiration* (1999) and *Culmination* (2001), a Grammy nominee. Both albums feature Rivers's original compositions, performed by artists like Steve Coleman, Greg Osby, Ray Anderson, Joseph Bowie, Bluiett, Baikida Carroll, Chico Freeman, and tubaist Bob Stewart. Several performers were veterans of the *Crystals* session and seemed right at home with Rivers's more accessible compositions. Rivers has continued to make waves into the new century with his trio and orchestra.

Roberts, Hank (b. Terre Haute, IN, 24 March 1955): cellist. An excellent performer on a comparatively rare beast in improvised music, Roberts began his cello studies at the age of ten. He dabbled a bit with piano, trombone, and guitar in high school but kept the cello as his principal instrument. While at Berklee College of Music, he began to develop a very personal style that encompassed various musical forms and techniques. In the mid-1980s, Roberts went to New York, where his career in free jazz took off. Guitarist Bill Frisell and altoman Tim Berne were two of his first employers in town, and Berne's *Fulton Street Maul* (1987, Columbia) was Roberts's first recording. Berne and Frisell both supported the cellist on *Black Pastels* (1987, JMT), his first release as a leader, and Berne in particular has worked closely with Roberts ever since (see Berne's entry). He partnered with Mark Dresser and Mark Feldman in the Arcado String Trio (*Behind the Myth*, 1990, JMT), which endured until 1992. Roberts gathered a trio with bassist Peter Chwazik and drummer Bill King but spent the mid-1990s working as a teacher. He returned to improvised music in 1997, recording the trio date *I'll Always Remember* and solo *22 Years from Now* (both on Level Green).

Robertson, Herb (b. Plainfield, NJ, 21 February 1951): trumpeter. Robertson graduated from Berklee College of Music in 1972, after which he made a living in rock and jazz bands around New York. In 1981, he made a connection with Tim Berne and played in several of the altoist's units since then (*Mutant Variations*, 1983; *Pace*

Yourself, 1990, both JMT). Bassist Mark Helias has also been a frequent partner. Through Berne, Robertson landed his own contract with JMT (*Transparency*, 1985; *Shades of Bud Powell*, 1988). His technique flawlessly blends traditional styles and edgy avant-garde explorations, enabling him to fit in well with employers as different as David Sanborn, George Gruntz, Ray Anderson, Bob Ackerman, and Anthony Davis. He has participated in several sessions for the Cadence Jazz and CIMP labels.

Robinson, Perry (b. New York, NY, 17 September 1938): clarinetist. One of the few free players aside from John Carter to specialize in the clarinet, Robinson has remained somewhat obscure despite his talents. He studied at the Lenox School of Jazz in 1959, concurrent with Ornette Coleman and Don Cherry, and made in-roads into free music with Henry Grimes's trio, Archie Shepp, Bill Dixon, and Paul Bley. In 1968, he recorded *Escalator Over the Hill* (JCOA) with Carla Bley's orchestra, and gigged with the Roswell Rudd Quintet. Since then, his wildly decorated resumé has included Charlie Haden's Liberation Music Orchestra, mainstream jazz with pianist Dave Brubeck and his son Darius, jazz-funk fusion with electric bassist Stanley Clarke, soul-pop with Joan Armatrading, and backing poetry recitals by Allan Ginsberg. On the freer side, Robinson has played and recorded with Gunter Hampel (*Angel*, 1972, Birth), drummer Lou Grassi (two sessions for CIMP), Ray Anderson, Grachan Moncur, Jeanne Lee, and Burton Greene's klezmer-jazz group Klezmokum. As a leader, Robinson debuted with *Funk Dumpling* (1962, Savoy) and cut a self-titled disc for ESP in 1965. He labored in near obscurity for most of the 1980s but returned in 1989 with the triumphant *Nightmare Island* (West Wind). In 2002, he appeared on William Parker's *Bob's Pink Cadillac* (Eremite) along with drummer Walter Perkins.

Romus, Rent (b. Hancock, MI, 6 January 1968): saxophonist, composer, and bandleader. A rising star of the San Francisco Bay Area, where he has lived since 1970, Romus has lately been a vital force in increasing free music's profile in the region. Romus studied at the Stanford Jazz Workshop in the 1980s, learning from Stan Getz, Dizzy Gillespie, and other major figures. At age sixteen, he organized the North Area Youth Jazz Ensemble. At UC Santa Cruz, Romus assembled the group Jazz on the Line (JOTL), which debuted with *Dark Wind* (1988, JOTL) and performed with Chico Freeman (*In the Moment*, 2000, Edgetone). Later the group, renamed 2 AM, helped to pioneer the "acid jazz" genre. Romus founded the Edgetone label in the early 1990s.

In 1993, Romus collaborated with cellist Kash Killion and drummer James Zitro, two lesser-known figures of 1960s free jazz, in the RKZtet. With additional personnel, the group became the Lords of Outland (*You'll Never Be the Same*, 1995, Jazzheads/Edgetone). Through the nonprofit Jazz in Flight, Romus performed with John Tchicai (*Adapt . . . or Die!*, 1997, Jazzheads/Edgetone). After a sabbatical, Romus reopened Edgetone and started the SIMM Music Series in San Francisco. PKD Vortex Project, inspired by the sci-fi writings of Philip K. Dick, released a self-titled album on Edgetone that year. With guitarist Ernesto Diaz-Infante, Romus coleads The Abstractions (*Sonic Conspiracy*, 2002, Edgetone).

Rose, Jon (b. 1951): violinist, instrument inventor, electronic musician, and composer. Rose has played the violin since the age of seven, when he was awarded a scholarship to the King's School in Rochester. He discontinued his formal studies as a teenager but continued to practice and study on his own. In the 1970s, before and after his move to Australia, Rose explored bebop, big band, classical sitar studies, highly academic avant-garde music, country, and other forms of music. Later in the decade, he assembled the Relative Band with like-minded Australian improvisers who explored the union of personal artistic philosophies and approaches. Rose then extended the "relative" principle to his violin methodology, creating new variations on the instrument, original stringed devices, and environmentally based recordings, which have often been enhanced by technology.

Rose has performed with many of the world's finest improvisers, including Derek Bailey, Jöelle Léandre, Miya Masaoka, Eugene Chadbourne, Butch Morris, Conrad Bauer, Fred Frith, and Otomo Yoshihide. One of Rose's more recent projects, *Violin Music in the Age of Shopping* (1994, Intakt), features Otomo, singer Lauren Newton, and drummer Chris Cutler. Among his other projects have been various duos, the rock-improv band Slawterhaus, the game-piece "Perks," and "The Chaotic Violin," which uses interactive software in live performance. Rose is also an independent filmmaker.

Rosenberg, Scott: reedman and composer. Since the mid-1990s, Rosenberg has been a favored sideman of Anthony Braxton, debuting with the Creative Music Orchestra in 1995, participating in the various Ghost Trance Music projects (*Six Compositions [GTM] 2001*, 2002, Rastascan), and duetting with his mentor now and then (*Compositions/Improvisations 2000*, 2001, Barely Audible). Rosenberg cut a couple of sessions with guitarist John Shiurba and drummer Gino Robair, and led a quartet. In 1997, he moved to Chicago and founded the Barely Audible label, which premiered with *IE (For Large Ensemble)* (1997), his composition for a twenty-seven-piece band inspired by the large orchestras of Braxton and Marco Eneidi/Glenn Spearman. Rosenberg has continued to compose, runs a nightclub in Chicago, and has recorded with fellow reedmen Jack Wright (*Rattle OK*, 2001, Secret Garden) and Kyle Bruckmann (*Six Synaptics*, 2002, Barely Audible).

Rothenberg, Ned (b. Boston, MA, 15 September 1956): reedman and bandleader. Rothenberg first made waves as a member of the Anthony Braxton Creative Music Orchestra, establishing a relationship that he has renewed several times. In the 1980s, he recorded a few sessions for Lumina (*Trials of the Argo*, 1980), and later led Power Lines (self-titled, 1995, New World) and his Double Band. Among his regular partners are Herb Robertson, flautist Robert Dick (both men in the ensemble New Winds), Kip Hanrahan, bassist Jerome Harris, and drummer Samm Bennett (as R.U.B., *Animul*, 2002, with guitarist Uchihashi Kazuhisa). Rothenberg is an enthusiast of the shakuhachi, having studied it extensively in Japan. He plays it along with most of the saxophones, clarinets, and flutes. He has toured most of the world over the past thirty years with various aggregations.

RoTToR: quartet of pianist Keith Tippett, his wife, vocalist Julie Tippetts, trombonist Paul Rutherford, and bassist Paul Rogers. The band was originally a trio called RoToR (the capital letters representing the players' surnames) until Julie Tippetts was invited to join. *The First Full Turn* (1999, Emanem) features accents of bells, maracas, and thumb piano on the nearly hour-long title piece.

Rova: sax quartet, one of the most significant groups to come in the World Saxophone Quartet's wake. Rova deftly combines free elements with a rainbow of other musical styles. The group's name derives from the surnames of its founders: Jon Raskin, Larry Ochs, Andrew Voigt, and Bruce Ackley.

Rova debuted on vinyl with *Cinema Rovaté* (1978, Metalanguage), a frighteningly potent recording that demonstrated Rova's brand of composition, wide open for interpretation yet structured enough to survive without a rhythm section. *Daredevils* (1979, Metalanguage) was their first work with Henry Kaiser, who has championed their cause along with Fred Frith. Kaiser's maniacal sound was a stirring complement to the winds' galumphing, though it was not an entirely successful matchup. Kaiser produced Rova's next effort, *This, This, This, This* (1979, Moers), featuring the original version of Raskin's popular "Flamingo Horizons": the staccato figures bounce off one another like pinballs, layers of purest sound fall in domino fashion.

As Was (1981, Metalanguage, reissued 2001, Atavistic) is a fascinating game piece of sorts, with each man interacting with and against the others according to predetermined rules. It contains a genuine *tour de force* in the long, modal "Paint Another Take of the Shootpop," a masterpiece of textural arrangement beginning with Ochs's brusque tenor statements. One of their most popular records is *Saxophone Diplomacy* (1983, HatHut), recorded live in various locales behind the Iron Curtain. "Strangeness" lives up to its name through its discomfortingly deliberate atonality. Appropriate for a group of saxophonic concentration, two intricate Steve Lacy compositions are assayed. The individual parts of "Sidelines" seem detached, then gently flow together like brooks into a river. Raskin's bari sax rips titanically through "The Throes" as if he were a bar-walking R&B tenorman.

Rova's devotion to Lacy continued on *Favorite Street* (1983, Black Saint), an ecstatic collection of seven Lacy compositions. The rhythmic and melodic devices that the soprano saxophonist had borrowed from Thelonious Monk and Cecil Taylor are recast yet again under the light of Rova, with an appealing payoff. The members keep a keen ear toward keeping out of each other's way and construct letter-perfect harmonies for compositions originally intended as solos, such as "Moon" and "Snips."

Composition and improvisation overlap almost imperceptibly on *The Crowd* (1985, HatArt), commissioned from the group by composer John Adams and based upon the writings of sociologist Elias Canetti. Rova alludes to the full history of jazz and twentieth-century classical music here, which is eminently enjoyable despite its rather heavy inspiration. The next disc, *Beat Kennel* (1987, Black Saint), turned back to their "roots" with an Anthony Braxton interpretation, an exhilarating improv ("Sportspeak"), and originals by Raskin and Voigt.

Following *Beat Kennel*, Voigt left the group and was replaced by altoist Steve Adams, an able substitute. In 1989, Rova collaborated with composer Alvin Curran, a founding member of Musica Elettronica Viva. *Electric Rags II* (New Albion) features ten complicated tracks, which range from an Ackley solo to impenetrable group blowing, with Curran electronically manipulating the results. Curran's "Other Brothers" was featured on *This Time We Are Both* (1989, New Albion), a return to the basic quartet and their own openly structured writing.

For the next album, *Long on Logic* (1990, Sound Aspects), Fred Frith wrote three tracks and Henry Kaiser one. This was another ambitious effort that featured notable studio processing of the saxophones, resulting in even richer textures. Rova returned to Black Saint in 1992 for *From the Bureau of Both*. Ochs's "The Floater" is too long and painful at eighteen minutes, and the tribute to John Cage is rather static. But there are plenty of well-assembled compositions here, and Adams's "What's the Frequency, Kenneth?" is the one real free-for-all.

In 1994, Ochs composed several pieces for saxophone octet, hoping to experiment with an expanded lineup. The Rova members teamed with four other saxophonists to form Figure 8. *Pipe Dreams* (1995, Black Saint) documents the results of their union with Dave Barrett, Vinny Golia, Glenn Spearman, and Tim Berne, all veterans of free music in their respective regions. The performers distinguished themselves on Ochs's complex stratifications, cycling through instruments as glasses of water and interspersing free passages with tightly orchestrated sections.

The following year, Spearman again worked with Rova in a very special expanded setting: a reenactment, as best as could be hoped, of *John Coltrane's Ascension* (1995, Black Saint). Also on hand for this unusual adoration were trumpeters Raphé Malik and Dave Douglas, pianist Chris Brown, bassists George Cremaschi and Lisle Ellis, and drummer Donald Robinson. The first track is a good performance of Coltrane's "Welcome" with just Ochs and the rhythm section. "Ascension" follows the basic format of the original, with wild group improvisations and barely composed segments linked by extended solos. Though all the performers deliver the goods, Spearman is the true star of the session. It is unfortunate that his premature death prevented further collaborations.

Rova has thus far issued three albums in their *Works* series, emphasizing episodic commissioned pieces as well as their own compositions. All of these recordings have the horns arranged in a particular sequence for stereo rendering: from left to right, soprano, baritone, alto, and tenor. *Works, Vol. 1* (1994, Black Saint) begins with Ochs's "When the Nation Was Sound," wherein the horns emulate the aching sound of bagpipes. *Vol. 2* (1995, Black Saint) contains three long works. *Vol. 3* (1999, Black Saint) presents Adams's geometric "The Gene Pool," Muhal Richard Abrams' "Quartet #1," and Robin Holcomb's Western nod "Laredo."

The commission fever continued on *Bingo* (1998, Victo). Ochs's chunky "Initials" shares space with works by British avant-jazzers: two by Lindsay Cooper, one by Fred Frith, and two versions of Barry Guy's "Witch Gong Game," which pitches players against each other on solos, melodic phrases, and exercises in microtones and sound manipulation. More recently the quartet recorded *Freedom in Fragments* (2002, Tzadik) with Frith.

Morphological Echo (1998, Rastascan) is another game-based album, stemming from experiments the four players held with John Zorn, himself a master musical gamesman. The big-picture title of the game is "Maintaining the Web Under Less than Obvious

Circumstances," with its sections rearranged into six separate tracks. The various cues are activated by the horns using methods unknown; it would be fascinating to have a thorough outline of the preestablished cues with which to follow along. The last piece, "Grace," is a slow, sensuous unveiling akin to an ancient Gregorian chant. The players rely upon the acoustics of San Francisco's Grace Cathedral to color their outlines with echo and natural harmonics.

Rowe, Keith: guitarist. Rowe, who usually places his guitar on a tabletop and plays it with an assortment of fans, sticks, radios, and other objects, has always been a forward thinker. In college, he devised a way of translating Paul Klee's artworks into guitar tablature; ambitious pursuits like that made his experience in the Mike Westbrook Orchestra seem less than satisfactory. In that light, he formed AMM in 1965 with Lou Gare and Eddie Prévost as an outlet for experimentation (see entry for AMM). He made sidesteps into Cornelius Cardew's Scratch Orchestra and People's Liberation Music as well. *Supersession* (1984, Matchless), with Prévost, Barry Guy, and Evan Parker, remains a particular favorite.

In the late 1970s, Rowe was a member of Trevor Watts's band Amalgam (*Wipe Out*, 1979, Impetus), but AMM remained his main stock-in-trade. In 1989, Rowe cut the solo record *A Dimension of Perfectly Ordinary Reality* (Matchless), and in 1997, he joined the electronic ensemble MIMEO (see entry). Rowe continued to translate art into music, notably the paintings of Jackson Pollock, and was a painter himself for a time. Besides his continued solo work (*Harsh*, 1999, Grob), Rowe has collaborated with Günter Müller and guitarist Taku Sugimoto (*The World Turned Upside Down*, 1999, Erstwhile), Evan Parker (*Dark Rags*, 2000, Potlatch), Oren Ambarchi, and computer musician Kim Cascone.

Rudd, Roswell (b. Sharon, CT, 17 November 1935): trombonist, composer, and bandleader. Roswell Hopkins Rudd Jr. was one of the very few trombonists to break into early free jazz. He was to his music as J.J. Johnson was to bebop, a master technician and creative soloist who triumphantly translated the physical demands of the style onto a truly difficult horn. Rudd was able to work the greasiness of early jazz trombone techniques into free music, which came easily to him since his background was in Dixieland. Most subsequent free trombonists have followed his lead. After a conspicuous absence for well over a decade, Rudd's comeback in the mid-1990s was a welcome one indeed.

Rudd, whose father was a drummer, studied the French horn at age eleven and learned about jazz from his dad's records. He moved to the trombone in high school, falling under the spell of Woody Herman's great slideman, Bill Harris. At Yale, he performed in a Dixieland sextet called Eli's Chosen Six, then landed an inspirational job with pianist Herbie Nichols who remained one of his greatest influences along with Thelonious Monk. In 1960, Rudd met soprano saxophonist Steve Lacy and drummer Denis Charles, who had both worked with Cecil Taylor a few years prior. The three formed a sort of Monk repertory group and explored more futuristic sounds on the side. Like Lacy, a fellow ex-Dixielander, Rudd found much to embrace in the exciting world of free jazz. From 1962 onward, when he and Charles joined Bill Dixon's unit, his whole focus was upon the exciting new style. There he met Archie Shepp, who became a steady partner in the mid-1960s.

The New York Art Quartet, which Rudd founded with altoist John Tchicai in 1964, was one of the city's most applauded post-Coleman ensembles. His debut as a leader, *Roswell Rudd* (1965, America), included Tchicai, bassist Finn von Eyben, and drummer Louis Moholo. (It has not yet been issued on CD.) As a sideman with Enrico Rava, Shepp, and Cecil Taylor, Rudd guaranteed his position as the principal trombonist in free jazz, practically eclipsing the equally talented Grachan Moncur III in the process. He also investigated musics of other cultures with Gato Barbieri and in Charlie Haden's Liberation Music Orchestra. Rudd joined the staff of ethnomusicologist Alan Lomax in 1964, giving him another chance to dig into the rich history of world music.

In 1966, Rudd waxed *Everywhere* (Impulse), with Haden and Louis Worrell on basses, reedmen Giuseppi Logan and Robin Kenyatta, and drummer Beaver Harris. The saxophonists provide some valuable textural support, but it is clearly the trombonist's show. After a while, the extended length of the four tracks becomes a bit tedious, but as an illustration of his formative days this recording is of interest. Rudd became involved with the Jazz Composers Orchestra Association upon its inception in 1965. About eight years later, he led the *Numatik Swing Band* (1973, JCOA) session with the collective. His five-part title suite forms the core of the recording, which features worthy performances by Harris, Rava, vocalist Sheila Jordan, and tubaist Howard Johnson. Ms. Jordan is also featured on *Flexible Flyer* (1974, Freedom), a Rudd quintet album with Barry Altschul on drums, pianist Hod O'Brien, and the fine Norwegian bassist Arild Andersen. *Inside Job* (1976, Arista) has different personnel (Enrico Rava, pianist Dave Burrell, bassist Stafford James, and drummer Harold White) but a similar aura of relaxed inventiveness.

Rudd's sense of adventure has led him to some interesting artistic extremes. On *The Definitive Roswell Rudd* (1979, Horo), hardly a realistic title, he performs on trombone, piano, drums, and percussion and recites poetry by Ralph Romanelli. On *Regeneration* (1982, Soul Note), a session organized by Misha Mengelberg, he interprets three tunes each by Herbie Nichols and Thelonious Monk in the company of Steve Lacy, Han Bennink, and bassist Kent Carter. This date might be said to mark the beginning of the Nichols resurgence in jazz.

Regeneration was Rudd's last significant session for many years, as he concentrated on more stable jobs to make ends meet. Rudd was a college professor for some time, teaching at the University of Maine at Augusta until he was disrespectfully denied tenure. His main musical activity was achieved in a hotel resort band until a flood of new interest brought him back into the spotlight. Fittingly, Rudd's return to form brought him right back where he had left off, right in the middle of the Herbie Nichols legacy. *The Unheard Herbie Nichols, Vol. 1* (1996) and *Vol. 2* (1997, both CIMP) finds Rudd working in an odd trio with guitarist Greg Millar and drummer/vibist John Bacon Jr., two unknowns who nevertheless click with the leader. Both albums contain rare compositions that Nichols never got around to recording before his death in 1963. These interpretations by Rudd's trio (and him solo as well) are not only fabulous, they make us regretful that we can never hear them played by their creator's hands.

The unpredictable *Broad Strokes* (2000, Knitting Factory) has the air of a what's-to-come sampler, as if Rudd were trying to decide what new direction to take. A great tentet with the trombones of Josh Roseman and Steve Swell, who plainly acknowledge Rudd's influence yet inevitably change our ideas about free trombone, bashes its way through Nichols's "Change of Season." Steve Lacy and Elton Dean, a pioneer of free, mainstream, and fusion styles in Britain, join Rudd for Monk's "Coming on the Hudson." The guest appearance by Sonic Youth is grotesque and the vocal spots by Rudd, his son Christopher, and Steve Ruddick could be done without (our man is no lyricist), but Sheila Jordan is as welcome as ever. Despite this album's wishy-washy content, it does promise good things to come from the trailblazer of free trombone. And on the evidence of *Monk's Dream* (2000, Verve), his latest high-quality meeting with Steve Lacy, we can bet that Rudd will keep his influences close to his heart. *MaliCool* (2003, Sunnyside) is an atypical but fascinating album with Barry Altschul and Malian kora player Mamadou Diabate.

Russell, Hal (Harold Luttenbacher; b. Detroit, MI, 28 August 1926; d. Chicago, IL, September 1992): multi-instrumentalist, composer, and bandleader. Russell made a surprising transition from obscure bop drummer to patriarchal hornman in the 1980s, reinventing himself as few other jazz musicians have. He began playing drums at the age of four and took up the trumpet later, majoring on the horn at the University of Illinois. After performing around Chicago as a drummer, he was hired by Woody Herman in the late 1940s and made his first recordings. Russell experienced the avant side of big-band jazz with the explorative groups of Boyd Raeburn and Claude Thornhill. For most of the 1950s, Russell did studio work and played in pickup bands behind visiting artists like John Coltrane and Dizzy Gillespie.

Russell's first serious taste of free jazz came in 1959, when he joined a trio with tenorman Joe Daley and bassist Russell Thorne. Daley's group stayed together for a few years, just long enough to wax *Trio at Newport '63* (1963, RCA). The next fifteen years or so were quiet and not especially productive for Russell, as he kept up the old pace of studio work and backup gigs. In the late 1970s, however, he was inspired to pick up the trumpet again and try playing the tenor sax. He briefly worked with a quintet he called Chemical Feast, which included reedman Mars Williams. He then assembled his NRG Ensemble in 1979 to explore his own high-energy concepts of free jazz. The initial personnel included Williams, bassist Kent Kessler, multi-instrumentalist Brian Sandstrom, and percussionist Steve Hunt, all of whom remained in the band after Russell's death. (See NRG Ensemble's entry.) Russell recorded with The Coctails and the Flying Luttenbachers, a free-rock ensemble titled after his original surname, in the 1990s. All Russell's efforts as a free musician were characterized by fearless ambition and large measures of humor, which helped endear him to audiences who did not quite know what to make of his music.

Russell's two final recordings were especially poignant in hindsight, almost as if he had forseen his death from heart trouble. *Hal's Bells* (1992, ECM) is a solo extravaganza on which Russell plays tenor and soprano saxes, trumpet, the double-reed musette, drums, bells, vibes, bass marimba, congas, gongs, and percussion as well as using his voice. Aside from the vibes solo "I Need You Now," all the tracks feature multiple overdubs of the instruments in different combinations. It is an erratic but profoundly personal overview of his career, all original works except for the nearly forgotten "Carolina Moon" and "Moon of Manakoora." *The Hal Russell Story* (1993, ECM), by the NRG Ensemble, was released posthumously. It intersperses narrations by Russell about his memories and thoughts in between usually short but always interesting musical segments. The album closes, in Russell's characteristically irreverent way, with a cover of Fleetwood Mac's "Oh Well," a somehow entirely fitting send-off to one of the most colorful characters in jazz.

Russell, John (b. London, England, 1954): guitarist. Russell is a brilliant improviser who has yet been somewhat overlooked. He began playing the guitar at age eleven and became a professional musician in the early 1970s. He became involved in free improv early, performing at the Little Theatre Club, Ronnie Scott's, London Musicians' Collective, and other forward-looking venues with the Incus Records cadre. His first recording for the label was 1975's quartet date, *Teatime*. By then, Russell was already teaching and working in broadcasting. He soon permanently abandoned the electric guitar in favor of a loud, vintage acoustic model. In 1979, Russell began playing in a trio with violinist Phil Durrant and saxophonist Mark Pickworth, who was replaced by John Butcher five years later. The trio hit its stride then and became one of Britain's most popular improvising ensembles (*Concert Moves*, 1992, Random Acoustics).

In the late 1980s, Russell helped Butcher establish the Acta label, which debuted with their fiery collaboration *Conceits* (1987, Acta), then set up the long-running Mopomoso concert series, which gave London's improvisers a big leg-up in the public eye. Over the course of his career, Russell has collaborated with Radu Malfatti's Ohrkiste, drummer Roger Turner, Toshinori Kondo, Chris Burn Ensemble, saxman Stephan Keune, the quartet London Airlift with Evan Parker, Luc Houtkamp, Günter Christmann's Vario, and others. His own recordings have been issued on Acta (*Excerpts and Offerings*, 2001) and Emanem (*From Next to Last*, 2002).

Rutherford, Paul (b. Greenwich, London, U.K., 29 February 1940): trombonist, euphonist, and pianist. One of the early British pioneers of free jazz, Rutherford is often said to have been the first trombonist to use multiphonics, predating Albert Mangelsdorff's own experiments. His earliest recordings were made with the Spontaneous Music Ensemble in 1966–1967. Besides his stellar solo trombone performances, Rutherford has performed in a vast number of musical settings: the Globe Unity Orchestra, London Jazz Composer's Orchestra, Peter Brötzmann's Tentet, Tony Oxley's Dedication Orchestra, Keith Tippett's Centipede, RoTToR, bands led by Mike Westbrook and Don Cherry, and duos and trios with Anthony Braxton, Paul Lovens, Sabu Toyozumi, and Evan Parker. Rutherford was a founder of Iskra 1903 and is a member of Quintet Moderne. His 1974 album *The Gentle Harm of the Bourgeoisie* (Emanem) could serve as a primer of extended trombone technique, so exotic and unexpected are the sounds he creates.

Ryan, Jim (b. St. Paul, MN, 29 June 1934): reeds player. Ryan received a philoso-
phy degree from the University of Minnesota in 1957 and moved to Paris in 1960.
For fifteen years, he played alto, tenor, and flute in free ensembles around the city.
He spent the next decade performing in Washington, D.C., then moved to Oakland,
California, in 1986. Since then, he has become an indelible fixture on the Bay Area
improv scene. Ryan now leads two bands, Forward Energy (*Configurations*, 2002,
Edgetone) and the Left Coast Improv Group (*April/May 2002*, Edgetone). The latter
group shifts in personnel according to the gig's needs and has included such exotica
as prepared guitar, koto, and electronics. Ryan has issued several albums on his own
label, Jimzeen, including the spoken word/improv CD-R *Subjects of Desire* (2002).

Rypdal, Terje (b. Oslo, Norway, 23 August 1947): guitarist and composer. Rypdal is
a stalwart fixture of the ECM label, having released twenty albums on the imprint
since his self-titled debut in 1971. His guitar tone is heavily rock-influenced, laden
with distortion and volume à la Hendrix. He studied classical piano as a youth and
learned the Lydian Concept of Tonal Organization from George Russell at Oslo University. His very first recording, *Dream* (1967, Karusell) is practically lost to history.
He performed alongside Jan Garbarek in Russell's group (*Electronic Sonata for Souls
Loved by Nature*, 1969, Flying Dutchman) and accompanied Garbarek on his early
ECM albums *Esoteric* (1969) and *Afric Pepperbird* (1970). The label association stuck.
In 1972, Rypdal formed his band Odyssey (self-titled, 1975, ECM) and has regularly
worked with Scandinavian improvisers. In addition, he has been a vital sideman with
John Surman, Don Cherry, Lester Bowie, Jack DeJohnette, and pianist Ketil Bjørnstad.
The widely separated *Eos* (1983) and *If Mountains Could Sing* (1994, both ECM) are
among his best sessions as a leader.

S

Sanders, Pharoah (Ferrell Sanders; b. Little Rock, AR, 13 October 1940): tenor and soprano saxophonist, composer, and bandleader. Sanders is renowned for his igneous attack on tenor and soprano saxes, an intimate appreciation for world musics, and a loving affection for the legacy of his former employer, John Coltrane. In the two brief years that the saxophonists worked together, Sanders was a vivid foil for the jazz giant, burning through the most intense solos and accompaniments imaginable while Coltrane explored the depths of his own soul. Sanders's ability to rend note-streams into undiscernable smears of sound was an organic extension of Trane's earlier experiments with playing extremely fast through convoluted chord changes on "Giant Steps" and "Countdown." He brought the intensity of Albert Ayler to Coltrane's quintet when the leader's chops could not quite attain that level of pure passion. (See the Coltrane entry.)

Both of Sanders's parents were music teachers, and they encouraged him to take up the clarinet. He learned about jazz through the guidance of his high school band director, Jimmy Cannon, who had him switch to tenor sax and played him recordings by Sonny Rollins, John Coltrane, Charlie Parker, and other premier jazz saxophonists. An after-hours gig with a blues band sustained Sanders until he worked up enough money to move out to Oakland, California. Local musicians like reed players Sonny Simmons and Dewey Redman got wind of the new kid in town, "Little Rock" Sanders, while he studied music at Oakland Junior College. His first dabblings in free jazz came in this period, after Ornette Coleman's early records for Contemporary had made an impact on the Bay Area scene.

In 1961, Sanders moved to New York but had a difficult time landing gigs in that crowded setting. Coleman alumni Don Cherry and Billy Higgins offered him sporadic work, as did Sun Ra when a temporary vacancy came up in the Arkestra. Higgins, pianist John Hicks, and legendary bebop bassist Wilbur Ware formed the core of his first band in 1963. When John Coltrane heard the quartet perform at the Village Gate, he was duly impressed by Sanders's high level of energy and intricate harmonic sense.

Later in 1964, Coltrane asked Sanders to sit in for the first time, and by the following year, he was an unofficial member of his mentor's group. Their combined strength made for a truly fearsome sound, alienating former fans but landing a new crop of adherents who adored the searing new music made by Trane and his associates.

Bernard Stollman, head of the ESP label, decided to give Sanders the chance to record as a leader in 1964. *Pharoah's First* (1965, ESP) was the result of a rather poorly thought-out session, no fault of Sanders. There is little chemistry between him, trumpeter Stan Foster, and pianist Jane Getz, their bop orientation being wholly unsuitable for what he was trying to accomplish. Sanders tries to soar as he preferred to with Coltrane's group, but Foster and Getz will have none of it.

ESP might not have been the best neighborhood for Sanders to settle down in, but Impulse definitely was. Producer Bob Thiele practically gave artistic *carte blanche* to the saxophonist in November 1966, when *Tauhid* was recorded. This date remains one of his enduring best, thanks to the patient, organic development of the themes and improvisations. The band is outstanding: pianist Dave Burrell, bassist Henry Grimes, drummers Roger Blank and Nat Bettis, and particularly furious guitarist Sonny Sharrock, whose frantic ten-second guitar solo on "Upper Egypt and Lower Egypt" is the stuff of legend. Sanders is remarkable on alto, tenor, and piccolo, which he uses for bright coloration at ideal times along with his voice. His interest in ethnic elements—bells, odd scales, exotic rhythms—is already manifest on this early date.

Sanders's world-music wildness was given further vent on *Izipho Zam* (1969, Strata-East), which marked his first recording with vocalist Leon Thomas. The singer's trademark, a sort of superhuman pygmy yodeling deep in the throat, is one of many ear-grabbing features of "Prince of Peace." "Balance" and the title track are full-band blowouts, which grants copious space to Sharrock, pianist Lonnie Liston Smith, tubaist Howard Johnson, and drummers Bettis, Billy Hart, and Chief Bey. This is an absolutely cathartic album to those who can appreciate Thomas's vocals.

Thomas, Hart, Smith, Bettis, reedman James Spaulding, and French horn player Julius Watkins are among the contributors to *Karma* (1969, Impulse), which moved Sanders even further toward Eastern motifs. His music in this period is a continuation of Coltrane's spiritual searching. A devout Muslim, Sanders also investigated Hindu and Buddhist thoughts in his early projects. "The Creator Has a Master Plan" is a passionate half-hour devotional on which Thomas ululates ecstatically for long periods, driven by and driving the saxophonist's own performance. It became one of free jazz's rare popular hits. Bassist Reggie Workman and Smith maintain a lovely ostinato beneath it all. A quote from "A Love Supreme" kicks off the track, revealing the inspiration of Coltrane.

Jewels of Thought (1969, Impulse), the next installment in Sanders's spiritual series, is more of the same. Thomas and Smith are again on hand; the bassists this time are Cecil McBee and Richard Davis; Idris Muhammad drums majestically except on "Hum Allah Hum Allah Hum Allah," a revamp of "The Creator . . ." with Roy Haynes on skins. Sanders spreads out a bit horn-wise, using bass clarinet and flutes for textural variety. "Sun in Aquarius" gives a typical impression of his bass clarinet work, just as boiling and abrasive as his tenor sax. *Deaf Dumb Blind (Summun Bukmun Umyun)* (1970), *Thembi* (1971), and *Village of the Pharoahs* [sic] (1971, all Impulse) present more of the same foreign intrigue, interlarded with sections of pure beauty, such as Sanders's tender soprano sax on "Thembi." Violinist Michael White was another important addition, polishing the music to a mirror finish.

On the extended work *Black Unity* (1971, Impulse), Sanders began exploring funkier rhythms in place of the tidal ebb and flow of his earlier ostinato-based patterns. Bassist Stanley Clarke, well before his breakout as a top fusion star, joins Cecil McBee on the low end; the drummers are Billy Hart and Norman Connors, with Lawrence Killian on percussion. Reedman Carlos Garnett, trumpeter Marvin "Hannibal" Peterson, and pianist Joe Bonner are the remaining sidemen on this long, difficult session. Bonner's intricate chords are the basic framework over which the deep groove is laid as the rhythm section cycles through various Afro-Latin beats and other ethnicities. Garnett's soulful flute and tenor work makes a nice contrast with the leader's sizzle, and Peterson shows off the chops that made him such an asset to the Gil Evans Orchestra. Thirty-seven minutes of mesmerizing motion is as hard to take from Sanders as it was from Miles Davis's electric band, but *Black Unity* is still an important achievement.

Throughout the 1970s, Sanders recorded similar dates for Impulse, Capitol, India Navigation, and Arista. As the years progressed, he moved closer to the popular mainstream, adding more dance beats and electric instruments to the impenetrable layers of percussion and winds. *Pharoah* (aka *Harvest Time*) (1977, India Navigation) marked an ebb in his creativity. It features one of his least interesting bands on lesser material. Bassist Steve Neil and drummer Greg Bandy are the only high points of Sanders's arrival at rock bottom.

Once he began moving away from the residue of disco and back into Coltrane's inspiration, Sanders's music took a turn for the better. *Heart Is a Melody* (1982, Theresa, reissued by Evidence), recorded live at the Keystone Korner in San Francisco, depicts the unpredictability of Sanders's set list from this period onward. A long, full burn through Coltrane's Latin opus "Olé" contains some jaw-dropping tenor blowing. Every time it seems that Sanders has hit the peak of his energy, he blasts through the ceiling with ever-higher squeals and roars. His fingers fly over the keys at nearly superhuman speed; he even yells with a primitive vigor at one point in his extra-long solo. A choir provides backup vocals on the title track, which takes its initial horn melody from "The Creator Has a Master Plan," and Sanders sings and shouts joyously on the highlife romp "Goin' to Africa." He even plays fairly straight tenor on tracks like "Rise and Shine."

Journey to the One (1980, Theresa, reissued by Evidence) cycles through a huge roster of personnel, which includes Joe Bonner, John Hicks, Bedria Sanders, Idris Muhammad, vocalist Bobby McFerrin, Eddie Henderson on flügelhorn, percussionist Babatunde Olatunji, and Mark Isham on keyboards. Coltrane's lovely "After the Rain" and a Rodgers and Hart cull, "Easy To Remember," are beautifully rendered.

Sanders and Leon Thomas enjoyed a rather average-sounding reunion on *Shukuru* (1985, Theresa, reissued by Evidence). Thomas's signature richness colors "Sun Song" and "For Big George," which are enjoyable for what they are, even though the power of their original collaborations is gone. "Jitu" and "Shukuru" are as fiery as expected from Sanders, but on "Body and Soul" and "Too Young to Go Steady," he drops back into Coltrane's shadow quite audibly. Sanders and John Hicks paid further homage to Coltrane on *Africa* (1987, Timeless), though only the starkly beautiful "Naima" was written by his old friend.

A potentially fatal interest in recording such pop fare as Whitney Houston's "The Greatest Love of All" has not kept Sanders from gaining new fans. If anything, being able to creatively interpret such tunes in his personal way has probably helped his reputation. That song is included on *A Prayer before Dawn* (1987, Theresa; reissued by Evidence) along with "The Christmas Song" and Dave Brubeck's "In Your Own Sweet Way," two uncharacteristic pieces that work well.

Welcome to Love (1991, Timeless) consists of the reedman's singular readings of standards: "My One and Only Love," "Polka Dots and Moonbeams," "Moonlight in Vermont," and others. His teamwork with William Henderson is priceless. *Crescent, with Love* (1992, Evidence) is an extension of the idea, with several Coltrane tunes included in the package. "Misty," "Too Young to Go Steady," and Anthony Newley's "Feelin' Good," despite their potential for cheesiness, are painted tenderly. Things steam up on the Coltrane material, but a spirit of loving devotion prevails.

In the mid-1990s, Sanders began an association with electric bassist, producer, and world music aficionado Bill Laswell. *Message from Home* (1996, Verve) is a fantasia of ethnic musics, true jazz, and avant-garde intensity. Foday Musa Suso, a Malian kora player who had previously worked with Herbie Hancock, is prominent on the ornate "Kumba." "Our Roots (Began in Africa)," Sanders's categorical homage to the Homeland, is loaded with deep chanted vocals and percussion, and the sheer beauty of "Tomoki" is reminiscent of "Thembi" from a quarter-century ago. Laswell also produced 1999's *Save Our Children* (Verve), a similarly lavish affair with Africanisms on the title track, a gorgeously straight "Midnight in Berkeley Square," and a synthesized "Kazuko." Henderson, percussionist Trilok Gurtu, bassist Alex Blake, and keyboard funkmeister Bernie Worrell stand out. The Laswell discs open new opportunities for Sanders and his fans, blending freedom with absolutely captivating global sounds.

Sanders is less encumbered but no less enlightened on *Spirits* (2000, Meta), a live date with percussionists Hamid Drake and Adam Rudolph. The reedman's wood flutes, hand drums, and tenor are blissfully assisted by the large array of devices used by his cohorts on this spiritually lush set. The meditative spirit present on many tunes is more reminiscent of his Impulse days ("Sunrise" could have been easily inserted into a number of those albums), but the less overblown ethnic elements are in the selective Laswell mode.

Sarin, Michael (b. Seattle, WA): drummer. Sarin came up in Seattle's improv scene but moved to New York in 1991. He joined Thomas Chapin's trio with Drew Gress in that year, replacing Michael Johns, and debuted on record with the trio's *Anima* (1992, Knitting Factory Works). Sarin remained with the trio until Chapin's death in 1998. He has worked with Gress in other settings as well, including Dave Douglas's String Group (*Parallel Worlds*, 1993; *Five*, 1995, both Soul Note). Sarin has also backed up Myra Melford, Andy Laster, Ned Rothenberg, Brad Shepik, Mark Feldman, Mark Dresser, bassist Ben Allison, John Zorn, Briggan Krauss, and other key NYC improvisers.

Saturn: record label established by Sun Ra in 1957. Saturn was one of the first labels established by a jazz musician to produce and distribute his own music. Recognizing the biases that permeated the record industry, Sun Ra saw self-production as the best way to bring his visionary albums to the market without unwanted input. Saturn Records was a seriously shoestring project for many years, given the economic difficulties of maintaining an ensemble like the Arkestra. Ra and manager Alton Abraham often pressed just seventy-five copies of an album at a time, selling them at concerts with hand-painted or mimeographed sleeves. Some pressings were bad, some track and personnel listings incorrect, and many "newly issued" tracks were several years old or duplicated from other albums. But today, original Saturn LPs can carry four-figure price tags on the collectors' market. Many classic Saturn records have been reissued by Evidence since the early 1990s, with shorter albums often paired up on single CDs.

Sawaï, Kazue: koto player, one of the few to freely improvise on the traditional Japanese instrument. She studied the seventeen-string bass koto at Tokyo University of Fine Arts and Music and began her career in 1978. In that year, Sawaï caught the ear of European improvisers when she appeared at the Festival d'Automne in Paris. She and her husband, Tadao Sawaï (d. 1997), founded the Sawaï Koto Institute in Tokyo to instruct others in the art of the long zither. John Zorn took notice of her in the late 1980s, and in 1989, she presented some of his compositions at the Bang On A Can Festival. The performance was highly acclaimed and she was invited back the following year. She has partnered with saxophonist Michel Doneda (*Temps Couché*, 1998, Victo), Japanese bassist Tetsu Saitoh, and composer David Behrman, among others. Recommended is *Live at Hall Egg Farm* (2000, Sparkling Beatnik).

Schiaffini, Giancarlo (b. Rome, Italy): tubaist and trombonist. Schiaffini has an educational background in both music, which he studied at Darmstadt after teaching himself to play, and physics, the field he finally abandoned in favor of music. He was a founding member of both Gruppo di Improvvisazione Nuovo Consonanza and Gruppo Romano Free Jazz in the 1960s (see separate entries). In the 1970s, Schiaffini performed with percussionist Michele Iannaccone and saxophonist Eugenio Colombo in the SIC Trio, whose albums now appear to be out of print. British reedman Lol Coxhill and percussionist Andrea Centazzo were other early partners (*Moot*, 1978, Ictus) with whom he has remained in contact (Centazzo's *Situations*, 2000, New Tone). Schiaffini and Pino Minafra cofounded the Italian Instabile Orchestra and have appeared on all their recordings. He stays active in the "classical" avant-garde, performing regularly with composer Luigi Nono's troupe, Prometheus. There is usually a palpable sense of jazz in his playing on either instrument, skills that he keeps honed as an instructor with the Siena Jazz Courses. Schiaffini has collaborated with top non-Italian improvisers including Barry Guy, Evan Parker, Maarten Altena, and Thurston Moore (*Three Incredible Ideas*, 2001, Auditorium). He has recorded a few albums as a leader, among them tributes to Thelonious Monk and Charlie Parker (*About Monk*, 1992; *As a Bird*, 1994, both on Pentaflowers).

Schiano, Mario (b. Naples, Italy, 1933): reedsman and vocalist. A primary force in Italian improvisation, Schiano began dabbling with free music in the mid-1950s, separately but concurrently with Cecil Taylor and Ornette Coleman. He was a cofounder of Gruppo Romano Free Jazz (see separate entry), one of the nation's earliest free ensembles, promoted the Contraindicazioni Festival in Rome, and is a cofounder of the Italian Instabile Orchestra. Like many European freemen, Schiano delights in fusing traditional folk forms with jazz, standards, and improvisation. Since 1973's *Sud* (Splasc(h)), he has released well over a dozen albums as a leader or coleader. Among his collaborators have been Evan Parker, Barry Guy, Paul Lovens, Sebi Tramontana (all of whom perform on *Social Security*, 1996, Victo), Paul Rutherford, Marcello Melis, Giorgio Gaslini, Peter Kowald, Joëlle Léandre, and Ernst Reijseger.

Schlippenbach, Alexander von (b. Berlin, Germany, 7 April 1938): pianist, composer, and leader. He began formal piano studies at the age of eight, following up with a stint at Köln's Staatliche Hochschule for Musik. He studied under Bernd Alois Zimmermann there, absorbing the underappreciated master's ideas of avant-garde music. In 1963, he met Gunter Hampel and began working with him in a duo. The pair may have toyed a bit with some of the free jazz concepts being pursued by Harriott or Coleman, but Schlippenbach did not seriously investigate such music until he joined Manfred Schoof's quintet in 1964. He stayed with Schoof for three years before he began to lead his own ensembles in a personal quest for jazz liberation.

In 1966, Schlippenbach assembled a fourteen-piece jazz orchestra to perform his extended composition "Globe Unity," which was commissioned by the Berlin Jazztage Festival. That piece was released on *Globe Unity* (1966, Saba) under Schlippenbach's name. Pleased with the project's success, Schlippenbach maintained the Globe Unity Orchestra off and on until their final performance at the 1987 Chicago Jazz Festival. (See separate entry for Globe Unity Orchestra.)

In 1970, Schlippenbach, saxophonist Evan Parker, and drummer Paul Lovens formed their highly influential trio, with bassist Peter Kowald stepping in at times to make it a quartet. The Schlippenbach Trio quickly became one of Europe's most beloved free units. The dichotomy of seriously jazzy piano and fervently outside sax is held in check by middleman Lovens, doling out equal measures of freedom and form as necessary. The pianist has also performed in duo with Sven-Åke Johansson since 1976, pursuing decidedly different directions in rhythm and form. As a composer, ensembles such as the Italian RIA Big Band have commissioned Schlippenbach, for which he has orchestrated works by Jelly Roll Morton and Thelonious Monk.

Hunting the Snake (2000, Atavistic) was recorded live in 1975 by the Schlippenbach Quartet. Parker is the most forward figure here, specializing in the sax technique he calls "The Snake": sinuous, consistently varied figures sustained indefinitely through circular breathing. But all four players engage in the truly democratic form of group interplay that makes for a good free-jazz performance. Lovens's drum kit is practically handmade, with all manner of found objects used as sound sources. Kowald is as forward as a free bassist should be, bowing frantically to stoke the fires ignited under Schlippenbach's piano. This early snapshot shows the pianist and friends in the early stages of their rapport, rough around the edges but with a definite unified conception taking shape.

In 1989, Schlippenbach landed the dream opportunity to work in a duo with drummer Sunny Murray. The brilliant Murray has lived in France since the 1970s and has developed a firm following among European improvisers and fans. The pairing on *Smoke* (1989, FMP) paints a different portrait than did his work with Taylor, but the results are just as appealing. Murray's deliberate tuning of his drums plays a vital role in settings like this, permitting him to function as melodically as Schlippenbach's forceful piano approach casts him in a Tayloresque percussive role.

Another duo of import is *Digger's Harvest* (1998, FMP), Schlippenbach's meeting with another favorite of Cecil Taylor: drummer Tony Oxley. The more European seasoning of Oxley's percussing, moderated by an abstruse understanding of the jazz continuum, pays off in pulling deeper jazziness out of the pianist. The long opening track, "Grains and Roots," almost exhausts the listener with its endless flow of sonic activity. The series of shorter improvs in various tints of blue and red grants us the second wind to endure the equally long and stimulating title track. It is a radically different set from *Leaf Palm Hand*, Oxley's 1988 duet with Taylor: fewer stylistic differences between the cuts, but no less raw power.

Of the Schlippenbach Trio's albums, perhaps the best executed is *Elf Bagatellen* (1990, FMP), a collection of two piano solos, one sax solo, and eight white-hot trio ventures. On the evidence of "Aries," Schlippenbach comes straight out of the Monk school of jazz piano, as he pours out hard-hitting chords and regularly warped melodic lines at stilted tempos. Parker puts "The Snake" to good use, and behind him, Lovens comments, trips, and builds up in a great surge of cymbal waves. The spaces here are not as wide as in some AACM projects, as these players are quick to develop new ideas and insert them brashly.

Physics (1993, FMP) contains two long group forays. On both tracks, the trio push themselves to the limits of human endurance, with periodic drops in tension so that they might catch their breath. That date is less coherent than *Complete Combustion/ Seven Fuels* (1999, FMP), a live set from the 1998 Free Music Workshop. Lovens all but brutalizes Schlippenbach's piano into submission on the long opener, cranking out horrifically powerful streams of sound for the pianist to respond to with a vigor comparable to Cecil Taylor's. Parker lingers on the sidelines for most of that action, acting as a sort of referee. On the shorter "Fuel" segments, Schlippenbach figuratively takes it all out on the saxophonist, engaging in fervent but good-spirited exchanges with Lovens as puppet master.

Even better yet is *Swinging the BIM* (2000, FMP), recorded live at Amsterdam's BIMhuis, the epicenter of free improvisation in Holland. Both sets from that night in 1998 are presented here as nonstop lava flows: searing primal forces sputter, collide, and coagulate into awe-inspiring wholes. The onslaught of the half-hour opening set would have been enough to drive lesser players into retirement, but on the second set, the trio doubled their stamina for another full hour of episodic dialogue. Lovens's use of the musical saw at one point is as hilariously endearing as some of the exotica Parker chokes out of his soprano.

Schoeppach, Brad: see **Shepik, Brad.**

Schoof, Manfred (b. Magdeburg, Germany, 6 April 1936): trumpeter and bandleader. Schoof was interested in jazz early in life, studying the trumpet and flügelhorn as a youth and arranging music before he graduated from high school. He attended the Kassel Musikakademie, then the Köln Musikhochschule, where he studied under bandleader and radio personality Kurt Edelhagen. Schoof worked extensively with Gunter Hampel and Edelhagen's Radio Big Band at roughly the same time, and in 1965, he began exploring free jazz in a quintet with Alexander von Schlippenbach, reedman Gerd Dudek, bassist Buschi Niebergall, and drummer Jaki Liebezeit. In 1966, the quintet recorded *Voices* (Columbia), one of the first enduring documents of free jazz by Europeans; *The Early Sessions* (FMP) also captures the group in action. Three years later, Schoof gathered an improvising orchestra that included Irène Schweizer and Evan Parker (*European Echoes*, 1969, MPS; reissued 2002, Atavistic). Schoof contributed to Globe Unity Orchestra, the Kenny Clarke–Francy Boland Big Band, and the orchestras of George Russell and George Gruntz. He has also performed on sessions by Stan Getz, Miles Davis, and Peter Brötzmann, and composed for the Berlin Philharmonic. Schoof has only recorded sporadically as a leader, his most recent album being *Shadows and Smiles* (1987, Wergo).

Schweizer, Irène: pianist and composer. Schweizer's expansive keyboard technique readily implies an academic background in classical music, but that is not the case. Her orchestral sensibilities stem not from the conservatory directly, but from her deep studies of Cecil Taylor's *modus operandi*. She learned to play both piano and drums as a teenager and later studied jazz with English pianist Eddie Thompson while working as a housekeeper.

By age twenty-one, when Schweizer came back to Switzerland, she was well versed in several aspects of the jazz piano vocabulary. Further life lessons came at the hands of South African expatriates like pianist Dollar Brand (now Abdullah Ibrahim), who performed in Zurich on occasion. At about the same time, wisps of freedom from Coleman and Taylor began to tickle her sensibilities. In 1966, her trio was invited to the Frankfurt Jazz Festival, and there she made the acquaintance of Peter Kowald, Peter Brötzmann, and other young Germans who followed similar paths. Once she saw Taylor himself in live performance, Schweizer had to decide whether to fish or cut bait. Her passion for the music soon gained her a faithful following among European musicians and fans. *Early Tapes* (1998, FMP) unveils the semi-free music of her 1967 trio with bassist Uli Trepte and drummer Mani Neumeyer. The first track, "Dollar's Mood," makes clear her indebtedness to Mr. Ibrahim.

In 1968, Schweizer formed a trio with Kowald and Swiss drummer Pierre Favre, with Evan Parker in as a fourth wheel on occasion. As influential as that group was, apparently they were never recorded. She later formed a friendship with Rüdiger Carl, whose refreshing notions about music's universality clicked with her own. They have worked together on many occasions, recording the duo recording *The Very Centre of Middle Europe* (1978, HatHut) under her name and the 3-CD ensemble set *Book/Virtual COWWS* (1978/1996, FMP) under Carl's. On *The Very Centre* Schweizer plays piano and drums, complementing the tenor sax, soprano and bass clarinets, and concertina of Mr. Carl. The squeezebox casts a folkish light, of course, but the results are vibrantly original.

In 1977, Schweizer joined the Feminist Improvisers Group (FIG), a phenomenal collective that counted among its members bassist Joëlle Léandre, vocalist Maggie

Nicols, and saxophonist Lindsey Cooper. All the players shared common interests in politics, women's rights, and, above all, the spirit of creativity. Though their name and stance did not help them land gigs all the time, the FIGs more than earned the praise of their fellow improvisers. In 1983, their name was finally changed to the European Women's Improvising Group, a bow to pressure that caused no harm to their outstanding music. Shortly thereafter Schweizer helped to found the Intakt label, which has issued a number of essential improvised sessions by herself and other artists, Swiss and non-Swiss. She also had a hand in founding the Taktlos and Canaille Festivals.

The trio on *Les Diaboliques* (1993, Intakt) is an offshoot of the FIG: Schweizer on piano, Lèandre bass, and Maggie Nicols contributing her inimitable horn-like vocals. Diabolical, maybe; crazy, perhaps; fun, no doubt about it. Schweizer lays the shifting, sliding groundwork for the other two to improvise over, scattering arpeggios and big, blocky chords about the floor. Nicols is nothing short of amazing, ululating and scatting and diatribing off the top of her head as Lèandre strums and pounds the bass into submission. The Diaboliques are also featured prominently on Schweizer's *The Storming of the Winter Palace* (1985, Intakt) with two men in the house this time, drummer Günter Sommer and American trombonist George Lewis. The Moers Festival usually draws the best out of its artists, and this session was no different. Lewis and Nicols mesh as a horn section should, calling, responding, and countering expertly throughout the three selections while Schweizer lays waste to notions of jazz piano decorum.

The pianist's interest in African music and its compatibility with modern improvisation bore succulent fruit on *Irène Schweizer and Louis Moholo* (1986, Intakt), a gorgeous collaboration with the South African drummer. He had been friends with the late Dudu Pukwana, an altoist of almost unparalleled talent, and Pukwana's tune "Angel" is given a passionate reading here by two big fans. A tribute to bassist Johnny Dyani is similarly heartfelt, and "Free Mandela!" carries all the drive and determination that the sentiment bore when it was pertinent. The stamp of Dollar Brand is consistently present in Schweizer's performance, while Moholo miraculously keeps an African sensibility even during his most outward excursions.

For an unobstructed view of Schweizer's essential techniques, *Piano Solo, Vol. 1* and *Vol. 2* (1990, Intakt), are just the ticket. Like most other solo efforts by free players, a different aspect of the artist's personal vocabulary is demonstrated on each track, a virtual roadmap of her musical mind. Africanisms abound on "Sisterhood of Spit," a play on the Brotherhood of Breath; she reaches in and plucks the piano strings on "Chüschtenplötz," gets way out rhythmically on "Backlash." An honorable interpretation of "Ask Me Now" ends the second release on a fresh note, Monk being an influence heard too infrequently in Schweizer's work. An interesting comparison of techniques can be made by listening to *Overlapping Hands: Eight Segments* (1990, FMP), her duo with Marilyn Crispell.

Sclavis, Louis (b. Lyons, France, 1953): reeds player. In particular, Sclavis is one of the most impressive clarinetists in free music. He studied the horn from age nine, came up in a local brass band, and graduated from the Lyons Conservatory. Henri Texier was an early partner, giving Sclavis an education in musical freedom (*Paris-Batignolles*,

1986, Label Bleu, with American tenorman Joe Lovano). The young reedman also served time in Chris McGregor's Brotherhood of Breath. In 1982, Sclavis united with several other Frenchmen to form Le Tour de France and soon began making the rounds of Europe with Peter Brötzmann, Tony Oxley, Wolfgang Fuchs (*Duets, Dithyrambisch*, 1989, FMP), Evan Parker, and Lol Coxhill. His solo debut, *Clarinettes* (1984, Ida), preceded the formation of his quartet, which endured for several years (*Rouge*, 1991, ECM). Sclavis has composed theater and film scores, and has recorded with his own trios and septets, Cecil Taylor's European Orchestra, the Klaus König Orchestra, Fred Frith, percussionist Trilok Gurtu, Arcado String Trio, Ernst Reijseger, Steve Lacy (*Work*, 2002, Sketch), choreographer Mathilde Monnier, and various clarinet ensembles. He received the Prix Django Reinhardt in 1988 and the British Jazz Award in 1991.

Seamen, Phil (b. Burton-on-Trent, Staffordshire, England, 28 August 1928; d. 13 October 1972): drummer. He was one of Britain's greatest jazz performers until his untimely death at age forty-four. In the late 1940s, Seaman played in British dance bands, then moved into bop with Tubby Hayes, Ronnie Scott, and free-jazz pioneer Joe Harriott (*Free Form*, 1960, Jazzland). Harriott's band was perhaps the primary source of his exposure to free music; otherwise, Seamen alternated between playing hot blues with Alexis Korner, rock with Ginger Baker, and bop with Scott and Stan Tracey. He recorded a few albums as a leader, including *Now! . . . Live!* (1968, Verve).

Sharp, Elliott (b. Cleveland, OH, 1 March 1951): guitarist and bandleader. Sharp is one of the premier guitarists in modern music and an important catalyst of experimental music in New York City. He lavishly blends jazz, rock, and various ethnic forms into a sonorous stew of musical bliss. A prodigy, Sharp began playing the piano at age six and was performing in concert two years later. Eventually he moved to the guitar, which has remained his primary instrument, although he also plays bass and saxes at times. At Cornell University, he studied both anthropology and music; one class with synthesizer pioneer Robert Moog made an especially strong impression on Sharp. Later on, he studied jazz with Roswell Rudd and was advised in graduate school by modern composer Morton Feldman. He has explored the mathematical aspects of music, basing some compositions on the Fibonacci number series.

Since moving to New York in 1979, Sharp has honed his craft to a razor keenness while remaining open to new ideas. His debut recording, *Hara*, was issued on Zoar that year, and several other albums followed on that label (*I/S/M*, 1981; *(T)here*, 1983) and SST (*Tesselation Row*, 1987; *Hammer, Anvil, Stirrup*, 1989, both with the Soldier String Quartet). His ensemble Carbon (self-titled, 1984, Atonal) was one of the most difficult, adventurous groups on the scene. The more recent Terraplane, featuring saxophonist Sam Furnace, updates the Delta blues with postmodern trappings. Sharp's circuit of collaborators has included Bobby Previte, John Zorn, Wayne Horvitz (all four appear on *Downtown Lullaby*, 1998, Depth of Field), Eugene Chadbourne, electronic drummer Samm Bennett, Zeena Parkins, Guy Klucevsek, flautist Robert Dick, and Butch Morris. Sharp collaborated with fellow guitarists Vernon Reid and David Torn in *GTR OBLQ* (1998, Knitting Factory Works) and has worked with avant-rockers God Is My Co-Pilot, among other members of the Knitting Factory stable. In 2003, Emanem issued *The Velocity of Hue*, an astonishing album of solo acoustic guitar experiments.

Sharrock, Linda: vocalist. An unnervingly powerful singer, Sharrock's unorthodox technique includes screaming, narratives, and producing noise effects. She appeared with her husband, guitarist Sonny Sharrock, on the peculiar yet popular *Black Woman* (1969, Vortex); her wordless vocal acrobatics on the title track alternately clash with and balance his bluesy, powerful playing. They worked together on a few albums under her husband's name (*Monkie-Pockie-Boo*, 1970, BYG; *Paradise*, 1975, Atco) before Mrs. Sharrock took an extended sabbatical. She returned to form in 1986 with saxophonist Wolfgang Puschnig's group, the Pat Brothers. The partnership has continued off and on ever since (*Then Comes the White Tiger*, 1995; the ensemble AM4's . . . *And She Answered*, 1989, both ECM). Sharrock has also collaborated with the Korean percussion ensemble SamulNori (*Red Sun*, 1993, ECM). While she has tempered her rather extreme approach to singing, her music still remains somewhat of an acquired taste.

Sharrock, Sonny (Warren Harding Sharrock; b. Ossining, NY, 27 August 1940; d. 26 May 1994): guitarist. Sonny Sharrock was perhaps outranked only by Derek Bailey as the premier guitarist in free music. In his all-too-brief lifetime, he created some of the most incendiary sounds of the modern era, using his own slide method and an almost violent right-hand technique to paint extremely loud sheets of sound. This was a radical departure from the original direction of his musical career, singing in a doo-wop group from the age of thirteen.

Sharrock was prevented by asthma from learning the saxophone, and he finally took up the guitar at age twenty. The following year he was admitted to Berklee but was quickly kicked out of the school's guitar department for a perceived lack of technique and direction. Undaunted, the young man pursued a new interest in avant-garde jazz and played with tenorman Wayne Shorter's group. Some of his earliest gigs on the free fringe were with saxophonist Byard Lancaster, who gave Sharrock his first recording opportunity on *It's Not Up to Us* (1966, Vortex), and Don Cherry (*Eternal Rhythm*, 1968, Saba). Sharrock spent the next two years with Pharoah Sanders's band, becoming (in)famous for his legendary ten-second guitar solo on the title track of *Tauhid* (1967, Impulse). Sharrock took part in the sessions for Miles Davis's famed pastiche *Tribute to Jack Johnson* (1970, Columbia), though his contribution was uncredited. From 1968 to 1971, Sharrock worked with flautist Herbie Mann and is mostly remembered for another furious guitar solo, this time on "Hold On, I'm Comin'" (*Memphis Underground*, 1971, Atlantic). His wall-of-static outro follows a powerful but pretty straight guitar solo by Larry Coryell; Sharrock steps up and effortlessly peels the remaining paint off the wall with his flailing right hand and neck-climbing slide. Such full-bore assaults astonished even the punk generation, forever altering the face of jazz guitar as both a sideman and leader.

During a break from Mann's band, Sharrock recorded his debut as a leader, *Black Woman* (1969, Vortex), which featured the otherworldly, often grating vocals of his wife, Linda. Though it has perhaps not aged well and the vocals can be downright frightening at times, the album gives an interesting look at the full scope of Sharrock's interests. Among the personnel, largely out of their expected medium, are Dave Burrell, Sirone, and Milford Graves. As of this writing, *Black Woman* is only available as half of a 2000 CD from Collectables Records (the other portion is a generic soul-jazz set by Wayne Henderson and the Freedom Sounds).

After his tenure with Mann, Sharrock was off the scene for several years. His 1975 album *Paradise* (Atco) was not well received, and he did little recording until 1982, when Bill Laswell hired the guitarist for his conceptual group, Material. Sharrock appeared on *Memory Serves* (1982, Enemy) then was tapped for a quartet with Laswell, drummer Ronald Shannon Jackson, and German saxophonist Peter Brötzmann. That ensemble, Last Exit, presented Sharrock in ideal form, blasting away in the company of three similarly spirited improvisers. (See the entry for Last Exit.) Both Last Exit's debut and Sharrock's own outstanding return, *Guitar*, were issued in 1986 on Enemy.

During the 1980s, Sharrock recorded several more albums, usually drawing from his preferred bag of funk, rock, and freedom. *Seize the Rainbow* (1987, Enemy) featured two electric bassists for a double-dose of rhythmic might. Sharrock's final album, *Ask the Ages* (1991, Axiom), perhaps best illustrates the compatibility of rock and avant-jazz, an unlikely wedding that continues to light up the scene in the new century. The session includes Sanders and drummer Elvin Jones, both Coltrane alumni, and bassist Charnett Moffett. Despite the jazzy personnel, many of these selections seem more akin to the progressive-rock feel of King Crimson and Yes than to jazz, or even to most fusion. Sanders is absolutely volcanic here in one of the most mercurial studio performances of his later career. This session is a fine document of Sharrock's intensive quest to inject free music with the maximum amount of energy.

At the time of his death, Sharrock held down a most unusual gig, playing regularly with the "house band" for the half-animated Cartoon Network talk show "Space Ghost: Coast to Coast." He had just signed a record deal with RCA when he succumbed to heart failure at fifty-three. His biography is Margaret Davis's *Sweet Butterfingers: Sonny Sharrock, 1940–1994* (self-published).

Shaw, Charles "Bobo" (b. Pope, MS, 5 September 1947): drummer and bandleader. Shaw is one of the most flexible drummers in free jazz, bending to suit rapid changes in musical mood. Also trained on bass and trombone, Shaw was a founder of the Black Artists Group in St. Louis. He and other BAG members went to Paris for a time, where they performed with Anthony Braxton, Alan Silva, Steve Lacy, and other expatriate jazzmen. After returning to St. Louis in the 1970s, he recorded with Oliver Lake and later formed the Human Arts Ensemble with Julius Hemphill and the Bowie brothers, Lester and Joseph. Besides his own sessions (1997's *Junk Trap* [Black Saint] was a welcome return), Shaw has recorded with Frank Lowe, Billy Bang, Hamiet Bluiett, Defunkt, Leroy Jenkins, and others.

Shepik, Brad (Schoeppach; b. Walla Walla, WA, 1966): guitarist and saz player. Like Briggan Krauss, Wayne Horvitz, and a number of other improvisers, Shepik came up in Seattle's improvising scene before relocating to the more fertile fields of New York after the rise of grunge rock. After a few years of having Schoeppach mispronounced, he changed the spelling of his name to the more phonetically friendly Shepik. His earliest records came in 1993, first with drummer Owen Howard, then in the trio Babkas with altoist Krauss and drummer Aaron Alexander (*Babkas*, Songlines). The trio's exciting improvisations helped get them noticed around NYC, and in 1994, Shepik was hired by Dave Douglas for the Tiny Bell Trio, with drummer Jim Black. That group specialized in a fusion of Balkan musics and jazz, with often captivating results. Shepik has since continued his pursuit of Eastern European forms with the quartet Pachora, reedman Matt Darriau's Paradox Trio, and The Commuters. Shepik has done a few albums under his own name, beginning with 1997's *The Loan* (Songlines), and has worked with the likes of Charlie Haden and Paul Motian on various projects. The intense technical demands of Balkan music have given Shepik an impressive degree of fluidity and accuracy, characteristics that are truly prized in improvising guitarists.

Shepp, Archie (b. Fort Lauderdale, FL, 24 May 1937): tenor and soprano saxophonist, composer, and bandleader. Shepp was, all at once, one of the most commanding and criticized players to emerge from the second wave of free jazz. In the liner notes of Shepp's Impulse recording *Fire Music* (1965, Impulse), a robust document of his quest for relevance, LeRoi Jones stated, "Shepp is one of the most committed of jazz musicians, old or young, critically aware of the social responsibility of the black artist, which, as quiet as it's kept, helps set one's aesthetic stance as well. In this sense, ethics and aesthetics are one." A compelling poet, Shepp creates bold characterizations with his horns and pen, relating stories of blacks in America without straying too far into caricature or exaggeration. His poetry inspired later artists like Kamau Daa'ood and 1970s icon Gil Scott-Heron. Some jazz writers have postulated that Shepp was so concerned with being an activist for his causes that he neglected to produce good music in support of them. Further reflection upon the bulk of Shepp's output shows the argument to be baseless. He was one of the more appreciably talented hornmen of his generation, despite the corrosive tone on which he chose to focus. His devotion to musical and social revolution did not last through the 1970s, however, and the resultant sea change in his music left many previously devoted listeners perplexed.

Archie Vernon Shepp spent his childhood in Philadelphia, aimed to be a playwright and actor, and studied dramatic literature at Goddard College. Following his graduation in 1959, Shepp moved to New York to seek work in the theater. It was not until this time that he began playing the saxophone as a sideline. He originally concentrated on the alto sax while working in dance bands around town, but Shepp switched to tenor under the influence of John Coltrane not long before he met Cecil Taylor. Swing tenorman Ben Webster's stout, breathy delivery was also a big influence on Shepp's tone.

Taylor offered Shepp his first recording opportunity and an entry into the exciting new world of free jazz. The young saxophonist showed early promise on albums like *The World of Cecil Taylor* (1960, Candid) and drew edification from the maverick pianist's experiments. Shepp's playing already exhibited some aspects of the guttural, R&B-inspired sound that would develop more fully over the next decade to become his signature. The Taylor band's participation in Jack Gelber's play "The Connection" brought Shepp back into his comfort zone, the stage, which was perhaps a further inspiration in this time of rampant learning. (See entry for Taylor.)

Shepp remained with Taylor for two years before forming a quartet with trumpeter Bill Dixon, another of Taylor's associates. John "Dizzy" Moore on drums and Paul Cohen on bass rounded out the early unit, with one or two other players added as desired. The band mostly played beatnik coffeehouses and dives, building a small cult following. In July 1962, the quartet performed to notable acclaim at a socialist festival in Helsinki, Finland, and found themselves a regular spot on radio once they returned to New York. They played original tunes and works by George Russell and Ornette Coleman in addition to more standard fare. Their debut album, *Archie Shepp–Bill Dixon Quartet* (Savoy), recorded in October 1962, was a rather shaky start. Shepp and Dixon composed and interacted well together, but their improvisational ideas were not yet on level ground, and the rhythm section was ill-suited to their objectives. The addition of Danish altoist John Tchicai added much-needed vitality, though Tchicai also had yet to reach his technical peak. The unit gave acclaimed performances until mid-1963, when embouchure problems forced Dixon into temporary retirement.

With Dixon incapacitated, Shepp and Tchicai formed a new unit with ex-Coleman trumpeter Don Cherry, bassist Don Moore, and drummer J. C. Moses. The New York Contemporary Five debuted at a coffeehouse show in August 1963. Just a few days afterward, excited by their reception, the quintet entered the studio to lay down one track. A two-month excursion to Denmark cemented the NYC5's popularity and unity, and their self-titled LP was recorded in Copenhagen on November 11, 1963. *The New York Contemporary Five* (Storyville) reveals the weighty influence of Ornette Coleman, thanks to Cherry's presence and covers of three Coleman compositions, but Tchicai's lighter approach to the alto sax freshens up the sound and leaves Shepp in charge. Shepp's original "The Funeral," dedicated to the memory of Medgar Evers, was a landmark of his career, which he later transformed into a tribute to Malcolm X. Dixon's difficult composition "Trio" was a staple of the NYC5's repertoire. Also of note are a pair of too-short Monk tunes, "Crepuscule with Nellie" and "Monk's Mood."

In March 1964, Shepp reunited the NYC5 with Cherry, Tchicai, and two new members who had outstanding free-jazz lineages by then: Sun Ra bassist Ronnie Boykins and ex-Taylor drummer Sunny Murray. Trumpeter Ted Curson joined the band for two of the tracks recorded that month. Dixon's 7-Tette and the NYC5 split the disc; each band was featured on a side and no personnel were shared. Significantly, Shepp had top billing in his unit, indicating his desire to be more fully in charge of his destiny. Side one of *Bill Dixon 7-Tette/Archie Shepp and the New York Contemporary 5* (1964, Savoy) features Dixon's suite "Winter Song 1964," which bears some resemblance to Miles Davis's 1949 cool-school nonet thanks to Howard Johnson's tuba, Dixon's lack of vibrato, and the larger-than-life sound resulting from Dixon's expansive arrangement. Among the other performers are bassist David Izenzon, fresh from the Ornette Coleman Trio, and reedman Ken McIntyre, who had worked with Taylor and Dolphy. The Dixon material does not seem to lean far outward much of the time, particularly during George Barrow's mainstream tenor moments, but McIntyre's oboe and Dixon's smeary tone draw things further afield. With the exception of the nine-minute "Section III-Letter F," the 7-Tette's tracks are snippets that seem as interludes without resolution. (The CD reissue includes two fine alternate takes of the long center segment.)

The three tracks by the NYC5-plus-Curson are cut from completely different cloth, illustrating just how far Shepp pulled away from Dixon's relative timidity. Murray acts like a fourth horn on "Where Poppies Bloom (Where Poppies Blow)," which features some of Shepp's best arranging of the era. His low-blatted vamp, answered by the other horns, leads into a razor-edged solo that calls forth the spirits of bar-walking R&B tenormen like Big Jay McNeely while warping their memories with rhythmic ambiguity. Shepp was now coming into his own conceptions more, adding plaintive wails and growls at emotional high points. It is difficult to tell Curson and Cherry apart at this time in their careers, except when Cherry's thinner tone becomes apparent. Curson had been hired by Charles Mingus a few years prior and was specifically told to play like Cherry in that context. Here he was brought in as a "ringer" in case Cherry didn't show up. Curson ended up on two tracks, Cherry on the closer, and they never play together. The motivic analysis on Cherry's "Consequences" is a classic characteristic of Cecil Taylor, which Shepp and the others continued to use for their solo development. Shepp's gutbucket improv is anguished at times, boppish at others, unveiling the duality of his jazz conceptions.

Shepp's next triumph came in August of 1964, when he landed an Impulse recording contract through John Coltrane's assistance. As a thank-you gift for his mentor, Shepp recorded the landmark *Four for Trane*. As the title suggests, Shepp interprets four of Coltrane's earlier compositions under the new light of free jazz. His rendition of "Syeeda's Song Flute" is worlds removed from the childlike original (found on Coltrane's classic disc *Giant Steps*), with parts of the thematic remarks in half-time. Shepp's tenor is hoarse and abrasive, his solos compact and bursting with the guttural power that dominated his sound. No sheets of sound for him; each note, or rather each vibration, is selected for the optimal visceral impact. The band included several rising stars of the new jazz: Tchicai, trombonist and arranger Roswell Rudd, trumpeter Alan Shorter (the brother of saxophonist Wayne), bassist Reggie Workman, and ex-Coleman drummer Charles Moffett. Rudd's arrangements are what sell the record, providing plenty of elbow room for all the players, and his glistering trombone sound brightens an otherwise murky session. "Naima" (which was regularly misspelled as "Niema" on prior issuings) is retooled by Rudd to better suit Shepp's strident tone, and the fugal separation of parts on the introduction is a masterstroke. "Mr. Syms" and "Cousin Mary" are both coolly abstruse, delivered with confidence.

The most disturbing track on *Four for Trane* is the sole Shepp original, "Rufus (swung, his face at last to the wind, then his neck snapped)." Not only does the title play up the subject of black injustice, which Shepp would continue to denounce throughout his career, but the tune itself is wild-eyed, fragmented, the tonalities clashing, the tempo positively breakneck (no pun intended). Shorter and Rudd are missing, but the saxophones provide more than enough flesh. Shepp's solo is by turns plaintive and furious—at one point he literally shouts through the horn—as if he were expressing combined bewilderment and rage at witnessing a lynching. Tchicai is similarly inclined, echoing Shepp's hoarseness and motivic investigations at his own pace. Coltrane had intimated that Shepp's music was, to him, "another beautiful manifestation of the love of God." On the evidence of this album, it must have been a deeply passionate side of God, one that loved justice and hated oppression on cosmic levels.

Shepp's next recording project was a different animal, not entirely successful but a classic in hindsight. *Fire Music* (1965, Impulse) presented two (three, on the CD reissue) different ensembles in bold textural experiments. Duke Ellington's "Prelude to a Kiss" shows the tender face of Shepp, a face shining with tears and scarred from hard battles. His tenor blurts the theme out painfully as if lamenting a lost love. Even more demented is "The Girl from Ipanema," Jobim's bossa nova as enacted by the inmates of Charenton Asylum, as it were. The originals are no less creative. "Hambone," inspired by a television mime, bears a woeful theme early on, out of sync with the rhythmic base built by bassist Reggie Johnson and drummer Joe Chambers. Curson's solo is rapturously free, exhorting the horns to higher ground. The music takes on an Off-Broadway swagger as Shepp blares the blues. "Los Olvidados" ("The Forgotten Ones") was inspired by Luis Buñuel's film and by Shepp's participation in a failed urban-youth project. Its theme flits every few bars from hurried groove to long, slow tones. Curson takes a cue from "West Side Story," musically evoking an alley-way brawl. "Malcolm, Malcolm, Semper Malcolm" is a reinvention of the NYC5 theme "The Funeral," augmented by Shepp's new recitation for the fallen black leader. The ensemble here is simply Shepp, Izenzon, and drummer J.C. Moses, a sparse setting for the poem's weighty message: "We are murdered in amphitheaters, on the podium, on the Autobahn . . . Malcolm! My people. Dear God, Malcolm . . ." The final track on the CD reissue is a live "Hambone." It is as frantic as the studio take, even if the less familiar hornmen don't fare as well with the material. Baritone saxophonist Fred Pirtle does shine brightly; it is a shame he is so obscure.

Next Shepp followed up with what seemed like two collections of studio floor-sweepings, compared with the relative unity of *Fire Music*. *Further Fire Music* and *On This Night* (both 1965, Impulse) gather selections recorded between March and August of that year. The former album features the Izenzon/Moses trio as centerpiece, blowing hard on three takes of "The Chased" (a wry alteration of the old two-tenor chase recordings of the 1950s, perhaps). "The Pickaninny" begins with a hilarious chicken-cluck rhythm followed by caustic, double-stopped bass bowing. Shepp and Izenzon trace each other's leads well as Moses plays good-natured mediator. Shepp's solo nods toward "Reveille" and folksong. *Further Fire Music* includes also five tracks from the 1965 Newport concert. "Rufus" boils furiously over Joe Chambers's ride cymbal, and Bobby Hutcherson's skewed vibraphone patterns recall a computer gone haywire. "Le Matin des Noirs" ("Morning of the Blacks") has a sumptuous, modal vibes foundation. Ametric trippings introduce the cat-footed theme, then a funky blues feel ensues. Shepp does not play on "Scag" but instead recites a poem about the hell of heroin addiction as the trio clatters beneath: "Where tracks is, money ain't. It's all in them tracks. . . . There is the stench of rotted blood and dried Philadelphia clay." "Call Me by My Rightful Name" is an abrupt change of pace, a light-hearted frolic in 6/8. Even Shepp's sandpaper tone can't diminish its cheeriness for long. "Gingerbread, Gingerbread Man" is Shepp's bilious take on a children's song. While it is simple as a nursery rhyme, there is little of comfort to be found in its disturbing alkalinity. "The Mac Man" is an alternate take from the sessions for *On This Night*. The combination of Hutcherson's chords and Henry Grimes's forcefulness is particularly interesting. A pretty waltz section on which Shepp opts for a more attractive tone is overcome by an urgent vamp on which Ed Blackwell pounds rhythm logs. Shepp quotes "It Don't Mean a Thing (If It Ain't Got That Swing)" in the midst of swelling fury, egged on by Hutcherson and Blackwell.

On This Night, Shepp's third Impulse release, was in a similar mold. The title track is a tribute to W.E.B. DuBois and features Shepp on piano accompanying classically trained vocalist Christine Spencer. Ellington's "In a Sentimental Mood" receives a loving if rough-edged treatment, and "The Original Mr. Sonny Boy Williamson" is a disquieting nod to one of Shepp's blues inspirations. Blackwell and Rashied Ali distinguish themselves with their rhythmic facility. The CD reissue overlaps earnestly with *Further Fire Music*. Since *Further* has not been issued on CD, one would do best to purchase the CD versions of *On This Night* and *Live at Newport '65* to cover its bases.

Sometime in 1965, Shepp produced his play "The Communist" in New York to reasonable acclaim. That side step into the theater did not hold him for long; in February 1966, he returned with the live *Three for a Quarter, One for a Dime* (Impulse). Barely half an hour long—any more music at this intensity would be hard to endure— the recording features Shepp's new quintet with Rudd, bassists Donald Rafael Garrett and Lewis Worrell, and drummer Beaver Harris. Vibrant versions of Ellington's plaintive "In a Sentimental Mood," Shepp's piano feature "Sylvia," and Herbie Nichols's "Lady Sings the Blues" mark the comparative rest stops. The title track and "Where June Bugs Go" meet the intensity quotient, and Rudd's "Keep Your Heart Right" is a gem.

The following year Shepp's group became an eclectic octet with Rudd, Harris, Grachan Moncur III, soul-jazz trumpeter Tommy Turrentine, Charlie Haden, Perry Robinson, and tubaist Howard Johnson. This band recorded *Mama Too Tight* (Impulse) in August 1966. Its centerpiece is "Portrait of Robert Thompson (As a Young Man)," a mind-bending suite that covers gospel, blues, and free jazz in the course of nineteen minutes. The remaining tracks all relate to the main suite in some fashion. The paired low brass of Rudd and Moncur adds a severe kick, principally on the blues-laden title piece.

More lineup changes ensued following this session, with Beaver Harris now the sole holdout. *The Magic of Ju-Ju* (1967, Impulse) was similar in concept to the prior date, with a long suite followed by subsidiary pieces, but this time the multiple horns were supplanted by percussionists: Ed Blackwell, Norman Connors, Denis Charles, and Frank Charles. Trumpeter Martin Banks, trombonist and trumpeter Mike Zwerin, and Reggie Workman completed this powerful group. As can be gathered from the title, the main suite draws inspiration from the tribal drumming of West Africa, an influence faithfully realized by Blackwell's rhythm logs and the other drums. Shepp is more furious than ever on tenor, dominating until the trumpets wind things down in the last few minutes.

Shepp's musical experiments up to 1968 were notable for the lack of a piano player other than the leader himself, and that on scarce occasions. Free jazz is not particularly well suited to the chord-based temperament of a piano unless the player is of Cecil Taylor's caliber. Having worked with Taylor early on, it is likely that Shepp knew of the instrument's limitations in lesser hands and deliberately avoided it until he was ready. At that time, he hired Walter Davis Jr., a lesser-known but gifted bebop pianist, for *The Way Ahead* (Impulse). The title is ironic, since some of the music here is more rooted in jazz traditions than most anything else Shepp had recorded up to that time. Moncur and Beaver Harris are still present and joined by bassist Ron Carter, trumpeter Jimmy Owens, and drummer Roy Haynes, a trio of skilled musicians with few free-leaning experiences on their resumés. Davis's tune "Damn If I Know (The Stroller)" is out of the hard-bop mold, and Shepp settles in by drawing from Ben Webster. His tenor solo is thematically intriguing on Moncur's forbidding "Frankenstein," and "Fiesta" is a free-bop updating of Latin jazz conceptions. The CD reissue tacks on two tracks from February 1969: Moncur's imposing "New Africa" and Cal Massey's "Bakai," with Dave Burrell, bassist Walter Booker, and baritone saxophonist Charles Davis included.

Some of Shepp's strongest recordings are those taped in live settings where enthusiastic crowds egged the saxophonist and his sidemen to highest intensity. *Live at the Donaueschingen Music Festival* (1968, MPS) consists of one long performance of "One for the Trane," broken into two parts. Once again, the group included the paired trombones of Rudd and Moncur. Jimmy Garrison and Beaver Harris get rhythm duties on this searing marathon, one of the leader's finest moments on record. Shepp's free power is as astonishing as his sense of humor. His wit is most acutely realized in his subtle shift into "The Shadow of Your Smile"; he tries his best to cram in that kitschy theme but finally leaves it to suffer and die. Also outstanding in a different way is *Live at the Pan-African Festival* (1969, BYG), which finds him with trombonists Moncur and Clifford Thornton along with a troupe of Algerian performers.

In August 1969, in a flurry of creativity, Shepp produced three full recordings in less than a week for the Affinity label. The first and best was *Yasmina, a Black Woman*, on which he teamed with three members of the Art Ensemble of Chicago: Lester Bowie, Roscoe Mitchell, and Malachi Favors. Joining that unit on the compelling twenty-minute title track were Sunny Murray, Art Taylor, and Philly Joe Jones, three drummers from various walks of the jazz life. Murray was a Taylor alumnus, while the others had served with Miles Davis and John Coltrane. Another unexpected juxtaposition was Shepp's meeting with hard-bop tenorman Hank Mobley on "Sonny's Back." Two-tenor battles had been popular in jazz for two decades, but rarely had there been a stylistic clash like this. The disc closes with Shepp briskly navigating the tenor sax anthem "Body and Soul," with middling results.

Philly Joe Jones became a regular partner of Shepp following *Yasmina*, and he was prominently featured on two other albums in August 1969, *Poem for Malcolm* and *Blasé* (both Affinity). The former includes a rematch between Shepp and Mobley on "Oleo," written by tenor titan Sonny Rollins, and the free blowout "Rain Forest." By now the effectiveness of Shepp's poetry was starting to wane, as evidenced by the less-than-convincing title track. *Blasé* fares better, given the presence of Bowie, Favors, and Dave Burrell. However, the inclusion of two obscure harmonica players is questionable, and Jeanne Lee is not used to the best advantage.

In November 1969, Shepp briefly switched allegiances, recording *Black Gypsy* for Prestige. The move to a well-established bop label might have been another attempt at slowly moving toward mainstream acceptance, but the two long tracks hardly represented Shepp's finest work as a composer. Nonetheless, the ensemble bristles with raw energy thanks to the presence of Burrell, Sunny Murray, Leroy Jenkins, Noah Howard, and other fierce players. That month saw Shepp reunite with the master drummer on *Archie Shepp and Philly Joe Jones* (Fantasy), which accomplishes little despite the bracing efforts of Jenkins and Anthony Braxton. Jones sounds out of his element this time, leading to a sense of aimlessness, and Shepp's recitations drag things further down.

The leader spent the next couple of years trying to find a new direction. In late 1969, he recorded an album of tunes inspired by the African American Kwanzaa celebration for Impulse, but the disc was not released for nearly five years. *Coral Rock* (1970, America) was a return to form, with two sidelong tracks featuring Shepp, Clifford Thornton, Alan Shorter, and Lester Bowie (though saxophonist Joseph Jarman, Bowie's Art Ensemble partner, was erroneously credited as the trumpeter on the initial release!) Shorter's title track is awash in percussion, with bassist Bob Reid bowing a lament as Shepp wails wordless blues over a Sahara beat. The trademark Bowie blare erupts, and the other horns blow dissociatedly around him. Shepp's tenor solo is neck-deep in the blues, filled with yelps and screams. On "I Should Care," Shepp's hard-hit piano chords give the tune a Monkish revision. Reid and drummer Muhammad Ali stick to something resembling a swing feel as Shepp wittily trills and trips his way along. The other horns emerge in a New Orleans funeral procession, setting the stage for another humorous Bowie solo.

Shepp returned to Impulse in May 1971 with *Things Have Got to Change*, another politically charged disc with one extended tune per side. He broke that stride with *Attica Blues* (1972, Impulse), a colossal effort inspired by the infamous prison riots. Funky, jazzy, bluesy all at once, it is one of the most consistently interesting releases in Shepp's discography. Among the cast are Thornton, Burrell, Garrison, drummers Beaver Harris (the coleader) and Billy Higgins, violinists Leroy Jenkins, John Blake, and L. Shankar, Marion Brown, and two fixtures of soul-jazz: bassist Jerry Jemmott and guitarist Cornell Dupree. Cal Massey played flügelhorn and contributed some tunes and arrangements, and his wife, Waheeda, was among the half-dozen vocalists. For all of the album's political viscerality, Massey's "Quiet Dawn" closes the album on a hopeful note.

The positivity that began to creep into Shepp's music at this time marked the eventual end of his scathing socially conscious rhetoric. Besides the changing tide of American society, another mitigating factor in his paradigm shift may have been Shepp's professorship at State University of New York in Buffalo. Shepp and Massey produced the stage play "Lady Day: A Musical Tragedy" in 1972, a look at Billie Holiday's legacy that was more loving than politically irate. Shepp became more deeply interested in the music of Ellington and other founding fathers of jazz, which contributed to his further withdrawal from freer music.

In September 1972, Shepp gathered another huge ensemble for *The Cry of My People* (Impulse), a lavish overview of "trans-African" musical styles. Garrison, Harris, Jenkins, Dupree, Burrell, trumpeter Charles McGhee, trombonist Charles Majeed Greenlee, bassist Ron Carter, and a gospel choir were part of the undertaking. Shepp's "Rest Enough (Song to Mother)" and Ellington's "Come Sunday" bookend the other material with gospel overtones, with plenty of free jazz and funk to be found as well. Many of the same players appeared on *There's a Trumpet In My Soul* (1975, Impulse).

In July 1975, Shepp got away from the large-ensemble kick and assembled an outstanding quintet for the Montreux Festival, where two discs' worth of music was recorded. Greenlee, Burrell, Harris, and bassist Cameron Brown practically tore down the house on the crushingly emotional "Lush Life," Shepp's Kwanzaa-inspired theme "U-Jamaa" (both on *Montreux, Volume 1*, Arista), and other originals. The following month Shepp went to Italy to record *A Sea of Faces* (Black Saint) with the same quintet.

A further departure came with *Steam* (1976, Enja), a spare but commanding trio with Brown and Harris. Standards dominated the program for the first time on a Shepp album. Shepp's piano playing is almost as prominent as his tenor and more broadly appealing. In the absence of additional horns, Cameron Brown is pressed to provide a melodic foil for Shepp when needed, but he succeeds nobly with Harris's bolstering. In an interview with the French *Jazz Magazine* that year, Shepp seemed to concede that the political motivations behind free jazz, and the black power movement in general, had become all but passé:

> The black people of America have adopted a more "reflective" political position, with everything that word implies. . . . It's unwise to take needless risks, to make yourself obvious, to mouth off on television. That makes us vulnerable on every level, easily identified by reactionary forces.

From the spring of 1977 onward, Shepp concentrated more fully on mainstream jazz and standards, pulling back from freedom's tide. He began a long duo collaboration with pianist Horace Parlan with *Goin' Home* (1977, Steeplechase), a splendid collection of spiritual interpretations. In 1978, Shepp became an associate professor at the University of Massachusetts, a position that afforded him more comfortable income and further chances to spread the jazz gospel through tours and records. It seems ironic that, although he taught a course entitled "Revolutionary Concepts in Afro-American Music," Shepp's music in the future would hardly seem revolutionary in itself. Perhaps the necessity of reflecting upon the music's long, rich history brought him a new realization of its joys, and no doubt it helped to facilitate his continued movement away from free jazz. In fact, Shepp concentrated so hard upon the old guard of jazz compositions that many wondered if he had lost his way entirely. It took some time for his acerbic sax tone to catch up to the sea change in his material. This made for uncomfortable juxtapositions in recordings like the Charlie Parker homages *Lady Bird* (1978, Denon) and *Bird Fire: A Tribute to Charlie Parker* (1979, Impro).

In 1979, Shepp made a brief return to the avant-garde with his *Attica Blues Big Band* (1996, EPM Musique), featuring a thirty-piece band interpreting some of his most popular material live, at the Palais de Glaces in Paris. The session was not released until seventeen years after its recording, but its raw power was breathtaking and undated. Old friends and young lions abounded in the group: Marion Brown, trombonists Charles Majid Greenlee and Steve Turre, trumpeters Malachi Thompson and Charles McGhee, and arrangements by Melba Liston, Cal Massey, Frank Foster, conductor Ray Copeland, and others. Over a dozen originals and covers roar by in a brisk flurry of blues, funk, and mainstream jazz. This release is difficult to come by in America but well worth the search.

In 1995, Shepp was granted the New England Foundation for the Arts Achievement in Music Award, an overdue honor for a man who, three decades prior, helped to re-shape the face of music for all time. A hopeful sign for the myriad fans of Shepp's pro-totypical freedom was the release of *Live in New York* (2001, Verve), marking his long-anticipated reunion with Rudd, Moncur, Workman, and Cyrille. "Keep Your Heart Right," "U-Jamaa," and "Steam" are called upon once again, along with more recent works like Rudd's "Bamako" and Shepp's "Déjà Vu." Amiri Baraka is even represented on the robust "We Are the Blues," the power of his words slightly diminished over time. This reunion was not truly meant to be nostalgic, as evidenced by Shepp's tamer sax attack and warm vocals, but there is plenty of power left in these longtime friends. Whatever his future directions, the twenty-first century continues to hold much promise for Shepp and the musical movement he helped bring into prominence.

Shipp, Matthew (b. Wilmington, DE, 7 December 1960): pianist, composer, and bandleader. Shipp is more than a decade younger than David S. Ware, his regular partner since 1990. The age difference is rendered moot largely by Shipp's maturity as an artist. He exhibits a musical wisdom well beyond his years, which enables him to relate to more experienced performers as easily as he keeps up with new develop-ments. Shipp is viewed as a beloved icon among young punk musicians and fans; the patronage of punk singer Henry Rollins led to the pianist's freak explosion in popu-larity in the 1990s. As rooted in the bop of Bud Powell and Thelonious Monk as in the freedom of Cecil Taylor, Shipp has an immediately identifiable technique that meshes with Ware's heady abandon while keeping the music fairly accessible.

Shipp began studying piano at age five and was surrounded by jazz in his home even before then. In his teens, he played electric piano for local rock bands but kept an active interest in jazz styles, especially bebop. He was fortunate to study music with Robert "Boisey" Lawrey, who had taught the late bebop trumpeter Clifford Brown. Shipp tarried only briefly at the University of Delaware, eventually ending up at the New England Conservatory as Cecil Taylor had many years before.

Not long after moving to New York in 1984, Shipp met bassist William Parker and struck up a friendship that has lasted into the new century. Alto saxophonist Rob Brown was another early associate; Shipp's first record session was a duo with Brown. *Sonic Explorations* (1987, Cadence Jazz) bears all the marks of his future prowess. His technique is slightly unfocused at times but already impressive in scope. Brown models his alto style upon Eric Dolphy, leaping across intervals and skipping over the usual expectations of meter or bar length. The six-part title suite finds the partners experi-menting with scales, runs, and tone color with differing degrees of success. On the two takes of Sonny Rollins's "Oleo" and Bill Evans's modal "Blue in Green," Brown forces the melody into a corner and reshapes it around Shipp's new chord structures. Working without the net of percussive support, Shipp expertly provides the rhyth-mic base that Brown needs while offering vital harmonic buttressing.

Shipp began his association with Ware in 1989, taking a spot in the quartet with Parker and drummer Marc Edwards. Whit Dickey, who later replaced Edwards in the Ware band, held the drum chair in Shipp's smart trio with Parker. *Prism* (1993, Brinkman, reissued by HatHut) consists of two live half-hour explorations by the trio on which they delve into the most primal spirit of improvisation. Shipp goes it alone on the first part of "Prism II," poking and prodding until his partners suddenly bash through the veil and haul him away on their surging tide.

Circular Temple (1995, Infinite Zero) was the trio's next recording, a four-part suite with subtle variations between the segments, a favorite compositional device of Shipp. The dark, fragmented melody is reshaped, resized, morphed by each player in turn or at once and sometimes completely ignored in favor of focused group interaction. The second section, subtitled "Monk's Nightmare," is downright boppish in its phrasing, a mirror image of Shipp's vaporous Monk/Powell heritage. Shipp and Parker seemingly read each other's minds more often than not, carrying on a brotherly dialogue while Dickey builds up groundwork beneath them.

Rob Brown sometimes supplemented the trio, as documented on *Points* (1990, Silkheart). The bassist and drummer are as fanciful as usual on the four selections, and Brown is a vital coloring agent, but Shipp completely dominates the proceedings. "Piano Pyramid" outlines the continuum of his influences from Powell to Taylor, ending up with the confirmation that Shipp has become a remarkably original artist in his own right. The two long "Points" tracks are full of exciting but still rather unfocused group improvisation, something that the rhythm team worked out more soundly behind Ware.

The Ware/Parker association has been especially inspirational to Shipp, coloring most of his recordings. In 1994, he and Parker recorded the impressive duo disc *Zo* (Thirsty Ear), and from that point, the bassist has been one of his most reliable cohorts. Some of Shipp's albums since the 1990s have seemingly been constructed with an eye toward the symmetry and beauty of science and mathematics: *Symbol Systems* (1995, No More), *Flow of X* (1997, Thirsty Ear), *Gravitational Systems* (1998, HatOlogy), *Multiplication Table* (1998, HatArt), and so on. He has also performed with Other Dimensions in Music, Nommonsemble, Roscoe Mitchell's Note Factory, Mat Maneri, Joe Morris, and other freemen. Shipp is a respected producer, recently working on discs by Roy Campbell, Maneri, and Tim Berne.

Since 2000, Shipp has been curator of the "Blue Series" for the Thirsty Ear record label, presenting cutting-edge improvised music for a new, technologically savvy audience. His own contributions to the imprint have varied greatly thus far: *Matthew Shipp's New Orbit* (2001) is a phenomenal project with Parker, Wadada Leo Smith, and Gerald Cleaver; the follow-up, *Nu Bop* (2002), was a comparatively disappointing venture into synth-enhanced jazz but has its own merits. Shipp also collaborated with the rap group Anti-Pop Consortium to appreciable reviews.

Shiurba, John: guitarist. Shiurba is an up-and-comer from the San Francisco Bay Area, utilized well by Anthony Braxton in his Ghost Trance Music projects (*Six Compositions (GTM) 2001*, Rastascan). He frequently works with reedman Scott Rosenberg and the indie rock-jazz band Eskimo, and has recorded with altoman Jack Wright (*Rattle OK*, 2001, Spring Garden) and koto player Brett Larner.

Silva, Alan (b. Bermuda, 29 January 1939): bassist, cellist, synthesizer player, composer, and bandleader. He studied piano and violin as a child, eventually finding his way to the New York College of Music, where he took up bass for the first time. In the early 1960s, Silva gained an interest in free jazz, and he soon partnered with pianist Burton Greene in the Free Form Improvisation Ensemble. In 1964, he worked with Bill Dixon in the "October Revolution in Jazz," and the two renewed their partnership off and on until the early 1980s. From 1966 to 1967, Silva was Albert Ayler's main bassman, taking part in the important Greenwich Village concerts and *Love Cry* (1968, Impulse) sessions. He was also an essential part of Cecil Taylor's unit in its seminal late-1960s phase of development. The sheer power of Silva's technique helped him to stand out well from the melée in both the Ayler and Taylor bands.

Silva's ensemble conjured many sounds reflective of nature on the album *Alan Silva* (1968, ESP), his debut as a leader. On the twenty-three-minute selection "Skillfullness," he set aside his main ax in favor of violin, piano, and cello. The selection is broken into several vignettes, beginning with the duo of Silva's violin and Dave Burrell's cascading piano. Burrell evokes a babbling waterfall while Silva flits about like a happy dragonfly, or perhaps a mosquito. For the second portion, the leader switches to piano to accompany the flute of Becky Friend. Her horn is run through a delay effect, and this combined with her vocalizations makes for unusual and captivating sounds. Over Silva's jittery piano, the effect is something like a moth being chased by a playful kitten. The selection progresses in like manner, some pieces of the puzzle more musically seditious than others.

In 1969, Silva assembled the first lineup of his big band, the Celestrial [sic] Communications Orchestra. The group debuted with *From the Luna Surface* (1969, BYG), a rather spotty yet impressive document of his notions for ensemble improvisation and composition. In the early 1970s, after some experiences with Sun Ra, Archie Shepp, and Sunny Murray, Silva settled in Europe where he remained active as a live musician but did little recording. Along the way, he became fascinated with the possibilities of synthesizers, and eventually he all but did away with the bass in favor of keyboard performance. Since his reemergence in the late 1990s (*A Hero's Welcome*, 1998, Eremite), Silva has still concentrated on synthesizers for the most part but has returned to the bass more frequently. His most recent large group is the Sound Visions Orchestra, captured on a 2001 release by Eremite.

Simmons, Sonny (Huey; b. Sicily Island, LA, 4 August 1933): alto saxophonist and bandleader. Simmons spent his youth in Oakland, California, where he played English horn and alto. His earliest professional gigs were in the blues bands of Amos Milburn and Lowell Fulson, followed by some straightforward bebop jobs. He worked briefly with Charles Mingus in 1961, then met flautist Prince Lasha and formed a working friendship. They recorded two classic albums, *The Cry* (1962) and *The Firebirds* (1967), for Contemporary Records. In between those sessions, Simmons lived in New York for a few years where he gigged with Elvin Jones and Eric Dolphy. Upon returning to California, the altoist married trumpeter Barbara Simmons and began performing with her. *Manhattan Egos* (1969, Arhoolie) is one of his best classic sessions.

Simmons's career then faced a steady decline; within ten years he was all but forgotten by the industry. He performed as a street musician whenever possible and kept busy with other jobs, his full-time music career evidently done. His sole album in a span of nearly twenty years was *Backwoods Suite* (1982, West Wind). In 1992, however, Simmons was signed to Quincy Jones's Qwest imprint, a Warner Brothers subsidiary, and kick-started his career with a strong comeback, *Ancient Ritual*. In 1996, he participated in two sessions for CIMP, *Transcendence* and *Judgment Day*, which betrayed no loss of his former creative power; he played tenor sax exclusively on the latter album. More recently, he has been a member of Cosmosamatics.

Sirone (Norris Jones; b. Atlanta, GA, 28 September 1940): bassist. Under his birth name, he worked with George Adams in "The Group" in Atlanta during the 1950s and early 1960s. Sirone then moved to New York and encountered pianist Dave Burrell, with whom he founded the Untraditional Jazz Improvisational Team. As his reputation spread, helped by his powerful sense of rhythm and a vibrant tone, the bassist found opportunities with some of free jazz's rising stars: Pharoah Sanders, Marion Brown, Sonny Sharrock, Gato Barbieri, Archie Shepp, Sunny Murray, and Sun Ra.

In 1971, Sirone, Leroy Jenkins, and drummer Frank Clayton formed the Revolutionary Ensemble (see entry), one of the most inspired units of the decade. During the Ensemble's six-year existence, the bassist recorded with Jenkins outside of the trio (*For Players Only*, 1975, JCOA), as well as Dewey Redman (*Ear of the Behearer*, 1973; *Coincide*, 1974, both Impulse) and Clifford Thornton. After the Ensemble folded up, Sirone continued to gig with artists like vibraphonist Walt Dickerson, Andrew Cyrille (both men play on *Life Rays*, 1982, Soul Note), Roswell Rudd, Cecil Taylor, and James Blood Ulmer's Phalanx, which reunited the bassist with George Adams. Sirone has released only two albums under his own name, both long deleted.

Slam: British label, established in 1989 and administered by saxophonist George Haslam. The catalog includes albums by Haslam, Elton Dean, Paul Rutherford, Steve Lacy, Lol Coxhill, Mal Waldron, and others.

Smith, (Ismail Wadada) Leo (b. Leland, MS, 18 December 1941): trumpeter, composer, and bandleader. Like many of his AACM associates, Smith had a background in R&B before moving into free jazz. As a young man, he had also studied French horn and drums before choosing the trumpet as his primary instrument. His wise usage of space and silence, coupled with an understated tone, made him an appropriate foil for Anthony Braxton and Leroy Jenkins in the Creative Construction Company. Following their period in Europe, during which time he worked fruitfully with Marion Brown (*Porto Novo*, 1968, Black Lion), Smith returned to America and settled in New Haven, Connecticut. He founded his own label, Kabell, in 1971 and issued his first album, *Creative Music 1*, in 1972. Smith established the New Dalta Akhri ensemble/ concept a few years later (see entry for New Dalta Akhri).

In the mid-1970s, while continuing to work with Braxton, Brown (*Geechee Recollections*, 1973, Impulse), and European improvisers, including Derek Bailey's Company cadre, Smith studied ethnomusicology at Wesleyan University, which led him to write a book on world music. Smith spent a good deal of time in Europe, recording for labels like FMP and Moers (*Budding of a Rose*, 1979), and converted to Rastafarianism while residing in Iceland. At that time, he took on the name "Wadada." *Rastafari* (1983, Sackville) was Smith's first solid exploration of reggae-tinged music. Smith's principal project for the next several years was the ensemble N'Da Kulture, which included Asian-American pianist Glenn Horiuchi. He endured a rather dry period in the late 1980s and early 1990s, finally broken when he landed a position at CalArts in 1993. Since that time, Smith has continued to work as a leader in various settings, most recently with the Golden Quartet of pianist Anthony Davis, bassist Malachi Favors, and drummer Jack DeJohnette (*Golden Quartet*, 2000, Tzadik; *The Year of the Elephant*, 2002, Pi Recordings). Over the years, Smith has collaborated with performers as diverse as Henry Kaiser (*Yo Miles!*, 1998, Shanachie), African vocalist Thomas Mapfumo, the String Trio of New York, What We Live, and Matthew Shipp (*Matthew Shipp's New Orbit*, 2002, Thirsty Ear). He has also worked with his wife, poet Harumi Makino Smith, in live performances.

Smith, Roger (b. Crawley, Sussex, England, 21 April 1959): acoustic guitarist. Smith is rather unique in improvised music in that he specializes in Spanish acoustic guitar. The extra resonance of the instrument gives a dark, majestic color to his playing, even in extreme circumstances. His recordings *Spanish Guitar* (1980, LMC; expanded edition 2002, Emanem) and *Green Wood* (2002, Emanem) present some typical explorations. Smith has recorded with the Spontaneous Music Ensemble (*Plus Equals*, 1975, Emanem), John Stevens apart from the SME, and Steve Beresford, among others.

Smoker, Paul (b. Davenport, IA, 1941): trumpeter and bandleader. In the mid-1960s, the classically educated Smoker moved to Chicago and jumped into the city's jazz scene. Though he was not a member of the AACM, the experiments of that movement influenced him to pursue free jazz even as he was working in settings like Bobby Christian's big band. Lester Bowie's tonal manipulations on trumpet were especially inspiring. He returned to Iowa long enough to obtain his doctorate in music, which led to a succession of collegiate teaching positions. In 1984, Smoker cut his first record, *Mississippi River Rat*, for the Sound Aspects label. Two years later, Smoker formed his wittily named Joint Venture, which included saxman Ellery Eskelin, drummer Phil Haynes, and bassist Drew Gress. The quartet made a few comparatively straight albums for Enja (self-titled, 1987; *Ways*, 1989; *Mirrors*, 1994). Smoker has occasionally worked with Anthony Braxton, Vinny Golia, and various artists in the CIMP stable (*Large Music, Vol. 1*, 2000; *Vol. 2*, 2001). Now a resident of upstate New York, Smoker has also established a solid reputation as an interpreter of contemporary classical music.

Sömmer, Günter (b. Dresden, Germany, 15 August 1943): drummer and percussionist. A true veteran of Europe's improvisation scene, Sömmer has been extremely active in new music since the early 1970s. One of his best discs is a partnership with Leo Smith and Peter Kowald, *Touch the Earth/Break the Shells* (1997, FMP). He has collaborated with Irène Schweizer, Cecil Taylor, Peter Brötzmann, Mario Schiano, Jost Gebers, Conrad Bauer, Paul Rutherford, bassist Klaus Koch, and many other improvisers. Sömmer has only rarely recorded as a leader, his first album being *Hörmusik* ("Music for Hearing," 1979, FMP).

Songlines: Canadian label founded by Tony Reif. Their respectable catalog has included releases by Babkas, Dave Douglas/Han Bennink, François Houle, and Ellery Eskelin.

Spearman, Glenn (b. Oakland, CA, 14 February 1947; d. 8 October 1998): saxophonist, composer, and bandleader. Spearman's untimely death robbed the San Francisco Bay Area of one of its most promising jazz figures. He had begun performing free jazz there in the late 1960s but moved to Europe in 1972. For over a decade, Spearman played in France (with Emergency), the Rotterdam Conservatory, and on several tours around Europe. In 1983, he returned to America and met Cecil Taylor, then performed in both the Unit and Taylor's large ensemble. There he established a friendship with Raphé Malik and appeared on some of the trumpeter's best albums (*Sirens Sweet and Slow*, 1994, Outsounds; *Short Form*, 1997, Eremite), his mighty tenor tone grinding against the leader's brassy roar.

In 1984, Spearman went back to California, where he worked with several of his own projects including the award-winning Double Trio with Rova saxophonist Larry Ochs (*Blues for Falasha*, 1999, Tzadik). Spearman began his recording career as a leader with *Utterance* (1990) on Cadence Jazz, then was signed to Black Saint for a series of fine albums (*Smokehouse*, 1993; the catch-all *Free Worlds*, 2000). Other albums followed on CIMP, Red Toucan, and Eremite. Spearman and Marco Eneidi assembled the Creative Music Orchestra for large-band experiments in the mid-1990s. Trio Hurricane, with William Parker and drummer Paul Murphy, was another well-received project (*Live at Fire in the Valley*, 1997, Eremite). Spearman guested on special projects by Rova and What We Live, and taught at Mills College in Oakland for the last few years of his life before succumbing to cancer.

Speed, Chris (b. Seattle, WA, 1967): clarinetist and tenor saxophonist. Speed came up in Seattle, studied piano and clarinet as a child, and took up the saxophone in high school. At the New England Conservatory, he met guitarist Kurt Rosenwinkel and his fellow Seattlean, drummer Jim Black. In 1991, the friends formed the adventurous quintet Human Feel (*Scatter*, 1992, GM Recordings), around which time Speed was hired by drummer George Schuller for his big band, Orange Then Blue. Two years later, Speed and his Human Feel bandmates moved to New York City, where further doors were opened. Speed soon began working with Dave Douglas in the trumpeter's own sextet and in pianist Myra Melford's group The Same River, Twice. Speed and Jim Black formed half of Tim Berne's quartet Bloodcount, and also work together in a Balkan-influenced quintet, Pachora, and Speed's like-minded quartet, Yeah No. *Iffy* (2000, Knitting Factory Works) teams Speed with keyboardist Jamie Saft and drummer Ben Perowsky. Speed's employers have included James Emery, Jerry Granelli, Satoko Fujii, Erik Friedlander, and Mark Dresser.

Splasc(h): Italian record label. Administrated by Peppo Spagnoli, it is the primary voice of contemporary improv in Italy, having recorded all of the country's major free improvisers since 1982. Its massive catalog houses albums by Stefano Battaglia, Carlo Actis Dato, Stefano Maltese, Paolo Fresu, Guido Manusardi, and many others.

Splatter Trio: improvising ensemble. The group was founded in 1987 after saxophonist Dave Barrett met bassist/guitarist Myles Boisen and drummer Gino Robair at a performance of John Zorn's "Cobra" in San Francisco. The trio formulated a concept that included live electronics alongside their usual instruments. *Splatter Trio* was issued in 1990 on Rastascan, Robair's own label. The group issued four more albums up through 1995, when they broke up in favor of separate projects. In 1998, the trio reunited briefly, and an out-take collection called *Splatterarities* (Limited Sedition) was issued that year.

Spontaneous Music Ensemble (SME): group formed in 1965, originally out of the experimental trio of drummer John Stevens, trombonist Paul Rutherford, and saxophonist Trevor Watts. In that year, the three men helped establish the Little Theatre Club in London. The club was one of Europe's earliest venues for free jazz, and its house band, so to speak, was a rough cooperative eventually named the Spontaneous Music Ensemble. The SME's music was even less structured than that of most American cooperatives, fairly typical of the Europeans' emphasis on collective improvisation over structural considerations. Interaction between performers was the principal guiding force in the development of much of their music; no head-solos-head formats were to be found, even when the group referred to the methods of Coleman or Taylor.

John Stevens was the ensemble's leader-by-default and its most consistent member over its lifetime. The personnel over the years included the cream of the British crop: Rutherford, guitarist Derek Bailey, bassists Barry Guy and Dave Holland, tenorist Evan Parker, trumpeters Ian Carr and Kenny Wheeler, among others. It varied in size from the simple Stevens-Watts duo to a twenty-piece incarnation dubbed the Spontaneous Music Orchestra. At times, the SME has also included vocalists such as Maggie Nicols and Julie Tippetts, imbuing the group with deeper textural possibilities. At heart, the SME's approach centered on listening and space: members paying close attention to what the others were doing, following leads as inspired to, and allowing room for reflection and absorption. Wheeler, who had moved from Canada to London a decade prior, had never before played freely and was reluctant, but, due to Stevens's encouragement, he eventually became one of the strongest players in the British free movement. Evan Parker also joined the group, although initially he was intimidated by the more powerful company he kept.

For the next year, the musicians were extremely busy, performing most every night of the week and moving from the early theme-and-solos structure to more collective improvisation. Early in 1967, the SME began developing along similar lines to, but totally independent of, the AACM in Chicago, adding more instrumentation to build the variety of tone colors available. Instead of the usual style of collective improvisation, in which everyone played his own thing despite the ensemble's actions, Stevens emphasized the importance of listening to the whole collective experience and deriving inspiration from the group interplay. Unlike other collectives, such as AMM, each musician played a distinctive role within the ensemble while maintaining an individual voice in the proper context. This new approach, plus Stevens's adoption of a quieter drum kit, did not sit well with many members, who soon dropped out.

Withdrawal (rec. 1966–1967, released 1997, Emanem) is the earliest document of the SME, the soundtrack for a film now lost to posterity. Each pseudosuite resonates with strange, impromptu beauty. The four segments of "Withdrawal Soundtrack" feature Wheeler, Stevens, Rutherford, Guy, Parker, and Watts in slow unfoldings over glockenspiel patterns. The governing forces seem to be Stevens and Wheeler, with Parker practically hiding behind the others and Guy sustaining simple drones. Derek Bailey joins on the remaining selections from 1967, as the group reconsiders the root motifs of the spontaneous soundtrack in three sections. Bailey and (again) Parker are difficult to hear amid all the clatter and tumble, especially when Watts gets worked up on flute. Despite the unevenness of the individual contributions, however, the disc is a completely fascinating document of the general SME process.

Challenge (1966–1967) (1967, Emanem) was the first officially released SME album. It is a much jazzier release than *Withdrawal*, sensible given the specific purpose of the latter; it's like comparing Ayler's *Spiritual Unity* with *New York Eye & Ear Control*. There are definite composed elements to most of the music here, and the front belongs to Watts, Wheeler, and Rutherford in phases. The title of Rutherford's "2. B. Ornette" pretty much indicates the objectives of this project. Barry Guy is not present, replaced by Bruce Cale and Jeff Clyne. Stevens is in constant flux as usual. The difference between the two saxmen is specifically audible on the long final track on which they are the only horns. Watts gives off an air of confidence on alto sax and scrabbling, soaring flute, while Parker's own ideas comparatively sound held together by spit and tape. That disparity did not last long, thanks to the persistence of Parker and Stevens in refining the group's central objectives.

The mercurial nature of just what constituted the SME is apparent on *Summer 1967* (Emanem), originally issued in 1995. Most of the tracks are duos by Parker and Stevens, with bassist Peter Kowald joining the battle on a pair of longer pieces. The impression is that Stevens recognized Parker's uncertainty about the SME's methods and decided to sit down with him one-on-one for an improv tutorial. As the two hash things out, beginning with the five takes of the edifyingly titled "Listening Together," Parker seems to blossom like a daylily. By the time they grapple with resounding responsiveness on the "Echo Chamber Music" tracks, the saxophonist and his mentor seem to be on the same page. "First Cousins" and "Second Cousins" benefit from the daunting prowess of Kowald, who helps egg Parker on to new heights.

The presence of bassist Dave Holland adds jazz credibility to *Karyōbin* (1968, Island), one of the SME's most popular recordings. Such favor is only appropriate given the high quality of these performances. The quintet of Holland, Stevens, Wheeler, Parker, and Bailey do move further away from jazz elements, but the building blocks of free jazz are still palpable. Bailey rides in the back seat for most of the six-part setting, while Evan Parker has finally found the gumption to assert himself confidently alongside Wheeler. Motifs rise and fall as the band members weigh their merits, musically arguing at length over some ideas. It is never clear what the end goal is for the performance, however, and some might be disheartened that the session ends on a somewhat unresolved note instead of the hoped-for big bang. A minor quibble, however; this is one for the ages.

Face to Face (1973, Emanem) is a duo outing for Stevens and Watts. The recording session was a planned exercise in attentive listening and response, the two musicians facing each other and focusing as hard as possible on the information streams poured out. There were no other hard-and-fast rules besides that locked attention, and by the end of the recording, the experiment seems to have paid off. Stevens plays as nonidiomatically as he could in this situation, with occasional recognizable dashes of jazz rhythm leaping from his cerebrum, and on one section he sets down the drumsticks in favor of the cornet. Watts sticks to soprano exclusively, and his light, uncluttered tone mixes well with Stevens's equal reservation. The energy swells at certain climactic points, and when the men let things die down again, it's not out of fear that the whole mess will career out of control.

Quintessence 1 (1973–1974) and *Quintessence 2* (both issued 1986, Emanem) capture two halves of a 1974 concert, along with a number of tracks from encounters in 1973. The lineup for the big concert was Bailey, Stevens, Parker, Watts, and bassist/ cellist Kent Carter, and the intuition guiding the improvisation leads to splendid intricacy. Bailey and Parker are both equal partners in the venture by now, holding their own in the chain of command. Bailey in particular crafts all manner of surprises, taking the guitar into alien territories while exhibiting the highest level of musicianship. His occasional use of a mutant acoustic guitar, with sympathetic strings like a sitar, completely alters the music's texture. Carter's cello playing is impressive in itself, attaining the quality of Dave Holland's better work with the instrument. The concert is spread out across three tracks. The remaining selections on *Quintessence 1* are by the trio of Stevens, Watts, and Carter. The two takes of the drummer's "Rambunctious" are less than satisfying after having heard the larger lineup, but "Daa-Oom" has some great moments when Stevens ululates like an African native while pounding out faux tribal rhythms behind Watts's torrid horn. An even better version of "Daa-Oom," *sans* Carter, is found on the second album.

On occasion, a further dash of jazz validity was blended into the SME in the person of trumpeter Bobby Bradford. A veteran of free units with Ornette Coleman, John Carter, and Eric Dolphy, Bradford moved to England in 1971 and fell in with the SME circles. He made a couple of fine albums with the ensemble, now sadly difficult to come by. *Bobby Bradford with the SME* (1971, Freedom) is an excellent illustration of how well Bradford's jazzy sensibilities mixed and collided with the Europeans' mindset. Drummer Rashied Ali and trumpeter Don Cherry also spent time with the SME in the 1970s, giving the Britons a taste of how it was done in the homeland.

Starting in 1970, Stevens got the idea of augmenting the SME with additional players to change the nature of the music. The Spontaneous Music Orchestra, as the larger groups were known, was not your average big band or symphony, of course. Few visionaries besides Stevens would attempt a premeditated performance for thirty or more musicians, but on *For You to Share* (1970) and *Mouthpiece* (1974, both Emanem) he did just that. Unfortunately, the names of all the players on *Mouthpiece* have been forgotten due to poor documentation, and it is next to impossible to pick out individual styles among the horde of instrumentalists and vocalists. Perhaps it is best to just let the music speak for itself, which it does with generally crystal clarity. Stevens's conception by now has taken on more of a Euro-avant air, with the leader trying out various aleatory or new-music techniques to direct the performers while permitting freedom.

Plus Equals (1975, Emanem), the next SMO-credited album, united some of Stevens's workshop students with old improvising friends to create an excellent larger unit. Watts and Parker are up front again, joined by Nigel Coombes on violin, guitarist Roger Smith, and other creative souls. Coombes and Smith were some of Stevens's favorite collaborators for most of the SME's existence. The guitarist is a jazzier player than Bailey but has plenty of avant-garde thoughts running through his head. The bigger surprise is Coombes, whose lovely, lyrical facility recalls Leroy Jenkins rising above the boiling cauldrons of Braxton and Taylor. The forty-minute principal selection is built upon the foundation of staticky string sections and achingly held notes. Parker, Watts, and harmonica player Chris Turner offer some of the best instances of pure inspired reaction on this underrated set.

Emanem has long had the habit of combining tracks from widely separated time frames onto the same disc. Usually the results are interesting, sometimes maddening. *Hot and Cold Heroes* (1991) falls into the first pigeonhole, as it presents performances by the same trio recorded more than a decade apart. Stevens sporadically teamed up with Nigel Coombes and Roger Smith to form a very special trio edition of the SME. "Boileau Road" is a 1980 recording by that lineup, which, being hornless, reveals bright new possibilities for Stevens's ensemble concepts. The other four tracks date from 1991 and are actually less ear-friendly because of the major changes in the leader's fancies over time. The music is still intriguing but less melodic and relevant to the untutored. The addition of flute and clarinet to one track helps buoy things up a bit, but the stylistic progression from "Boileau Road" to "One for Terry Day" speaks almost of a devolution.

The final SME release before Stevens's untimely death was *A New Distance* (1994, Acta). The personnel on the last roundup were Stevens, Smith, and saxophonist John Butcher, who issued the disc on his own label. Butcher is a genius when it comes to extended techniques, such as multiphonics, yet he can temper his playing with a profound subtlety akin to Derek Bailey. He is a consummate purveyor of what has come to be known as "kitchen music," a form of improv consisting of small, untraditional sounds that recall the tinkling of silverware and plates in a kitchen. On this date, the saxophonist was high on mettle and battled Stevens and Smith with a frenetic tension through six prime cuts of improvised meat: a magnificent swansong for John Stevens and his inconstant brainchild, the SME.

Spontaneous Music Orchestra: see **Spontaneous Music Ensemble**.

Stangl, Burkhard (b. Vienna, Austria, 1960): guitarist and composer. Stangl's academic studies included guitar, musicology, and cultural anthropology. In 1985, he cofounded the Ensemble Ton Art, and in 1990, he formed a long partnership with Franz Koglmann (*A White Line*, *Orte der Geometrie*, both 1990; *L'Heure Bleue*, 1991, all HatArt; *Affair with Strauss*, 2000, between the lines). Stangl is a member of Polwechsel, Dachte Musik, SSSD, efzeg, and the chamber ensemble Maxixe. In 1996, he recorded *Ereignislose Musik (Loose Music)* (Random Acoustics), and in 1997, his opera *Der Venusmond* (2000, Quell) debuted on top of the Empire State Building. He has partnered live and on disc with Taku Sugimoto, Werner Dafeldecker, and koto artist Brett Larner.

Stánko, Tomasz (b. Rzeszów, Poland, 11 July 1942): trumpeter, composer, and bandleader. Stánko's earliest major association was with Krzysztof Komeda, with whom he worked from about 1963 until Komeda's death in 1969. The experience left a lasting cinematic imprint on Stánko's style as both a player and composer. In the 1970s, Stánko kept busy with a number of European and American performers, including Cecil Taylor's large groups, Gary Peacock, and Finnish drummer Edward Vesala. His career as a leader began with 1970's *Music for K* (Power Brothers), and his best work has been for ECM (*Matka Joanna*, 1994; *Balladyna*, 2000). Komeda has remained a prime inspiration for the trumpeter, who recorded *Litania: The Music of Krzysztof Komeda* (ECM) in 1997. His style as both a horn player and composer is somewhat reminiscent of Michael Mantler in its darkness and spectacular scope.

Stevens, John (b. London, U.K., 10 June 1940; d. London, 13 September 1994): bandleader, drummer, and percussionist. Stevens learned to play and read music formally during his time in the Royal Air Force, where he met like-minded musicians such as Paul Rutherford and Trevor Watts. When he wasn't performing with the RAF band, he and his comrades listened passionately to bebop and the music of Ornette Coleman, then a young American upstart.

After his service, Stevens returned to London, becoming a devout fan of master jazz drummer Phil Seamen. He frequented Ronnie Scott's club and led his own septet until 1965, when he reunited with Rutherford and Watts. Their group performed after hours at the Little Theatre Club in London's West End, one of the few places willing to support free music. This group evolved into the Spontaneous Music Ensemble (see entry), which Stevens united and disbanded as time, money, and personal interest led him for a couple of decades. When the SME was not his highest priority, Stevens dabbled in other avant-jazz musings like his Freebop band (*Freebop*, 1985, Affinity) and jazz-rock fusion with Away and Folkus. Aside from the SME, Stevens's most popular collective was Detail (see entry), a hot collaboration with altoist Frode Gjerstad, which was occasionally active until Stevens's death.

String Trio of New York: chamber-jazz ensemble founded in 1977 by violinist Billy Bang. His original partners in the trio were guitarist James Emery and bassist John Lindberg. Bang departed the group in 1987 and was replaced by Charles Burnham, then Regina Carter.

Studio RivBea: loft at 24 Bond Street in New York City, owned and administered by reedman Sam Rivers and his wife, Beatrice. It was the site of many free concerts, individual and in series. The five-volume *Wildflowers* record series (1977, Douglas/ Casablanca; reissued 1999, Knitting Factory Works) was taped at Studio RivBea during the course of eight nights in 1977. It was closed in the 1990s upon Rivers's relocation to Florida.

Sugimoto, Taku (b. Tokyo, Japan, 20 December 1965): guitarist and cellist. Sugimoto came to free improvisation from a background of psychedelic rock and blues, having played in the Velvet Underground–inspired band Piero Manzoni from 1985 to 1988. At the end of that period, he issued his debut recording, *Mienai Tenshi* (1998, independent). He took up the cello in 1991, but after one solo recording (*Slub*, 1994, Slub Music) and some work with the trio Henkyo Gakudan, he gave up the instrument. In 1994, Sugimoto formed a guitar duo with Tetuzi Akiyama, with whom he has gigged in America. He began to embrace the extremely quiet aesthetic of nmperign or Radu Malfatti, keeping the decibel level as low as possible. Since the mid-1990s, Sugimoto has worked with Otomo Yoshihide, Toshimaru Nakamura, Günter Müller, Keith Rowe, Jim O'Rourke, Kevin Drumm, Borbetomagus guitarist Donald Miller, and Burkhard Stangl. In 2001, he released *Italia* (A Bruit Secret), drawing from solo concerts in Bologna and Milan.

Sun Ra (Herman "Sonny" Blount; b. Birmingham, AL, 22 May 1914; d. 30 May 1993): bandleader, composer, and keyboardist. Rarely in any genre has there been such a colorful and enigmatic figure as Sun Ra. Driven by the boundless human imagination and pure creative energy, claiming to be a visitor from Saturn who traveled in a craft powered by music, Ra fabricated his own peculiar sonic universe. His innovations as a composer, arranger, and performer affected the spectrum of jazz substyles in his lifetime, none more than the nascent free-jazz movement.

Sometime after his expatriation from the Ringed Planet, the entity yclept Sun Ra landed in Birmingham, Alabama, and assumed the persona of Herman "Sonny" Blount. He founded a band at the age of twenty and spent a few years gigging around the Midwest. Early on, Blount was an appreciable pianist with a commendable sense of jazz history and practicum, capable of firm swing and imaginative improvisation. He was given a book on chords by a member of Erskine Caldwell's big band, with little instruction on "correct" ways to structure chord progressions. The naïve experimentation that followed skewed his artistic development, as Ornette Coleman's erroneous self-learning on the saxophone later led him to develop his own methodology. At Alabama State College, Blount quickly gained prominence as a star student, and eventually he was permitted to act as a surrogate teacher.

In 1946, Blount landed a job arranging and playing piano for bandleader Fletcher Henderson, an undersung great of big-band jazz. He spent about a year with Henderson's aggregation, bringing more than a few complaints from sidemen who griped that his charts were too damned difficult to play. Hardly put off by the criticism, Blount continued to develop radical levels of harmony and texture in his arrangements.

Around that time, Sun Ra's cryptic mythology began developing as Blount and producer Alton Abraham mixed fragments of pulp sci-fi, Holy Scripture, and Egyptian legend to form a mythical microverse centered on the bandleader. By the mid-1950s, Herman "Sonny" Blount had been forever transformed into Sun Ra, Traveler of the Spaceways. Ra soon assembled the first incarnation of his big band called, at its most basic level, the Arkestra. The name derives in part from Noah's Ark, which saved all of Earth's creatures from a great flood by floating until dry land was found. In like fashion, Sun Ra claimed to roam the galaxies seeking a sustainable homeland for the black race. His mythology was thus a microcosm, or rather an altercosm, of the American civil rights movement. The ensemble's moniker was frequently supplemented according to Ra's whims: Intergalactic Solar-Myth Arkestra, Myth-Science Arkestra, Astro-Infinity Arkestra, and so forth.

In the 1950s, Ra and his band performed around Chicago, serving as an early influence on the burgeoning avant-garde developments there. The music they created was unusual to say the least, blending atonal improvisations with straight-ahead swing and Latin elements, including large groups of percussionists. Ra's music was performable enough that he did not have to scrounge for loyal, functional sidemen. Yet the adherents who remained faithful to Ra for decades were fairly small in number and indispensable in successfully interpreting his music. The Arkestra's front line from the late 1950s on was the three-saxophone brigade of altoist Marshall Allen, tenorist John Gilmore, and baritonist Pat Patrick. All three doubled on flutes, clarinets, bassoon, percussion, and what-have-you. Bassist Ronnie Boykins was another key cog in the Arkestra's machinery, a technical virtuoso who interconnected amazingly with the bandleader. Boykins's duets with Ra, live and on record, were frequent highlights of the band's performances, on a par with those of Ornette Coleman and Charlie Haden.

Ra could be an iron-fisted disciplinarian, admonishing his subjects to renounce the world's vices and live completely inside the hermetic shell of Artistry. He frightened many players away but was instrumental in helping others kick their destructive lifestyles; for one, pamphlets distributed by Arkestra members led saxophonist Joseph Jarman to clean up his drug habit and seek spiritual guidance before he joined the Art Ensemble of Chicago. The Arkestra was a family in the communal sense, often all residing under the same roof to experience their patriarch's wisdom and leadership constantly. While Ra encouraged and provided ample room for individual expression, in the long run, his disciples conformed their musical efforts and their lives to his own whims and visions. His philosophy epitomized the idea of "walking the walk and talking the talk."

On July 12, 1956, the Arkestra recorded the sessions for *Jazz by Sun Ra* (occasionally reissued as *Sun Song*), which was released in 1957 on Transition. This milestone album, discussed earlier in this book, already bore many hallmarks that would make the Arkestra one of the most singularly interesting, if misunderstood, ensembles working in jazz: unusual instrumentation, heavy emphasis on percussion, sweeping charts that united old-school jazz theories with futuristic notions. (Some sides recorded from 1953 to 1957 were eventually released on the 1973 Saturn collection *Deep Purple* and under the alternate title *Dreams Come True*, but there is not much of free-jazz interest therein.)

Super Sonic Jazz (1957) was the first release on Ra and Abraham's Saturn label. Some tracks predated *Jazz by Sun Ra*, others were taped later in 1956, hence the slight changes in personnel between tracks. "India" instantly catches the ear: Ra's Wurlitzer electric piano tiptoes amid gongs and slowly rising percussion. Tympani conjure images of a rajah's procession through the streets of Delhi. The Wurlitzer's funky modern tone cannot be escaped as it complements Art Hoyle's countermelody on muted trumpet. "Kingdom of Not" has a tribal drumbeat accented by handclaps and a charmingly syncopated melody. Ra's piano work recalls past masters: Art Tatum, Ahmad Jamal, Ellington, and Fats Waller. Ra's compositions on this date were more complex than the hard bop that was taking hold in the jazz industry, a formidable challenge that his sidemen addressed fearlessly.

Jazz in Silhouette (1959, Saturn) extended Ra's big-band modernization with one of his most quick-paced recordings. The tentet's presentation is often beautiful, especially on the cool opener, "Enlightenment." Trumpeter Hobart Dotson is charming in a restricted Miles Davis vein, and Ra's piano is classily traditional. The Mingusian "Saturn" carries a sort of up-tempo tango beat, with hard thumps from the bass drum accenting the sinewy sax lines. A pretty, free-metered piano introduction brings in "Images" before the horns blow on the cool theme.

The most avant-leaning track on *Silhouette* is "Ancient Aiethiopia." It bears a North African caravan feel; Ra's piano ventures off the rhythmic path at times, and melody gives way to rigid drums, a lone gong bash, stutter-scraped guiro, and an exultantly exotic flute duo. Dotson takes a cloudy solo of long, thoughtful tones and motivic analyses over Boykins's ostinato, followed by Ra's piano improv, which slides between the beauty of Bill Evans and thundering atonality. The importance of percussion in Ra's overall concept becomes more evident on this session. "Blues at Midnight" is a different animal, a fast, straight blues in the old jam-session style on which everyone has a chance to solo at length. *Silhouette* is an excellent entry into the crossover of Ra's influences, the spot at which his cosmic interests began to bleed more deeply into his big-band sensibilities.

In 1960, Ra relocated Saturn and the Arkestra to New York, looking for better employment opportunities. Ra's free ideas left Chicago's jazz scene with a lingering impression of their vast potential, which Muhal Richard Abrams later blended with the innovations of Ayler, Taylor, and Coleman to create another new movement in jazz. Once in the Big Apple, Ra located an appropriate rehearsal and recording venue, the Choreographer's Workshop. This was the cauldron in which the Arkestra's creations stewed for years, often augmented by mammoth waves of studio reverb to accentuate the cosmic aura that Ra desired. The sound effects and tape manipulations of electronic composers in the day's avant-garde circles affected Ra, who easily translated these methods to his own work.

The Arkestra recorded one session for the Savoy label in October 1961, released as *The Futuristic Sounds of Sun Ra*. Tom Wilson, their former producer at Transition, supervised the production. Kashmiri percussionist Leah Ananda is featured prominently, particularly on "The Beginning," where his congas front a percussion ensemble that transforms Ellington's "jungle music" into something more primal. Bernard McKinney's euphonium adds a warmer timbre to the horn section. Ethnic flavors abound in other tracks.

In 1965, Saturn issued some 1961–1962 sessions from the Choreographer's Workshop under the title *Art Forms of Dimensions Tomorrow*. It begins with the sparse trio of Ra on "sun harp" and "spiral percussion gong" with Pat Patrick and Tommy Hunter playing "thunder drums." This is akin to what was then happening in electronic music and sci-fi soundtracks: Ra scrapes up small insect sounds and gongs; the drums, heavily processed into thumping echoes, beat out a far tattoo. The gong increases in force briefly but remains distant, the drums rise and fall in abyss-deep cosmic vibration. String twinkles from the "sun harp" appear before the galaxy recedes. "Ankh" sounds like an old Henderson swinger played at too slow a speed, a disconcerting effect. Ra's piano is grossly out of tune, building upon the nightmarish sound. Ra's solo on "Lights on a Satellite" indicates his debt to Monk and the stride pianists, and how far he had chosen to move away from them. *Art Forms* was reissued in 1992 (Evidence) in combination with *Cosmic Tones for Mental Therapy* (orig. 1967, Saturn), which contained five live tracks from 1963. Beneath all the bizarre sound quackery lay some of Ra's most intriguing concepts of the period.

Sun Ra Visits Planet Earth/Interstellar Low Ways (1992, Evidence) combines two 1960s Saturn releases with other material; the dates range overall from 1956 to 1960. "Reflections in Blue" (no relation to the title track of a later album) is a pretty straight blues with funky electric piano and Jim Herndon's wonderful, zooming tympani. "El Viktor" carries an unusually stiff beat, like a mutant tango. The seductive Spanish tinge of "Saturn" melts into a bop drive, an amazing feat of arrangement, and "Planet Earth" circles the globe to blend African, Latin, and Oriental influences into one. The tracks from *Interstellar Low Ways* (originally titled *Rocket Number Nine*), dating from around 1960, have a different flavor. Ra's piano is poorly recorded, the ill resonance wiping out note clarity, but the horns are scintillating. "Somewhere in Space" is assembled around a simple three-note motif, which clashes violently with the atonal harmonies and Gilmore's modal solo. The closer is "Rocket Number Nine Take Off for the Planet Venus," reminiscent of the old bebop novelty "Salt Peanuts" in its melodic structure and silly vocal lines: "Zoom! Zoom! RTA! RTA!" and the final shout, "All out for Jupiter!" It was here that the space-travel theme began to really saturate Ra's music, accompanied by his pulling back from the big-band traditions. *When Angels Speak of Love* (1966, Saturn) draws from further sessions held in 1963. The requisite reverb is still present, cosmicizing the drums and horns like an infinity mirror. This octet was one of Ra's furthest-out offerings, demonstrating the potential for free-form exploration within a composed structure for larger ensemble.

In April 1965, the Arkestra recorded *The Heliocentric Worlds of Sun Ra, Volume 1* (ESP), which became one of the band's most innovative releases. (*Volumes 2* and *3*, unfortunately, have been notoriously hard to find as of this writing.) The textural contrasts and dense complexity of Ra's compositions reached a zenith, and the band once again lived up to his formidable expectations. "Heliocentric" means "suncentered," implying that the world(s) revolved around Ra and his unique artistic conceptions. The track by that name is composed mostly of percussion sounds, with Boykins holding down the beat and the sporadic emergence of bass clarinet or trumpet. Out of nowhere, Danny Davis's flute sails in, like a bird lost in a magic forest, to which the trombonists respond with vitriol. Ra makes like Cecil Taylor on "Other Worlds," zipping through arpeggios and complex chordal runs that incite the band to an Aylerish intensity. The fearsome spatiality in "Of Heavenly Things" is only occasionally relieved by the tympani or bass marimba, then torn asunder by a sudden rush of brass and flute. "Nebulae" has inconsequential noodling by Ra on electric celeste; he gets back to the meat on the Mingusian "Dancing in the Sun."

The Magic City (1966, Saturn) further advanced Ra's cosmic atonality, embodied in a suite of nearly half an hour in length. It is a warped look back at Ra's earthly birthplace of Birmingham, Alabama, an important black community seat and the site of significant civil rights struggles. Marshall Allen's twittering piccolo weaves through the web of reverbed piano and Roger Blank's sparse percussion. There is no solid rhythmic underpinning at all, just continuous waves of improvisation directed by Ra's hand signals and keys. On occasion, the energy rises to the level of Coltrane's *Ascension* before the rickety scaffold collapses. A powerful baritone sax solo by Patrick is overrun by sax-section brutality, from which Davis runs blithely away. The final onslaught of horns wipes out the peacefulness.

On *Atlantis* (1969, Saturn), Ra debuted the Hohner Clavinet, a funky keyboard that later became a signature sound for Stevie Wonder ("Superstition"). It burbles skankily on "Mu," over faux tango beats and Gilmore's quiet, Indian-influenced tenor. The sound quality is terrible, adding a weirder timbre to the quacking clavinet (which Ra dubbed his "solar sound instrument"). These are said to be rehearsal tapes, perhaps held so that Ra could figure out what to do with his new toy. There are two different tracks called "Yucatan," one originally issued by Saturn and another that was included on the 1973 Impulse reissue; they are differentiated on CD by the issuing label's name. The full Arkestra is only present on the twenty-two-minute title track.

Singer June Tyson joined the Arkestra in about 1970 and eventually became sort of the ambassador to the audience, leading the vocal chants that became an ever-larger part of the Arkestra experience. On *Space Is the Place* (1973, Blue Thumb), Tyson fronts the Space Ethnic Voices and shares vocal duties with Gilmore and trumpeter Akh Tal Ebah. The twenty-one-minute title track is built on a relentless vamp over which the vocalists chant "Space is the place," as Tyson blurts arcane verse with oddly accented delivery. "Sea of Sounds" brings more group improvisation over a thundering mass of percussion. Ra sweeps his hands back and forth quickly across the synthesizer's keys as if he were punishing a chain of wrongdoers. There are also unidentifiable death-throe sounds, possibly from Thompson's overblown baritone.

The indescribably odd soundtrack to the 1972 film *Space Is the Place* (reissued 1993, Evidence; not to be confused with the above Blue Thumb album) contains all the standard elements of Ra's music in the early 1970s: repetitive vocal themes chanted by Tyson and the sidemen; traditional sounding swing-based arrangements for truly unconventional instrumentation; powerful percussion sections; Ra's progressive use of electronics, specifically the Moog synthesizer; and abstract, hovering solos from key players like Allen and trumpeter Kwame Hadi. Most of the pieces are under four minutes long, the main exception being the seventeen-minute opus "Blackman/Love In Outer Space." The music is eminently suited to the film, a bizarre cinematic spectacle about Ra's travels around the universe as he seeks a new home planet for the black race. In that era of oddball Blaxploitation films, *Space Is the Place* was the queerest of the queer. It started out to be a mere half-hour documentary about the bandleader from Saturn but was transformed by Ra's cosmic hand into something unique.

Ra engaged in similar experiments throughout the 1970s, stratifying Tyson's vocals with large volumes of percussion, complicated horn passages, and his own electronic soundscapes. He tried out new electronic keyboards as they came out, finding a niche for each of them within the Arkestra's massive song catalog. *Lanquidity* (1978, Philly Jazz; reissued 2000, Evidence) is one of the period's more accessible releases, finding Ra leaning closer to jazz-rock fusion. This is not, however, the kind of electrified music with which Miles Davis would have had truck.

Later in 1978 came an unusual venture for Ra: a quartet session with Gilmore, drummer Luqman Ali, and trumpeter Michael Ray. *New Steps* was recorded in Italy and issued on Aldo Sinesio's Horo label. The band boldly recorded Coltrane's theme song, "My Favorite Things," with Gilmore on tenor. Ra's left hand maintains the blocky bassline; his right hand thumps out broken figures like Monk with a hangover. Ray's muted horn offers commentary on the keen, masterful lines pouring from Gilmore's tenor, and Ali's drums bubble and swell in pinpoint reaction. A cover of "Exactly Like You" is truer to the jazz spirit, with straightforward swing and fine horn interactions.

The Atavistic reissue in 2001 of *Nuclear War* (orig. 1984, Music Box/Y Records) does not live up to the hyperbole. The title track is a seven-minute snoozer, an inane call-and-response chant about the effects of nuclear war: "When they push that button, yo ass got to go . . ." Other tracks suffer from Ra's choice of keyboard sounds. It is a shame, since this lineup was one of Ra's most potentially interesting. There is a return to prior form on the second half. "Blue Intensity" is a fun retro thing, Ra's organ nodding to Richard "Groove" Holmes and Jimmy Smith over the rhythms of Samarai Celestial and Atakatune. The chestnut "Shine" is interpreted weakly by Tyson, with shaky intonation and dry delivery.

In the 1980s, Ra waxed more nostalgic than ever, revisiting the music of Ellington, Henderson, and the vast catalog of standards with not only regularity, but also a more traditional approach to arrangement. His music began to lose its exciting freedom, becoming nearly kitschy in its content, and much of the mystique drained out of his live shows and albums. Most typical is *Reflections in Blue* (1987, Black Saint), a great ensemble effort that has little in common with Ra's past achievements. The title track (no relation to the one from the 1950s) dives into the rifftide to feature several performers in the solo spotlight: trumpeter Randall Murray, Allen, bassist Tyler Mitchell, electric guitarist Carl LeBlanc (pulling out an unexpected surf tone), with Ra's piano improvisations divvying up the shares. Though brilliantly recorded, this session typified the end of Ra's notoriety as a pioneer of free-jazz development. What original compositions the Arkestra did record from this time onward tended to be less interesting derivatives of their past accomplishments.

Ra's health began to fail in 1990 when he suffered a stroke. Two others followed this over as many years, and he was eventually reduced to minimal playing and conducting from his wheelchair. But the Arkestra lived on, in abbreviated forms, bowing to Ra's every command for the rest of his days. As might be expected, some later sessions hold up better than others. Many records took on the air of mainstream bebop or swing dates, with Ra's synthesizers simply getting in the way. An example of this shift is *Sun Ra Sextet at the Village Vanguard* (1993, Rounder) recorded in New York in November 1991. Most of these tunes might as well have been lifted from a good quintet date led by Gilmore. Ra finally gets his first wind halfway through, becoming more prominent on "Autumn in New York" and "'S Wonderful." The closing "Theme of the Stargazers" is the only reminder of the Arkestra's powerful spaciness. Recommended for the sidemen's uniformly good playing, but it's not the most representative or best Ra by any stretch.

Following further strokes, Sun Ra finally left his adoptive planet on May 30, 1993. He died nearly broke, but he was enriched by the love of his devoted sidemen and fans across the little blue globe that was his temporary home. The tradition of Ra's music is carried on by his devoted sidemen. Michael Ray's Cosmic Krewe blends funk and Dixieland elements with Ra's tunes and inspiration. Samarai Celestial and Ken Vandermark formed like-minded ensembles to advance the Ra legacy, and Your Neighborhood Saxophone Quartet and Trey Anastasio's Surrender to the Air have recorded apropos tributes. As for the Arkestra, it carries on with shifting personnel under the faithful direction of Marshall Allen.

One posthumous collection that is well worth pursuing is *The Singles* (1996, Evidence), a double-disc set compiling forty-nine tracks recorded between 1954 and 1982. Beginning with a pretty straight take on Gershwin's "A Foggy Day" and ending with the "Western Union"–style punctuation of the piano solo "Outer Space Plateau," the collection gives a marvelous overview of Ra's full range of work. Several tracks feature the Arkestra backing up unusual "space age vocalist" Yochanon, the "Batman" theme pops up unexpectedly, and blues guitar legend Buddy Guy joins in the fun. Gilmore's vibrant tenor is featured prominently throughout the set, and the intergalactic vibe of Ra's synthesizers permeates most of the second disc. Two CDs of Ra is a lot for a beginner to handle, but this might be the very best place to start learning to appreciate the heliocentric sounds of Sun Ra. Two recommended books are Hartmut Geerken's *Omniverse Sun Ra* (Wartaweil, Germany: Waitawhile Press, 1995) and John F. Szwed's *Space Is the Place: The Lives and Times of Sun Ra* (New York: Pantheon Books, 1997).

Surman, John (b. Tavistock, England, 30 August 1944): reeds player, synthesist, composer, and bandleader. He is an impressive performer on all his instruments, but especially on baritone sax and bass clarinet. Surman began his jazz studies in high school and continued his schooling at the London College of Music and London University Institute of Education. Some of his earliest pro jobs were with British white bluesman Alexis Korner and bandleader Mike Westbrook. In 1968, Surman issued his self-titled debut album on Deram and was named best overall soloist at the Montreux Jazz Festival. Like vibist Gary Burton in America, Surman found a strong audience among rock fans, a niche market he continued to satisfy in projects with John McLaughlin (*Where Fortune Smiles*, 1971, Pye). Later gigs followed under Chris McGregor, Graham Collier, Dave Holland, and Mike Gibbs.

In 1970, after touring Europe with the Kenny Clarke-Francy Boland Big Band, Surman recorded *The Trio* (Dawn) with bassist Barre Phillips and drummer Stu Martin.

The unit continued as a threesome for a few years, then changed its name to Mumps with the addition of Austrian trombone master Albert Mangelsdorff. In 1974, Surman broke new ground for all-horn ensembles by performing with his fellow saxmen Mike Osborne and Alan Skidmore (*S.O.S.*, 1974, Ogun). After that sax trio's too-short lifespan, Surman worked with Morning Glory, fusion bassist Miroslav Vitous, pianist Stan Tracey, and Azimuth with Kenny Wheeler and vocalist Norma Winstone.

Surman spread out in new directions after signing with ECM in 1979. His first album for that label, *Upon Reflection*, was enriched by multiple overdubs on several horns and tasteful, atmospheric synthesizers. Almost all of his subsequent recordings as a leader have been on ECM (*The Amazing Adventures of Simon Simon*, 1981, re-mains quite popular). His musical partnerships have included Norwegian vocalist Karin Krog (*Such Winters of Memory*, 1982, ECM), Archie Shepp, Pierre Favre, cool tenorman Warne Marsh, Gil Evans's British Orchestra, Lester Bowie, the Dolmen Orchestra, oud player Anouar Brahem, Christine Collister, and Paul Bley, with whom Surman has made several strong ECM sessions (*In the Evenings Out There*, 1991). While he has moved away from free jazz since the 1970s, Surman still regularly refers to freedom in his singularly ambitious projects.

T

Taj Mahal Travellers: Japanese improvising ensemble. Between 1969 and 1975, the Travellers were the Japanese counterpart of the Grateful Dead, performing extended, free-form pieces that united psychedelic rock and jazz, albeit with ethnic instrumentation and drones in the mix. The group was founded by violinist Takehise Kosugi, a former Fluxus participant; other members included trumpeter Seiji Nagai, guitarist Michihiro Kimura, vibraphonist Yukio Tsuchiya, bassist Ryo Koike, and vocalist Tokio Hasegawa. Their standard instruments were augmented with sheet metal, oscillators, harmonicas, and other sound sources. Most of their handful of recordings are scarce; *August 1974* (Sony/Columbia; reissued 2000, P-Vine) and *Live Stockholm July 1971* (Drone Syndicate) have become available on CD. After the group's demise, Kosugi gained renown as a solo performer (*Improvisation*, 1975, Iskra) and composer, collaborating with Merce Cunningham's company on dance pieces.

Takayanagi, Masayuki "JoJo": guitarist. Takayanagi, who began playing jazz straight in the 1950s, was well ahead of his time in exploring free music in Japan. His 1960s noise experiments predated those of Sonny Sharrock. He and Kaoru Abe recorded the important session *Kaitai Teki Kohkan: New Direction* (2000, DIW) in 1970. Two more DIW reissues, *Mass Projection* and *Gradually Projection* (both 2001) also present Abe and JoJo in a powerful live context. The groundbreaking *Call in Question* (1996, PSF) was recorded in 1971 with Takayanagi's New Direction Unit. When he passed away in 1996, the Flying Luttenbachers recorded *Tribute to Masayuki Takayanagi* (Grob).

Tammen, Hans: guitarist. Tammen is a serious experimenter in the Keith Rowe mold, altering his guitar's tonal qualities and engaging in multimedia and environmental events. In the early 1970s, he played both rock and classical guitar, but hearing Sonny Sharrock with Herbie Mann's band led him to explore other forms. Tammen has variously dabbled in swing, free jazz, bebop, and contemporary avant-garde music. He utilizes specialized software in live performances and has even bowed his guitar with pieces of styrofoam. *Endangered Guitar* (1998, Nur/Nicht/Nur) gives a good impression of his aesthetic. He has performed and recorded with Denman Maroney (*Billabong*, 1999, Potlatch), the Statements Quintet, Dominic Duval (*The Road Bends Here*, 1999, Leo Lab), Herb Robertson (*Music for Long Attention Spans*, 2000, Leo), and a number of European creative musicians.

Tapscott, Horace (d. 27 February 1999): pianist, composer, and bandleader; perhaps the most consequential figure in West Coast free jazz following Ornette Coleman's move to New York. A forceful pianist in the Thelonious Monk mold, Tapscott was a beloved mentor to a number of younger players, including saxophonists Azar Lawrence and Arthur Blythe. Tapscott and several friends formed the Union of God's Musicians and Artists Ascension (UGMAA) in 1961, four years before the AACM came into being. UGMAA's mission was basically the same as the subsequent collectives, to find solid work and promotional opportunities for creative black musicians. The collective's main satellite band was Tapscott's Pan-Afrikan People's Arkestra, a group with shifting personnel that performed his finely crafted compositions and arrangements.

Tapscott's first recording was the seminal *The Giant Is Awakened* (1969, Flying Dutchman), unfortunately unavailable. Blythe was featured prominently in the ensemble, negotiating the leader's compositions with confident ease. This session was briefly available on CD under the title *West Coast Hot* (1991, Novus), paired with a date by Bradford and Carter, but that too is now deleted. In fact, aside from a number of albums for the small Nimbus label, most of Tapscott's recorded output is no longer available. It's a sad testimony to his underappreciation that began in the 1970s, as his social activism cost him playing opportunities. A steady gig at the Troubadour in L.A. was barely enough to keep Tapscott afloat, along with occasional church or Parks and Rec concerts. When he decided to revive the Arkestra around 1977, Tapscott revamped the concept to include poetry and dance, an interdisciplinary effort that offered more opportunities to local performers.

The best of Tapscott's recordings with the Arkestra can still be found from time to time. *The Call* (1978, Nimbus) is a fairly good representation of the Arkestra's sound. One striking feature is the complete absence of any trumpets, almost heretical for a large jazz ensemble. The group includes six reeds, two trombones, tuba, cello, two pianos, two basses, drums, and percussion. Altoist Michael Session and tuba/bass player Red Callender are among the featured performers. The centerpiece is "Nakatini Suite" by Cal Massey, a former collaborator of Coltrane and Shepp. *Flight 17* (1978) and *Live at the IUCC* (1979, both Nimbus) are equally fine. The former features excellent solos by the leader, while the personnel shifts from tune to tune on the latter to surprisingly good effect. Other issues of note are the seven volumes of *The Tapscott Sessions* (1981–1984, Nimbus), two volumes of *The Dark Tree* (1989, HatArt), and two later releases on Arabesque, *aiee! The Phantom* (1995) and *Thoughts of Dar es Salaam* (1997). The last two albums marked a comeback for the iconoclastic pianist, who was just beginning to reclaim some limelight when he passed away from lung cancer. Steven Isoardi edited Tapscott's autobiography, *Songs of the Unsung: The Musical and Social Journey of Horace Tapscott* (New York: Duke University Press, 2000).

Tarasov, Vladimir (b. 29 June 1947): percussionist, one of the founding members of the G-T-Ch Trio (see entry). Since his work with G-T-Ch, Tarasov has recorded several solo albums, the *Atto* series, for Sonore. On these discs, he again distinguishes himself as a nonpareil percussionist with incredible polyrhythmic ideas.

Taylor, Cecil (b. Long Island City, NY, 25 March 1929): pianist, composer, poet, and bandleader. Taylor was in several ways a unique figure in the nascent free-jazz movement, partly in that he came from a clear-cut academic background in music without the anticipated life experience of playing in blues and R&B bands. Though he became notorious for his outspokenly Afrocentric views of musical history, Taylor initially had a deep-seated interest in twentieth-century Western classicism: the works of Igor Stravinsky, Bela Bartók, and French impressionists like Darius Milhaud and Claude Debussy. He also intensely studied the time manipulations and ethnic references of cool jazz pianist Dave Brubeck, who was himself a student of Milhaud.

The combining of classicism, jazz traditionalism, and his own unique conceptions has made Taylor's body of work matchless and seriously controversial. Given the geodesic intricacies of his compositions, Taylor, like his idol Monk before him, has had to rely on a small but devoted core of gifted sidemen for support in settings beyond solo recitals. Because his concepts have been pretty well set in stone since the 1960s, much ado has been made in recent years of his perceived lack of stylistic evolution. The point is moot: Taylor has been so far ahead of his time for so long, the rest of the world has yet to catch up with him.

Taylor's genealogy was a distinctive blend of black, Scottish, and American Indian roots. He studied piano from age five and later took up percussion as well, which had a noticeable and lasting impact on his piano playing. His mother, a pianist herself, encouraged him to study music as a serious vocation. This was another anomaly in the jazz scene, as so many musicians took up the career over their parents' declamations about dead bodies.

In 1950, after some studies at the New York College of Music, Taylor moved to Boston to attend the New England Conservatory, where he studied piano, composition, harmony, and arranging. There he listened intently to new modern jazz recordings by Erroll Garner, Lennie Tristano, Horace Silver, Thelonious Monk, and other pianists. He especially favored the keyboard techniques of Monk, Ellington, and Fats Waller, influences that are still audible in his work today. He also kindled a deep fondness for poetry, ballet, and opera, which would inform his own musical performances. Taylor began to develop his own highly unorthodox piano technique, which contradicted the "proper" methods he was being taught at the Conservatory. He adopted the position that any technique that produces musical sounds is acceptable, whether or not it conforms to instituted traditions for the instrument in question. He savored both creativity and tradition in the arts without contradiction. Though he admired John Cage's conceptions, he looked upon Cage's fawning acolytes with disdain because they chose to simply imitate their chieftain instead of advancing their own ideas. Taylor also disagreed with Cage's contempt for improvisation, and he took the music establishment to task for its ignorant denial of the aesthetic beauties of the black culture's music. Taylor's attitudes toward the status quo gained him few friends, his musical approach even fewer, but those perspectives played a principal role in shaping both the man and his art. In time, Taylor turned his back on most Eurocentric ideas of musical formality, which he has discounted due to a belief that the roots of all Western music were planted in Africa. He developed a style more suggestive of percussion than piano, treating the keyboard like, as author Valerie Wilmer put it, "eighty-eight tuned drums." Taylor uses his instrument to create variegated hues and textures, as a painter might with gesso and gouache, putting down layer upon layer according to the sweet inspiration of the moment.

After graduating from the Conservatory, Taylor began to expand on his own ideas in jazz contexts. He got unlikely gigs with the bands of Johnny Hodges, the renowned alto saxophonist from Duke Ellington's orchestra, and trumpeter Hot Lips Page. Taylor briefly had a group with vibraphonist Earl Griffiths, but after its demise, he formed a quartet with some adventurous young New Yorkers: bassist Buell Neidlinger, West Indian-born drummer Denis Charles, and soprano saxophonist Steve Lacy, a former Dixieland musician who was outgrowing the footprints of his idol, Sidney Bechet. As he taught them the new principles he had begun to develop, from this motley assemblage Taylor shaped one of the most empathic, innovative, and misunderstood units in modern jazz. Lacy in particular was a rare commodity, the first jazzman to specialize in the soprano sax since Bechet in the 1920s.

Nineteen fifty-six was a banner year for Taylor. The quartet recorded their first album, *Jazz Advance!*, for the Boston label Transition (discussed in the front matter) on December 10, 1955. It received mixed reviews; some lauded the pianist as a prophet, others as a quack with worse rhythmic sense than Monk. Soon the band landed a six-week engagement at the Five Spot in New York, starting the tradition of avant-garde jazz there. The following year, Taylor and company made a controversial showing at the Newport Jazz Festival, and in February 1958, the band played their first concert hall set at Cooper Union in New York. These were prestigious opportunities, but for the most part, the audiences just didn't understand. Taylor started getting used to uphill battles.

In June 1958, Taylor cut *Looking Ahead!* for Contemporary, the California label that gave Ornette Coleman his first shot at recorded immortality that same year. Neidlinger and Charles completed the rhythm section, but Earl Griffiths replaced Steve Lacy in the fourth chair. It is unique in Taylor's catalog, sad since the vibes-piano combo worked so well at this stage of the leader's development. Monk and the classical avant-garde meet up in the opening track, the starkly minor "Luyah! The Glorious Step." Taylor's comping behind Griffith's solo is marvelous, as he sculpts little thematic noodles out of the dough kneaded by the vibes. The pianist's note clusters on "Of What" are prophetic of his impending move into theme-and-variations analysis that would become a Taylor hallmark. Other tracks are all homages to the earlier spirit of jazz. The piano on "Toll" flits between Monk and the stride of James P. Johnson, but the immediate switch to atonality dampens the nostalgic spirit. "Wallering," intended as a tribute to Fats Waller, reduces the stride-piano aesthetic to its bare bones, while "Excursion on a Wobbly Rail" futurizes the Duke Ellington legacy by revamping the rail-ride groove of "Take the 'A' Train."

In October 1958, Taylor joined hard-bop trumpeter Kenny Dorham, tenor saxophonist John Coltrane, bassist Chuck Israels, and drummer Louis Hayes for a largely unsatisfactory date. *Hard Driving Jazz* (United Artists) has been reissued under the saxophonist's name as *Coltrane Time* on a few occasions, most notably on Blue Note, but Taylor was the original session leader. Coltrane and Dorham were rumored to have been hired for the date to help sales; in fact, Ted Curson was the first choice for trumpeter. It is said that Dorham clashed repeatedly with both the pianist and tenorman over the direction that the set should take, so Dorham stuck to the kind of bop he excelled at, making little attempt to go with the others' flow. The spirit of the original title is reflected in the two driving-related originals, Dorham's "Shifting Down" and Israels' "Double Clutching"; also included are uncomfortable versions of "Just Friends" and "Like Someone in Love." The record is interesting as a historical piece, the first meeting of two minds that would later come to define free jazz, but in 1958, their individual conceptions were simply incompatible and Dorham's unbending presence didn't help.

The follow-up album for United Artists, *Love for Sale* (1959, reissued 1998, Blue Note), was not nearly as disappointing. Taylor, Neidlinger, and Charles reinvented three Cole Porter tunes, devoting special attention to the rhythmic structures rather than the chords. "Get out of Town" begins ear-catchingly, with heavy-handed six-note figures breaking up the melody. Trumpeter Ted Curson and tenorman Bill Barron join in on the three originals. The bass/piano counterpoint on "Little Lees (Louise)" is a special highlight of this frequently overlooked session.

Despite the exposure that Taylor received through his first few albums and widely discussed concerts, the audience for his music did not grow at an appreciable rate, and further work opportunities became rare. Some of the band's next recordings were issued under Buell Neidlinger's name, because Taylor was *persona non grata* in certain circles. The members also found occasional work in Jack Gelber's legendary jazz-and-drugs play "The Connection," which constantly rotated musicians in and out of its combination cast and pit band. In that show, Taylor made the acquaintance of tenorman Archie Shepp, who would play a significant role in his next couple of projects.

One of the Candid albums issued under Neidlinger's name was *New York City R&B*, recorded in January 1961. The visionary release included four tracks centered on Taylor, Neidlinger, and drummer Billy Higgins. That trio plays on "O.P.," the bassist's tribute to bebop figure Oscar Pettiford, and "Cindy's Main Mood," which is loosely based upon "I Got Rhythm" (as were, ironically, so many of the bebop chestnuts that Taylor was trying to rise beyond). Shepp was added on "Cell Walk for Celeste," which has a magnificent orchestration that reveals itself through close listening. Shepp's hard-core approach to the tenor sax was not yet in full bloom, but his promise as an eventual powerhouse was beginning to bud. Shepp was also on board for a remarkable take on Ellington's "Things Ain't What They Used To Be," which also added Lacy, trombonist Roswell Rudd, baritone saxman Charles Davis, and ex-Ellington trumpeter Clark Terry. Though Taylor had drastically reinvented the piece, his love for Ellington's genius is indisputable.

The World of Cecil Taylor (1960, Candid) is not quite as satisfying as the above album, but it illustrates further how admirably Taylor's concepts were evolving. The originals "Air," "E.B.," and "Port of Call" share the bill with two brilliant covers, "Lazy Afternoon" and the Rodgers and Hammerstein ballad "This Nearly Was Mine."

Several tracks show off Shepp's singular flair at twenty-three, and show how well this group had learned to mesh. A companion album, *Air*, includes "Port of Call," two takes of "Number One," and three takes of the title track.

Taylor received moral support from some musicians who recognized his genius when the booking agents did not. In 1961, Impulse released the album *Into the Hot* under the name of arranger/bandleader Gil Evans, though Evans had nothing to do with the music: half of the disc featured Taylor's band, the other half a cool-jazz group led by trumpeter Johnny Carisi. Evans clearly saw the need for Taylor's music to be brought to a wider audience, and he arranged for the sessions to be released under his own, more marketable name. Perhaps this was not the most upright example of music marketing, but it got Taylor's musings into a few more hands. Taylor's septet on the date included Rudd, Shepp, Curson, altoist Jimmy Lyons, bassist Henry Grimes, and drummer Sunny Murray. The three Taylor compositions "Pots," "Bulbs," and "Mixed" sound otherworldly compared with Carisi's cool-based trio of tunes, and the tones of Shepp and Curson all but steal the show. These tracks were briefly reissued on CD as *Mixed* along with some other Rudd material.

Despite the well-intentioned efforts of friends like Evans, times remained strenuous for the pianist. A few critics offered sporadic praise, but promoters and booking agents avoided him like the plague. A.B. Spellman's *Four Live in the Bebop Business* details the hypocrisy of clubowners like the Five Spot's Joe Termini, who was hesitant to book Taylor because he thought drinks didn't sell during two-hour sets, even though Taylor invariably packed his house to overflowing. In 1962, Taylor did receive an award from *Down Beat*, hailing him as the best new piano star of the year. Ironically, at that time he was unemployed as a musician and working as a dishwasher. Later that year, Taylor embarked on a tour of Scandinavia with his group, including Lyons and Murray. He also worked with Albert Ayler during this time, though there is no recorded evidence. Typical of European audiences, the people were more open and accepting of Taylor's innovative music than the jazz fans at home. But instead of expatriating to Paris or Scandinavia as many of his countrymen had done, Taylor returned to America when the tour was over, his sense of home overriding his disillusionment.

November 1962 found Taylor at the Café Montmartre in Copenhagen, Denmark, laying down a landmark performance issued as *Nefertiti, the Beautiful One Has Come* (1962, Freedom; also issued as *Trance*). The recording quality is muddy (an alternate take of "Call" is almost unlistenable), but Lyons shines like a supernova. His Parker-bred tone blends surprisingly well into the Taylor *oeuvre*, and, in fact, the opening notes of "Call" could be mistaken for a Bird recording from the late 1940s. Murray is also vibrant, showing the unfettered conception of percussion that made him a luminary of free jazz over the next several years. He ensures that the pulse is always present, no matter how many washes of sound he might lay over it.

Lyons and Murray became important foils for Taylor, as much for their deep-rooted jazz sensibilities as their open ears. A fan of Sonny Stitt as well as Charlie Parker, Lyons brought a strong notion of swing and bebop logic to Taylor's free music. Besides the technical elements, even the timbre of his horn instantly recalled Parker for many years until he developed his own unique voice. As a youth, he had befriended Bud Powell, Thelonious Monk, and clarinetist Buster Bailey, who gave Lyons his first alto saxophone. He strode the line between bop and free more successfully than most any other musician since, and those qualities helped temper the fury of Taylor's music with a dose of accessibility. Lyons, in short, gave listeners something familiar to grab onto in the midst of perceived chaos.

Murray's tenure with Taylor was more sporadic but hardly less inspiring. He literally reinvented the role of the drummer in the ensemble context, subjugating time in favor of expressive equality within the band. He had held more traditional jobs on both ends of the jazz spectrum, from stride pianist Willie "The Lion" Smith to Ted Curson's creative exploits, before meeting up with Taylor in 1959. A short stint with John Coltrane in 1963 put the finishing polish on Murray's concepts. He owed much of his later acclaimed work with Ayler, Shepp, and his own bands to the early tutelage of Taylor and Coltrane. Unfortunately, very little of his work with Taylor (and none with Trane) is documented on record.

Though he could easily have compromised his principles in order to find steady work, Taylor instead chose to move further from the jazz mainstream. He began his performances in a state of deep relaxation, then let the flow of internal energy move him in a manner that inspired later pianists like Keith Jarrett. Where he once used single-note lines as melodic statements and occasionally relied on standard rhythms, Taylor was now pounding out weighty tone clusters and rippling arpeggios at both ends of the keyboard. He hit the piano with his open palms, fists, and arms, using any manner of unorthodox rhythmic structures that recalled European avant-garde music and, above all, certainly did not "swing" in the traditional sense.

In April 1964, Taylor gave a solo performance at Bennington College in Vermont. That concert was taped and intended for release under the title *Cathedrale*, but the record never appeared. In May, Taylor was attacked and left with a broken wrist, which prevented him from playing much for the remainder of the year. He lacked a working unit anyway. Murray had left and was eventually replaced in the autumn by young Tony Williams, who moved on to fame with Miles Davis. Though Williams did not play with Taylor for long, he returned the favor fifteen years later by arranging a guest spot for the pianist on *Joy of Flying* (1979, Columbia), by his fusion band Lifetime. It need not be said that this is a singular item in Taylor's discography!

Also in 1964, Taylor became a founding member of the Jazz Composers Guild, a well-intentioned but poorly accomplished union of souls gathered by Bill Dixon in an attempt to foster support for avant-garde jazz musicians in New York City. The Guild sponsored a series of concerts, "Four Days in December," at Judson Hall. One of those shows, on December 28, featured Taylor with Lyons, Neidlinger, drummer Andrew Cyrille, and trumpeter Mike Mantler, an Austrian immigrant who would continue building upon the Guild's concepts after its folding. No recording of the show is known, but apparently, Taylor's wrist was back in working order.

On May 19, 1966, Taylor's band entered engineer Rudy Van Gelder's studio in Englewood Cliffs, New Jersey, to record *Unit Structures*, his first album for Blue Note. This probably remains the most outward-looking session the legendary label has ever issued, as the avant-garde was never its strong suit. The leader's rhythmic, arpeggiated style began to blossom more fully, although the coherent development that marks his later work was still slightly lacking. The ensemble consisted of Taylor on piano and bells, Lyons on alto sax, trumpeter Eddie Gale Stevens Jr. (who is mostly subsidiary, quite unusual for that horn), Ken McIntyre on alto, oboe, and bass clarinet, drummer Cyrille, and two bassists: Henry Grimes and Alan Silva. The tracks are difficult and Taylor's arcane liner notes offer little lucid revelation. On first listen, "Steps" evokes an often-repeated criticism of free jazz, that it seems the band is merely warming up for long stretches. Slight twinges of bebop coloration come and go, but the piano ripples, saxophone fragments, and unpredictable percussion seem wholly separate. As time goes by, definite sections of melody can be recognized and things start becoming clearer. Taylor launches into a rapid, short piano break that recalls the agility of Bud Powell but is quickly supplanted by Lyons. Alto, piano, and drums tumble and romp furiously together as the remaining players fight to keep up. McIntyre's solo is slightly blurrier, but he earns his chair in the ensemble, using even more "outside" techniques than Lyons had. The gangly "Enter Evening" has some moments of beauty: McIntyre's oboe conjures up exotic landscapes over Silva's bowed bass, and Taylor's piano is a pool at the base of a waterfall. In an alternate take on the CD release, Lyons's role is upfront counterpoint while McIntyre maintains the theme. "Unit Structure/ As of Now/Section" begins with a Latin-scented rhythm from Cyrille, a keening statement by the alto, then wildly undulating arco bass with a single long tone from McIntyre's bass clarinet. Taylor introduces a thematic structure, which the horns pick up on, following new avenues as Cyrille nudges them along. The hornless "Tales (8 Whisps)" bears the kind of percolating theme that characterized Taylor's later solo work: clusters of a few notes at a time, repeated, varied, then set aside with the option to return. He and Cyrille work in duo at first, and the pianist dominates in a whirl of stride, bebop, and classical inklings. Somewhere in there are quiet bass bowings, and the basses emerge full force at the four-minute mark. Taylor takes the piece out in his own sweeping fashion. This is one of his masterworks, though real appreciation may require several deep listens.

On October 6, the band returned to the Van Gelder studios for the *Conquistador!* sessions. McIntyre was gone and Eddie Gale (who eventually dropped his last name, Stevens) was replaced by Bill Dixon. The material for this album was significantly less chaotic than *Unit Structures* had been, as if Taylor had gotten some things off his chest and settled down a bit. The spiritual kinship between Taylor and Lyons became more apparent now, and the pianist assimilated Ellington's strategy of fashioning works around individual musicians' personalities. Dixon's solo on the title cut, tender and pained, is the antithesis of Lyons's fury. "With (Exit)" illustrates just how nicely the sound of bowed instruments complemented Taylor's piano style. Silva's arco bass harmonics on these albums may have paved the way for the inclusion of violinists in later units. Bubbling piano and alto generate a gently suspended feel, supported by Dixon's remote cries and the vibrant combination of Silva's bowing and Grimes's wandering pizzicato.

Paris was the setting for *Student Studies* (1966, Affinity), a live date by the quartet of Taylor, Lyons, Silva, and Cyrille. A steady pulse from Lyons's alto is the first sound heard, backed by Silva's bowing as the volume swells and dies out. Taylor steals in on dark chords, the bass and drums exchange a few shots, then Lyons launches into a manic little circle dance with the piano. Silence is important in the two parts of "Student Studies," the occasional spaces offering kind respite from the mayhem, and again Silva's bowing adds a critical texture. Cyrille judiciously experiments with percussion instruments on "Amplitude," inducing smiles amid the sparseness. This is a high-water mark of his tenure with Taylor, rich with whistles and objects that clatter and bang against the piano strings à la John Cage's prepared pianos. "Niggle Feuigle" is wonderfully jazzy, a clashing exaltation that features Lyons squealing and puttering like Coltrane was in the same period. Taylor's deep blue chords keep this track tenuously grounded in a passable jazz frame.

The year 1967 to 1968 was a comparatively quiet time for Taylor, with an interesting new opportunity for exposure in the latter year. After the Jazz Composers Guild's quick demise, Taylor stuck around for its reincarnation, the Jazz Composers Orchestra Association, which was fronted by Michael Mantler and pianist/composer Carla Bley. Taylor was prominently featured on the Orchestra's self-titled album on their own JCOA label, another small step toward better appreciation within the community. Don Cherry, tenorists Pharoah Sanders and Gato Barbieri, and energetic guitarist Larry Coryell had their own features on the disc, but the definitive climax was Taylor's furious assault on the half-hour "Communications #11." Taylor, granted top billing on the album cover, asserted his right to that honor with an overwhelmingly ecstatic performance.

In July 1969, a festival at the Fondation Maeght in St. Paul de Vence, France, featured such free luminaries as Sun Ra and Taylor's quartet with Lyons, Cyrille, and saxophonist Sam Rivers (there was no bassist on this date). The pianist's set was documented and released as *The Great Paris Concert* (1969, Black Lion) and was recently available as *Fondation Maeght Nights, Volumes 1-3*, on the Jazz View label. These discs break the quartet's long interpretation of Taylor's work "Second Act of 'A'" into three parts. On the first disc, the saxes harmonize, first with short honking tones that swell and fade, then into the linear boplike theme. Cyrille's surges are coupled with piano and horns, building to a massive sustained climax that dissolves into low skulking by the piano. Disc 2 begins with immediate piano and drum percolations, then scarcely contained screams from the saxophones. Rivers's frantic tenor solo sounds as if he is about to fly into bits. Lyons's solo turn begins in a more linear fashion, but soon he is back to trading roars with Rivers over an unrelenting piano and drum avalanche. The third disc returns to the ominous piano figures, then unison saxes on a recurring line as Cyrille keeps a third distinct rhythm going. Taylor's majestic octave passages lean once again toward classical forms. The Fondation Maeght show was one of the most exhausting live concert experiences on record, and much of the energy is translates well on disc.

Taylor retreated for a time into college instruction to pay the bills, an artistically frustrating period for him. He spent 1970 to 1973 at the University of Wisconsin in Madison and later held residences at Antioch College and Glassboro State College. Antioch was the most comfortable, since Lyons and Cyrille were also on staff. During this period, Taylor slowly began to garner attention as a performer once again, and by 1973, he was out of academia and back on the road with Lyons, Cyrille, and bassist Sirone. A Guggenheim Fellowship in that year helped to further boost Taylor's confidence and financial security.

The band recorded *Spring of Two Blue J's* (originally released on Taylor's own Unit Core label) at New York's Town Hall in 1973. In previous years, Town Hall was the site of controversial concerts by Charles Mingus and Ornette Coleman, which shook jazz to its foundation. While Taylor was fairly well established by the time he walked through its doors, this performance was no less shocking. The disc bears two wildly different interpretations of the title composition: a solo rendition, and one with the quartet. Taylor's solo take is lavish and pastoral; one can imagine water tumbling over rocks, leaves falling, birds in song. Classical influences like Debussy and Scriabin are apparent. The full-quartet version is a different animal, indeed. The piano cascades and rumbles before Lyons begins the melody. His tone is again akin to Parker's, injecting a bebop sensation and putting the classical essences aside. Taylor's playing is highly abstracted; Sirone and Cyrille punctuate each declamation from the alto and piano, trading off diatribes with each man in turn. The disc offers a special chance to see just how radically Taylor's compositions can be interpreted in different settings, a method employed by Coleman with similar success.

In July 1974, Taylor appeared solo at the Montreux Jazz Festival, a set documented on the ever-popular *Silent Tongues* (Freedom/Black Lion, 1975). There are five total tracks (the later Freedom CD reissue mistakenly lists six; "Crossing (Fourth Movement)" is not divided into two tracks as it was on LP), containing five movements and two variations, each with conspicuous differences and similarities to the others. There is a classical majesty to the first suite of three movements, "Abyss/Petals & Filaments/Jitney," with emphasis on the piano's low end. Soon patterns of repetition and variation peek forth, some sounding unconsciously like the call of Woody Woodpecker. The small thematic devices become easy to identify as Taylor returns to them throughout the performance. The two versions of "After All" bear a Spanish tinge, filtered through Ellington, while "Jitney No. 2" recalls a jostling cab ride through third-world urban streets. The set's evocative emotionality has kept it perennially popular.

On August 20, 1976, Taylor performed solo at the Moosham Castle Festival in Austria, a concert that was documented on *Air above Mountains* (Enja, 1992). This is one of his more satisfying solo forays on record. In that same year, he recorded *Dark unto Themselves* (Enja) with the bassless quintet of Lyons, tenor saxophonist David S. Ware, trumpeter Raphé Malik, and drummer Marc Edwards. The hour-plus "Streams and Chorus of Seed" features outstanding solos, and Ware in particular shines. Within a few years of his apprenticeship with Taylor, the tenorman would be a rising star in another wave of free jazz.

In April 1978, the Unit went into the Columbia Studios to record *Three Phasis* (New World, 1979), a single hour-long piece that is separated on CD into five tracks at various convenient "entry points." Lyons and Malik state widely spaced melodic segments in unison. Sirone's bowed bass takes on almost a bassoon quality; drummer Ronald Shannon Jackson, fresh from Coleman's Prime Time, is powerfully loud; and violinist Ramsey Ameen offers subtle scrapes. At the second entry point, Ameen is most prominent. Taylor's concentration on rhythm is especially evident as he nails regular accents in each passage. Part 3 marks the start of a typically hefty piano solo. At mark 4, a blues feel emerges below the somber horn melody, and Taylor strikes his figures almost like a stride pianist. The mood at mark 5 is tense, minor, underscored by rattling, hard-swinging percussion. Malik's disaffected bebop lines contrast with Lyons's free statements; Sirone howls and harasses Jackson in an almost pugilistic fashion. Exhilarating.

Just as exciting is the album simply titled *The Cecil Taylor Unit* (1978, New World). The quintet tackles Taylor's "Idut" and "Serdab," each over fourteen minutes long, and the half-hour "Holiday En Masque." The first sounds heard are crunchy bowings by Sirone and Ameen, giving off a lofty classical air. Alto and trumpet soon join in with scattered runs, followed by cacophonous thumping from Taylor. A *film noir* aura hangs in the mist for a time; everything moves in unpredictable waves, energy swelling and falling with all players in complete accordance. On "Serdab," Malik and Lyons are quite attentive to one another's moods. The introduction to "Holiday" is painted in jazzier hues. Taylor's interaction with Jackson is stupefying, as is the middle section with the furiously bowing strings flanking the piano. The musicians wail and pound until they seemingly haven't a drop of energy left, and the music winds down like a rubber-band toy on its last legs.

Malik and Jackson left the Unit in 1978. Their swansong was the superior *One Too Many Salty Swift and Not Goodbye* (1991, HatArt, 2 CDs), recorded live on June 14, 1978, in Stuttgart, Germany. The CD includes two previously unissued duets: fun-spirited trading between Lyons and Malik, and a more vibrationally centered meeting between Ameen and Sirone, who plays masterfully abrupt pizzicatos in response to the violin's chordal stabs. These duets offer a glimpse into how well the Unit members could interact with their leader out of the picture. A rollicking Jackson drum solo is also included. The full Unit section of *One Too Many* begins almost as a dirge, in the vein of Coleman's "Lonely Woman" or "Broken Shadows." There is an angrier edge to Taylor's playing, partially because he was not permitted to play upon a better-quality grand piano, which the venue claimed was reserved for classical pianists. Perhaps the finest performance is Sirone's, his tambura-like resonance moving the ensemble toward a new plane of vibration. The final section belongs to Ameen, as pastoral tenderness unfolds from his strings and splashes into Taylor's limpid pools.

In 1979, another special event occurred that further propelled Taylor into the national spotlight: he was invited to perform at the White House for President Jimmy Carter. Reaction to the program was positive, a further step toward building up Taylor's confidence and ambitions. Performance opportunities, which had already been on the rise over the past few years, now comparatively flowed like champagne on New Year's Eve. Thankful for such overdue recognition, Taylor again stepped up his efforts to further develop new musical vocabularies. He recorded a triumphant duo date with bop drummer Max Roach (*Historic Concerts*, 1979, Soul Note) at Columbia University in December of that year. Each performer soloed for about five minutes in turn, then the duo dove into a manic eighty-minute cathartic assault exhibiting all the best elements of their respective approaches. Roach, who had backed Bird and Dizzy at the advent of bebop thirty-odd years prior, proved he had the right stuff to handle the avant-garde.

In 1980, the Unit was briefly expanded to include two drummers: Jerome Cooper, who had just served with Taylor alumni Sirone and Leroy Jenkins in the Revolutionary Ensemble; and Sunny Murray, who had returned after eighteen years for a quick reunion with Taylor. This Unit, rounded out with Lyons, Ameen, and bassist Alan Silva, recorded *It Is in the Brewing Luminous* (1990, HatArt) at Fat Tuesday's in New York in February 1980. The added rhythmic power of the double drummers made a strong difference, even on more subdued material. The show begins with comparative restraint, as the pianist ushers in Lyons with the barest flutters. The melody is lighter than in many of Taylor's pieces, moreover buoyed by the rhythms of Cooper's balafon (a small African xylophone). There is a lot of space within this performance, with tiny trickles of rhythm dribbling behind Taylor's spare figures. Some of this spareness, admittedly, might be due to feeble recording quality more than conscious effort by the musicians. Ameen and Silva may as well not even be present; Lyons and Taylor utterly dominate the show. Also worth tracking down from this same period is the solo showpiece *Fly! Fly! Fly! Fly! Fly!* (1980, MPS), a collection of eight shorter works that present the pianist in a more introspective mode.

Around 1981, Taylor's bizarre poetry and stage personality began to play a prominent role in his live shows. *The Eighth* (1989, HatHut) is an early document of Taylor's theatricality, recorded live at the Freiburger Jazztage in West Germany on November 8, 1981. The set begins with the sound of hands drumming on the body of the piano, and vocal chanting by all the Unit members: Taylor, Lyons, bassist William Parker, and drummer Rashid Bakr. The rhythm duo were new to Taylor's Unit, and Lyons's tone on this recording is, for once, less reminiscent of Parker than of Steve Lacy's soprano sax sound. Bakr does not rumble across the entire kit as much as Jackson or Murray had before him. Instead, he focuses on smaller units of sound: a tom here, snare and one cymbal there. Parker's broad ideas were just what Taylor needed in the wake of Sirone and Silva. The bassist has successfully applied Taylor's percussive technique to his own instrument, approaching each string as if it were a bass drum, tom, or snare. Despite the session's obvious freedom, its combination of rhythmic elements brought a sense of bop's more focused energy that Taylor's music had lacked for some time.

The solo double-disc set *Garden* (1981, HatArt; reissued on CD in 1990 as *Garden, Part 1* and *Part 2*) was recorded live in Basel, Switzerland, eight days after *The Eighth*. At first, Taylor's voice is heard offstage, reciting nonsense syllables inspired by Japanese drama. He emerges, singing half-strangled runs like a drowning operatic baritone, spitting out abstractions about "the pressure that comes too soon," stomping his feet rapidly as if running upstairs. Finally, after chattering like a bat taking flight, Taylor takes the bench and begins the minimalist theme of "Êléll." Such drama, difficult to capture in true spirit on a recording, has been a key part of Taylor's performances since the 1980s. "Driver Says" and "Stepping On Stars," on *Part 2*, look back again to past notions of jazz, while "Points" and "Pemmican" stare awestruck into the future.

Nineteen eight-five saw the release of Taylor's first recording for a larger ensemble. *Winged Serpent (Sliding Quadrants)* featured a united European-American group billed as "Segments II (Orchestra of Two Continents)": Enrico Rava, Tomasz Stánko, Frank Wright, John Tchicai, Gunter Hampel, Karen Borca, percussionist André Martinez, and the ubiquitous Lyons, Parker, and Bakr. The music is often reminiscent of Charles Mingus's work in the 1960s or perhaps Ellington as channeled through Mingus, with its bustling, quavering structures and prominent bari sax. The opening of "Taht" is especially Mingusian, but after the thematic statements, Taylor's serious freedom pours out. Obviously, the larger the group, the more chance for freedom to become unintelligible chaos. However, the leader's rhythmic concentration and the drummers' confluence steadfastly keep things from flying apart. "Womb Waters Scent of the Burning Armadillo Shell" has a simple theme that is echoed all about the hall by the various players, and "Cun-Un-Un-Un-An" features the voices of all the participants, chanting and grunting amid a rainfall of exotic percussion. On the closing "Winged Serpents," Rava summons up dark spirits over a bottomless cascade of piano arpeggios and splashing drums. This album is one of the most uniformly intriguing and approachable in Taylor's catalog, revealing new dimensions to his composing and arranging skills.

In April 1986, the Workshop Freie Musik in Berlin, sponsored by FMP Records, held the Cecil Taylor Festival. The man himself performed a solo set that was documented on *For Olim* (Soul Note, 1987). *Olim* is an Aztec hieroglyph that indicates movement or even an earthquake. It's an apt title for the first track, as Taylor begins with restrained, minor-key stirrings that wouldn't quite register on the Richter scale. Little motifs that recall Ravel and "Jaws" in equal parts pop up and fade, and pointillistic bursts flop about inside the piano. After a fashion, Taylor focuses on a few select clusters, pumping them back and forth across octaves, interjecting tiny fleeting runs before moving to other fragments. At times he chooses individual chords that recall Duke, Monk, or Jelly Roll Morton in small ways. The remaining seven tracks are of a similar bent but differ in mood. "For The Death" is battling and short, as if Taylor is questioning the reasons behind sickness and death but soon withdraws out of bitter exhaustion. "The Question" is tender at the onset, plumes of Debussy-drawn beauty scented with probing inquiry and self-dialogue. It is a wild, cathartic ride through memories of joy and the pain of loss. A second recording from that festival, *Olu Iwa* (1986, Soul Note), captures Taylor, Parker, and Wright with Steve McCall, Thurman Barker, Peter Brötzmann, and trombonist Earl McIntyre. Different lineups are featured on two energetic extended pieces, "B Ee Ba Nganga Ban'a Eee!" and the quartet tune "Olu Iwa (Lord of Character)." The track titles, if not the music itself, portray Taylor's interest in both African cultures and nonsensical verse.

At the Berlin fest, no doubt Taylor had on his mind Jimmy Lyons, who was desperately ill with lung cancer after many years of chain-smoking. Lyons's death on May 19, 1986, ended an era. As the passing of the young bass virtuoso Scott LaFaro had absolutely devastated pianist Bill Evans, the death of Taylor's longtime foil and empathic doppelgänger left a similar void in his life and creative motivation. Upon its release, *For Olim* was dedicated to the memory of Lyons. Subsequently, Taylor seemed to have a difficult time finding a solid replacement for "Little Bird" in his ensembles, often settling for players with willing hearts but much less technique. Then again, replacing Lyons was rather like replacing himself, so close were the two musically and emotionally.

On November 3, 1987, the Unit was recorded live in Bologna, Italy, for what became the second release on the Leo label. *Live in Bologna* features Taylor, Parker, Barker, reedman Carlos Ward, and violinist Leroy Jenkins. Taylor seems a bit more soulful than usual, perhaps injecting a little gospel inflection into his playing. Jenkins is the most prominent melodic voice here while Ward is almost secondary, as if he were unsure of his worthiness as Lyons's successor. As the set wears on, however, Ward emerges with a sure, vibratoed tone that helps to finally assert his belongingness.

Tzotzil Mummers Tzotzil (Leo Records) was unusual in several respects. It is a single, very long piece that overdubs Taylor's multitracked poetry and grotesque vocalizations onto a Unit performance recorded several days prior. His dada verses, psychobabble, marching instructions, and such are accented by percussion, tiny bells, and bass drum thumps. Odd as the session may be, these are some of the most appealing Unit sounds on disc, a different form of ritual than Taylor had engaged in before. Another Leo release, which should be left as a last resort only after one has come to terms with Taylor's poetic side, is *Chinampas* (1987). There is no piano at all, only Taylor reciting nine tracks of surreal verse and accompanying himself with various percussion instruments.

In 1988, Taylor was duly venerated as a monthlong festival devoted to his music was held in Berlin. This was one of free jazz's supreme ironies: that a man who had openly declared his dissatisfaction with European musical traditions would be honored there a quarter-century later with a festival in his name. The inaugural event resulted in eleven CDs' worth of live recordings on the FMP label. These were made available in the limited-edition boxed set *Cecil Taylor in Berlin '88*, as well as individually.

For each set of the festival, Taylor partnered with various other musicians for spontaneous explorations. The results vary, yet each disc reveals implications of Taylor's vision and its adaptability to different circumstances. Among the discs are five duets with European drummers: South African expatriate Louis Moholo (*Remembrance*), Han Bennink (*Spots, Circles, and Fantasy*), Günter Sommer (*Riobec*), Tony Oxley (*Leaf Palm Hand*), and Paul Lovens (*Regalia*). Each set is successful to a different degree, given the serious differences between the drummers' backgrounds and personalities. Equally successful is the duet with guitarist Derek Bailey on *Pleistozaen Mit Wasser*. Bailey's interest in microtonal music is evident from the start, as he picks out blissfully clashing notes just a hair off parallel. The trio session with saxophonist Evan Parker and cellist Tristan Honsinger, *The Hearth*, is just as good and perhaps a bit more accessible to the casual listener. High-bowed cello figures charm us immediately, then Parker's tenor skitters in. Rapid-fire interplay dissolves briefly into relaxation, whereupon a dose of blues feeling is infused. After nearly seven minutes of delightful cellotenor interchange, Taylor's voice pops forth, groaning, swooping, and ululating. Once the piano arrives, Parker holds on for dear life until he simply has to drop out and catch his breath.

Two large-band recordings are included in this set as well. *Legba Crossing* is by the Workshop Ensemble, a group of mostly unknowns, which includes vocalist Trudy Morse, reed player Brigitte Vinkeloe, violinist Harald Kimmig, Canadian pianist Paul Plimley (Taylor sticks to conducting and vocalizing), bassist Alex Frangenheim, and drummer Peeter Uuskyla. Taylor begins this forty-eight-minute ritual with poetic chanting, "Bay-bay-bay-bay . . . ," then the ensemble slowly sticks its collective head out of the sand with bass groans and sinuous sax. Kimmig, who has more recently performed with Taylor in the ensemble Corona, alternates between pointed pizzicatos and lovely bowing, interacting with the flute as bees around a hive. It is a different experience than Taylor's prior large-ensemble works, fascinating in its own right. Stranger yet is *Alms/Tiergarten (Spree)*, spread out over two CDs. Instead of the eager trainees of the Workshop Ensemble, this set features the seasoned pros of Taylor's European Orchestra: trumpeters Tomasz Stánko and Enrico Rava; reed players Parker, Peter van Bergen, Brötzmann, Hans Koch, and Louis Sclavis; trombonists Hannes Bauer, Wolter Wierbos, and Christian Radovan; French hornist Martin Mayes; vibist

Gunter Hampel; cellist Honsinger; drummer Bennink; and bassists Peter Kowald and William Parker. The leader performs on piano. The session moves from otherworldly ensemble vocals to Bennink's quiet little rolls and patters, the entry of the bassists, then a building of tension until the train is barreling downhill for a long period. About forty-eight minutes along a blessed relief comes, the energy dying off to reveal tinkling piano, tumbling toms, and occasional short trumpet blares. When the end is near, Taylor, Kowald, and Bennink take it out until all that is left is tapping percussion and exotic vocalizing. This is an exhausting performance, and the second disc ("Weight-Breath-Sounding Trees") gives little quarter. Of particular interest there is the ripping duet between Sclavis's clarinet and Bauer.

Finally comes *Erzulie Maketh Scent*, Taylor's solo performance toward the end of the month-long festival. He concentrates on the low register early, sounding at times as if the piano is sliding slowly down a staircase. Earlier in the festival, Taylor had spoken about the concept of magic as it applies to music, and the ways he skillfully blends all of the disparate elements of his global piano technique are indeed enchanting. The barren force of twentieth-century classicism is united with stride, Monk, Ellington, and all things Taylor. The result is a wholly satisfying performance of the tripartite "Erzulie," along with two shorter, jazzier pieces that close out the session: "Water" and "Stone," with which he had closed out the duet with Moholo.

Around this time, Taylor conveyed his "Feel Trio" with William Parker and Tony Oxley. A marvelously interactive unit of great power, it is one of the few threesomes Taylor has worked with in recent memory and most certainly a successful partnership. *Looking (Berlin Version): The Feel Trio* (1990, FMP) is the third setting in which Taylor has recorded that particular work for the label, the others being solo and with the multicultural group Corona. All three men share an incredible gift of rapt concentration right down to streams of 32nd notes, and their unrivaled techniques blend seamlessly on this exhilarating production. It captures all the drama of its time and locale, having been taped a few days before the Berlin Wall was demolished. *Celebrated Blazons* (1993, FMP), also recorded at the Berlin Workshop in 1990, contains equally praiseworthy interplay.

In September 1990, a new lineup of Taylor's Workshop Ensemble recorded *Melancholy* (1990, FMP). This time around, the ensemble included trumpeter Tobias Netta, soprano saxophonist Harri Sjöström, reedman Wolfgang Fuchs, altoist Volker Schlott, tenorman Thomas Klemm, trombonists Thomas Wiedermann and Jörg Huke, and a trio of prominent British improvisers: Evan Parker, Oxley, and bassist Barry Guy. Broken into three "Spheres" of twenty to twenty-eight minutes each, the performance is not as successful as earlier large-group efforts like *Winged Serpents*, but it has plenty of excellent moments.

On that six-month visit to Berlin, Taylor cut two solo records. The title track of *Double Holy House* (FMP) is one of his most magnificent ballad performances. The nearly hour-long second track, "Squash People," starts with an overlong bout of poetry and percussion before Taylor tackles the piano. The other solo album, *Tree of Life* (1991, FMP), was a parting gift to the devoted festival crowds. After a minute-long incantation, Taylor gave an astonishing performance that, more than most of his prior releases, clearly reflected his debts to both the European classical and avant traditions and to the American jazzmen who preceded him. A flurry of jazz piano styles is intercut with atonal and serial elements to result in a dazzling sonic confection.

Taylor's fourth record from that season in Berlin, *Nailed* (FMP), is a quartet with Oxley, Parker, and Guy. This disc is a battle royal, due in part to squabbles among the musicians before the tape started rolling. Despite the tangible one-upsmanship that runs through the session like an ugly varicose vein, the performers do not let their egos get in the way of the collective good for long. All four men turn in some of their best performances of the period, confirming the fruitfulness of hostility in certain situations. *Always A Pleasure* (1993, FMP) documents yet another Free Music Workshop session, this time in April 1993. The band is a blend of old friends and new: Sirone, Bakr, Honsinger, Sjöström, tenorman Charles Gayle, and French trumpeter Longineu Parsons. Gayle's rage could almost supplant the tremendous energy of Jimmy Lyons, and young Sjöström holds his own well. Sirone and Bakr, as one might expect, help gird the younger lions for the pianist's headlong attack. Honsinger and Parsons end up as second bananas, though in other settings they are more than capable of taking charge.

On March 29, 1998, Taylor performed two savage, bracing sets at the Iridium in New York with Sjöström, bassist Dominic Duval, and drummer Jackson Krall. These sets are beautifully documented on the albums *Q'ua* and *Q'ua Yuba* (both 1998, Cadence Jazz). It's the open-eared interaction of Duval and Krall that sets these discs apart, as the rhythmists permit plenty of breathing room for the manic pianist and soprano saxophonist to parry and thrust. Sjöström remains a bit of an unknown quantity, having recorded almost nothing outside these sessions with Taylor, but he shows promise as a bright new voice on soprano.

A surprising meeting of the minds occurred on *Momentum Space* (1999, Polygram), which teamed Taylor with ex-Coltrane drummer Elvin Jones and ex-Coleman tenorist Dewey Redman. This is just barely a trio effort at all. Each man has his own solo track, with Redman's a piddling forty-five seconds in length. "Spoonin'" is a groovy drum-tenor duet, and Taylor and Jones spar together on "It" without Redman. When all three work together, on "Nine" and "Is," the results are spellbinding. Had this trio been recorded in the 1960s or 1970s, it's not likely that their interplay would be nearly as respectful or accurate. The seasoning of experience definitely helped the performers relate and follow each other's leads. It's a shame that only two tracks were devoted to the full trio, though most of the album is rewarding overall. Perhaps another, better conceived session will come in the near future.

Taylor has continued to record and perform into the twenty-first century, both solo and with various units in America and Europe. Though he is still not a household name among American fans, his worldwide following has swelled tremendously. He still frequents European and American festivals, making lauded appearances at the annual "What Is Jazz?" Festival, conducted by the Knitting Factory in New York. His group performances continually redefine the concept of the jazz ensemble. In 2001, he performed several shows in duo with drummer Elvin Jones, followed by a trio reunion with Dixon and Oxley. However, his most popular recordings and performances tend to be those where he is alone at the piano, creating the overwhelming tide of sound that is his signature.

Tchicai, John (b. Copenhagen, Denmark, 28 April 1936): saxophonist. Of Danish and Congolese heritage, Tchicai would appear to be somewhat of an outsider in free jazz. As a minority of European birth, he could not relate well to the socioeconomic difficulties faced by his black American contemporaries, but he was welcomed into continental free circles with open arms. He began his musical studies as a violinist at the age of ten, moving on to reeds in high school. He spent three years as a saxophone student at the Royal Conservatory, then began his professional career in the late 1950s. Much of his work has been on tenor sax, though he is an equally capable altoist. Like Sonny Rollins, Tchicai is appreciated for his deft motivic improvisations, working the dickens out of selected phrases for effect.

Upon meeting Archie Shepp in Helsinki in 1962, Tchicai found his entryway into the free-jazz movement. He moved to New York the following year, built up a reasonable reputation, then joined Shepp and Don Cherry in the New York Contemporary Five. Not as fluid a player as Ornette Coleman had been, Tchicai nevertheless worked quite well with Cherry in the quintet. Shortly thereafter, he moved to the New York Art Quartet, honing his sense of rhythm in front of Milford Graves's drums. Tchicai was a member of the Jazz Composers Guild during its short life and recorded with many of its members. Two more plum recording opportunities arose for the young Dane: the *New York Eye and Ear Control* soundtrack (1964, ESP) with Cherry and Albert Ayler, and John Coltrane's monumental *Ascension* (1965, Impulse), on which Tchicai blew brave if unsteady alto sax in the seething ensemble, sounding not unlike Eric Dolphy at times. This pair of albums could have firmly established Tchicai as a serious force in America, but in 1966, he returned home to Denmark armed with a new wealth of knowledge.

In 1967, Tchicai began performing with Cadentia Nova Danica, a jazz workshop of sorts, which explored free areas as much as other jazz textures. His association with that group lasted about four years, after which he stepped sidelong into a teaching career. In 1977, he returned from near-obscurity with two fine albums, *John Tchicai Solo Plus Albert Mangelsdorff* (FMP) and *Real Tchicai* (Steeplechase). On the first disc, his blissful interaction with the genial trombonist betrays little of the underconfidence heard on *Ascension*. The second session finds him in a prime trio with with guitarist Pierre Dørge and bassist Niels-Henning Ørsted Pedersen, assaying compositions that draw from his studies of Asian and African musics. In 1982, he began performing with Dørge's New Jungle Orchestra, becoming an essential voice in the daring ensemble, and later with De Zes Winden ("The Six Winds"). Tchicai has contributed to sessions by Cecil Taylor, Kristian Blak's Yggdrasil, Famoudou Don Moye, guitarist John Ehlis, Rent Romus (*Adapt . . . Or Die!*, 1997, Jazzheads), and the Either/Orchestra, among others. *Willi the Pig* (1975, Intakt) is a classic session with pianist Irène Schweizer; on *Infinitesimal Flash* (2000, Buzz) he points to further new directions. Since the early 1990s, Tchicai has lived and taught in the San Francisco area.

Teitelbaum, Richard (b. New York, NY, 19 May 1939): electronic musician and composer. Teitelbaum graduated from Yale's music masters program in 1964, then went to Italy on a Fulbright scholarship. There he studied with electronic music pioneers Luigi Nono and Goffredo Petrassi, which sealed his artistic fate. Already inspired by

John Cage and LaMonte Young, Teitelbaum was headed inexorably into the electronic avant-garde. He returned briefly to the United States, then brought an early Moog synthesizer over to Europe, where he began exposing baffled audiences to its sonorous potentials. In 1966, he teamed up with Frederic Rzewski and Alvin Curran to form Musica Elettronica Viva (MEV), one of the first and most important electronic improvising ensembles. He met Anthony Braxton in the early 1970s when the reedman briefly worked with MEV, and the two have performed together many times since then. Teitelbaum's first recording under his own name was *Time Zones* (1977, Arista). He has also performed with Scott Fields, Andrew Cyrille, Company, Carlos Zingaro, Marilyn Crispell, Luc Houtkamp, and other free improvisers. Teitelbaum has taught at Vassar and Bard Colleges. In 1995, Tzadik issued a recording of *Golem*, an opera that the composer had debuted in Austria in 1991. He remains at the forefront of experimental music, developing interactive performance systems for computers.

Terroade, Kenneth (b. Jamaica): flautist and tenorman. Terroade was a fringe player, a reliable sideman and solid soloist who never achieved much recognition. He came to London at the age of fourteen and played in local R&B groups. Exposure to Chris McGregor's Blue Notes and other African expatriate bands led him to explore jazz, and McGregor became one of his first employers in the field. Terroade also worked with John Surman and John Stevens but is best known for a series of albums led by Sunny Murray (*Sunshine, [Never Give a Sucker] an Even Break, Homage to Africa*, all 1969, BYG). He also recorded with Dave Burrell, Alan Silva's Celestrial [sic] Communications Orchestra, and Louisiana pianist and singer Dr. John. The sole album issued under Terroade's leadership was the good, overlooked *Love Rejoice* (1969, BYG). He returned to Jamaica shortly afterward and effectively retired from music while still in his twenties.

Test: improvising quartet consisting of drummer Tom Bruno, bassist Matthew Heyner, saxophonist Sabir Mateen, and multi-instrumentalist Daniel Carter. While working in the Music Under New York program, performing in the subways, Bruno and Carter met and decided to form a partnership. They originally worked in a trio with bassist Dan O'Brien, who was soon replaced by the fluidly adaptive Heyner from the No Neck Blues Band. The fiery Mateen, who had come out of Horace Tapscott's circle in Los Angeles and later worked with Raphé Malik, completed the quartet in the early 1990s. Test played together in the streets and subways for several years before the opportunity to record arose (*Live*, 1998, Eremite). The quartet has issued two self-titled albums, one each on the Aum Fidelity and Ecstatic Peace labels. All are marked by a tremendous level of spontaneous energy and utter absence of clear form.

Thomas, Ijeoma Chinue: see **Positive Knowledge**.

Thomas, Leon (or **Leone**) (Amos Leone Thomas, Jr.; b. East St. Louis, IL, 4 October 1937; d. 8 May 1999): vocalist. After graduating from Tennessee State University, Thomas went to New York in 1958 and began working with the mainstream jazz artists of the day: Grant Green, Mary Lou Williams, Hank Crawford, even Count Basie. Jobs with Oliver Nelson and Roland Kirk opened his ears to more outward-facing music. Thomas finally broke through in his work with Pharoah Sanders, recording "The Creator Has a Master Plan" (on Sanders's *Karma*, 1969, Impulse), which became one of the new jazz's very few hits. Its most fascinating aspect, out of many, was the incredible pygmy-style yodel that the singer inflected, his ululations sending emotional waves high in the air. That same year saw Thomas's debut as a leader on *Spirits Known and Unknown* (Flying Dutchman). His career subsequently saw many hills and valleys, including projects with artists as diverse as Louis Armstrong, bop drummer Louis Hayes, singer Jeri Brown, and Latin rock titans Santana. In 1974, he changed the spelling of his name to Leone, which stuck for over a decade. After a long period out of the spotlight, Thomas returned with the live album *Precious Energy* (1987, Mapleshade) on which he still displayed a firm command of his vocal cords. *Leon Thomas Blues Band* (1988, Portrait) marked another promising new direction. After another unfortunate career decline, Thomas died of heart failure in 1999.

Thomas, Oluyemi: see **Positive Knowledge**.

Thomas, Pat (b. 27 July 1960): pianist and electronic musician. His first interests were classical music and reggae, which he played as a teenager. A TV appearance by bebop giant Oscar Peterson sold him on jazz, which he began playing in the late 1970s. He gigged around for most of the next decade, playing in the band Ghosts, guitarist Mike Cooper's Continental Drift, and his own ten-piece electroacoustic group, Monads. A faithful partner over the years has been reedman Pete McPhail. In 1988, Thomas was granted a Jazz Bursary from the Arts Council to compose new music for Monads. He performed in the 1990 Company event, then was invited back for the marathon gathering in 1991. He joined Tony Oxley's quartet that year (*The Tony Oxley Quartet*, 1992, Incus) and was carried over to the drummer's Celebration Orchestra (*The Enchanted Messenger*, 1994, Soul Note). It was not until 1997 that Thomas issued a full album under his own name (*Remembering*, newjazz.com).

In solo performances, Thomas often plays along with tapes of random TV bites and other sounds. He has played most of Europe's major festivals and has recorded and performed with Steve Beresford, his quartet Scatter with Phil Minton, Evan Parker, Carlos Zingaro, Jim O'Rourke, Thurston Moore, Thomas Borgmann, Sweethearts In A Drugstore, Eugene Chadbourne, Lunge, and the London Improvisers Orchestra. Especially successful have been his duos and such with Lol Coxhill (*Halim*, 1993, Nato; *One Night in Glasgow*, 1994, Scatter) and the trio And with Derek Bailey and drummer Steve Noble (*And*, 1997, Rectangle). Thomas exchanges ideas with fellow pianists Steve Beresford and Veryan Weston on *3 Pianos* (2001, Emanem).

Thornton, Clifford (b. Philadelphia, PA, 6 September 1936; d. Geneva, Switzerland, 1989): trombonist and trumpeter. In his youth, Thornton studied under some of Philly's best brassmen, including trumpeter Donald Byrd and tubaist Ray Draper. After serving in the army in the late 1950s, he landed in New York and began working with Sun Ra's unusual ensemble, the Arkestra. His bop training served him quite well in the setting, and at the same time he began opening his ears to more forward-looking jazz forms. In 1967, he recorded his debut as a free jazzman, *Freedom and Unity* (Third World; reissued 2001, Atavistic/Unheard Music). Two years later, he found himself at the Actuel Festival in Algeria, where he made important connections. He recorded *Ketchaoua* for the BYG label and appeared on several of the label's other albums led by Archie Shepp, Sunny Murray, and Dave Burrell. Besides continuing to work with Shepp and issuing his own records, Thornton collaborated with Sam Rivers and Joe McPhee while teaching music. He cut *The Gardens of Harlem* (JCOA) under that organization's auspices in 1974, which was his final album as a leader. After facing difficulties in France for his political views, Thornton settled in Switzerland where he stayed for the rest of his life, very rarely recording again.

Threadgill, Henry: reedman, composer, and bandleader. A founding member of the AACM, Threadgill first gained public attention through his work with the trio Air. (See entry for Air.) He is acclaimed as both an alto saxophonist and flautist, not to mention being one of the most impressive composers in post-bop jazz.

Despite the success of Air, Threadgill fostered a long interest in larger groups, crafting classic albums with his sextet and septet. His first recording under his own name was made almost a decade prior to Air's demise. *X-75* (1979, Arista/Novus) was an excellent release with an early version of "Sir Simpleton" and a revisited "Air Song." The ensemble included reedmen Joseph Jarman, Douglas Ewart, and Wallace McMillan, vocalist Amina Claudine Myers (also a renowned composer and organist), and no less than four bassists. This ensemble was Threadgill's first dabbling in unusual instrumentation.

When Was That? (1982, About Time) was the debut of Threadgill's Sextett [sic], an inaccurate name since the leader made seven. (Perhaps that extra T was to indicate "sextet + T(hreadgill).") Cornetist Olu Dara, trombonist Craig Harris, drummer John Betsch, and piccolo bassist Brandon Smith joined Hopkins, Ak Laff, and Threadgill on a dizzying set of originals. On *Just the Facts and Pass the Bucket* (1983, Axiom) Smith was replaced by cellist Diedre Murray, a subtle textural switch that added a bit of balance to the ensemble. *Subject to Change* (1984, About Time) replaced Olu Dara and Harris with the equally proficient Rasul Siddik and Ray Anderson, respectively. The album features Amina Claudine Myers singing Cassandra Wilson's lyrics to "A Piece of Software" and Ak Laff's arcane recitation on "Homeostasis."

One of the best records of the Sextett era is *You Know the Number* (1986, Novus), with yet another lineup change: percussionist Reggie Nicholson in for Betsch, and Frank Lacy in the trombone chair. Threadgill's amusing calypso mutation "Bermuda Blues" starts off this raging set; it is complemented by "To Be Announced." Siddik and the drummers distinguish themselves on the vivacious "Those Who Eat Cookies" and "Theme from Thomas Cole." This lineup remained intact on *Easily Slip Into Another World* (1987, Novus), with Indian singer (and Ornette Coleman veteran) Asha Puthli contributing a queer vocal on "My Rock." Influences from all across the American musical spectrum abound: island groove, postmodern cartoon, New Orleans parade, and flat-out weirdness.

Rag, Bush and All (1988, Novus) was the Sextett's swansong, and a fine one at that. Threadgill, Hopkins, Murray, Nicholson, drummer Newman Baker, trumpeter Ted

Daniels, and bass trombonist Bill Lowe judiciously interpret four intricate tunes by the leader, with the level of energy approaching Ornette Coleman's best free units. "Gift" has a feeling of Sun Ra about it, with its slow, impressive horn lines straddling percussion masses. For all its energy, this seems to be the most directionally challenged Sextett disc; the full-group unity of their prior sessions is missing to a degree. Perhaps it was the right time for Threadgill to move on to a fresh concept, and that he did.

The leader's next project was kindred to Ornette Coleman's Prime Time ensemble, with paired instruments and a firmer symmetry of composition and freedom. Very Very Circus consisted of Threadgill, trombonist Curtis Fowlkes, electric guitarists Masujaa and Brandon Ross, tubaists Edwin Rodriguez and Marcus Rojas, and drummer Gene Lake. The group's first effort, *Spirit of Nuff . . . Nuff* (1990, Black Saint), was a rather uneven affair with the low registers weighing heavily on the music. Some tunes are of a piece, martial structures bogged down in muddy bass and reverbed guitars. Lake sounds as if he is plunging through quicksand because of the skewed tone balance. The Caribbean tinge of "Hope A Hope A" and Threadgill's gripping flute feature, "First Church of This," are among the high points. The next Very Very Circus project, *Too Much Sugar for a Dime* (1993, Axiom), corrected the imbalance somewhat by replacing Fowlkes with French horn player Mark Taylor for new buoyancy through higher range. Masujaa and Ross, too, spend more time in the upper range of the guitars, increasing the equilibrium further. Certain tracks feature vocalists (not to very good effect) and added strings and percussion, but the best are those with the core band.

Song Out of My Trees (1993, Black Saint) was an unusual one-off project that saw Threadgill dabbling in other waters. The leader does not even perform on "Crea" or "Over the River Club," content to conduct. The former track features Ted Daniels on valveless hunting horns to striking effect, while on the latter Threadgill's fascination with guitars was given full release by Ed Cherry, James Emery, and Brandon Ross. Amina Claudine Myers's organ levitates the studio on the gospel-inflected title track, and pianist Myra Melford and accordionist Tony Cedras shine.

Like Arthur Blythe, altoist Tim Berne, and a number of other freemen, Threadgill worked all too briefly for Columbia Records. *Carry the Day* (1994) was the first of three discs he cut for the big label, with the band billed as Very Very Circus Plus. On three of the tracks, the core ensemble was augmented variously by Cedras, violinist Jason Hwang, Chinese *pipa* player Wu Man, percussionists Johnny Rudas and Miguel Urbina, and singers Mossa Bildner and Sentinela Toy. The three tunes by the expanded unit tend toward unmanageable density, so much so that Wu Man and Cedras tend to get lost in the shuffle. Nonetheless, it is an extremely absorbing release.

Makin' a Move (1995, Columbia) was Threadgill's last project with Very Very Circus before he moved on to new horizons. It was an exceptional point at which to fold the band's cards, with some of their best-ever performances on four searing tracks. The disc also overlaps a little with *Song Out of My Trees*; Myra Melford appears on "Noisy Flowers" and the three *Song* guitarists, along with fourth wheel Ayodele Aubert, appear both on that track and "The Mockingbird Sin." Cellists Akua Dixon Turre, Diedre Murray, and Michelle Kinney deliciously augment two tracks. The album's blend of jazz, freedom, funk, motivic variation, and chamber music again affirm Threadgill's status as a premier composer and arranger.

Threadgill made another seditious move with his next ensemble, appropriately named Make A Move. Ross, Cedras, electric bassist Stomu Takeishi, and drummer J. T. Lewis seem like the oddest of bedfellows. Yet *Where's Your Cup* (1996, Columbia) confirms that appearance does not equal essence. Ross is particularly versatile, moving from crunching metal to lyrical acoustic picking with ease. The group's sound can be unnerving at first take, even for one accustomed to Threadgill's unpredictable musings, but soon the beauty of the musical conception takes hold. The first sound heard is Cedras's warm squeezebox, humming a reedy mantra with classical, jazz, and South African flavors. Threadgill's alto enters subtly and becomes lost within the accordion wash. Then a rigid tango beat pumps from the bass and Threadgill transports us to Buenos Aires, circa 2050.

For the next few years, Threadgill lay low, drafting new visions while recording sporadically with other projects: the flute quartet Flute Force Four (*Flutistry*, 1997, Black Saint), Douglas Ewart and the Inventions Clarinet Choir (*Angels of Entrance*, 1998, Aarawak, with Braxton, Mitchell, Favors, and others), and electric guitarist Jean-Paul Bourelly (the likably strange *Boom Bop*, 1999, Jazz Magnet). Threadgill also spent much time in Goa, a former Portuguese colony on India's west coast, where he absorbed all manner of exotic musical notions.

Finally, in March 2001, the second album by Make A Move was recorded. On *Everybody's Mouth a Book* (PI Recordings), Tony Cedras was replaced by vibraphonist Bryan Carrott, resulting in a drastic mood swing. Cuban drummer Dafnis Prieto's flexibility is a pleasant change from the comparative firmness of J. T. Lewis. Much promise remains in the ensemble's concept, and one hopes that Threadgill will return to this lineup time and again. Given the optimistic spirit of this album compared with the prior one, it is a safe bet he will.

Issued simultaneously with the above disc was *Up Popped the Two Lips* (2001, PI Recordings), a markedly different album by Threadgill's new project, Zooid. The music itself harkens back to the multilevel complexity of Very Very Circus, but the ensemble blends elements of many past units: guitarist Liberty Ellman, Tarik Benbrahim on the middle Eastern *oud* lute, cellist Dana Leong, tubaist José Davila, and Prieto underscoring the whole schmear. The leader's persistent interest in martial music takes a powder in favor of Arabic, Indian, Latin, and even classical seasonings. Apparently this ensemble was slapped together hurriedly when some members of Make A Move were unavailable for a live gig. Whatever its genesis, Zooid is a remarkably zestful entity, yet another project of promise, ensuring that Threadgill will be a major force in creative music for the foreseeable future.

Tilbury, John: pianist and composer. Long a member of AMM (see entry), Tilbury is one of the most respected pianists in contemporary classical and improvised music. On *Cornelius Cardew Piano Music: 1957–1970* (1996, on his label, Matchless), he interprets the compositions of his late friend and ex-AMM cohort. Beyond most of AMM's albums from 1983's *Generative Themes* (Matchless) onward, one of his most interesting records is *Another Part of the Story* (2003, Emanem) with fellow pianists

Keith Tippett and Howard Riley. Also high in interest level are *Two Chapters and an Epilogue* (1998, Matchless), his rapt duo with Evan Parker, and *The Hands of Caravaggio* (2002, Erstwhile), wherein he plays alongside AMM colleague Keith Rowe in MIMEO.

Tippett, Keith (b. Bristol, U.K., 25 August 1947): pianist, composer, arranger, and bandleader. Tippett arrived in London in 1967 and first recorded as a leader two years later (*You Are Here, I Am There*, 1969, Polydor). He was influenced early on by the African sounds of The Blue Notes, several members of which became Tippett's recording partners. In 1970, he recorded three albums with progressive-rock icons King Crimson, then moved on to one of his most ambitious projects, the fifty-piece megaband Centipede (*September Energy*, 1971, RCA). Tippett's other groups have included Ovary Lodge (self-titled, 1973, RCA), The Ark (*Frames [Music for an Imaginary Film]*, 1978, Ogun), the Dedication Orchestra with Tony Oxley, Tapestry, and various duos and ensembles with artists like pianist Stan Tracey, Louis Moholo, and his wife, Julie Tippetts (the "s" on the end is intentional). His "Mujician" concept, often including the use of prepared piano, has been expanded from a solo conception (*Mujician*, 1981, FMP) to ensemble recordings (*Birdman*, 1995, Cuneiform).

Tippetts, Julie (Julie Driscoll; b. London, England, 8 June 1947): vocalist. Ms. Tippetts and her husband, pianist Keith Tippett (no "s"), have been vital components of British improvised music for over three decades. Originally performing under her maiden name of Julie Driscoll, she has performed with artists as diverse as Carla Bley, John Stevens, Harry Miller, Robert Wyatt, Brian Auger, and pianist John Wolf Brennan. She has only rarely recorded as a leader (*Sunset Glow*, 1975, Utopia; *Shadow Puppeteer*, 2002, Resurgent). Projects with her husband have included Mujician, Centipede, and the quartet RoTToR with trombonist Paul Rutherford and bassist Paul Rogers.

Tommaso, Bruno (b. Rome, Italy, 1946): bassist and composer. Widely respected as a writer and music advocate, Tommaso's *oeuvre* ranges from ancient music to the most modern jazz. He has been a key contributor to Gruppo Romano Free Jazz and the Italian Instabile Orchestra. Some of his recordings are difficult to find outside of Italy, but the Splasc(h) albums *Su Un Tema Di Jerome Kern* (1981, a set of Kern variations) and *Barga Jazz* (1987) are worth seeking out. Tommaso teaches at the Naples Conservatory, cofounded Rome's Testaccio school of music, and has arranged and composed many exciting, complex works.

Tonic: New York performance venue, located at 107 Norfolk Street in Manhattan's Lower East Side. Tonic originally gained notoriety as the club that "stole" John Zorn and his cadre from the Knitting Factory after the tempestuous reedman/composer had a falling-out with Michael Dorf. Since the mid-1990s, Tonic's reputation has outstripped its small size, making it one of the principal venues for avant-garde expression in the city.

Tononi, Tiziano (b. Milan, Italy, 1956): drummer and percussionist. As a young man Tononi studied with Andrew Cyrille, for whom he has also produced albums, and other jazz and classical artists. His studies with percussionist Jonathan Scully led to the contemporary classical trio Moon on the Water. In 1990, Tononi cofounded the Italian Instabile Orchestra with Pino Minafra and Daniele Cavallanti. The drummer and Cavallanti have a long history of collaboration, having performed together in the Jazz Chromatic Ensemble, Nexus, the duo Udu Calls, and Tononi's Society of Freely Syncopated Organic Pulses. With the Society he has paid homage to several primary influences, including Don Cherry (*Awake Nu!*, 1996), Rahsaan Roland Kirk (*You Did It, You Did It*, 2000, both Splasc(h)), and John Coltrane (*Coltrane's Infinity Train*, 1998, Musica Jazz).

Total Music Meeting: improvisation festival held annually in Berlin, Germany, since 1968. The festival is managed by Free Music Production (FMP) and has featured the cream of European and American improvisers including Peter Brötzmann, Alex von Schlippenbach, Han Bennink, and Cecil Taylor. Early in 2003, the city of Berlin withdrew all financial support for the festival, forcing the promoters to seek other funding. Its sister program, the Workshop Freie Musik, was conducted annually from 1969 until its funding was withdrawn in 1999.

Town Hall: New York performance venue, at 123 W. 43rd Street in New York City, between 6th & 7th Avenues. Acoustically excellent, it first gained renown as the site of women's rights activities in the 1920s under feminists like Margaret Sanger. Marian Anderson started her career at Town Hall in 1935, the same year that the America's Town Meetings radio program began there. It has since been the location of several significant jazz performances, some earth-shaking (Ornette Coleman) and some disastrous (Charles Mingus). Since 1988, the Not Just Jazz series at Town Hall has presented performances by the likes of Don Cherry, the Art Ensemble of Chicago, Allen Ginsberg, Cassandra Wilson, and the Lounge Lizards.

Toyozumi, Sabu (b. Tsurumi, Yokohama, Japan, 1943): drummer and bandleader. Toyozumi played with a drum-and-fife band as a child and became a professional musician after college. He was one of the very few foreigners to officially join the AACM in Chicago, studying with the collective in the early 1970s before moving to Paris for a year. His duo with altoist Kaoru Abe brought Toyozumi major attention (*Overhang Party*, 1978, ALM). He has worked with many improvisers who have visited Japan, including Leo Smith, Derek Bailey, Paul Rutherford, Marco Eneidi, Misha Mengelberg, and Peter Brötzmann (*Duo*, 1982, Improvised Company).

Tramontana, Sebi (b. Rosolini, Sicily, Italy, 12 December 1960): trombonist. Tramontana explored guitar and soprano sax in his youth before claiming the trombone as his principal instrument. He studied under Giancarlo Schiaffini at the Casella Conservatory in L'Aquila and became immersed in Rome's avant-jazz society. His first recording was Stefano Maltese's *Music From the Island* (1986, TMR). The following year he established a trio with Daniel Studer and Roberto Altamura, which performed at various Italian festivals. In 1988 he joined Mario Schiano and two-thirds of the G-T-Ch (Ganelin) Trio, Vladimir Tarasov and Vladimir Chekasin, for the exciting *Red and Blue* (Splasc(h)). In 1990, Tramontana joined the Italian Instabile Orchestra in time for its first concerts and recordings. Georg Gräwe has also been a frequent partner, in duo and ensemble settings (*Concert in Berlin 1996*, Wobbly Rail). Besides his solo efforts, Tramontana has performed with many Europeans and Americans, including Barry Guy, Evan Parker, Ken Vandermark, Paul Rutherford, the Südpool Project, Joëlle Léandre, and Carlos Zingaro (recording with the last pair on *The Chicken Check in Complex*, 2001, Leo).

Transition: Boston-based record label. Little is documented or remembered about the tiny label, which had a small catalog of bebop albums by Donald Byrd, Lucky Thompson, Curtis Fuller, and Pepper Adams in the 1950s. Though it was fairly minor in a field of giants, Transition holds a place of honor in the annals of free-jazz history for two iconoclastic releases: *Jazz by Sun Ra* and Cecil Taylor's *Jazz Advance!* These were the first available documents from two men who would soon ride high in the pantheon of creative music. While neither might sound especially adventurous in the twenty-first century, in their time these records marked a significant departure from jazz orthodoxy. Transition's in-house producer at the time was Tom Wilson, who later gained fame as a producer for Bob Dylan and the Velvet Underground. Wilson gave Taylor spacious rein to develop his music as he saw fit. Wilson realized that successful recordings often depend upon such grace by studio personnel, whose agendas and hang-ups can make or break a session. Were it not for Wilson and his employers, the tide of jazz might not have turned so quickly by the decade's end. (See entries for Cecil Taylor and Sun Ra.)

Trio-X: trio of multi-instrumentalist Joe McPhee, bassist Dominic Duval, and drummer Jay Rosen, born out of the CIMP label's experimental groupings. Three albums have been released on Cadence Jazz since the trio's inception: *Watermelon Suite* (1999), *Rapture* (2000, with violinist Rosi Hertlein added), and the superb *On Tour . . . Toronto/Rochester* (2002). The live set includes some of the trio's best work, especially on "Trail of Tears (for Jim Pepper)" and revamps of "Blue Monk" and McPhee's "Old Eyes." Trio-X epitomizes the incredible degrees of listening and intuition that make free-jazz sessions truly successful.

Trovesi, Gianluigi (b. Nembro, Italy, 1944): reeds player, composer, and bandleader. Trovesi completed his formal musical studies in 1966, well versed in the fullest range of styles. In 1977, he assembled his first unit (*Baghet*, 1978, Dischi Della), joined the Giorgio Gaslini Quintet, and soon began teaching at the Milan Conservatory. Trovesi was a member of the RAI TV Big Band for well over a decade in addition to his other teaching and performing activities. His project *Les Boîtes à Musique* (1988, Splasc(h)), with Tiziano Tononi, united improvisation with taped backing and electronic processing. Since the early 1990s, Trovesi has performed with the Italian Instabile

Orchestra, Nexus, and his own octet (*From G to G*, 1992, Soul Note). Collaborators include Anthony Braxton, Conrad Bauer, Steve Lacy, Han Bennink, Paolo Damiani, Andrea Centazzo, Misha Mengelberg, Marc Charig, John Carter, Horace Tapscott, and Evan Parker. Trovesi has received several national and worldwide music awards. *Let* (1992, Splasc(h)) is an uplifting trio session with Giancarlo Schiaffini and drummer Fulvio Maras.

Tsahar, Assif (b. Tel Aviv, Israel, 11 June 1969): reedman. Originally a guitarist, Tsahar switched to saxophone at age seventeen. Inspired greatly by Albert Ayler, Tsahar moved to New York City in 1990 to begin working with the city's freemen. He began playing bass clarinet in 1998 and founded the Hopscotch record label the following year. Tsahar was married to drummer Susie Ibarra for several years, recording with her on *Home Cookin'* (1998, Hopscotch) and adding William Parker for a trio on *Shekhina* (1996, Eremite) and *Ein Sof* (1998, Silkheart). The saxophonist has performed with Parker in his Little Huey Creative Music Orchestra and In Order To Survive. *Soul Bodies, Volume 1* (2002, Ayler) is an earthshaking duet between Tsahar and Hamid Drake. Other partners include Peter Kowald, Ken Vandermark, Rashied Ali, Butch Morris, Cecil Taylor, Rob Brown, Mat Maneri, and Jim Black.

Tyler, Charles (b. Cadiz, KY, 20 July 1941; d. Toulon, France, 27 June 1992): baritone and alto saxophonist. Tyler studied piano as a child but switched to clarinet and saxophones as a teenager. In 1960, he moved to Cleveland and began playing sometimes with Albert Ayler, whom he had briefly met in high school. Tyler continued to build his outstanding chops on local gigs, and he joined Ayler in New York in 1965. After a couple of recording sessions and some tense tours with Ayler, Tyler grew tired of playing second fiddle and quit the group. He had led two dates for ESP himself (*Charles Tyler Ensemble/First Album*, 1966; *Eastern Man Alone/Second Album*, 1967), but those got scant attention. Tyler spent a year studying under David Baker at Indiana University, then he got involved in the increasingly hot jazz scene in Los Angeles. David Murray, Arthur Blythe, and Bobby Bradford were regular partners until Tyler went back to New York in 1973. His album *Saga of the Outlaws* (1976, Nessa) became a minor classic that influenced many younger freemen. One of his best regular gigs was in Billy Bang's ensemble, with which he made three albums in 1981 and 1982. By the time of his death, not long after recording *Midwestern Drifter* (1992, Adda), Tyler had never found the measure of fame he truly deserved. Unfortunately, most of his albums are out of print.

Tyner, McCoy (Alfred McCoy Tyner, b. Philadelphia, PA, 1938): pianist with John Coltrane's inventive 1960s ensembles. His brocaded style was well suited to Coltrane's post-Miles Davis experiments but Tyner left the tenorist in 1965, no longer willing to play in the atonal, drum-heavy atmosphere that predominated the quartet as Coltrane moved further into free music. Tyner worked as a sideman and leader for Blue Note during the rest of the 1960s, but he gained his overdue recognition after signing with Milestone in the early 1970s.

U

Ullmann, Gebhard (b. Köln, Germany, 1957): reedman, composer, and bandleader. After coming to Berlin in 1983, Ullmann began his career in earnest. His debut album, *Out to Lunch* (Nabel, 1985), hinted at his love for Dolphy's music but only scratched the surface of Ullmann's vision. The group known as Tá Lam (Songlines, 1998) united musicians from both sides of the Berlin Wall and received a number of awards. He has contributed to ensembles like Friedemann Aquamarine, Springtime, and Die Elefanten in Europe, and Conference Call and Basement Research (with Ellery Eskelin) in America. One especially ambitious project was *Trad Corrosion* (1995, Nabel), his trio with American drummer Phil Haynes and German acoustic guitarist Andreas Willers. Ullmann has also performed with bassist Joe Fonda's quintet.

Ulmer, James "Blood" (b. St. Matthews, SC, 2 February 1942): electric guitarist, vocalist, composer, and bandleader. Ulmer was one of the first musicians to apply Ornette Coleman's harmolodic theory to his own music after leaving the altoist's band. Like Coleman, his music tends to be steeped heavily in blues and performed with a nearly human kind of expressiveness. He has taken hold of the early promise of electric free music as demonstrated by Coleman and headed off in his own direction, with a good degree of success.

Ulmer's career began in Pittsburgh's R&B circles, and he spread out into funkier sounds after moving to Columbus, Ohio, in the mid-1960s. A period in Detroit further fueled his desire to experiment with rock-derived forms, and his discovery of Jimi Hendrix during that period left an indelible mark on his guitar style. In 1971, Ulmer came to New York and worked in bebop bands, including Art Blakey's, for a couple of years. He soon discovered, however, that free jazz held a stronger appeal. Ulmer met drummer Rashied Ali in 1973 and recorded an album with Ali's quintet on the

Survival label. Ali directed him to Coleman, and another element of Ulmer's eventual musical identity was put into place. The repetitive rhythms and thematic development native to harmolodics became part and parcel of Ulmer's aesthetic for the next several years.

Ulmer's debut as a leader was *Revealing* (1977), issued on the small In & Out label. The album made few waves but easily demonstrated the guitarist's ability to straddle the line between jazz and rock. His approach was not as cacophonous as Sonny Sharrock's but reasonably accessible even during his most outrageous moments. *Tales of Captain Black* (1978, DIW) issued the following year was more successful and focused. It remains one of the more popular items in Ulmer's catalog and features the impetuous guitarist with Ornette and Denardo Coleman and electric bassist Jamaaladeen Tacuma. The organic, nearly modal feel that unifies the eight funky tunes confirms that harmolodics could work well in contexts other than Coleman's own compositions.

His friendship with David Murray led to the establishment of the Music Revelation Ensemble (MRE) in 1980. The MRE was more of a concept than a set unit; bassist Amin Ali has been a regular participant, but several reedmen and drummers have come and gone as Ulmer has revisited the idea over the years with generally sound results. Phalanx, a later group with Ali, bassist Sirone, and saxophonist George Adams, was equally explorative and arguably more successful than the MRE (*Phalanx*, 1986, Moers).

In 1981, Ulmer landed an unlikely contract with Columbia Records, becoming one of several free musicians that the major label tried out and dumped after a few years. The resulting three albums were not exactly Ulmer's most inspired work. *Black Rock* (1982), the second, is an especially confused mishmash of poorly conceived ideas and high-volume chops demonstration. He fared better as a sideman on two of Arthur Blythe's Columbia records. A one-off session for Blue Note (*America, Do You Remember the Love*, 1986) was rather weakly recorded but more accessible than Ulmer's prior efforts.

Since the mid-1980s, Ulmer has steadily withdrawn from free jazz but has kept up his harmolodic interests (*Harmolodic Guitar with Strings*, 1993, DIW). He has successfully recast himself as a forward-thinking bluesman, beginning with *Blues All Night* (1989, In & Out). *Music Speaks Louder Than Words* (1997, Koch Jazz) blends his twin loves, Ornette Coleman's music and the blues. In 2001, Ulmer again surprised his critics by releasing *Memphis Blood: The Sun Sessions* (Label M), a straight blues disc recorded in the very cradle of rock-and-roll, Sun Studios, by funk-rock-jazz guitarist Vernon Reid. Besides his own projects, Ulmer has worked with Third Rail, Karl Berger, Joe Henderson, Samm Bennett, and eclectic guitar man Ry Cooder, among others.

Uncool Festival of International Contemporary Music: annual festival held at Lago di Poschiavo, Switzerland. The festival has featured the best American and European improvisers since its founding in 1999. Among the major artists have been Peter

Kowald, Amiri Baraka, Les Diaboliques, Alan Silva's Celestrial Communications Orchestra, Charles Gayle, Cecil Taylor, and Evan Parker.

Unit Records: Swiss independent, musician-owned label, directed by Lucas Niggli. Featured artists in their catalog include Urs Leimgruber, Pierre Favre, Hans Koch, and other Swiss and middle-European performers.

V

van der Schyff, Dylan (b. Johannesburg, South Africa, 1971): drummer and percussionist. One of Canada's premier free improvisers, van der Schyff is the husband and frequent performing partner of cellist Peggy Lee (*These Are Our Shoes*, 1999, Spool). He studied percussion at the University of Victoria and jazz at McGill University in Montreal. Van der Schyff moved to Vancouver in 1991 and fell in love with the city's bold jazz scene. A member of the NOW Orchestra and Talking Pictures, he has performed with John Butcher (*Points, Snags and Windings*, 2001, Meniscus), François Houle, Tony Wilson, Scott Fields Ensemble, Barry Guy, and most of Canada's finest. Van der Schyff is especially influenced by Han Bennink and has experimented with electronic enhancements of his minimal kit. His International Project includes Mark Helias, Michael Moore, and trumpeter Brad Turner.

Van Hove, Fred (b. Antwerp, Belgium, 1937): pianist and composer. Classically trained at the Music Academy of Belgium, Van Hove embraced free improvisation in the early 1960s as the wave spread across Europe. In 1966, he began working with Peter Brötzmann, taking part in the legendary *Machine Gun* (1968, FMP). The two men formed a trio with Han Bennink (*Brötzmann, van Hove, Bennink*, 1973, FMP) that lasted until the mid-1970s. All three men continued to work on other projects with various personnel (*Nipples*, 1969, Calig; reissued 2001, Atavistic). He was also a key player on Manfred Schoof's important *European Echoes* (1969, FMP) and in Don Cherry's New Eternal Rhythm Orchestra. From 1970 onward, Van Hove gave impressive solo concerts all across Europe, approaching free improvisation with the technical aplomb gained through his academic studies. He has also made a sideline career out of accompanying silent films.

In 1972, Van Hove and friends founded WIM (Werkgroep Improviserende Musici), a collective similar to the JCOA, which promoted free music and fair employment practices for musicians. He has led his various "ML" (Musica Libera) ensembles since about 1980, uniting performers from across Europe in different combinations. An interest in duo performances has resulted in great concerts and recordings with Brötzmann, Steve Lacy, Lol Coxhill, Albert Mangelsdorff (*The Berlin Concert*, 1971, FMP), Barry Guy, Evan Parker, Philipp Wachsmann, and the like. Van Hove has played with piano quartets, string ensembles, poets, painters, and vocalists, occasionally stretching out on accordion or church organ. In 1996, he was made a Cultural Ambassador of Flanders, and two years later he founded the Nuscope record label. In 2002, a compendium of his 1970s solo and duo recordings for the Vogel label was issued by Atavistic Unheard Music.

Vandermark, Ken (b. Warwick, RI, 22 September 1964): reedman, composer, and bandleader. Vandermark's interest in improvised music stems from a wealth of influences: Anthony Braxton, Charlie Parker, Eric Dolphy, John Cage, and most every major tenor saxophonist. At present, he might well be Chicago's highest-profile free musician, perhaps second only to Fred Anderson. He is an appreciated cheerleader of sorts for improvised music, regularly dedicating compositions or bands to the many free performers who have influenced his career.

Vandermark started out on trumpet but switched to sax in junior high. In his late teens in Montreal, he led the band Fourth Stream from 1983 to 1986 while attending McGill University. He then relocated to Boston, where he led the group Lombard Street for three years. In 1989, Vandermark settled in Chicago and became a major force in the city's new music community. He joined Hal Russell's NRG Ensemble in 1992 (see entries for Russell and NRG Ensemble), the same year in which he established the group Caffeine and his own highly popular quartet.

Vandermark's first recording as a leader was *Solid Action* (1994) on the small Platypus label. Since the quartet's breakup the following year, Vandermark has maintained membership in, or leadership of, several other improvising units: Steam, Cinghiale, Vandermark 5, DKV Trio, and Steelwool Trio. He wears his influences on his sleeve by participating in a number of impressive tribute projects: Witches and Devils (for Albert Ayler), Spaceways Incorporated (Sun Ra and George Clinton), School Days (Steve Lacy), and the Joe Harriott Project. He has also been a member at different times of the Flying Luttenbachers, the Boxhead Ensemble, Territory Band, the Sinister Luck Ensemble, and the Crown Royals.

The Vandermark 5 has been his most heralded ensemble, and with good reason. Trombonist/guitarist Jeb Bishop, reedman Dave Rempis, bassist Kent Kessler, and drummer Tim Mulvenna reflexively ignite fires under the leadership of Vandermark. Typical of their fare is *Burn the Incline* (2000, Atavistic), on which the quintet interprets eight compositions dedicated to William Parker, Misha Mengelberg, Joe Morris, and other major and minor figures of improvised music. Every moment of the group's interaction is spot-on, their moves directed by an incredible level of intuition and creativity.

The first thousand copies each of *Burn the Incline* and the slightly less jazz-based *Acoustic Machine* (2001, Atavistic) included limited-edition second discs, featuring the quintet covering classic free-jazz compositions by Don Cherry, Joe McPhee, Ornette Coleman, Eric Dolphy, Archie Shepp, Cecil Taylor, Anthony Braxton, Sun

Ra, Lester Bowie, Frank Wright, Carla Bley, Julius Hemphill, and Jimmy Giuffre. In 2002, Atavistic collected both discs into one double package, *Free Jazz Classics, Vols. 1 and 2*, so that fans of the Van 5 who were not lucky enough to score those original releases could finally enjoy this exciting music. Both discs bear the Van 5's marks of distinction, but it is bliss to hear one of today's cutting-edge ensembles addressing music that inspired their path.

The DKV Trio, with Kessler and drummer Hamid Drake, is a radically different animal. Recordings like *Baraka* (1997, Okkadisk) are almost unbearably intense at times, finally relieved by the simmering "Consequence" that closes the album. Disc one of *Live in Wels and Chicago 1998* (Okkadisk) presents the trio's vital recasting of Don Cherry's seminal "Complete Communion"; disc two offers three extended original works of differing moods. The trio has also recorded albums in support of the Aaly Trio (*Double or Nothing*, 2002, Okkadisk), Joe Morris, and Fred Anderson.

Vandermark formerly conducted the monthly "Head Exam" improv concert series in downtown New York and received a MacArthur Foundation "genius grant" in 1999 for his contributions to American arts. He has worked with the Aaly Trio on several concerts and recordings (*Stumble*, 1998, Okkadisk) and has been a featured sideman with Morris, Anderson, and Peter Brötzmann's Chicago Octet and Tentet.

Vario: pseudocollective founded by German trombonist Günter Christmann. Perhaps inspired by the success of Derek Bailey's Company experiments and the Instant Composers Pool, Christmann founded this loose aggregate in 1979. The name obviously implies a wide variety of performers and modes of musical expression within the group. Though Company often included both European and American performers, Vario was more exclusively European in its makeup. The group has recorded some studio albums but was primarily intended as a live performance ensemble. The personnel has included not only top-rung improvising musicians such as Dutch bassist Maarten van Regteren Altena and German drummer Paul Lovens, but also a varying number of actors, singers, and mimes.

Varner, Tom (b. Morristown, NJ, 17 June 1957): French horn player. One of the few specialists on his instrument in the free-jazz field, Varner is a superb technician on a par with Vincent Chancey. He began with piano studies in his youth, then moved to the horn. He drew inspiration from the recordings of Julius Watkins, who had brought the French horn into bebop and cool jazz settings with excellent results. Varner studied at New England Conservatory of Music and relocated to New York after graduation. The following year he recorded *The Tom Varner Quartet* (Soul Note), surprising critics and free jazzmen alike with his versatility and improvising skills. He has issued several more albums on Soul Note, Omnitone, New Note, and New World, and has worked with John Zorn, Lee Konitz, Steve Lacy, the George Gruntz Concert Jazz Band, Franz Koglmann, Anthony Braxton, Orange Then Blue, the East Down Septet, New Age musician Scott Cossu, and other artists. He supported Miles Davis in a 1991 Montreux Jazz Festival performance and even backed Beat writer William S. Burroughs on *Dead City Radio* (1990, Polygram).

Velvet Lounge: Chicago jazz club owned by saxophonist Fred Anderson. Located at 2128 1/2 S. Indiana Avenue, the venue opened in 1982 following the closure of Bird-house, Anderson's previous club. It is one of the city's most respected venues for outward-reaching music.

Vesala, Edward (Martii Juhani Vesala; b. Mäntyharju, Finland, 15 February 1945): drummer and percussionist. Vesala was a Finnish counterpart of Miles Davis, in a way, given his propensity for uniting jazz and rock with elements of his native culture. After coming out of the Sibelius Academy, he explored fusion of that ilk with Eero Koivistoinen and "Baron" Seppo Paakkunainen. In 1972, Vesala began his associa-tion with ECM by appearing on Jan Garbarek's *Tryptikon*. He built up a cadre of close associates including Charlie Mariano, Juhani Aaltonen, and Tomasz Stánko (*Nan Madol*, 1974, ECM, perhaps his triumph). Vesala and Stánko collaborated with American free jazzmen J. D. Parran, Bob Stewart, and Reggie Workman on *Heavy Life* (1980), issued on his own Leo label (not to be confused with Leo Feigin's im-print). *Ode to the Death of Jazz* (1989, ECM) was a strike against the conventional-ism of artists, like Wynton Marsalis, who sought to restrict the boundaries of jazz. His ensemble Sound & Fury was birthed from his series of workshops in the 1980s. Vesala composed for the Helsinki Philharmonic and collaborated with Kenny Wheeler and saxman Gary Windo before his death from heart failure at the age of fifty-four.

Victo: record label associated with the Victoriaville Festival in Québec, Canada. Many of the label's releases have been recorded at the festival, others simply feature artists who have performed there. Among the headliners are Fred Frith/René Lussier, John Butcher, Chris Burn, and Derek Bailey.

Vienna Art Orchestra (VAO): experimental ensemble founded by pianist Mathias Rüegg. The VAO has a particularly eclectic track record, having paid tribute to minimalist classical composer Erik Satie, Mozart, Brahms, Ellington, and Mingus in their recordings. Of its historical members, perhaps only saxophonist Wolfgang Puschnig has a solid reputation in America, but other outstanding performers within its ranks include pianist Uli Scherer, trumpeters Karl Fian, Herbert Joos, and Hannes Kottek, and trombonist Christian Radovan. Puschnig has been one of the VAO's principals since its inception, having worked in a duo with Rüegg for several years beforehand. The group's most surprising contributor was vocalist Lauren Newton, an American expatriate who functioned primarily as an extra "horn" within the en-semble. Newton remained with the band until 1989 and was eventually replaced by Polish diva Urszula Dudziak, whose own live concerts frequently feature multiple real-time overdubs of her clarion voice.

Concerto Piccolo (1980, HatArt) was the Vienna Art Orchestra's debut disc, and an auspicious one at that. Rüegg certainly wears his inspirations on his sleeve, from staunch classics to Charles Mingus. The American bassist gets loving attention on "Jelly Roll, But Mingus Rolls Better." It's a step beyond "My Jelly Roll Soul," Mingus's own tribute to jazz pioneer Jelly Roll Morton, and the VAO isn't too humble about moving away from the signature Mingus sound after a few moments. Newton beams as her spontaneous vocal darts in and around the group figures. (Another brilliant rendition of "Jelly Roll" can be found on *From No Time to Rag Time* (1982, HatArt), the VAO's second disc.)

Herbert Joos could be Europe's answer to Lester Bowie, so pliable and witty is his trumpet technique. He is heard in peak form on *Suite for the Green Eighties* (1983, HatArt), Rüegg's bang-up accolade for the Green Party's politicoenvironmental success across Europe in that era. Joos creates his own tone vocabulary on the cool-school-inspired "Plädoyer for Sir Mayor Moll," showing utter disregard for conventional intonation or the chord changes. Serialism is one coloring device used in the five-part title suite, incredible in harmonic and rhythmic inventiveness. The suite begins almost as an afterthought, adapts to its surroundings, and eventually becomes an unstoppable swing blowout, one of the many distinguished peaks of Rüegg's career as a writer and bandleader.

Dudziak is featured on *Artistry in Rhythm: European Suite* (2000, TCB), yet another cross-pollination of European and American theses. This time around, Rüegg molds the VAO into an ersatz, late-period Stan Kentonish organization, with ponderously heavy but appealing charts, complex time signatures, and crunchy electric guitar by Wolfgang Muthspiel. The fifteen selections are inspired by various European capital cities. Each tune is completely different from the next, reflecting the individual characters of the honored cities.

There are myriad other excellent discs in the VAO canon, some now hard to find due to HatArt's cutbacks. *A Notion in Perpetual Motion* (1992, HatArt) prominently features the agile Newton on "Voices Without Words" (one of the most "out there" selections) and "Lady Delay." Monk's "Round Midnight" is handled faithfully by Joos and Scherer, and "H. M. Blues," written by clarinetist (and King of Thailand) Bhumibol Adulyadej, is pulled out of its Benny Goodman insipidness by Joos. *Tango from Obango* (1997, Extraplatte) showcases saxman Harry Sokal on the charming "Polish Contrasts," and Newton on the title track and "The World of Be-Band and Big Bop," an over-the-top jazz eruption. *Duke Ellington's Sound of Love* (2000, TCB) is another update of jazz traditions, Duke as seen through Mingus's eyes and then heard through Rüegg's ears. The orchestra lavishes love on each gem.

The best entry point, perhaps, for truly learning to appreciate the VAO is *Highlights: Live in Vienna* (1993, Polygram), which revisits many of the band's finest moments in one incendiary concert performance. "Perpetuum Mobile" (aka "A Notion in Perpetual Motion"), "Two Little Animals," and "Haluk" are among the pinnacles of this eminently satisfying release featuring Newton, Joos, Sokal, and guest trombonist Joseph Bowie.

Vinkeloe, Biggi (Brigid; b. Germany): alto saxophonist and flautist. Now based in Sweden, Vinkeloe has enjoyed a long rapport with drummer Peeter Uuskyla, particularly in trios with bassists such as Barre Phillips (the outstanding *Mbat*, 1994, LJ), Peter Friis Nielsen (*Sweet Odd*, 1995, Horizon), Georg Wolf, and Peter Kowald. In 1988, Vinkeloe performed with Cecil Taylor's European Orchestra in Berlin (*Legba Crossing*, 1989, FMP). She has also played with Gino Robair, Perry Robinson, Miya Masaoka,

Steve Swell, Ken Filiano, a special American trio with Lisle Ellis and Donald Robinson, church organist Karen Nelson, and in multimedia events. Her sax tone tends toward the light and melodic, unlike many free jazzers.

Vision Festival: annual New York City festival, produced by bassist William Parker and his wife, dancer Patricia Nicholson, since 1996 under the Arts For Art umbrella. Parker's first attempt at assembling such a gathering, the 1984 Sound Unity Festival, was not successful financially, but the lessons learned have made the Vision Festival one of the world's greatest jazz/improv events. Concerts are usually held in more than one location throughout the ten-day (usually) festival, including the Knitting Factory and the Orensanz Arts Center on Norfolk Street. Special associated events have included dance companies, painters, and other extramusical artists.

   Vision One: Vision Festival 1997 Compiled (1997, Aum Fidelity) contains two-CDs worth of performances from the fest's second year: Trio Hurricane (with Parker, Glenn Spearman, and drummer Paul Murphy), Parker's Little Huey Creative Music Orchestra, John Zorn with Susie Ibarra, the David S. Ware Quartet, Borah Bergman with Denis Charles and Roy Campbell, Rashied Ali's Prima Materia, Bill Cole's Untempered Ensemble, Butch Morris's conduction unit, Other Dimensions in Music, and other artists. The 2002 fest, subtitled "Vision Against Violence," featured Positive Knowledge, Little Huey, Rob Brown's quartet, Joe McPhee, a Don Cherry Memorial Band, Dewey Redman's quartet, Roy Campbell's "Buhaina" (a tribute to bop drummer Art Blakey), and dozens of other artists.

Voice Crack: electronic improvising ensemble centered around electronic musicians Norbert Möslang and Andy Guhl. Since the early 1980s, they have specialized in using "cracked everyday electronics"—that is, short-circuited synthesizers, toys, and gadgets—as sound production devices. Drummer Knut Remond made the ensemble a trio on *Earflash* (1990, Dexter's Cigar), while Gunter Müller joined on percussion for *buda_rom* (2002, For 4 Ears). Guhl, Möslang, and Müller are also members of poire_z (see entry). Voice Crack have partnered with Otomo Yoshihide, Borbetomagus, and Jim O'Rourke.

Vu, Cuong (b. Vietnam): trumpeter. Vu came from a musical family, which moved from Vietnam to Seattle when he was six. He took up the trumpet five years later and excelled on the horn, earning a scholarship to New England Conservatory. Saxophonist Joe Maneri was one of Vu's instructors and a powerful influence upon his development as an artist. Vu moved to New York upon graduation and became a popular fixture on the avant-jazz scene, working with Dave Douglas, Gerry Hemingway, Andy Laster, Mark Helias, Chris Speed's Yeah No, Bobby Previte's band Weather Clear Track Fast, and the big band Orange Then Blue. Recently he has recorded with Pat Metheny, Laurie Anderson, and Satoko Fujii. *Bound* (2000, Omnitone) features Vu's quartet including keyboardist Jamie Saft, bassist Stomu Takeishi, and drummer Jim Black.

Vysniauskas, Petras: reedman. Vysniauskas is a rising star of Lithuanian jazz whose notions of freedom were directly in line with the original G-T-Ch Trio; he played a prime role in Slava Ganelin's subsequent trio (see G-T-Ch Trio's entry). His quintet on *Viennese Concert* (1989, Leo) includes Ganelin, Mika Markovich, pianist Kestutis Lusas, and percussionist Gediminas Laurinavicius. He is devoted to both classical forms and to the folk music of his homeland, both of which are evident on this solid recording. Lusas seems to be better attuned to the saxophonist than Ganelin, tastefully building synthetic backdrops for Vysniauskas's keening improvisations. The leader has also recorded in a duo with Arkadi Gotesman on *Lithuania* (1990, ITM), where his bass clarinet and flute stroll through quiet dreamscapes of shrewdly delicate percussion.

W

Wachsmann, Philipp (b. Uganda, 1944): violinist, violist, and electronic musician. Wachsmann was steeped early on in the avant-classical movement. He first began experimenting with electronic manipulation of his violin sound as a member of Yggdrasil, which interpreted the music of Cornelius Cardew, Morton Feldman, John Cage, and other avant composers. He stepped away from formal classicism into free improvisation in about 1970, beginning with the ensemble Chamberpot. Tony Oxley provided him with entry into Europe's wider free improv circles, leading to gigs with Derek Bailey's Company, Paul Lytton (*The Balance of Trade*, 1996, CIMP), Keith Tippett's Ark, Barry Guy, Fred Van Hove (*Was Macht Ihr Denn?*, 1984, FMP), Evan Parker, and Rüdiger Carl. He has been a member of Iskra 1903 (replacing Bailey), Quintet Moderne, King Übü Orchestrü, London Improvisers Orchestra, and the London Jazz Composers Orchestra. Wachsmann's first recording was 1973's *Balance* (Incus). *Chathuna* (1996, Bead) is an impressive solo outing.

Wadud, Abdul (Khabir; b. Cleveland, OH, 30 April 1947): cellist. Wadud has played cello exclusively since he was nine years old and has been a vital member of many jazz aggregates. He studied music at Youngstown University and later Oberlin, where he met Julius Hemphill. Wadud spent a few years in the New Jersey Symphony and entered free music in the early 1970s. Besides Hemphill, who was one of Wadud's most regular employers up until the altoists' death, one of Wadud's strongest associations was with altoist Arthur Blythe. From 1976 through the 1980s, the cellist was a prime player in Blythe's unusual quintet with tuba, electric guitar, and drums (*Light Blue*, 1982, and several other Columbia albums). Wadud debuted as a leader on *By Myself* (1977, Bishara) but has only rarely led his own dates. From 1982 to 1984, Wadud, Anthony Davis, and James Newton performed as a trio and in the octet Episteme (self-titled, 1981, Gramavision); Davis has remained a consistent partner. Wadud's other employers include Oliver Lake, Muhal Richard Abrams, Leroy Jenkins, Cecil Taylor,

Frank Lowe, David Murray, the Black Swan Quartet, Marty Ehrlich's Dark Woods Ensemble, and Sam Rivers.

Waldron, Mal (Malcolm Earl Waldron; b. New York, NY, 16 August 1926; d. 2 December 2002): pianist, composer, and bandleader. Waldron ably straddled the line between free and mainstream jazz, accompanying Billie Holiday in her final days and inaugurating the ECM label with *Free at Last* (1969). Early in his career, Waldron's piano interests lay chiefly in classical music while he played jazz on alto sax. While studying at Queens College he dropped the sax entirely and spread out into jazz piano. His marvelous, classically trained technique combined with an interest in the harmonic innovations of Monk and Mingus (with whom Waldron worked in the mid-1950s) to result in a unique and easily identified personal style.

Waldron's early resumé included stints with saxman Ike Quebec and blues singer Big Nick Nicholas. Once he got into Mingus's band, the pianist's ears were opened further to a wealth of possibilities for jazz interpretation. In the 1950s and 1960s, Waldron was a house pianist and recording supervisor for Prestige Records; he also performed on a series of successful "Music Minus One" instructional records. A short but influential period with Eric Dolphy gave Waldron a deeper interest in free music, which he explored on albums like *The Quest* (1961, New Jazz/OJC).

After some time with singer Abbey Lincoln and some jobs as a film scorer, Waldron moved to Europe in 1965 and remained there until his death. He led his own groups almost exclusively on an impressive string of discs (*Sweet Love, Bitter Love*, 1967, Impulse; *Black Glory*, 1971, Enja; *Dedication*, 1985, Soul Note) and occasionally made duo sessions with Steve Lacy (*Sempre Amore*, 1986, Soul Note) and George Haslam (*Waldron-Haslam*, 1994, Slam). His records are a mixed bag stylistically, some much freer than others, but performance-wise all are brilliant.

Ward, Carlos (b. Ancon, Panama, 1 May 1940): alto saxophonist. Ward grew up in Seattle, where he learned the clarinet in high school. While stationed at a naval base in Germany in the mid-1960s, Ward became aware of free jazz upon working with Albert Mangelsdorff and witnessing Eric Dolphy in action not long before Dolphy's death. Ward returned to Seattle, where he had the fortune to sit in with John Coltrane and form a brief, sadly unrecorded relationship with the saxophone giant. Upon moving to New York, Ward played funk jazz with B.T. Express while honing his free chops with Don Cherry, Rashied Ali, Sam Rivers, and other prominent figures. In 1973, Ward began a lasting partnership with pianist Abdullah Ibrahim, and in 1986 he replaced the late Jimmy Lyons in Cecil Taylor's unit. Ward was a fairly able replacement for Lyons, tentative upon first entry into Taylor's realm but well versed in the hard blues that Lyons had successfully plied in that setting. Since then, Ward has worked with Carla Bley's big band, Ahmed Abdullah, Karl Berger, and others. He has only led a few dates, the best being *Lito* (1988, Leo).

Ware, David S(pencer) (b. Plainfield, NJ, 7 November 1949): saxophonist, composer, and bandleader. Ware is a major force in free jazz in the new century. He combines the technical wisdom of Coltrane with the sheer passion, fury, and gutbucket-blues sense of Shepp. From the time that he first made waves with the Cecil Taylor Unit in the 1970s, Ware has steadily climbed up the ladder of free-jazz prominence to claim his seat in its uppermost echelons. His mammoth tone is possibly more concentrated than even that of Pharoah Sanders, one of his main rivals for the tough tenor title. Ware's main quartet with Matthew Shipp on piano, William Parker on bass, and a sequence of drummers from Marc Edwards up to Guillermo Brown, was one of the most vitally important bands of the 1990s. He feels that working and rehearsing regularly with a consistent ensemble is indispensable for honing one's craft, and that the art of holding together a steady group is too often missing in modern free jazz.

Ware studied tenor, alto, and baritone saxophones in high school and at Berklee College of Music, where he started the band Apogee with Marc Edwards and multi-instrumentalist Cooper-Moore. The band members moved to New York in 1973, but the unit quickly broke up as they found separate work opportunities. His association with Cecil Taylor began the following year when he took part in one of the pianist's large-group undertakings at Carnegie Hall. In 1976, he and Edwards joined Taylor for *Dark Unto Themselves*, then Ware remained with the group for about eighteen months. Ware then regularly played with two other Taylor alumni, Raphé Malik and Andrew Cyrille. His appearance with Cyrille's ensemble Maono on the essential *Metamusician's Stomp* (1978, Black Saint) furthered his reputation. Ware also worked in a surprisingly effective duo setting with bop pianist Barry Harris in this period.

Ware's debut as a leader came with a HatHut session in 1977. That was followed by a second release on Palm in 1978. Sadly, both are now as scarce as snail hair. A decade later, he contracted with the small, visionary label Silkheart for his third name release. *Passage to Music* (1988) is a trio date with Marc Edwards and ex-Taylor bassist William Parker, two tremendous rhythm players whose intensity directly paralleled Ware's. Edwards, probably the most extreme and flexible drummer Ware has had to date, is titanic in this spare setting. Parker is equally pliable, plucking out fleet single-note runs as easily as multiple-stop chords and screechy bowing. Ware's compositions are as terrifying as his sound: bare templates for furious improvisations blared at high volumes. Their titles recall Sun Ra's mystic, linguistic Afrocentricity: "An Ancient Formula," "The Elders' Path," the incredible "African Secrets."

Besides the tenor sax, on his earliest dates Ware played saxello, a slightly curved soprano sax, and stritch, a straight alto, which was favored by Rahsaan Roland Kirk a quarter-century before. All of the horns receive the same level of abuse in his imposing hands, belching out bell-loads of passionate frenzy. On *Great Bliss, Vol. 1* (1990) and *Vol. 2* (1994, both Silkheart), the additional horns are utilized in their own special features. *Volume 1* debuted the Ware quartet and heralded the arrival of pianist Matthew Shipp, whom Parker recommended to the leader. Ware was uncertain of the younger man's capabilities at first, but once they played together and talked about their common visions, the bond was permanent. Shipp can be as animated on piano as Taylor, but his unerring melodicism leads to more accessible music without hindering the collective energy.

Flight of i (1991, Columbia/DIW), Edwards's last disc with the saxophonist, is one of the more restrained performances in Ware's catalog. Not that he was bowing to the harsh criticisms of the jazz press; the impression is of an experiment in softer textures. Wide-open modality characterizes the title cut, and Ra-like embellishments color "Infi-Rhythms Number 1." The group does something surprising for such a free unit: tackling two standards, "There Will Never Be Another You" and "Yesterdays." Needless to say, both gems are reset into Ware's own findings; like Coltrane, he is a master at maintaining the core empathy of a ballad, even under crushing power.

Before cutting *Third Ear Recitation* (1992, DIW), Ware hired drummer Whit Dickey away from tenorman Charles Gayle's band. Dickey is more rhythmically stable than Edwards had been, sustaining a regular pulse or stiff beat as desired beneath the group tumult: Ed Blackwell compared with, say, Sunny Murray. His debut with the quartet features a few more covers. Ware's own works are generally built upon arpeggios that vary in speed and power; on the destructive title track, Ware updates Ayler's presence. By now, Ware had dumped the saxello and stritch to focus fully on developing his personal tenor sax vocabulary. Parker is a principal figure again, either bowing frantically or plucking with darting precision.

Cryptology (1994, Homestead) contains six compositions inspired by Far Eastern mysticism. Suitably, the vibe is more cosmic, somewhat in a Pharoah Sanders manner but without the filigreed pretense. A firm blues sense grounds "Direction: Pleiades," thanks to Shipp's reliable left hand. The textural variety in "Panoramic" reveals the on-the-spot versatility of each member. *Cryptology* is a pivotal point in Ware's development as an individual voice.

The steps in Ware's conceptual growth become more evident on *Earthquation* (1995, DIW) and *Dao* (1996, Homestead). The first date includes two more standards one would never expect from an incendiary free jazzer, the over-baked "Tenderly," played twice with markedly different results, and the stodgy "Canadian Sunset." Again, his group's talent for cutting down to the bare bones of a tune and building a diorama for the skeleton serves Ware well. On *Dao*, the quartet's inherent democracy is put to the test on one of their most mystically expansive improvisations. The seven tracks are connected by soul and nature instead of by strictly composed guidelines. Tempos, meters, and harmonic foundations are transitory, changing in an evanescent burst whenever a particular player decides the time is right. Ware and Parker give some of their most profoundly personal performances here, digging up deep emotions instead of always going for a hard, fast sell. On the subsequent *Oblations and Blessings* (1996, Silkheart), Ware and friends began a return to their former severity, but the wisdom borne from their brief spiritual searching gave new spit and polish to the half-dozen originals.

In 1997, Dickey was replaced by Susie Ibarra, a virtual phenomenon who belies the silly notion that women can't play drums, can't play jazz, and can't play free. Married to Israeli-born saxophonist Assif Tsahar, the cherubic Ibarra is one of the most torrential, technically proficient drummers in today's music. In all contexts, especially the Ware quartet, she contributes an inspirationally vital pulse. Combined with the pinpoint intuition between Shipp and Parker, and Ware's sheer volcanism, Ibarra becomes almost a supernatural force. Her style is not all about volume, however, as her regular use of small bells and percussion instruments for texture reveals. Whereas Dickey was more reserved and predictable, Ibarra's drumming is a fluid ballet broken up by forceful spurts.

Wisdom of Uncertainty (1997, Aum Fidelity) was the quartet's ninth album, perhaps their most perfectly conceived session yet, confirming the quartet's status as one of free jazz's tightest working units. On "Acclimation," Ware attacks the theme with searing intensity, roaring like a war machine and scanning the fragments for signs of survivors. Ibarra takes a brief improvisation reminiscent of her mentor, Milford Graves, ideas flying by like racing swallows. A theme returns, soon overcome by a tense mantra highlighted by Ware's trilling tenor, then Shipp takes a solo. His playing is well informed by hard bop and early free jazz, stylistic nods, which he combines in fresh new forms. Melodic almost to a fault, he is the antithesis of Cecil Taylor in most ways. Parker's cranky bowing leads into his own solo, wherein he revisits the theme between meditative drones. The theme of "Antidromic" cycles through modulations of the skittery melody, a format retailored in the subsequent improvisations. "Sunbows Rainsets Blue" is introduced by the rhythm trio, with Shipp as a surging, rippling geyser. Then Ware's buzzsaw entrance flips our consciousness from pastoral lull to bitter wailing. Ibarra is the key to the band's shift in disposition, loosening reins and opening windows for her cohorts.

On *Godspelized* (1998, DIW), Ware pays somber homage to the inspirations of Coltrane and particularly Ayler, wedding church influences and old-style free blowing to dazzling effect. Shipp's rolling, tumbling piano style is perfectly suited to such religious pursuits, setting up a matrix of opulent chords on the title cut for Ware to weigh and expound upon. The sax investigations are just as bloody visceral as Ayler's, as Ware pours his soul into the horn with moans and blasts. Ware often seems to trade off roles with Parker and Ibarra, holding down hard-core rhythms with his horn while they scurry about in a round of musical chairs.

Though *Flight of i* had been released by Columbia, it was licensed from the Japanese imprint DIW. Ware's official debut for the fickle major label was *Go See the World* (1998), possibly the most daunting thing ever issued by the company that had only briefly retained Ornette Coleman, Henry Threadgill, Arthur Blythe, and Keith Jarrett before recanting their interest in such forward-thinking jazz. Ware's disc is harnessed in temperament compared with most of his prior releases, even *Flight of i*, but his furious tone and the scalar simplicity of his writing are mostly unchanged. Instead of venturing too far from the melodic materials, the quartet choose to stick a little closer to home than usual through chordal focusing or thematic variations. Shipp's Lego-like architecture and Ware's abrasiveness balance on "The Way We Were," another standard gone punk. "Mikuro's Blues" is the most conventional piece, and even it is pretty outside once the unit gets past the pounding melody.

With the century's turn came Ibarra's departure. In came the quartet's fourth drummer in its dozen years of existence, Guillermo Brown, who brought light seasonings of rock and hip-hop to the group sound. His greatest gift lies in allowing room for free expression while structuring consistently reliable rhythms. Brown's impact is clear on *Surrendered* (2000, Columbia). Ware's "Glorified Calypso" is just about that, full of humor and Caribbean groove, and the leader has a ball with his newfound percussionist's conjurations. Charles Lloyd's "Sweet Georgia Bright" is different from Ware's usual fare, even given his propensity for bulking up featherweight standards, but the doubling of tempo at solo time adds meat to its bones. Beaver Harris's "African Drums" is treated with high respect even as its harmonies are reshaped. The three other originals are more typical of the skeletal forms Ware favors, granting Shipp and Parker permission to seek further horizons.

Both of Ware's Columbia albums were produced by Steven Joerg, who turned around and founded his own label, Aum Fidelity, with the tenorman as his first signing. The quartet's face is drastically altered on *Corridors and Parallels* (2001), foremost through Shipp's use of synthesizer and organ. Engineer Chris Flam's trickery turns parts of the date into near-techno productions. Surprisingly, Ware takes to the new sounds like a trout to water, and a sort of Sun Ra vibe emerges. The band gets practically goofy on the danceable "Superimposed," in sharp contrast to the profundity of "Mother May You Rest in Bliss" and "Somewhere."

Also in 2001, Ware took another bold step, following the path of sax forefathers like Anthony Braxton and Steve Lacy. He released his first solo recording, *Live in the Netherlands* (Splasc(h)), to reasonable acclaim. The disc barely comes to forty minutes, which might seem like a cheat were it not for the sheer strength of the music. The four tracks are not very well developed in a melodic sense, often a shortcoming of one's first attempts at total solo performance. However, the exposure of his deepest personal emotions without any support from his loyal rhythm team reveals new depths of logic and thought. Ware laid bare is more fragile than we have ever seen him, but the quiet beauty of this offering speaks volumes about his inspiring character.

Waters, Patty: vocalist and pianist. Waters was one of several artists who recorded for the ESP label in the 1960s and 1970s, only to descend into obscurity. She began as a nightclub performer and was directed to ESP by Albert Ayler. Her first album, *Patty Waters Sings* (1965), combines solo piano pieces with a long, at times frenetic, version of "Black Is the Color" that is reminiscent of Linda Sharrock's impassioned vocal work. On *College Tour* (1966, ESP), Waters reached further into the free-jazz pool, vocalizing wordlessly and turning piano duties over to Burton Greene and Ran Blake. Following an appearance on a Marzette Watts album in 1968, Waters disappeared from the radar screen. She finally reemerged in 1996 with a new album of standards, *Love Songs* (Jazz Focus).

Watts, Marzette: reedman, now deceased. Within New York's free circles, Watts was best known as a recording engineer whose handiwork appeared on a number of albums. He was also an accomplished painter and a self-taught hornman who led a couple of record dates. *Backdrop for Urban Revolution* (1967, ESP) features a heavy ensemble anchored by Byard Lancaster, Karl Berger, Henry Grimes, Sonny Sharrock, and J. C. Moses. A rarer offering is *The Marzette Watts Ensemble* (1968, Savoy), produced by Bill Dixon.

Watts, Trevor (b. York, England): alto and soprano saxophonist and bandleader. Like Coleman, Watts is a master of almost human expression on the alto saxophone and a deft-fingered technician. His work with bluesmen (Sonny Boy Williamson) and rock performers (Rod Stewart, Long John Baldry) considerably widened his vision. Largely self-taught, Watts met and played with John Stevens and Paul Rutherford while stationed in Germany in the Royal Air Force from 1959 to 1963. After his service, he helped found the New Jazz Orchestra and performed with various blues and rock players. In 1965, he and Rutherford led a quintet, eventually adding Stevens as the drummer. By 1966, this group had become the first incarnation of the Spontaneous Music Ensemble (see separate entry).

After about a year of performing with the SME, Watts left to form the band Amalgam with bassist Barry Guy and trombonist Paul Rutherford. From 1967 to 1979, Amalgam dealt in a unique blend of free jazz, folk, and rock music; subsequent members included Bobby Bradford, Keith Tippett, South African–born bassist Harry Miller, and AMM guitarist Keith Rowe. *Wipe Out* (1980, Impetus) is a boxed set that captures all the energy of the group at its peak. Watts created the Arc label in 1982 to document his projects; its very first release was Amalgam's classic *Over the Rainbow* (1983).

After Amalgam dissolved, Watts assembled his Drum Orchestra to explore new concepts of free rhythmic expression. In 1982, he assembled the tentet Moiré Music as a vehicle for compositional exploration, performing layered works colored with African and Eastern elements, which began moving away from free music. *Trevor Watts' Moiré Music* (1986, Arc), the group's debut album, remains the best entry point into their swirling musical world. In 1990, those two projects were merged to become the Moiré Music Drum Orchestra, a popular fixture on the festival circuit. In 1994, Watts broke off the core of the Drum Orchestra to form The Moiré Music Trio, recently consisting of himself, electric bassist Colin McKenzie, and drummer Marc Parnell. Watts has led his Celebration Band (*The Celebration Band*, 2001, Arc), a reed quartet plus rhythm section and String Ensemble as well.

As a sideman, Watts has worked with Louis Moholo, Bobby Bradford, John Stevens's Away, Stan Tracey's Open Circle, the London Jazz Composers' Orchestra, Steve Lacy, Archie Shepp, Don Cherry, and Jayne Cortez. He has regularly duetted with violinist Peter Knight and pianist Veryan Weston, and has received several commissions to compose for festivals and broadcasts.

Werner, Kenny (b. Brooklyn, NY, 19 November 1951): pianist, composer, and bandleader. Werner began his career very early, taking part in an orchestral recording session and playing stride piano on a New York television show at age eleven. While in high school, he continued his piano studies at the Manhattan School of Music, then moved to Berklee after graduation.

As Ken Werner, he recorded his first album in 1977 (*The Piano Music of Bix Beiderbecke, Duke Ellington, George Gershwin and James P. Johnson*, Atlantic). His relationship with Atlantic producer Ilhan Mimaroglu brought more work, including a Charles Mingus date, *Something Like a Bird* (1977, Atlantic). Mingus was too ill to play but directed the session from his wheelchair. In the 1980s, he became interested in free jazz, playing with Archie Shepp, Jaki Byard, and Chico Freeman along with mainstream dates with the Mel Lewis Orchestra, Joe Henderson, and Tom Harrell.

Werner's famed trio with bassist Ratzo Harris and drummer Tom Rainey was born early in the 1980s but was only recorded twice (*Introducing the Trio*, 1989; *Press Enter*, 1991, both Sunnyside). He formed rewarding associations with tenorman Joe Lovano, which increased his studio experience and exposure to outward ideas, and Broadway singer Betty Buckley, whom Werner served as musical director. In the 1990s, he received two NEA grants to produce tribute concerts to Ellington and Mel Lewis, and moved over to the Concord Jazz label for three exciting albums. Werner returned to a trio format twice in the decade, cutting *A Delicate Balance* (RCA) with Dave Holland and Jack DeJohnette, and *Unprotected Music* (Double-Time, both 1998) with Marc Johnson and Joey Baron. His European trio, with bassist Johannes Weidenmueller and drummer Ari Hoenig, recorded *Beat Degeneration* (2002, Sunnyside) live in Paris.

Werner champions the idea that free improvisation can be taught as a serious discipline. In collaboration with the jazz-education pioneer Jamey Aebersold, Werner developed the book/video set *Effortless Mastery* in 2001, presenting his lectures on jazz history and the importance of spontaneous creativity. In 2003, Aebersold issued *Free Play*, a play-along book/CD set intended to encourage free exploration. Except for bassist John Voigt's more spartan *Free Jazz Improvisation Play-A-Long* (2001, Moonfood Records), Werner's materials for Aebersold are unique in the jazz marketplace.

Weston, Veryan (b. Cornwall, U.K., 1950): pianist and composer. Weston honed his skills at London's Little Theatre Club, the birthplace of the Spontaneous Music Ensemble. He was granted a fellowship with Digswell Arts Trust, Hertfordshire, which enabled him to explore the arts in myriad ways from revising his book on piano improvisation to working with visual artists and composing film scores. In the mid-1970s, he began working with Lol Coxhill, who has remained a key parrying partner (*Digswell Duets*, 1978; *Boundless*, 1998, both Emanem). Weston has won many awards as a performer and composer, has lectured at schools around Britain, and has performed with Trevor Watts's Moiré Music, Phil Minton, Eddie Prévost, the group Stinky Winkles, Steve Beresford, London Improvisers Orchestra, Ntshuks Bonga, and John Butcher. His first album as a leader was the solo date *Underwater Carol* (1986, Matchless). *Mercury Concert* (1998, Emanem), with bassist John Edwards and percussionist Mark Sanders, is one of the exciting highlights of a vital and still young career.

What We Live: the trio of bassist Lisle Ellis, saxophonist Larry Ochs, and drummer Donald Robinson. Based in the Bay Area of Northern California, the group came together after the members had worked together in saxman Glenn Spearman's Double Trio. They have since recorded on their own (self-titled, 1996, DIW) and with guest artists like Dave Douglas and Wadada Leo Smith (both appear on *Quintet for a Day*, 1999, New World).

Wheeler, Kenny (Kenneth Vincent John Wheeler; b. St. Catherine's, Ontario, Canada, 14 January 1930): trumpeter, flügelhornist, composer, and bandleader. Canadian by birth and a graduate of the Royal Conservatory in Toronto, Wheeler has lived in Britain since the early 1950s. In 1959, he was hired by John Dankworth for his popular orchestra. He remained with the Dankworth band until 1965, then became involved in the earliest exploits of the Spontaneous Music Ensemble. Wheeler quickly became one of the most exciting and promising voices in British free music. His debut as a leader was 1968's *Windmill Tilter* (Fontana), an apt title for such a quixotic player.

In 1969, Wheeler joined both Mike Gibbs's fusion big band, playing an early hybrid of rock and jazz, and Tony Oxley's free jazz sextet (*The Baptised Traveller*, 1969, CBS). The following year, he joined the nascent Globe Unity Orchestra, then fell under the influence of Anthony Braxton. Wheeler and Braxton were impeccable matches on a number of the innovative reedman's 1970s albums (*New York, Fall 1974*, Arista; see Braxton's entry).

In 1975, Wheeler signed on with ECM and issued *Gnu High*, which remains one of the most popular items in his catalog. At direct odds with Wheeler's free leanings was his membership in Azimuth, the deep-thinking trio with vocalist Norma Winstone and pianist/percussionist John Taylor (*Azimuth*, 1977, ECM). From 1983 to 1987, the trumpeter was a member of Dave Holland's quintet (*Jumpin' In*, 1983, ECM). Wheeler continued to lead excellent recordings on ECM, Justin Time, and Soul Note. His *Music for Large and Small Ensembles* (1990, ECM), although unusual in his discography, is an outstanding release. Wheeler's resumé also includes concerts and recordings with John Abercrombie, Bill Frisell, David Sylvian, Joni Mitchell, Keith Jarrett, Phil Woods, vocalist Georgie Fame, Ian Carr's fusion group Nucleus, and Bob Brookmeyer.

Whitecage, Mark (b. Litchfield, CT, 1937): reeds player. One of the more under-appreciated players in modern improv, Whitecage has seen an appreciable career boost thanks to his participation in projects on the CIMP label. A pro musician since the age of twelve, Whitecage's style on various horns runs from pretty lyricism to Aylerish intensity. He dabbled in psychedelia with The Godz at the end of the 1960s, performed at Lincoln Center with Paul Bley and Annette Peacock in 1970, and began working with Gunter Hampel in 1972 (*Angel*, Birth). With bassist Saheb Sarbib, he recorded one of the first albums on the Cadence Jazz label, which led to his eventual association with CIMP. In the 1980s, after a stint with Jeanne Lee, Whitecage performed as a solo artist for a few years. In 1988, he formed two separate bands, Liquid Time (*Mark Whitecage and Liquid Time*, 1990, Acoustic) and the Glass House Ensemble. As a member of the New York Improvisers Collective, he made the acquaintance of William Parker, Jackson Krall, and clarinetist Perry Robinson, with whom Whitecage and his wife, Rozanne Levine, formed the trio Crystal Clarinets. When Anthony Braxton chose to perform as a pianist for several years in the 1990s, Whitecage was tapped as the reedman for his groups (*Trillium R – Composition 162*, 1999, Braxton House). He has performed with the Joe Fonda/Michael Jefry Stevens band, Dominic Duval, and Sun Ra saxman Marshall Allen (*Mark-N-Marshall: Monday*, 1998; *Mark-N-Marshall: Tuesday*, 1998, both CIMP). More recently, Whitecage resurrected his Acoustic label and issued several recordings along with gigging around Europe.

Wierbos, Wolter (b. Holsten, Netherlands, 1 September 1957): trombonist. Wierbos started as a trumpet player in his small community's fanfare band, to which many family members belonged. He eventually switched to trombone and continued to play while attending college in Groningen. Wierbos was inspired to explore extended techniques on his instrument after seeing performances by Albert Mangelsdorff and Ray Anderson. Determined to make a new career as a professional musician, Wierbos set a five-year deadline for himself. About three years later, he joined the band Cumulus with saxophonist Ab Baars, his first step toward a respectable niche in Dutch avant-jazz. His friendship with Maarten Altena led to participation in many of the bassist's sessions from *Veranda* (1982, Claxon) on. Wierbos has been a fixture in Altena's best ensembles ever since. He has performed with Misha Mengelberg's ICP Orchestra, the Gerry Hemingway Quintet, Michael Moore, Ernst Reijseger, Available Jelly, Steve Beresford, Evan Parker, and other improvisers. *X Caliber* (1996, ICP) was his first album as a leader.

Wild Mans Band: European ensemble centered around the titanic trio of reedman Peter Brötzmann, drummer Peter O. Jørgenson (a.k.a. P. O. Jørgens), and bassist Peter Friis Nielsen. Trombonist Johannes Bauer made four on their first album, *Peter Peter Peter und Johannes* (1997, Ninth World). The recording overflows with textures, from delicate tone paintings to the usual *sturm und drang*, with Jørgenson flailing like a beached octopus and Nielsen all but lost in the shuffle. Bauer was replaced by reedman Mats Gustafsson for *Three Rocks and a Pine* (1999, Ninth World).

Wilkerson, Ed: composer, arranger, bandleader, and multi-instrumentalist. Wilkerson is part of the newer wave of creative musicians in Chicago, a past president of the AACM, and teacher at the collective's school of music. He is principally a saxophonist but is also capable on clarinet and piano. Wilkerson runs the Sessoms label and leads two notable bands, the octet Eight Bold Souls and the large performance group Shadow Vignettes. Since 1977, he has been an occasional member of the Ethnic Heritage Ensemble and has performed with Roscoe Mitchell, Douglas Ewart, Muhal Richard Abrams, George Lewis, and other Chicago avant-gardists.

Wilkinson, Alan (b. Ilford, U.K., 22 August 1955): saxophonist and vocalist. Wilkinson briefly pursued a career as a librarian before studying painting. After graduation, he took up the alto sax and joined a quartet with drummer Paul Hession. Excited by the prospects of the musical life, Wilkinson dropped his painting ambitions and formed the trio Art, Bart, and Fargo with Hession and saxophonist Pete Malham. At a 1982 summer music gathering, Wilkinson met many of Europe's principal free improvisers, including Keith Tippett, Fred Van Hove, and Peter Brötzmann. With Lol Coxhill and friends, he helped found the Termite Club, a Leeds-based improvisation center. Since then he has worked on occasion with Brötzmann, Tippett, Louis Moholo, and Phil Durrant. He plays in a fine trio with Hession and bassist Simon H. Fell, and has taken part in several Company events.

Williams, Davey (b. 1952): guitarist. Williams spent his younger days playing in rock and blues bands in the South. He began working as a solo performer in the 1970s, established his Transmuseq label in 1978, and in 1986 he joined Curlew (see entry), which gave him his widest exposure. Within the group, Williams was able to stretch his blues, rock, jazz, and avant-garde chops to the limit while making the final products palatable. His other projects include work with Col. Bruce Hampton, the punk band Fuzzy Suns, and OK, Nurse. Williams edits *The Improviser* and has been a news-paper music critic, writer, and an NEA consultant. He has collaborated frequently with violinist/singer LaDonna Smith since the early 1970s, as well as Eugene Chadbourne (*Wild Partners*, 1997, House of Chadula), Jim Staley, and Günter Christmann. *Criminal Pursuits* (1985, Transmuseq) is one of Williams's finest record-ings.

Wilson, Peter Niklas (b. Hamburg, Germany, 1957; d. 27 October 2003): bassist. Wilson studied with John Tchicai, Barre Phillips, and other avant-gardists and ma-jored in musicology at Göttingen and Hamburg, but as a bassist he was mostly self-taught. Wilson helped found the Ton Art Collective in Hamburg and performed and recorded with Anthony Braxton (*8 Duets (Hamburg 1991)*, Music & Arts; *2 Compo-sitions 1991*, HatArt), Evan Parker, Fred Frith, Marion Brown, Derek Bailey, Keith Rowe, trumpeter Rajesh Mehta, and others. Wilson was a respected educator, pro-ducer, music journalist, and the author of several books on major jazz artists.

Wilson, Philip (b. St. Louis, MO, 8 September 1941; d. New York, NY, 1 April 1992): drummer. Excellent as timekeeper and improviser alike, Wilson was a favored mem-ber of the Art Ensemble of Chicago's circle of friends. Wilson was one of the nascent group's first drummers, appearing on the *Old/Quartet* sessions (issued under Roscoe Mitchell's name, 1975, Nessa; full sessions appear on discs A and B of *The Art En-semble 1967/68*, issued 1993, Nessa). In the same period Wilson was active in the modern soul and blues scene, drumming for the Rance Allen Group and Paul Butterfield Blues Band.

Although he left the Art Ensemble before they went to Paris and began their im-portant evolution, Wilson continued his close relationship with Lester Bowie for the remainder of his life. Wilson and Bowie took part in duos (*Duet*, 1978, Improvising Artists), Bowie-led dates like *All the Magic!* (1982, ECM), and several of the trumpeter's groups: Brass Fantasy (*The Great Pretender*, 1981, ECM), From the Root to the Source, and the New York Organ Ensemble (*Funky T, Cool T*, 1991, DIW). Wilson contributed to recordings by Julius Hemphill (*Dogon A.D.*, 1972; *Coon Bid'ness*, 1975, both Arista/Freedom), David Murray, James Newton, Hamiet Bluiett, Frank Lowe, Anthony Braxton (*Town Hall [1972]*, Pausa), and the Last Poets. He was also one of Bill Laswell's preferred drummers, with roles in many of Laswell's world-electronic fusion projects. *Live at Moers Festival 1978* (Moers), with a hot quartet including Frank Lowe, Olu Dara, and bassist Fred Williams, is the sole album issued under Wilson's name.

Wobbly Rail: label founded in 1998 by Mac McCaughan and based in Chapel Hill, North Carolina. Their catalog includes releases by Whit Dickey, Georg Graewe, the Aaly Trio, Steve Lacy, and John Butcher.

Wolf Brennan, John (b. Dublin, Ireland): pianist and composer. Wolf Brennan adeptly blends the best of traditional and contemporary classical technique with

Celtic and avant-garde elements, his sound reflecting his varied academic background in musicology, literature, and film. His studies have been extensive: the University of Fribourg, Lucerne Conservatory, the Academy of School and Church Music, Karl Berger's Creative Music Studio, and the Royal Irish Academy of Music. His first recording was *Mountain Hymn* (1985, L&R). Wolf Brennan has participated in several environmentally structured musical events, performing outdoors in acoustic settings including forests, rivers, and swimming pools. He is a member of Pago Libre (*Extempora*, 1990, Splasc(h)) and has collaborated with Robert Dick (*Aurealis*, 1995, Victo) and Christy Doran (*Henceforward*, 1988, Core). *The Beauty of Fractals* (1986, Creative Works) and *Momentum* (1999, Leo) are among his better recordings.

W.O.O.: ensemble and improvising pool led by reeds player Bonnie Kane. The acronym stands for "Whole Other Orbit," a fitting indication of Kane's musical visions. W.O.O. was the spawning ground for several outward-looking groups, including World of Tomorrow and W.O.O. Revelator, the trio of Kane, drummer Ray Sage, and guitarist Chris Forsyth. Outside the umbrella of W.O.O., Kane has performed in a quartet with saxophonists Daniel Carter, Sabir Mateen (both members of Test) and Blaise Siwula; bassist Scott Prato's Thundering Lizards; San Francisco guitarist Ernesto Diaz-Infante; and the Jon Spencer Blues Explosion. Her own music stands at the extreme edge of improvisation, often gratingly amelodic and abrasive.

Workman, Reggie (b. Philadelphia, PA, 1937): bassist, composer, and bandleader. He is one of the most important jazz bassists of the past forty years, having performed with major stars from hard bop through free jazz. Workman began playing the bass in high school and made his first recording, with saxophonist Gigi Gryce, at age twenty-one. That date was a springboard to working with Art Blakey and the Jazz Messengers, Thelonious Monk, John and Alice Coltrane, Booker Little, Freddie Hubbard, Mal Waldron, and many of the artists associated with them. His work with Coltrane gained him particular renown and pointed him in new musical directions. Among his more outward-looking projects since then have been sessions with Butch Morris, David Murray, Max Roach, and Abdullah Ibrahim.

Workman has led several excellent ensembles, beginning with Top Shelf in the late 1970s. His own Reggie Workman Ensemble, formed around 1982 and still cooking today, is a primary outlet for his compositional skills. *Cerebral Caverns* (1995, Postcards) features reedman Sam Rivers in an outstanding role. The bassist also fronts the electronic-jazz unit Groove Ship and performs with Trio Three, Mal Waldron's trio, Brew, New York Jazz Quartet, and the newly reformed New York Art Quartet with Roswell Rudd, Milford Graves, and John Tchicai. Workman has fronted several tributes to John Coltrane since 1987, when he also began teaching in the New School University Jazz and Contemporary Music Program. He has collaborated with dance troupes, toured worldwide, and received the Eubie Blake Award for musical excellence, a Lifetime Achievement Award from the Jazz Foundation of America, and the Kennedy Center's Living Legacy Award.

World Saxophone Quartet (WSQ): all-sax group founded in 1975. The WSQ's original lineup included altoists Oliver Lake and Julius Hemphill, tenorman David Murray,
and baritonist Hamiet Bluiett. The four were originally hired for a series of workshops
at Southern University in New Orleans; all but Murray had recorded with Anthony
Braxton in quartet format the prior year. Following appearances in New York as the
"Real New York Saxophone Quartet," the band changed its name and began to build
an appreciative audience. The quartet has drawn as much inspiration from Ellington,
Mingus, and Oliver Nelson as from Coleman and Ayler, and they have moved further away from freedom into elaborate composition. Nevertheless, there is abundant
freedom within their music. Hemphill was most oriented toward European contem-
porary-classical techniques, while Bluiett stays closer to Mississippi blues and funk.
Lake and Murray are perhaps the most global-minded of the lot, handling hard bop
and swing as easily as freedom, ethnic flavors, or anything else. Such variety in composition and performance made the WSQ one of the most successful avant-jazz entities
since Coltrane.

Point of No Return (1977, Moers), the quartet's debut, is one of their most daunting documents. A prime cut is the twenty-four-minute "Scared Sheetless," a series of
increasingly abrasive solos. Perhaps realizing that this approach was a little too overboard for their target audience, the men chose to temper their energy just a bit in
future projects. Their follow-up on Black Saint, *Steppin' With . . .* (1978), gives a better
overview of their group philosophy. The four men flaunt their ability to move in and
out of discernable pulses without losing the meter, an intimidating task with no
rhythm section at hand. The centerpiece of *W.S.Q.* (1980, Black Saint) is Bluiett's
short but tantalizing "Suite Music," with more high points in Hemphill's "Pillars
Latino" and Murray's "Fast Life."

With each new release, until Hemphill's departure, the WSQ keenly honed their
craft while experimenting with form, beat, and tone. *Revue* (1980, Black Saint) consisted of nine shorter pieces, including two from Murray's non-WSQ repertoire,
"Ming" and "David's Tune." The bracing *Live in Zurich* (1981, Black Saint) has six
Hemphill works bookended by short renditions of Bluiett's "Hattie Wall." Four years
passed before their next album, *Live at Brooklyn Academy of Music* (1985, Black Saint),
but the quartet's sheer might had only grown stronger.

After 1985, the WSQ started loosening their hold on the avant-garde, tackling
material seemingly selected for market impact more than creativity. *World Saxophone
Quartet Plays Duke Ellington* (1986, Nonesuch) contains intriguing takes on the classic Ellington/Strayhorn songbook. But their association with Elektra/Nonesuch seems
to have been misguided. Much of *Dances and Ballads* (1987) could be called boring
due to static compositions and too little group coagulation. The next disc, *Rhythm &
Blues* (1988, Elektra), interspersed a few good originals in with questionable versions
of Motown soul and Otis Redding hits. It reveals attractive possibilities for jazz
interpretation of soul songs but doesn't come close to the gripping qualities of earlier
releases.

Hemphill's poor health forced him into retirement in 1989, and the quartet's fourth
chair was quickly filled by altoist Arthur Blythe. He is an excitingly original performer
whose approach updates Eric Dolphy, but his debut with the WSQ was ill-conceived.
Metamorphosis (1990, Elektra/Nonesuch) burdens the quartet with well-meaning

African percussionists and electric bassist Melvin Gibbs with mixed results. Mor Thiam, Mar Gueye, and Chief Bey push the saxes to dizzying heights on rare occasions, but the album often gets bogged down. Blythe puts up a valiant effort, particularly on his title track, but he could hardly have debuted in a worse situation.

Moving Right Along (1993, Black Saint) brought the quartet back to the Italian label that had released most of their best material. Flavio Bonandrini worked his usual magic, pulling new reserves of quality out of the saxmen. Young altoist Eric Person briefly replaced Blythe, and hard-bop veteran James Spaulding was also on board. Their compositions moved toward a more traditional head-solos-head format, usually with the soloist backed by the other horns in close ranks. Blythe returned on *Breath of Life* (1995, Elektra/Nonesuch) but again was denied the chance to record within the basic quartet. Instead, the band was augmented by organists Donald Smith and Amina Claudine Myers, with Myers and Fontella Bass singing on two tracks. *Breath*, however, was better than *Metamorphosis* had been, all participants shining brightly.

In 1996, the WSQ were signed to Justin Time, which has also issued recordings by the quartet's individual members. The resulting records have varied widely in character, from *Four Now* (1996), with the African drummers returning, to the funked-up rhythm section on *Takin' It 2 the Next Level* (1996), to the basic four of Murray, Lake, Bluiett, and John Purcell paying homage to Hemphill on *Requiem for Julius* (2000). Purcell's principal horn is the saxello, an unusually bent variation on the soprano sax, and its unorthodox tone adds a new dimension to the WSQ's sound. Lake's compositions are the principal highlights, and the improvised blues that closes *Requiem* nods back to the quartet's original visions of spontaneity.

Wright, Frank (Rev.; b. Grenada, MS, 9 July 1935; d. Germany, 17 May 1990): tenor saxophonist. Wright started out as an R&B bassist but switched to the tenor sax after seeing Albert Ayler in action. That encounter was a life-changing experience that determined Wright's path for the rest of his days. In the early 1960s, he lived and worked in New York City, gigging with John Coltrane, organist Larry Young, Noah Howard, and Sunny Murray. Wright was contracted to ESP in 1965 and issued two powerful albums for the label, *Frank Wright Trio* (1965) and *Your Prayer* (1967). Like many American freemen, Wright had moved to Paris by the decade's end and was soon working in a quartet with drummer Muhammad Ali, pianist Bobby Few, and Noah Howard. The band cut *One For John* (1969) for BYG Actuel, and a couple of years later Howard was replaced by bassist Alan Silva.

The tenorman spent the remainder of his career in Europe, with only a few brief returns to America. Some of his most enduring work was as a sideman with Cecil Taylor (*Winged Serpent [Sliding Quadrants]*), 1984; *Olu Iwa*, 1986, both Soul Note), Peter Brötzmann (*Alarm*, 1981, FMP), and Silva's ensemble, Center of the World. Grossly underappreciated by the jazz community at large, Wright was a major inspiration to tenormen like Glenn Spearman and Charles Gayle.

Wright, Jack (b. Pittsburgh, PA, 1942): saxophonist and pianist. He began his musical studies at age ten but concentrated on history and literature in college. In the late

1970s, after teaching history for a spell, Wright returned to music and started play-ing free jazz around the New York area with artists like William Parker. By the mid-1980s, he was touring America in support of free improvisation. He settled in Boulder, Colorado, and in 2000 began to collaborate with Bhob Rainey (*Signs of Life*, 2001, Spring Garden). More recently he settled back in Pennsylvania. Wright has been a regular performer at the High Zero Festival in Baltimore and has worked with John Butcher, Michel Doneda, John Russell, Thomas Lehn, Joe McPhee (*Mister Peabody Goes to Baltimore*, 2001, Recorded), Lê Quan Ninh, Axel Dörner, Andrea Neumann, Phil Durrant, Greg Kelley, Michael Zerang, John Shiurba (*Mutable Witness*, 1999, Limited Sedition), and many others. He administers the Spring Garden label (*Double Double*, 1999; *Rattle OK*, 2001). Wright and Rainey perform with cellists Fred Lonberg-Holm and Bob Marsh on *The Darkest Corner, The Most Conspicuous* (1999, CIMP).

Y

Yoshizawa, Motoharu (b. Tokyo, Japan; d. 12 September 1998): bassist. One of the most important figures in Japanese improvisation in the 1970s, Yoshizawa had a resurgence in the 1990s but died with much of his promise unspent. He collaborated with Kaoru Abe, Masayuki Takayanagi, and Toshinori Kondo in the 1970s, and his own records, *Inland Fish* (1974, with percussionist Yoshisaburoh Toyozumi) and *Outfit* (1975, both Trio), are excellent when they can be found. Yoshizawa took part in several of Butch Morris's conductions (like *Conduction 50*, 1996, New World) and met up with Barre Phillips (*Uzu*, 1996, PSF), Derek Bailey, Otomo Yoshihide, Steve Lacy, Lê Quan Ninh, and Evan Parker. Morris, Elliott Sharp, and drum machinist Ikue Mori sparred with the bassist on *Gobbledygook* (1990, PSF).

Young, Larry (Khalid Yasin Abdul Aziz; b. Newark, NJ, 7 October 1940; d. New York, NY, 30 March 1978): organist, composer, and bandleader. Best known for his excellent work in soul-jazz and early fusion, the latter as a member of drummer Tony Williams's Lifetime with guitarist John McLaughlin, Young moved into free-jazz territories in the 1970s. *Lawrence of Newark* (1973, Perception), which debuted guitarist James Blood Ulmer, is his best recording on freedom's edge. (Pharoah Sanders also appears on the visceral free-form jams he directly influenced; he is billed as "Mystery Guest" due to a contractual conflict.) Young died of pneumonia at the age of thirty-eight, much of his promise yet unspent.

Z

Zankel, Bobby (b. Brooklyn, NY): alto saxophonist and composer. Cecil Taylor hired Zankel in 1971 to fill in for Jimmy Lyons, giving the young altoist a sizable break. Zankel continued to apprentice under Taylor while making the New York loft scene with Sunny Murray, Ray Anderson, and William Parker. He moved to Philadelphia in 1975 and found work with Odean Pope, bop tenorman Hank Mobley, Ellington bassist Jymie Merritt's Forerunners, Sun Ra drummer Samarai Celestial, and NRBQ. Since 1991, Zankel has been associated with Cadence and issued five albums under their umbrella, including *Seeking Spirit* (1991, Cadence Jazz) and his best yet, *Prayer and Action* (1996, CIMP). In 2000 he cofounded the Collective Voices Festival in Philadelphia.

Zerang, Michael (b. Chicago, IL, 1958): percussionist and composer. Zerang is one of his city's finest first-call percussionists, a favorite associate of Ken Vandermark, Hamid Drake, and other Chicagoans. He has recorded a few albums under his own name but is best recognized as a vivacious, colorful sideman who readily shapes the outcome of recording sessions. He has taught at Northwestern University and the Art Institute of Chicago, directed the Link's Hall Performance Series, and written for films and dance and theater companies. He has performed as a member of Peter Brötzmann's Chicago Tentet, Liof Munimula, and many other ensembles.

Zingaro (Alves), **Carlos** (b. 1948, Lisbon, Portugal): violinist. Very early on, Zingaro studied at the Conservatory in Lisbon, practically perfecting his craft by the time many youth begin to learn an instrument. Prior to graduation, Zingaro joined the Lisbon University Chamber Orchestra where he became a favored member. Shortly thereafter, he assembled the short-lived, free-leaning band Plexus, one of the only avant-garde ensembles in Portugal at that time. Work with theater companies as both a musician and designer led to opportunities to work with some of Europe's best improvising musicians. Thanks to a Fulbright Grant, Zingaro came to America in 1979 to study with Karl Berger at the Creative Musicians Workshop in Woodstock, New York. There he formed bonds with Anthony Braxton, Leo Smith, and Richard Teitelbaum, who became a frequent musical partner. Other collaborators include Peter Kowald, Kent Carter, Derek Bailey, Jöelle Léandre, Daunik Lazro, and the Canadian cellist Peggy Lee. *Western Front* (1996, HatOlogy), his duet disc with Lee, is a particular favorite.

Zorn, John (b. New York, NY, 12 September 1953): reedman, bandleader, composer, and arranger. Zorn is a key figure in the Downtown movement that developed in New York in the late 1970s, blending elements of free jazz with rock, klezmer, and ethnic forms. Besides jazz artists, including the underrated pianist Sonny Clark, to whom he has paid tribute, Zorn has been inspired by Japanese culture, film noir, and Carl Stalling's cartoon soundtracks. Perhaps one of modern America's most original and creative composers, Zorn has written works that rely on various gaming principles to determine the directions of the music; charted wackily anarchistic arrangements of tunes by Clark, Ornette Coleman, and Italian film composer Ennio Morricone; and developed compelling suites based on the Jewish experience for his ensemble Masada. His early work included the clarinet and the use of mouthpieces and birdcalls as special effects, but in recent years he has performed on alto sax almost exclusively.

Zorn studied piano, flute, and guitar in his youth, then continued learning instruments through high school. He became interested in avant-garde musics at age fourteen, after attending a gig by his French teacher, free trumpeter Jacques Coursil. He recorded his first experimental compositions while in college in St. Louis (*First Recordings 1973*, issued 1995, Tzadik). His college days did not last long; Zorn soon dropped out, went back to New York, and fell in with the Downtown scene that was being spawned from within the loft-jazz circles and early punk rockers. From 1977 to 1980, Zorn recorded a number of discs for the small Parachute label, including the game-based pieces that garnered him his original fame. Some, like 1981's *Archery* and 1983's *Locus Solus*, have since been reissued on his Tzadik label. A later move to Elektra/Nonesuch made possible a series of tribute albums to Morricone (*The Big Gundown*, 1984), Mickey Spillane (*Spillane*, 1986), and Coleman (*Spy vs. Spy*, 1988). In 1984, Zorn met British guitarist Derek Bailey, with whom he has performed in Company and recorded on occasion (*Yankees*, with George Lewis, 1984, OAO Celluloid/Charly; *Harras*, with William Parker, 1996, Avant).

In 1989, Zorn gathered the controversial quartet Naked City, which included guitarist Bill Frisell, drummer Joey Baron, and bassist Fred Frith. The band mostly played original pieces, sometimes featuring maniacal Japanese vocalist Yamatsuka Eye, as well as Zorn's own takes on Italian and American movie music. The disturbing images which adorned Naked City's record packaging—violent Japanese porn, dismemberings—caused more of a stir than the music once the novelty began to wear off. Their self-titled debut (1989, Elektra/Nonesuch) remains the best documentation of Naked City's aesthetic. The closest Zorn has come to that style since is with Painkiller, a trio with electric bassist Bill Laswell and grindcore drummer Mick Harris.

Around 1993, Zorn began exploring his Jewish heritage in earnest, particularly focusing on the Diaspora and the Holocaust. *Kristallnacht* (Tzadik), recorded that year, was the first recording on which Zorn addressed the violence and misunderstandings directed at his people for millennia. Not long afterward, Zorn created the quartet Masada (see separate entry), which has become his primary performance outlet. Zorn continues to record and produce albums at a staggering pace, including a growing body of independent film scores, regularly reshaping the face of contemporary music.

Suggested Readings

This is a listing of recommended books and periodical articles, which provide information on free jazz, its practitioners, and the multitude of issues surrounding the music. I recommend them to anyone who wishes to further research free jazz and improvisation. Some of these are biographies or autobiographies, but the majority are general works pertaining to free music and the political, social, and historical contexts in which it developed.

GENERAL REFERENCE BOOKS AND BIOGRAPHIES

Backus, Robert. *Fire Music: A Political History of Jazz.* Chicago: Vanguard Books, 1977.

Bailey, Derek. *Improvisation: Its Nature and Practice in Music.* Ashbourne, UK: Mooreland Publishing, 1981.

Balliett, Whitney. *Dinosaurs in the Morning.* New York: J. B. Lippincott, 1962.

Baraka, Amiri (LeRoi Jones). *Black Music.* New York: William Morrow and Co., 1969.

Berendt, Joachim-Ernst, revised by Gunther Huesmann. *The Jazz Book.* 2d ed. Brooklyn: Lawrence Hill, 1992.

Berliner, Paul F. *Thinking in Jazz.* Chicago: University of Chicago Press, 1994.

Berry, Lemuel, Jr. *Biographical Dictionary of Black Musicians and Music Educators.* Guthrie, OK: Educational Books, 1978.

Bley, Paul, and David Lee. *Stopping Time: Paul Bley and the Transformation of Jazz.* New York: Vehicle Press, 1999.

Bley, Paul, and Norman Meehan. *Time Will Tell: Conversations with Paul Bley.* Berkeley: Berkeley Hills Press, 2003.

Buckner, Reginald T., and Weiland, Steven, eds. *Jazz in Mind: Essays on the History and Meanings of Jazz.* Detroit: Wayne State University Press, 1991.

Budds, Michael J. *Jazz in the Sixties: The Expansion of Musical Resources and Techniques.* Iowa City: University of Iowa Press, 1990.

Buhle, Paul, Jayne Cortez, Philip Lamantia, Nancy Joyce Peters, Franklin Rosemont, and Penelope Rosemont, eds. *Free Spirits: The Insurgent Imagination.* San Francisco: City Lights, 1982.

Carles, Philippe, and Jean-Louis Comolli. *Free Jazz, Black Power.* 2d ed. Paris: Editions Galilee, 1979.

Carner, Gary. *Jazz Performers: An Annotated Bibliography of Biographical Materials.* Westport, CT: Greenwood Press, 1990.

Carr, Ian. *Music Outside: Contemporary Jazz in Britain.* New York: Da Capo, 1977. Previously issued by London: Latimer New Dimensions, 1973.

Carr, Ian, Digby Fairweather, and Brian Priestley. *Jazz: The Essential Companion.* London: Grafton, 1987.

Cole, Bill. *John Coltrane.* New York: Da Capo, 1976.

Collier, James Lincoln. *The Making of Jazz: A Comprehensive History.* Boston: Houghton Mifflin, 1978.

Corbett, John. *Extended Play: Sounding off from John Cage to Dr. Funkenstein.* Durham, NC: Duke University Press, 1994.

Davis, Francis. *In the Moment: Jazz in the 1980s.* Oxford: Oxford University Press, 1986.

Davis, Francis. *Outcats: Jazz Composers, Instrumentalists, and Singers.* New York: Oxford University Press, 1990.

Day, Steve. *Ornette Coleman: Music Always.* London: Soundworld, 2000.

Denisoff, R. Serge, and Richard A. Peterson, eds. *Sounds of Social Change: Studies in Popular Culture.* Chicago: Rand McNally, 1972.

Feigin, Leo, ed. *Russian Jazz: New Identity.* London: Quartet Books, 1985.

Feinstein, Sascha, and Yusef Komunyakaa, eds. *The Jazz Poetry Anthology.* Bloomington: Indiana University Press, 1991. (A collection of poems inspired by jazz themes, many of which reflect upon the free jazz legacy.)

Fischlin, Daniel, and Ajay Heble. *The Other Side of Nowhere: Jazz, Improvisation, and Communities in Dialogue.* Middletown, CT: Wesleyan University Press, 2004.

Gerard, Charley. *Jazz in Black and White: Race, Culture and Identity in the Jazz Community.* Westport: Praeger, 1998.

Giddens, Gary. *Rhythm-A-Ning: Jazz Tradition and Innovation in the 80s.* Oxford: Oxford University Press, 1985.

Gray, John. *Fire Music: A Bibliography of the New Jazz, 1959–1990.* Westport: Greenwood Press, 1991.

Heble, Ajay. *Landing on the Wrong Note: Jazz, Dissonance and Critical Practice.* New York: Routledge, 2000.

Heffley, Mike. *The Music of Anthony Braxton.* Westport: Greenwood Press, 1996.

Hentoff, Nat. *Jazz Is.* New York: Ridge Press/Random House, 1976.

Jones, Andrew. *Plunderphonics, Pataphysics and Pop Mechanics: An Introduction to Musique Actuelle.* London: Plenum, 1995.

Jones, LeRoi (Amiri Baraka). *Blues People: Negro Music in White America.* New York: William Morrow & Co., 1963.

Jost, Ekkehard. *Europas Jazz 1960–1980.* Frankfurt am Main: Fischer Taschenbush Verlag, 1987. (In German.)

Jost, Ekkehard. *Free Jazz.* New York: Da Capo Press, 1981.

Kahn, Ashley. *A Love Supreme: The Making of John Coltrane's Classic Album.* New York: Granta, 2003.

Kernfeld, Barry, ed. *The New Grove Dictionary of Jazz.* 2d ed. New York: Grove's Dictionaries Inc., 2001.

Kofsky, Frank. *Black Nationalism and the Revolution in Music.* New York: Pathfinder Press, 1970.

Larkin, Phillip. *All What Jazz: A Record Diary 1961–71.* New York: Farrar, Straus and Giroux, 1985.

Levey, Joseph. *The Jazz Experience.* Englewood Cliffs, NJ: Prentice-Hall, 1986.

Litweiler, John. *The Freedom Principle: Jazz after 1958*. New York: William Morrow & Co., 1984.

Litweiler, John. *A Harmolodic Life*. New York: William Morrow & Co., 1992.

Lock, Graham. *Blutopia: Visions of the Future and Revisions of the Past in the Work of Sun Ra, Duke Ellington and Anthony Braxton*. Duke University Press, 1999.

Lock, Graham. *Chasing the Vibration: Meetings with Creative Musicians*. New York: Da Capo, 1994.

Lock, Graham. *Forces in Motion: The Music and Thoughts of Anthony Braxton*. New York: Da Capo, 1989.

Luzzi, Mario. *Uomini e Avanguardie Jazz*. Milan: Gammalibri, 1980. (In Italian.)

Lyons, Leonard S. *The Great Jazz Pianists*. New York: William Morrow & Co., Inc., 1983.

Lyons, Leonard S., and Don Perlo. *Jazz Portraits: The Lives and Music of the Jazz Masters*. New York: Quill, 1989.

Mandel, Howard. *Miles, Ornette, Cecil*. New York: Taylor & Francis Group, 2004.

McRae, Barry. *The Jazz Cataclysm*. London: J. M. Dent, 1967.

Nisenson, Eric. *Ascension: John Coltrane and His Quest*. New York: Da Capo, 1995.

Noglik, Bert. *Jazzwerkstatt International*. Berlin: Verlag Neue Musik, 1981. (In German.)

Nyman, Michael. *Experimental Music: Cage and Beyond*. London: Schirmer Books, 1974.

Ostransky, Leroy. *Understanding Jazz*. Englewood Cliffs, NJ: Prentice-Hall, 1977.

Porter, Lewis. *John Coltrane: His Life and Music*. Ann Arbor: University of Michigan Press, 1999.

Radano, Ronald M. *New Musical Figurations: Anthony Braxton's Cultural Critique*. Chicago: University of Chicago Press, 1993.

Ramsey, Doug. *Jazz Matters: Reflections on the Music and Some of Its Makers*. Fayetteville, AR: University of Arkansas Press, 1989.

Robertson, Alan. *Joe Harriott: Fire in His Soul*. London: Northway Publications, 2003.

Rockwell, John. *All American Music: Composition in the Late Twentieth Century*. New York: Borzoi/Alfred A. Knopf, 1983.

Saul, Scott. *Freedom Is, Freedom Ain't: Jazz and the Making of the Sixties*. Cambridge: Harvard University Press, 2003.

Schwartz, Jeff. *Albert Ayler: His Life and Music*. Online at http://www.geocities.com/ jeff_l_schwartz/ayler.html.

Simosko, Vladimir, and Barry Tepperman. *Eric Dolphy: A Musical Biography and Discography*. New York: Da Capo, 1971.

Sinclair, John, and Robert Levin. *Music and Politics*. New York: World Publishing, 1971.

Smith, Martin. *John Coltrane: Jazz, Racism and Resistance*. London: Redwords, 2003.

Spellman, A. B. *Black Music: Four Lives*. New York: Schocken Books, 1970. (Originally published as *Four Lives in the Bebop Business*. New York: Pantheon, 1966.)

Such, David G. *Avant-Garde Jazz Musicians: Performing "Out There."* Iowa City: University of Iowa Press, 1993.

Szwed, John H. *Space Is the Place: The Life and Times of Sun Ra*. New York: Da Capo, 1998.

Taylor, Arthur. *Notes and Tones*. New York: Perigee Books, 1982.

Thomas, J. C. *Chasin' the Trane: The Music & Mystique of John Coltrane*. New York: Da Capo, 1975.

Vuijsje, Bert. *De Nieuwe Jazz*. Baarn, Holland: Bosch & Keuning, 1978. (In Dutch.)

Willener, Alfred. *The Action-Image of Society: On Cultural Politicization*. New York: Pantheon, 1970.

Williams, Martin. *Jazz Changes*. Oxford: Oxford University Press, 1992.

Williams, Martin. *Where's the Melody?: A Listener's Introduction to Jazz*. New York: Pantheon, 1966.

Wilmer, Valerie. *As Serious As Your Life: The Story of the New Jazz.* 2d ed. New York: Serpent's
    Tail, 1992.
Wilmer, Valerie. *Jazz People.* New York: Bobbs-Merrill, 1970.
Wilson, Peter Niklas. *Ornette Coleman: His Life and Music.* Berkeley: Berkeley Hills Press, 1999.

GENERAL PERIODICAL ARTICLES ON FREE JAZZ
AND IMPROVISATION

Baker, Malcolm Lynn. "Black Nationalism and Free Jazz Collectives: The Black Musician's
    Approach to Economic Self-Determinism." *Jazz Research Papers* 6 (1986): 24–29.
Bass, Milton. "Non-Jazz Jazz." *Atlantic Monthly,* October 1962.
"Bob Thiele Digs 'New Thing' Jazz." *Variety,* April 21, 1965.
Cole, Bill. "The New Music." *Down Beat,* December 23, 1971.
Cooke, Jack. "The Avant-Garde." *Jazz Monthly,* June 1966.
Dance, Stanley. "Lightly and Politely." *Jazz Journal,* April 1971.
Dawbarn, Bob, and Ross Russell. "For and Against the Avant-Garde." *Melody Maker,* September 14, 1968.
Dixon, Bill. "Contemporary Jazz: An Assessment." *Jazz & Pop,* November 1967.
D'Lugoff, Art. "Experimentation in Public: The Clubowner's Viewpoint." *Down Beat,* April
    8, 1965.
Easter, Gilbert. "So What Is Jazz?: A Mainstream View of the Avant-Garde." *Jazz & Blues,*
    June 1972.
Ellis, Don. "The Avant-Garde Is Not Avant-Garde!" *Down Beat,* June 30, 1966.
Ericsson, M. H. "Experimentation in Public: The Artist's Viewpoint." *Downbeat,* April 8, 1965.
Feather, Leonard. "Feather's Nest." *Down Beat,* February 15, 1962.
Feather, Leonard. "Hierarchy of the Jazz Anarchy: Symposium." *Esquire,* September 1965.
Feather, Leonard. "Jazz: Going Nowhere." *Show,* January 1962.
Fine, Milo. "Social Aspects of Free Jazz." *Jazz Forum* 30 (June 1975).
Fox, Ted. "Success Story: Self-Made Records." *Jazz Magazine* (N.Y.). 2, no. 4 (1978): 48–55.
Gitler, Ira. "Chords and Discords: To Hentoff from Gitler." *Down Beat,* September 9, 1965.
    In this forum, Gitler lambastes critic Nat Hentoff for suggesting that new jazz players
    be given the more popular evening performance slots at the Newport Jazz Festival in-
    stead of the afternoon slots. Hentoff's rebuttal is in "Second Chorus," *Down Beat,*
    October 21, 1965.
Green, Benny. "A Matter of Form." *Jazz Journal,* June 1962.
Heckman, Don. "The New Jazz: A Matter of Doing." *Down Beat,* February 9, 1967.
Hentoff, Nat. "Learning to Listen to Avant-Garde—A Basic Problem." *Down Beat,* December
    2, 1965.
Hentoff, Nat. "New Directions in Jazz." *International Musician,* September 1960.
Hentoff, Nat. "New Jazz—Black, Angry, and Hard to Understand." *New York Times Magazine,*
    December 25, 1966.
Hobson, Wilder. "Another Abstract Art." *Saturday Review,* October 28, 1961.
Hodeir, Andre. "Free Jazz." *The World of Music* 10, no. 3 (1968).
Hunt, David C. "Black Voice Lost in White Infrastructure." *Coda* 11, no. 6 (February 1974):
    12–14.
Jones, LeRoi. "Jazz: The Avant-Garde." *African Revolution* 1, no. 1 (May 1963).
Jones, LeRoi. "White Critics, Black Musicians, New Music." *African Revolution* 1, no. 6
    (October 1963).
Knox, Keith. "Sounds from the Avant Garde: the Aesthetic Problem." *Jazz Monthly,* February
    1967.

Levin, Robert. "The New Jazz and the Nature of Its Enemy." *Sounds & Fury*, April 1966.

Miles, Robert. "Understanding the New Thing." *Pieces of Jazz*, no. 4 (Autumn 1968).

"The New Thing." *Time*, April 6, 1970.

Palmer, Robert. "Respect." *Down Beat*, January 31, 1974.

Pekar, Harvey. "The Critical Cult of Personality, or, Stop That War—Them Cats Are Killing Themselves." *Down Beat*, January 13, 1966.

Pekar, Harvey. "Experimental Collective Improvisation." *Jazz Journal*, November 1963.

"Points of Contact: A Discussion." *Down Beat's Music '66*, 11 (1966).

Radano, Ronald M. "The Jazz Avant-Garde and the Jazz Community: Action and Reaction." *Annual Review of Jazz Studies* 3 (1985).

Tynan, John. "Take Five." *Down Beat*, November 23, 1961.

Williams, Martin. "The Bystander." *Down Beat*, March 10, 1962.

Williams, Martin. "The Jazz Avant-Garde: Who's in Charge Here?" *Evergreen Review* 10, no. 41 (June 1966).

PERIODICALS SPECIFICALLY ORIENTED TOWARD FREE MUSIC

Cadence magazine, Cadence Building, Redwood, NY 13679-3104. Phone: (315) 287-2852. A monthly periodical, associated with Cadence Jazz and CIMP labels and North Country Distribution. http://www.cadencebuilding.com.

Signal to Noise magazine, 416 Pine Street, Burlington, VT 05401. Phone: (802) 658-4267. A quarterly focusing on all manner of improvised and experimental music. http://www.signaltonoisemagazine.org.

Index

Page numbers for all main Encyclopedia entries are given in **bold** type. All album titles appear in *italics*. All individual persons are alphabetized by surname ("Ayler, Albert"). In cases where an artist has undergone a name change, all listings for that person will be under the most recent or familiar appellation (i.e., all references to Dollar Brand are listed under "Ibrahim, Abdullah"; all those for LeRoi Jones are under "Baraka, Amiri"). In those cases a small entry will redirect the reader to the appropriate listing ("Brand, Dollar. *See* Ibrahim, Abdullah"). The Oriental artists are alphabetized here by family name, regardless of how the artist generally sequences it (Otomo Yoshihide is listed under "O," Lê Quan Ninh under "L," and Toshimaru Nakamura under "N"). As an assumed name, Sun Ra is a special case and is alphabetized under "S" as per standard practice.

If an artist's name appears at the beginning of an album title, the title will still be alphabetized according to its first word (*Albert Ayler in Greenwich Village* is under "Al-"). If titles or other references begin with numerals that are not spelled out, they are indexed as if the numbers were spelled out (i.e., Air's album *80 Below '82* is listed under "E" for "Eighty"; Chicago Underground's *12 Degrees of Freedom* is listed under "T" for "Twelve"). Album titles beginning with "A," "An," or "The" are alphabetized according to the second word in the title ("*Love Supreme, A*"); however, non-English titles which begin with foreign equivalents ("Le," "Der," etc.) are listed by the first word of the title ("*Le Voix d'Itxassou*"; "*Der Venusmond*"). Due to the considerable size of this index, some of the more obscure record labels have been omitted.

About the Author

TODD S. JENKINS is a freelance writer who has contributed to *Down Beat*, *Route 66*, and *Signal to Noise*. A lifelong fan of jazz, he is a director of the American Jazz Symposium, a nonprofit arts organization.